THE NATURAL CITY:
RE-ENVISIONING THE BUILT ENVIRONMENT

Edited by Ingrid Leman Stefanovic and Stephen Bede Scharper

Today more than half of the world's population lives in urban areas. Meanwhile there is growing recognition that the environmental crisis, as in the case of global climate change and declining biodiversity, does not relate simply to 'natural' wilderness areas, but arises from, and affects, urban areas in a significant way. Yet, despite recent shifts in thinking, the perception persists that environmental issues are principally concerned with plants, animals, and pristine wilderness areas, while human settlements are the exclusive domain of architects, planners, and urbanists. Both at the conceptual and pragmatic levels, the implicit division of urban and natural environments serves to perpetuate myths of two separate entities, with nature seen as benevolent and the city as evil.

The Natural City is an interdisciplinary collection of essays that merges architectural theory and urban design with philosophy, religion, humanism, and environmental policy to present an alternative vision of urban life. The contributors argue that the deeply rooted urban/nature philosophical divide must be healed as a condition of building life-enhancing communities. Today new technologies promise to provide renewable energy sources and 'greener' designs. But it is fundamental values, attitudes, and perceptions that drive policy decisions. The aim of this volume is to redefine the meaning of cities as urban ecosystems and to encourage a more thoughtful philosophical and spiritual questioning of what it means to genuinely dwell in the cosmos that sustains us.

INGRID LEMAN STEFANOVIC is a professor in the Department of Philosophy at the University of Toronto.

STEPHEN BEDE SCHARPER is an associate professor with the Centre for the Environment and the Department of Anthropology at the University of Toronto.

Edited by
Ingrid Leman Stefanovic and
Stephen Bede Scharper

The Natural City

Re-Envisioning the Built Environment

UNIVERSITY OF TORONTO PRESS
Toronto Buffalo London

© University of Toronto Press 2012
Toronto Buffalo London
www.utppublishing.com
Printed in Canada

ISBN 978-0-8020-9160-4 (cloth)
ISBN 978-1-4426-1102-3 (paper)

∞

Printed on acid-free, 100% post-consumer recycled paper with vegetable-based inks.

Library and Archives Canada Cataloguing in Publication

The natural city : re-envisioning the built environment / edited by
Ingrid Leman Stefanovic and Stephen Scharper.

Includes bibliographical references.
ISBN 978-0-8020-9160-4 (bound).   ISBN 978-1-4426-1102-3 (pbk.)

1. Urban ecology (Sociology).   2. City planning – Environmental
aspects.   3. Sustainable urban development.   I. Leman Stefanovic,
Ingrid.   II. Scharper, Stephen B.

HT241.N38 2011   307.76   C2011-905601-1

This book has been published with the help of a grant from the Canadian
Federation for the Humanities and Social Sciences, through the Aid to
Scholarly Publications Program, using funds provided by the Social
Sciences and Humanities Research Council of Canada.

University of Toronto Press acknowledges the financial assistance to its
publishing program of the Canada Council for the Arts and the Ontario
Arts Council.

 Canada Council Conseil des Arts
for the Arts du Canada   ONTARIO ARTS COUNCIL
CONSEIL DES ARTS DE L'ONTARIO

University of Toronto Press acknowledges the financial support of the
Government of Canada through the Canada Book Fund for its publishing
activities.

Contents

Acknowledgments

We would like to acknowledge the support of both the Social Sciences and Humanities Research Council of Canada and the Dean's Office of the Faculty of Arts and Science at the University of Toronto, who provided research funding for this project.

We are also grateful for the editorial acumen and assistance of Anne Louise Mahoney, whose careful eye and irenic spirit helped not only to provide stylistic continuity but also ensured effective and timely communication among all the contributors.

Mona El-Haddad from the Centre for Environment, University of Toronto, also provided invaluable administrative assistance throughout the editorial process, and the Centre graciously provided funding to support the book as well.

We are especially indebted to Virgil Duff, Executive Editor, University of Toronto Press, whose seasoned editorial counsel and genteel demeanour helped to humanize the process of preparing this volume. We are also appreciative of the constructive insights from the two, anonymous external reviewers.

In addition, we are grateful to the contributors for their insights and willingness to work collaboratively in finalizing this collection.

Finally, a debt of gratitude is owed to our respective spouses, Michael Stefanovic and Hilary Cunningham, for their patience, goodwill, and unremitting support.

INGRID LEMAN STEFANOVIC AND STEPHEN BEDE SCHARPER

THE NATURAL CITY:
RE-ENVISIONING THE BUILT ENVIRONMENT

Introduction: Cultivating the Terrain

The past half century, demographically speaking, might well be termed 'the age of urbanization.' In 1950, only 30 per cent of the population lived in urban areas; today, over half do, and, by 2030, according to projections by the United Nations, 60 per cent of the world's population will dwell in cities.[1]

While many are there by choice, countless people live in cities in order to find work, even if it is sporadic, poorly paid, or unhealthy. The shift to urban living comes at great social and ecological cost. The Intergovernmental Panel on Climate Change, which presents the conclusions of thousands of top scientists, suggests that human activities, including rapid urbanization, are dramatically affecting the health of the planet and the survival of contemporary society as we know it.[2]

Philosophers and humanists share these concerns. Religious leaders met in 2008 in Sweden at an Interfaith Summit on Climate Change to sign a manifesto urging extensive reductions of carbon dioxide emissions in all parts of the world, particularly within developed nations. Christians, Buddhists, Daoists, Muslims, Sikhs, Jews, and Aboriginals reached consensus: 'We all share the responsibility of being conscious caretakers of our home, planet Earth. We have reflected on the concerns of scientists and political leaders regarding the alarming climate crisis. We share their concerns.'[3]

Amid environmental destruction, global climate change, air and water pollution, and dangers to human and ecological health, is there hope? Can cities become centres of life-enhancing community rather than sources of environmental degradation? In the words of these faith leaders, 'Can planet Earth be healed? We are convinced that the answer is yes.'[4]

It is in a similar spirit of positive possibilities for change that the current volume is presented within a new vision of what we call 'the natural city.' Certainly, there is growing recognition of the fact that the environmental crisis does not relate simply to 'natural' wilderness environments, but arises from, and affects, urban areas in a significant way. The natural city points to the need to move beyond any conceptual bifurcation or artificial compartmentalization and instead acknowledge the need to integrate urban and ecological concerns in a sustainable manner.

As human beings, we dwell; it is 'natural,' therefore, that we build. It is, in fact, in our human settlements that historical records have generally emerged. Encapsulated in cities are many of our testimonials to *civitas*, to culture, to science, to philosophy. While our dwelling places, particularly in the modern era, damage nature, they also record humanity's aspirations, needs, and failings, and perforce become a central locus for responding to our present and future environmental challenges.

This book describes the natural city – 'natural' not only because it is embedded in the ecological systems within which we work, but also because it embodies humanity's essential spiritual and cosmological quests. The natural cities we strive to build certainly pose technical questions of auto-use restrictions and renewable energy sources, but they also raise larger cosmological questions: Who am I? What is my purpose here? And what is my relationship to the rest of the created universe? As we hope that this book demonstrates, the natural city is at its core not only a technological and architectural concern, but also an ontological, cosmological, and spiritual project.

The natural city similarly evokes the notion of social justice. Such a perspective takes seriously the social, political, economic, cultural, and moral dimensions of human–earth relationships, pointing to a dynamic, rather than a dichotomy, in the intersection of human and ecological communities. A human ecology reminds us that an abstract, metaphysical notion of interrelatedness is insufficient; as human agents, we are called not only to be aware of our interconnectedness with non-human nature and each other, but also to advance this interconnection according to the demands of social and economic justice. In this sense, recognizing the spiritual, ontological, and cosmological dimensions of the natural city is also, inherently, a political enterprise.

The natural city must be one that respects and heeds historical, sociological, cultural, economic, environmental, political, and ontological origins. It opens up the possibility of dwelling among people and built spaces that are understood as more than mere objects. A narrow vision of instrumental rationality sees planning as no more than the technical ordering of residential, commercial, and industrial complexes, together with appropriate infrastructure. On the other hand, the natural city calls for another kind of thinking and planning, an 'originative thinking,' whereby buildings become other than discrete monuments to human ingenuity.[5] Instead, they seek to commemorate meaningful spatial and temporal contexts – indeed, cosmological contexts. These natural dwelling places restore to us a sense of human dignity and sacred belonging to the earth and to the cosmos. They remind us of the grace of creation and invite us to look up at the stars and reflect upon our place in the universe. And in so doing, they bestow upon us a sense of belonging – to the natural world as well as to our dwelling places.

There is much more to be said about the meaning of the natural city: hence, this volume. We each can sense already that many of our urban ecosystems are not sustainable, nor are they humane dwelling places. The sparrows' songs are drowned out by the din of car engines. Architecture becomes functional, seen purely from a narrow utilitarian point of view. While it may be aesthetically pleasing to some, we often feel emotionally alienated from these spaces; we feel that we do not belong. Grinding poverty stalks a disturbingly high percentage of the world's urban residents. We sense that there is, in fact, something 'unnatural' about city living in such circumstances.

Where do we search for an alternative vision? Wherein does the richness of the living, natural city reside? Many of the essays in this volume address this question – if not to answer it conclusively, then at least to enlarge our dialogue and understanding.

Philosopher Joseph Grange suggests that 'the city deserves a cosmology benefiting its grandeur, a semiotics worthy of its values and a praxis effective for all its citizens.'[6] The natural city certainly deserves no less. Ideally, the essays in this book will constitute some first steps in moving us in this important direction.

The Structure of This Book

The structure of this book is explicitly interdisciplinary, merging architectural theory and urban design with philosophy, religion, humanism, and environmental policy. The volume is divided into four parts that emphasize somewhat unique directions within this interdisciplinary conversation. Part I, 'Adjusting Our Vision: Some Philosophical Reflections,' sets the ontological grounding for the book.

In chapter 1, philosophy professor Ingrid Leman Stefanovic replies to some of the philosophical objections to the term 'natural' and advances the case for a phenomenological rethinking of the traditional metaphysical urban–natural divide. In chapter 2, phenomenologist W.S.K. Cameron considers whether we are describing an oxymoron when we portray cities as both natural and successful. Political philosopher Frank Cunningham moves in chapter 3 to describe cities as 'grue'-like – diverse and complex, defying universalizing definitions. He suggests that environmentalism calls for a holistic ecosystem perspective in the development of public policy, and discusses the challenges of defining a natural city against the background of diverse philosophical paradigms. Environmental studies professor Peter Timmerman then shows us in chapter 4 how the Western literary tradition has helped both to entrench, as well as to mirror, a long-standing separation of built environments from the natural world. Timmerman points to future directions of thought that might help to heal the divide.

Part II moves away from strictly philosophical concerns to consider how we might move 'From the Stars to the Street: Cosmological Perspectives.' Chapter 5, written by co-editor Stephen Bede Scharper, a professor of religion and ecology, reflects on the meaning of ecological integrity, garnering insights from Aldo Leopold's land ethic as well as Thomas Berry's concept of a universal communion of subjects. In chapter 6, phenomenologist and philosopher of Orthodox religion Bruce V. Foltz looks to clues for building a natural city through lessons learned from the holy city of Constantinople. In chapters 7 and 8, philosophy professors Vincent Shen and Kenneth Maly consider how Daoism and Buddhism respectively might help to shed light on the challenges of sustainability in a world increasingly defined by a Western technological world view.

Part III recognizes the need to look for ways of embedding these philosophical and cosmological concerns in social and institutional structures by 'Expanding Our Collective Horizons: Societal Implications.' Anthropology professor Hilary Cunningham's thought-provoking chapter shows how contemporary interpretations of the 'global city' miss out on essential elements that are more appropriately captured within the notion of a 'natural city.' In chapter 10, musician and phenomenologist Richard Oddie introduces an essential moment in the interpretation of a natural city by focusing on what is often most taken for granted – the impact of soundscapes on the meaning of our urban environments. Phenomenologist Trish Glazebrook brings an important ecofeminist contribution to the table in chapter 11, while, in chapter 12, internationally renowned process theologian and ethicist John B. Cobb, Jr, describes his vision of self-sufficient urban and rural areas, offering China as a case in point. Anthropologist Shubhra Gururani closes part III with a discussion of how Gurgaon, a growing city in India, provides important clues to the challenges of configuring urban nature against the background of new knowledge and power discourses that emerge around the practice of capitalist production and consumption.

In the book's final section, part IV: 'Building on the Vision: Reflecting on Praxis,' we recognize that it will be the cities that we actually build on the ground that truly bear witness to our dialogue about natural cities. In chapter 14, Aboriginal architect William Woodworth *Raweno:kwas* describes how Toronto itself implicitly reflects long-standing Aboriginal land traditions within its built form. Geographer David Seamon suggests, in chapter 15, ways in which one can seek to build 'lively urban spaces,' drawing from the work of architectural space theorist Bill Hillier and listening to lessons of colour that arise from Goethean phenomenology. Robert Mugerauer, a philosopher and professor of architecture, takes new lessons, in chapter 16, for urban design from the continuity in organism–environment interactions found within the natural world.

In chapter 17, environmental engineers Gaurav Kumar and Bryan W. Karney explore the vital issue of energy use, recognizing the importance of embodied knowledge of consumption and production costs as a necessary condition of behaviour change. The final chapter, by Sarah J. King and Ingrid Leman Stefanovic, reflects on a research project that investigates children's perceptions of nature in the city. We cannot forget that the actions that we undertake today will influence the world of tomorrow. Our decisions are not simply our own, for our young will inherit our mistakes as well as our successes.

Each section of this book contains important insights and expands further on the philosophical, cosmological, socio-political, and practical demands of constructing natural cities. We are keenly aware, however, that the chapters of this book constitute only some first steps towards building a natural city – one that appreciates the givenness of a world that we did not create but for which, in many respects, we are responsible. The authors and editors invite our readers to give careful consideration to the ideas raised here, and then to continue to find new ways of building more respectfully. Each one of us has a part to play in moving the environmental agenda forward in fertile, life-enhancing ways. Let us ensure that we continue the dialogue in a meaningful and constructive way, with an eye to leaving the planet in a healthier state than it was in when we arrived on it.

NOTES

1 *World Urbanization Prospects: The 2001 Revision*, prepared by the United Nations Population Division: http://www.un.org/esa/population/publications/wup2001/wup2001dh.pdf (accessed 20 January 2010).
2 Intergovernmental Panel on Climate Change, *Climate Change 2007: Synthesis Report*. Contribution of Working Groups I, II and III to the Fourth Assessment Report of the Intergovernmental Panel on Climate Change [Core Writing Team, with R.K. Pachauri and A. Riesinger, eds.,], IPPC: Geneva, 2008, http://www.ipcc.ch/ipccreports/ar4-syr.htm (accessed 3 December 2008).
3 See the complete report of the meetings in Uppsala, Sweden, 30 November 2008, at the Environment News Service: http://www.ens-newswire.com/ens/nov2008/2008–11–30–01.asp (accessed 3 December 2008).
4 Intergovernmental Panel on Climate Change, *Climate Change 2007*.
5 For a discussion of the meaning of originative thinking, see Ingrid Leman Stefanovic, *Safeguarding Our Common Future: Rethinking Sustainable Development* (Albany: State University of New York Press, 2000).
6 Joseph Grange, *The City: An Urban Cosmology* (Albany: State University of New York Press, 1999), 209.
7 The editors are indebted to James Conlon's work *From the Stars to the Street: Engaged Wisdom for a Brokenhearted World* (Ottawa: Novalis, 2007), for this section heading.

PART ONE

Adjusting Our Vision:
Some Philosophical Reflections

Not that we can have no recourse to philosophy, to its concepts or conceptions. But it cannot be our point of departure.

– Henri Lefebvre, *The Production of Space*

In the quote above, Lefebvre is critical of a philosophical tradition that aims at 'abstract (metaphysical) representations of space,' independent of a description of embodied, lived places.[1] He has a point. If philosophical reflection upon the meaning of a natural city remains simply at the level of theoretical abstraction, it is no more than a description of utopia – 'no place.'

And yet, contrary to Lefebvre's stand, it is precisely within philosophy that this book takes its point of departure. Is such a beginning at all problematic?

Philosophy is admittedly understood here as something other than rationalistic, abstract speculation. Rather than formulating theoretical constructs, the aim is to uncover foundational, taken-for-granted paradigms and world views that ground our ways of understanding the world.

Our interpretive horizons frame the way in which we see and understand our built and natural environments. Often, these *Weltanschauungen*, embedded in the historical traditions that we appropriate unthinkingly, are hidden, and yet they are fundamental to everything we do on a daily basis, including the way we envision cities and our place within them.

The chapters that introduce this volume are philosophical in the sense that they seek to bring to light some of the implicit world views that frame our policy making and planning initiatives. In chapter 1, Ingrid

Leman Stefanovic addresses what she sees to be a deeply rooted schism between 'nature' on the one hand and 'cities' or urban dwellings on the other. After showing how this dualism finds expression both empirically and conceptually in the modern world, she points the way towards a more integrative framework to ground the discussion of a 'natural city.'

W.S.K. Cameron continues to address this schism by acknowledging that contemporary human settlements exert huge ecological pressures upon the earth and that, in this sense, 'cities' and 'nature' may be seen to constitute an 'oxymoron.' He suggests that there may be a possibility of identifying a more 'organic' model of a city, rather than one that defies natural cycles as a detached 'machine.' He suggests pragmatic requirements, such as new regulations and policies that are the condition of moving us forward in a more meaningful way.

In chapter 3, Frank Cunningham describes the challenges that arise when one recognizes that cities fall into what he calls a 'grue-like category.' 'Grue,' a term that emerged from the philosophy of science, is coined from the combination of 'blue' and 'green.' If things are grue-like (never simply green or wholly blue), they are non-static, non-uniform. When environmental agendas aim to attain a balanced, 'holistic' vision, they cannot do justice to cities that can never conform to such essentializing categories. Cunningham explores the possibility of moving beyond these differences between a reified 'ecosystematicity' and a more fluid 'grueness' so that, ultimately, through a transformed civic culture, we may be more effective in greening the 'urban grue.'

The final chapter in this section similarly recognizes the challenges of integrating the natural and the urban and looks to the appropriation of our historical tradition for guidance. Peter Timmerman takes us back to the ancient roots of our literary interpretations, exploring images of nature and the city as they emerge through key classical texts. As he notes in the end, his survey reveals how not only fossil fuels, but fossilized categories, threaten natural cities.

All four authors recognize that a 'natural city' defies static, universalizing, and definitive categories. At the same time, they would likely all agree that this unencompassability of the term is not an indication of its paucity, but instead points to its very richness.

NOTE

1 Henri Lefebvre, *The Production of Space*, trans. Donald Nicholson-Smith (Oxford: Blackwell Publishing, 1991), 14.

1 In Search of the Natural City

INGRID LEMAN STEFANOVIC

> Admittedly, the distinction between the natural and the non-natural re-
> quires detailed working out.
>
> – Robert Elliot, 'Faking Nature'[1]

The term 'natural city' integrates two concepts that have a long history
of separation and even opposition. Reflecting a dualistic paradigm that
divides pristine notions of wilderness from the city, 'nature' is frequently seen primarily and benevolently as unsullied and salvific wilderness,
while cities are viewed as baleful, concrete dens of ecological iniquity.

This chapter argues that a condition of any meaningful interpretation
of the concept of the 'natural city' requires that we necessarily move
beyond such a deeply rooted dualistic paradigm. As a first step, we will
examine how the dualism manifests itself both empirically in current
institutional settings, and in contemporary philosophical discourse.
The continuing debate as to whether nature is a 'real' entity, existing
independently of human awareness, or is socially constructed will be
shown to assume the very bifurcation described above between natural
environments and urban culture.

The aim, however, is also to explore ways in which we can begin
to productively move beyond this deeply seated dualistic world view.
A number of authors have begun to take innovative steps towards a
more promising ontological paradigm that should better orient us in
the search of a natural city.

Challenging the Nature/City Divide: Some Pragmatic Reflections

As cottagers seek their weekend escapes from the city, the bifurcation between the 'natural' and the 'urban' continues to be deeply rooted in our everyday institutions and in our language. The United Nations *Environment* Programme, for instance, continues to function as a distinct entity from the United Nations Centre for *Human Settlements*. Urban planning and environmental programs are, typically, housed in different departments at our post-secondary institutions, and academics appear to identify with either 'urban' or 'environmental' issues rather than with their interface. For instance, 'between 1995 and 2000, of the 6,157 papers in the nine leading ecological journals, only 25 (0.2%) dealt with cities.'[2] Environmental ethicists persist in defining their field in terms of ethical responsibilities towards the *natural* environment – almost always excluding any mention of built places. Municipal, provincial, and federal governments typically separate environmental ministries or departments from those related to housing or urban issues.

To some degree, distinguishing diverse environmental experiences is only reasonable. One cannot deny that the sense of place that emerges in the midst of a pristine rainforest is markedly different from that of a bustling downtown metropolitan core. The very origin of these experiences reminds us that we did not have a hand in creating the planet or the rainforest, though human beings certainly play a significant role in the creation of cities.

Nevertheless, diverse as these experiences are, it is becoming increasingly evident that extremes of pristine nature, on the one hand, and artificially constructed environments, on the other, are, to use Finnish philosopher Helena Siipi's words, only 'abstractions.' Naturalness is not, in her words, 'an all-or-nothing affair but a continuous gradient … Total naturalness is an abstract state at the end of a continuum and some ecosystems are closer to that ideal than others.'[3] One can intuitively distinguish between an unploughed prairie and a shopping mall in terms of how closely they approximate 'ideal naturalness,' but to suggest that 'nature' and 'cities' are wholly separate, self-contained, and different entities is to engage in nothing less than simplistic abstraction.[4]

Certainly, while humans did not create this earth, we now know that humans are able to impact its climate, its landscapes, and the air and waters on a planetary scale. Similarly, cities themselves do not subsist independently of the vagaries of the natural world: urban areas are hardly immune to the effects of natural disturbances, a fact to which the residents of New Orleans and other cities that have been subjected to natural disasters can attest all too well. The case for linking human and ecosystem health integrity is increasingly evident.

In fact, the essential belonging of human and natural systems is now more and more recognized to be integral to the meaning of sustainability itself. As far back as 1987, with the publication of the Brundtland Report, the important point was made that to build sustainably means to factor in socio-economic as well as environmental matters.[5] No longer is it possible to mindlessly construct human settlements in isolation from the effects of natural environment constraints.

The fact is that cities simply do not subsist independently of the natural world. The water we drink and the air we breathe have passed through generations of living entities. Our urban gardens are nourished through the soil. On a grander scale, we now begin to see that our habits, polluting as they are, cannot be viewed independently of the health and well-being of the planet as a whole. 'Nature' is more than simply an escape from the concrete jungle; on the contrary, it sustains and permeates our existence – whether that is rural, urban, or situated in a northern wilderness that is now home to PCB residuals and glacial warming.

The natural environment envelops us, as is clearly reflected in the French word *environs*, meaning 'surroundings.' In our city gardens, the cardinal is a regular visitor, delighting us on a summer's day. His song awakens us to the trees, the lush green grasses, the aroma of the flowers, the bewildering meandering of insects along the rocks, and the broader ecosystem within which this remarkable bird rests. In my case, all of this occurs within the shadow of the Toronto megalopolitan setting – the largest urban conglomeration of settlements in Canada.

Urban naturalist and award-winning journalist Wayne Grady recalls his childhood in Windsor, Ontario, just across the border from Detroit, Michigan. 'Although I am a city boy,' he writes, 'I don't recall my parents or my teachers taking me out of the city to get fresh air.'[6] While family stories revisit swimming trips and holidays to surrounding areas, Grady recollects little of those moments. He reflects,

What I remember is playing in an open field across the street from our house on Factoria Avenue, whole summers spent lying in tall grass beside a stream that ran through the field, watching grasshoppers and crickets, tadpoles and garter snakes. I blew the heads of dandelions, checked to see if my mother liked butter by holding a buttercup under her chin (she always did), and punched air-holes in the lids of jam jars so I could collect the chrysalides of monarch butterflies and watch them hatch.[7]

Such memories are not uncommon for many who spent their childhoods in Canadian urban settings.

Grady reminds us that cities are not garrisons – 'or at least, if they are,' he adds, 'they are highly ineffectual ones, for there is as much nature in the city as out of it.'[8] He describes the antics of squirrels ('tree rats'), sparrows, snakes, raccoons, gulls, and termites. He explores coyote dens hidden in the valleys of the city. He reminds us that over 300 species of birds are in residence in or regularly passing through Toronto. Grady also points to the world's largest ring-billed gull colony, which exists on the Leslie Street Spit – built by humans from the 1970s construction rubble that was moved to accommodate many of the high-rises in the city's downtown. That human-engineered spit is now home to 46 species of wildfowl, 258 species of birds (including Caspian terns, black-crowned night herons, and falcons), 34 species of plovers, and 283 species of vascular plants.[9]

According to Grady, 'there is actually more nature in Toronto now than there used to be' before the city evolved to this stage of urban development.[10] Bats have been attracted to urban attics. Coyotes appeared first in Ontario in the 1940s only when they associated suburban parkland with their native Great Plains. Cockroaches would never have been a part of Toronto had they not travelled on slave ships from Africa, and would not have strayed north to Canada had we not invented central heating. Underground power cables and subway lines have provided accessible habitats for ever-evolving species of termites. Rabbits regularly grace our neighbourhoods. While not uniformly welcome in our cities, plant and animal species continue to emerge in complex, unexpected ways.

To be sure, it is naive to deny that many species have also been displaced or destroyed by the building of Toronto. That being said, the natural world is more resilient than we might have imagined. 'Nature loves change,' writes Grady. And nature pervades our urban experiences in ways that are closer than we might expect. It just may be the case that

to watch a dandelion head open and turn to the sun, or a pigeon pecking at grass seeds in the park, is to experience in one minute the history of life on this planet. And perhaps, by realizing that neither the dandelion nor the pigeon nor the grass would be there were it not for us, we become aware of our own place in the great web of life.[11]

'Cities are artifacts,' writes planner Witold Rybczynski – which may be true.[12] At the same time, as Grady reminds us, cities are also rich eco-systems that, thankfully, nature ultimately refuses to ignore. It is time that we began to recognize this fact, both within our academic settings and in our governmental institutions and public policies.

The Example of Urban Ecology: A New Vision of Integrative Planning

It must be said, of course, that recent decades have certainly brought a growing awareness of the earth's rich and varied ecology, and of the serious threats posed to it by human activity. We now know that environmental degradation – including species extinction, habitat destruction, contaminated air and water, and global climate change – affects the health of both the planet and our species. Whether this knowledge is adequately being translated into positive action is open for debate; it is clear, however, that the environment is a growing element of public discussion.

Moreover, one is equally obliged to acknowledge that urban ecologists and other proponents of green cities are beginning to uncover ways of reintegrating nature into our human settlements, thereby taking important steps forward in challenging the engrained paradigm of a nature/city dualism. As celebrated anthropologist Margaret Mead once observed, cities are to humans what hives are to bees and dens are to foxes; cities can thus be viewed not as environmental aberrations, but rather as necessary moments in the unfolding of the human story. As such, they can be positive and ecologically sustainable, rather than environmentally malignant, developments – provided ecological integrity is both preserved and fostered within city limits.[13]

In the words of Charles Redman, director of Arizona State University's Center for Environmental Studies, 'the study of urban ecology is taking off in … cities like Baltimore, Seattle, New York and especially abroad in Berlin, Sydney and many others.' Redman challenges the common wisdom that there is 'either nature or there are cities.' On the contrary, he concludes, 'There is nature in the city. The city is part of nature.'[14]

The field of urban ecology is now investigating the city in terms of flows of energy, natural capital, biophysical cycles, biotic communities, and the 'ecological footprint' that human settlements assume.[15] As journalist Alexander Stille points out,

> ecologists are finding that cities are interesting, legitimate environments, with surprisingly high levels of biodiversity, and what's more, that understanding and protecting them may be crucial to our environmental future. From Paris, Rome and Cairo to New York, Baltimore and Phoenix, cities are all subjects of intense ecological study. Unesco is even thinking of making several major cities, including New York, biospheres, important natural areas to be protected.[16]

Ecologists have been surprised to find over 3,000 plant species within an 80-kilometre radius of the New York metropolitan area. The marshy wetlands near Kennedy Airport are cited as one of the largest nesting areas on the east coast.[17] Empirically speaking, it is evident that nature infuses the city and, therefore, that separating the two concepts simply does not do justice to our lived experience.

The trend towards viewing the city as integrally linked to the natural environment is manifesting itself along many diverse fronts.[18] Consider, for instance, the call to 'Smart Growth,' a term popularized in 1997 in the state of Maryland when its governor established a set of policies to direct resources at retrofitting existing infrastructure and preserving farmland and natural resources while discouraging investment that promoted urban sprawl.[19] Across the national border, the Smart Growth Canada Network was launched in 2003 in an effort to 'help advance the implementation of smart growth and sustainability principles across the country through education, research and capacity building strategies for the broad range of decision makers.'[20] The network advocates 10 principles: encouraging affordable housing, walkable communities, smart building design, community renewal, green infrastructure, preservation of green space, integrated planning, varied transportation options, community involvement, and planning processes to facilitate investment in sustainable solutions. Provincial initiatives similarly tout smart growth: for example, the Ontario Smart Growth Network aims to 'help design compact and healthy communities – places you'd be proud to call "home."'[21] In each such instance, 'smart growth' symbolizes an initiative that promotes environmental sustainability and richer community viability in the development of urban settlement planning and design.

Urban planners and designers themselves are conceiving of their profession differently in light of environmentalism. Architect Ken Brooks described in a recent presentation to the Toronto Green Building Festival his vision of a 'biologically inspired city,' with biology driving decision making around water, energy, transportation, building systems, standards, neighbourhoods, and land use.[22]

In fact, one of the most renowned examples of an urbanist's commitment to a new vision is Andres Duany, an outspoken critic of traditional suburban sprawl and subdivision development, and an advocate of sustainable design.[23] His 'New Urbanism' supports an empathetic, nostalgic revitalization of old urban centres with higher densities; mixed-use, walkable neighbourhoods; social diversity; and low-rise developments. In actual practice, places such as Seaside, Florida, designed by Duany and his partner, Elizabeth Plater-Zyberk, while lauded by many, have also been subject to the criticism that they cater to the middle and upper classes, producing densities far too low to support the ideals of sustainable walking communities to which they aspire. Nevertheless, the ideals of this 'New Urbanism' are felt by many to be moving in a more positive direction than many suburban developments, because of their emphasis on values such as community, environmental sustainability, and a strong sense of place.

Across the Atlantic, initiatives respecting the 'greening' of urban environments have been advancing in full force. In 1994, more than 2,000 local and regional authorities signed the charter of the European Sustainable Cities and Towns Campaign, acknowledging that they 'shall integrate the principles of sustainability in all our policies and make the respective strengths of our cities and towns the basis of locally appropriate strategies.'[24] The Slow City movement similarly has member cities from across Europe. Targeted at urban scales with populations of less than 50,000, the movement aims to 'reinvent every aspect of urban life, by putting pleasure before profit, human beings before head office, slowness before speed.'[25] Integrating environmental with social, cultural, economic, and lifestyle concerns, the Slow City Manifesto supports over 50 pledges, such as 'cutting noise pollution and traffic, increasing green spaces and pedestrian zones, backing farmers who produce local delicacies and the shops and restaurants that sell them, and preserving local aesthetic traditions.'[26]

In Canada, similar efforts to integrate environmental sustainability into urban planning are becoming increasingly evident. One example is the Toronto and Region Conservation Authority, whose staff is working to build 'a new kind of community – the Living City – where human settlement can flourish forever as part of nature's beauty and diversity.'[27] The City of Toronto itself is actively promoting a new policy to encourage citizens to 'Live Green.' The aim is to help 'neighbourhoods and communities turn green ideas into action.'[28] 'Green building,' 'green houses,' 'greening of the city' – each of these terms reflects widespread initiatives that are commendable. Seeking to minimize resource use and the production of waste, integrating open spaces, supporting local food production and alternative transportation systems – many of these initiatives are becoming mainstream, and they are specific instantiations of much of the essence behind any 'natural city.'

Important as these initiatives are, however, there is a risk that something essential is missing. Is the building of a 'natural city' simply a matter of integrating more parks into urban spaces? Of reducing the ecological footprint? Of encouraging local food production? Of mixed-use zoning? Moving forward will require more than assembling a compendium of such discrete initiatives. More important will be to consider a repositioning of fundamental values, paradigms, and world views that sustain these efforts in the long term. In the following section, we look to philosophers for some guidance on the meaning of the word 'nature' in the hope that we can begin to build a fuller understanding of what it is about the natural city that is particularly significant and unique.

Some Philosophical Reflections on the Nature/City Relation

The very words 'nature' and 'natural' have become suspect in contemporary philosophical discourse. To refer to human 'nature' is often seen to be an insidious slipping back into substance metaphysics – into a universalizing, essentializing language that denies cultural, linguistic, and social diversity. In a postmodern age of moral pluralism, talk of a uniform, hypostatized human 'nature,' for instance, is seen to be either philosophically naive or misguided.[29]

To be sure, despite this critical trend, discussion of the meaning of the word 'nature' has filled journals and libraries. Debates rage over a variety of issues. For instance, in an era when society has planetary environmental impacts, is it naive to speak of the value of pristine nature? In fact, is virgin nature 'better' than nature cultivated and, if so, on what basis?[30] While environmentalists often glorify the notion of pristine nature, what is natural is not always seen to be of value.

Disease is 'natural,' as are volcanic eruptions and earthquake disasters – but instead of welcoming such events, we seek to avoid or to control them.[31] The natural, in such cases, is not always to be equated with an unequivocal good.

Yet we do tend, nevertheless, towards some kind of positive valuation of the natural world. As environmental philosopher Robert Kirkman notes, 'nature is everyone's favourite weapon: it is common practice to label something as "natural" in order to establish its value beyond dispute.'[32] In fact, philosophers such as Aldo Leopold have developed their environmental prescriptions by linking moral virtue specifically with the environment. In his famous pronouncement, Leopold states that 'a thing is right when it tends to preserve the integrity, stability and beauty of the biotic community. It is wrong when it tends otherwise.'[33] Critics charge that Leopold here commits a logical fallacy (the so-called naturalistic fallacy) by confusing the description of what 'is' with the prescription of what 'ought to be': for instance, just because a neighbourhood *is* designed around the residents' collective support and reliance upon automobiles does not mean that it *ought to be* so designed. Similarly, just because an initiative preserves the beauty of a biotic community does not necessarily imply that it is an initiative we *ought* to support. Perhaps criteria other than beauty or biotic integrity are more important. Still, Leopold's supporters are not convinced, and they continue to argue instead that there is a certain moral order that nature reveals to the attentive listener.[34]

Another sort of debate that rages throughout the literature relates to the question of whether nature is simply a social construct, or whether wilderness has an objective 'reality' of its own, independent of the human, valuing consciousness.[35] In many ways, this debate assumes a subject/object dualism that is mirrored in the conceptual bifurcation of cities and human culture on the one hand, and untouched, 'objective' nature on the other. Does nature exist as intrinsically valuable, independent of the human consciousness, or is nature only meaningful by virtue of human interpretive horizons?

In a postmodern era, there has been growing scepticism about the validity of describing any reality as 'objective' or independent of human valuation and interpretation, when such independence is meaningful only within the very framework of conscious awareness. For instance, Phil Macnaghten and John Urry argue against the theory of 'environmental realism,' which holds that 'the environment is essentially a "real entity"' that operates separately from human practice and thereby 'has the power to produce unambiguous, observable and rectifiable outcomes.'[36] Instead, the authors maintain that 'there is no singular "nature" as such, only a diversity of contested natures,' and that 'each such nature is constituted through a variety of socio-cultural processes from which such natures cannot be plausibly separated.'[37]

To be sure, the authors' critiques extend also to other reifying tendencies in philosophy, such as 'environmental idealism,' which claims that the best way to understand nature is to address various 'underlying, stable and consistent' values that support, in some universalizing fashion, our interpretation of nature.[38] Finally, they are equally set against 'environmental instrumentalism,' which is built upon 'straightforwardly determined calculations of individual and/or collective interests' and is linked to a standardized, 'marketized naturalistic model of human behaviour.'[39] In each of these areas, the authors make a strong case for an alternative understanding of nature that avoids the tendency towards universalizing abstractions and a denial of the 'sheer messiness of the "environment" and the diverse species which happen to inhabit the globe,' arguing instead for an approach that recognizes 'the significance of embedded social practices.'[40]

In many ways, arguments such as Macnaghten and Urry's are compelling: they recognize that 'nature' is meaningful in many different ways, because of divergent social, cultural, linguistic, and historical perspectives. Who can deny that the modern-day real estate developer sees Toronto's Lake Ontario waterfront from a fundamentally different perspective from that experienced by the Haudenosaunee people who lived on these same lands prior to their colonization by European settlers? One may wish to say that the lake remains a lake, but it is obviously understood and constituted differently by divergent societal perspectives.

On the other hand, critics of the social construction of nature argue that collapsing the natural world within human social and linguistic categories is deeply problematic. David Kidner, for example, suggests that the inevitable result is a denigration of nature, a reduction to exclusively human, 'anthropocentric' categories that only distance us further from the richness of the natural world.[41] Eileen Crist similarly criticizes the social construction of nature as indirectly supporting the human 'colonization' of the earth. She argues that in its privileging of human cognitive sovereignty, and in collapsing science into mere discourse, the constructivist approach is thereby unable to take the scientific study of environmental biodiversity seriously.[42]

To this day, the debate continues to rage between those who, on the one hand, feel that 'nature' is a 'reality' unto itself, independent of the human valuing consciousness and thereby subject to rational, objective scientific scrutiny; and those who, on the other hand, feel that interpretations of the 'natural' are always socially embedded and culturally dependent.[43] Even surveys of professional philosophers, such as the 'PhilPapers Survey' of 3,226 respondents, are framed in a way that recognizes these tendencies, noting, for instance, that when it comes to epistemic justification, 42.7 per cent 'accept or lean toward externalism,' while 26.4 per cent 'accept or lean toward internalism' – and 30.8 per cent choose an 'other' alternative.[44] Whether defining one's epistemic tendencies or aesthetic values, they are typically framed to this day within a dualistic subject/object context.

Certainly, until one is clear about where one stands on this issue, trying to provide a firm philosophical foundation for an understanding of the 'natural city' is a challenge, to say the least. For instance, one might wonder: Is the concept of a 'natural city' simply another instance of reification and modernist essentializing tendencies? Is 'nature' in the city socially constructed in similar ways to our constructions of pristine environments? Do rat colonies in subway systems bear witness to the hidden, but very 'real' manifestations of nature in urban areas? And how, in the end, do these questions affect a philosophical justification of a 'natural city'?

My own view is that neither a subjectivistic nor objectivist stance can do justice, either to the meaning of the natural world or to cities. In fact, an interesting alternative take on this debate is offered by Adrian Ivakhiv, a professor of religious studies and anthropology, who suggests that this very polarization between epistemological realists and social constructivists is itself reflective of the long-standing modernist tradition that distinguishes subjective and objective realities. Just as the father of modern philosophy, René Descartes, posited a dualism between the rational human subject and the non-thinking world of objects, 'a parallel dichotomy underpins the modern idea that things natural and things cultural constitute two different orders of reality, with humans on one side of the boundary and nonhuman animals (and everything else) on the other.'[45] The debate between the scientific realists and the social constructivists parallels a nature-culture dualism that 'has in turn given rise to the basic intellectual division of labor in academia, that between the natural sciences and the humanities and social sciences.'[46]

Not only is the conversation about the social construction of nature (or its independent existence) entrenched in a long tradition of Cartesian dualism but, from a practical perspective, that conversation is ill suited to the real challenges we face in today's environmental crisis. As Ivakhiv explains, 'phenomena like global climate change, ozone holes, AIDS and other viruses, genetic and reproductive technologies and so on, are merely the latest in a long line of phenomena that cannot be fully understood from within the segregated vantage points of either scientific realism or social constructivism.'[47] Since these phenomena (no less than the challenges of sustainability and natural cities) are both 'real' as well as subject to narrative discourse, we must look to transdisciplinary research that spans the sciences, social sciences, and humanities in order to best understand and address them.

In fact, Ivakhiv raises an important challenge to explore the space between the natural and the cultural, and begins to describe what he terms a 'multicultural ecology' as a new direction for thought – one that would 'recognize the nonessentialist, processual and dialogical nature of cultural-ecological interaction, which is always embedded within significatory and discursive practices and materially embodied ecological relations.'[48] Building upon a variety of perspectives, including the phenomenological recognition that intentional consciousness is always 'consciousness *of*,' Ivakhiv is hoping to avoid focusing on 'nature' and 'culture' as two distinct entities, acknowledging instead the need to attend to the relationship between them.

Certainly, such a shift carries some risks. Consider, for instance, Bruno Latour's contention that 'the very notion of culture is an artifact created by bracketing Nature off. Cultures – different or universal – do not exist, any more than Nature does. There are only naturescultures.'[49] There is merit in Latour's stand but, at the same time, philosopher Holmes Rolston III also has a point when he argues that 'we do not want entirely to transform the natural into the cultural, nor do we want entirely to blend the cultural into the natural. Neither realm ought to be reduced to, or homogenized with, the Other.'[50] In Rolston's view,

It is only philosophical confusion to remark that both geese in flight, landing on Yellowstone Lake, and humans in flight, landing at O'Hare in Chicago, are equally natural, and let it go at that. No interesting philosophical analysis is being done until there is insightful distinction into the differences between the ways humans fly in their engineered, financed jets and the ways geese fly with their genetically constructed, metabolically powered wings. Geese fly naturally; humans fly in artifacts.[51]

Rolston reminds us that 'answers come in degrees, with Times Square on one end of a spectrum and the Absaroka Wilderness on another.'[52] He is wary of those philosophers who simply collapse the distinction because, in so doing, there is a danger that the givenness of the natural world will be forgotten and subsumed simply within human constructs.

Both Ivakhiv and Rolston raise important issues here. In describing the 'natural city,' we neither wish to collapse the natural within the urban, nor to confound their tenuous relationship. What I think is helpful is to recognize, with phenomenology, that nature is not simply a reality 'out there' any more than it is merely a matter of subjective 'discourse.'[53] It makes good sense to ensure that the 'natural' encompasses both a recognition of the fact that we did not create the earth and that, in that sense, it is *given*, and, at the same time, a recognition that we do certainly actively engage and impact upon the earth. And we do so in multiple, diverse ways inasmuch as we are socially, culturally, and linguistically embedded in an ontological relationship with the world that defines us in our very way of being.

Towards an Ontology of the Natural City

How can we begin to explore the natural city in non-dualistic terms, focusing instead upon the diverse spaces that emerge between the 'natural' and the 'cultural'? Phenomenology has always aimed to avoid lapsing into a reified description of either a solipsistic subjective world or an apparently 'objective' reality that is said to subsist independently of interpretive structures of understanding. Might we take some clues from phenomenology in an effort to shed new light on the meaning of a natural city?

German thinker Martin Heidegger offers us some guidelines when he describes the essential belonging together of building and dwelling. 'The way in which you are and I am,' he writes, 'the manner in which we humans *are* on the earth, is *Buan*, dwelling.'[54] Inasmuch as we exist, we exist somewhere and, in that sense, we are fundamentally implaced.[55] Cities are not merely artificial, material artifacts but are the incarnation of our existence. 'I am the space where I am,' writes Noël Arnaud, emphasizing the integral belonging of human existence to built place.[56]

In that vein, a natural city is not simply a reference to a geographical location or physical spatial scale but, instead, it points to the phenomenon of human dwelling. Decades ago, Greek architect and planner Constantinos A. Doxiadis indicated that to be human means to settle: even when we seek refuge under a single tarp, that shelter reminds us that to live is to bide our time – even if only temporarily – in place.[57] Such settlement can occur on many scales – from tent to villages and towns, to cities, and even to ecumenopolis, the urbanized planet or what Doxiadis called 'the inevitable *city* of the future.'[58] Like Doxiadis here, we use the term 'city' metaphorically, not to indicate a particular population size but to suggest a mode of settlement that is ultimately respectful of civic engagement and, thereby, of social, cultural, regulatory, technological, economic, and ecological functions.

Moreover, the metaphor of the natural city also aims to pay heed to the ontological roots of human experience – to the multiple and diverse ways of human *being* in the world. To be in place, as I have shown elsewhere, is to engage with one's environment both rationally and calculatively – as well as pre-thematically.[59] When the city evokes a sense of disorientation, confusion, stress, or apprehension; when building indiscriminately gorges on resources; when social inequalities breed discrimination; when cultural prejudice breeds hatred; when inappropriate technologies are wasteful and heavy handed; when economics are short-sighted, and when a sense of place is at risk, we implicitly know that this 'unnatural' place is not one to which we belong.

Some years ago, architect Christopher Alexander defined natural cities as those that have arisen 'more or less spontaneously over many, many years.' By contrast, artificial cities have been 'deliberately created by designers and planners.'[60] Alexander felt that there was growing recognition that something essential was missing from artificial cities such as the British New Towns or Levittown. The human mind, he argued, was structured in such a way as to reduce ambiguity by categorizing and grouping mental constructs into simplified patterns. In the neat, compartmentalizing designs of artificial cities, we trade the 'humanity and richness of the living city for a conceptual simplicity which benefits only designers, planners, administrators and developers.'[61] A natural city is one that respects diversity; one that arises organically; one that invites local community engagement; one that respects not only ecological limits but the richness and diversity of historically grounded, ontological roots of human well-being.

To be sure, the kind of 'natural cities' that Alexander describes typically did arise through a long, intergenerational process of building, and one that was not always thematically, explicitly understood or articulated in terms of specific design principles. The challenge of dwelling in contemporary cities – especially in light of the speed and scale of their development – is to try to elicit a fuller understanding of how to self-consciously recreate these robust urban places that previously emerged spontaneously and unself-consciously.

Certain thinkers are addressing this very issue. Geographer and environment-behaviour researcher David Seamon speaks to the need to 'make design students more aware of the importance of the natural and built environments in human life.'[62] He is convinced that efforts at 'place restoration must be comprehensive existentially and incorporate both intellect and feeling, both knowledge and intuition, both scientific understanding and an instinctive sense of what is right for nature and for particular places.'[63] Citing phenomenologist Ted Relph's earlier works, Seamon reminds us that 'as the deepest kind of lived involvement with place, existential insideness is a situation in which people are normally unaware of the importance of place in sustaining their everyday world. They experience their place without direct attention, yet that place is rife with overriding but tacitly unnoticed significances.'[64]

The challenge is to better understand such 'insideness' and elicit design guidelines in order to thematically incorporate such an understanding within the natural cities that we build. In thinker Ronald H. Brady's words, 'the activity of intentionality, like other potential perceptions, escapes detection in ordinary consciousness because it is not brought into focus.'[65] How might the pre-thematic, taken-for-granted, intentional activity of building natural cities be better articulated and 'brought into focus'?

In some sense, architects such as Christopher Alexander have already begun such work. In both *A Pattern Language* and *The Nature of Order*, Alexander articulates a theory of wholeness in urban design while also suggesting how specific design elements can reflect a sense of belonging and order.[66] Similarly significant work has been undertaken by Bill Hillier, who also attempts to articulate a holistic sense of place by identifying essential networks that reveal a 'space syntax' in urban settings.[67] In each of these cases, the attempt is made to bring to light an ordering of built spaces that reflect essential existential structures, as well as broader environmental and even cosmological meaning.

How might philosophers contribute to this conversation? Presumably, there is always more to learn about how the unself-conscious process of building 'natural cities' occurs. There is always more to learn about how to better articulate that process and what sort of world views are best incorporated into the design of a natural city. It is particularly in terms of this latter task that phenomenologists may have significant insights.

Philosopher Mark Sagoff has suggested that one can understand the 'natural' in four senses: (1) in opposition to the 'supernatural' and, in that sense, somewhat trivially as 'everything in the universe'; (2) as sacred creation; (3) as the opposite of the 'artificial'; and (4) as 'that which is authentic or true to itself.'[68] Personally, I am particularly interested in how the city might remain 'authentic or true to itself.'

Again, perhaps Heidegger can guide us here, by reminding us that *natura* comes from the Latin *nasci*, meaning '"to be born, to originate" … *Natura* means "that which lets something originate from itself."'[69] Robert Elliot asks us to consider why environmental restoration projects ('faking nature') are so rarely able to return mined areas to their authentic, 'natural' condition. He rightly suggests that the manner of a landscape's genesis matters, just as much as or more than the number of replanted trees.[70] When we speak about something being 'natural,' we are implicitly saying something about the depth of its origins.

Delving further into the roots of Western metaphysical history, Heidegger reflects on how the ancient Greek roots of the word lead us back to the notion of *physis* – more than merely the root of physics but, rather, 'the realm of emerging and abiding … a shining appearing … The essence of Being is *physis*.'[71] Nature as *physis* refers to the process of self-emergence that arises and endures, that appears while also withdrawing into the mystery of self-concealment. The origins of nature, in this sense, refer to the temporal unfolding of Being itself – 'the self-concealing revealing, *physis* in the original sense.'[72] Nature, in this reading, guides us to the very origins and legacy of our cosmos.

Recognizing the givenness of nature as *physis* takes us back to the reflections of Holmes Rolston III, who invites us to teach the people visiting Yellowstone Park and other wilderness areas that 'nature is the ground of culture, that culture transcends nature, that humans emerge from nature. But teach them too that nature is a womb that humans never entirely leave.'[73] It is important that we act with humility: our sense of technological empowerment often hides the fact of our originary dependence upon a natural world that exceeds our control and precedes our own appearance upon this planet. To that extent, we must pay heed to the wonder of the world as *given*. Whether we stop to reflect upon the fact that *Homo sapiens* emerged only about 195,000 years ago, upon a planet whose geological time preceded that appearance by billions of years, or whether we stand in wonder at the opening of the magnolia blossom or the spectacle of each unique sunrise, in every case, we sense, with delight, that the world proceeds independently of our will. In such moments, the grace, the givenness of the natural world is evident. Such moments, somehow, must be preserved, rather than forgotten or hidden, within the natural city.

In the words of ecologist Jarmo Jalava, we must find ways to move towards a 'repositioning of the human species to a place of humility within the cosmos.'[74] In Jalava's view, 'a key part of the solution to humanity's great predicament is a new cosmological paradigm, one that places the intelligence and beauty of nature first, one that reveres the unfathomably complex web of self-organizing interactions that keeps ecosystems healthy.'[75]

Why engineered cities are often not 'natural' has much to do with the fact that nature as *physis* remains hidden within these manicured, manufactured landscapes. Wildness itself is kept in check. As Robert Kirkman reminds us, 'wild nature, in this sense, is very much like what Derrida calls "excess," that from which all meaning springs but which itself threatens the destruction of meaning. Wild nature is a threat to human aspirations, simply because it is profoundly indifferent to those aspirations.'[76] In many of our cities, comfort and convenience provide both a sense of invulnerability and a cocky but misguided assurance that the world is ours to control.

Yet we need not relinquish being open to the grace and mystery of existence within our human settlements. In fact, recalling that sense of the wild into our cities can also bring the promise of richer, healthier environments. When we invite wildness into our cities and thereby speak of the city's 'origins' in wildness, it is not a universalizing 'wilderness' that we evoke. Rather, in philosopher Wade Sikorski's words, such wildness of dwelling 'cultivates difference, includes alterity, nurtures diversity, protects ambiguity, spares multiplicity, frees irony, and makes it possible to understand it all as the world's worlding.'[77] Sikorski has it right, to my mind, when he explains how

the wilderness, or anarchy, of Being is not the opposite of civilization, as it has long been characterized in the Western tradition, virginal, unhandled, inhuman, untouched, but rather a building that we dwell in, that we have built because of what we, as earthly and mortal beings, are. In Being's wilderness, we do not strip away our earthly connections, our belonging with human and nonhuman others in biotic communities, becoming a lonely outcast in the world's vastness, at last free of ourselves, but rather, we find a place where we learn of our life's connections with our earthly situation, with the others and shadows we think we are not, resituating ourselves in the community of life we humans have long tried to escape.[78]

To be sure, the original sense of exposure and vulnerability to a cosmos within which we are all simply *thrown*, to use Heidegger's expression, is often hidden today in our cities. In earlier societies, comfort in the face of the vagaries of nature was perhaps sought within a deification of that world. In such a cosmological era, the gods appeared through thunder, fire, water, and through nature herself.

In many ways, the gods fled upwards and away through the medieval epoch. Lynn White argued years ago that Christianity was responsible for a vision of nature to be conquered.[79] Certainly, the story is not a simple one. But stand sometime in a European cathedral and see whether your gaze is not spontaneously drawn upwards through the grand height, towards the skies. Church spires point us towards the heavens. The theo-logic of the medieval holds the promise of an otherworldly salvation. Some would argue that, on some level in such a moment, the earth risks being left behind.

And it risks being left behind once again, and more radically, in a modern era when Descartes proclaims the indubitable ground of existence to be located in the human form. The egoism of his claim *Cogito, ergo sum* overwhelms. Nature is no longer seen to be the very ground and condition of my being. On the contrary, it is there as an instrument, as little more than a resource for human consumption. Human reason, technology, and culture hold nature at bay – or, so it seems in the arrogance of a modern moment.

Our cities today light up the night and banish the stars. We turn our backs on the grace of the cosmos and are entertained. Yet, to return to Sikorski, wilderness is 'as easily found in the city as the vast rain forest … because wilderness is the place where we recover the things that are most ourselves, but that we have denied, repressed, forgotten.'[80] To be-at-home is to ensure that such wildness is preserved within our cities.

The Natural City and the 'Fourfold'

In the end, a city remains 'natural' precisely because it preserves the interplay between the unencompassability of wildness and the very essence of being human. There is no thematic prescription to draw upon, for the mystery of a natural city cannot be reduced to a neatly circumscribed inventory of sustainability principles, nor is it a static accomplishment. Instead, as evolving and historically implaced, a natural city must pay heed to our essential, often taken for granted connection with the earth and with other living beings with whom we are share our time.

In fact, a natural city is perhaps best informed by Heidegger's ontological understanding of building and dwelling as a sparing and preserving of 'the fourfold' – understood as the relation between earth, sky, divinities, and mortals.[81] Earth is seen in terms of the 'serving bearer, blossoming and fruiting, spreading out in rock and water, rising up into plant and animal.'[82] The dense soil beneath our feet reminds us that the grace of the earth itself is never a simple, wilful product of human creation but is given fundamentally as mystery.

Dwelling under the sky is seen by Heidegger in terms of the 'vaulting path of the sun, the course of the changing moon, the wandering glitter of the stars, the year's seasons and their changes, the light and dusk of day, the gloom and glow of night, the clemency and inclemency of the weather, the drifting clouds and blue depth of the ether.'[83] In many of our cities today, the lights blind us from the stars. With the odd exceptions, we do not build to accommodate the weather but to hide from it.[84] Our city corners are often wind tunnels, constructed oblivious of wind currents and changing weather patterns. Tall buildings cast long shadows, blocking the sun as well as the horizon.

And what of the divinities – 'the beckoning messengers of the godhead'?[85] At the centre of many medieval Western settlements is the cathedral or church. North American city centres, on the other hand, build monuments to banks, business, and telecommunications. The divinities withdraw in an age where idolatry usurps faith, dogma displaces mystery, and consumerism supplants cosmological awareness.

Might we not bring different voices nearer – ones that invite a sense of place, of caring, of community belonging, of being-at-home? Perhaps a natural city is one that allows the divinities to appear through a sense of being-at-home, through sense of place, through spaces that we love and protect, and that protect and shelter us as well.

Finally, Heidegger speaks to us of the dwelling of *mortals*.[86] Chairs and tables ultimately perish, but human beings know that life is temporal and that finite existence defines their mortality. To be alive is to be aware of death, even if only implicitly.

Our cities, however, often seem to help us deny these temporal roots.

Daylight may pass, but our urban centres are ever artificially lit: 'the city never sleeps,' as the saying goes. The perpetual availability of services ensures a permanent, apparently immutable *presence* of the city. The glitter obscures the mortality of all life.

In a sense, that perception of permanence is reassuring and the entertainment of the city can also be invigorating in its denial of death. In the end, however, the city is an artificial construct if it projects itself as neatly circumscribed within the static confines of the present (ever-present?) tense. Cities that lack a historical embeddedness in place and environmental receptivity to their landscapes have no hope of qualifying as natural, in any sense of the word.

Closing Reflections

The natural city, then, must be one that respects and heeds historical, sociological, cultural, economic, environmental, and ontological origins. It opens up the possibility of dwelling among people and built spaces that are understood as more than mere objects. A narrow vision of instrumental rationality sees planning as no more than the technical ordering of residential, commercial, and industrial complexes, together with appropriate infrastructure. The natural city calls for another kind of thinking and planning, an originative thinking, whereby buildings become other than discrete monuments to human ingenuity.[87] Instead, they seek to commemorate meaningful spatial and temporal contexts – indeed, cosmological contexts. These natural dwelling places restore to us a sense of human dignity and sacred belonging to the earth and to existence itself. They remind us of the grace of creation and invite us to look up at the stars and reflect upon our place in the universe. And in doing so, they bestow upon us a sense of belonging – to the natural world as well as to the heavens, to earth, and to our oneiric visions of how best to dwell.

NOTES

1 Found in *Environmental Ethics*, ed. Robert Elliot (New York: Oxford University Press, 1995), 79.
2 Lisa Benton-Short and John Rennie Short, *Cities and Nature* (New York: Routledge, 2008), 141.
3 Helena Siipi, 'Naturalness in Biological Conservation,' *Journal of Agricultural and Environmental Ethics* 17 (2004): 469.

4 Siipi, 'Naturalness in Biological Conservation,' 469.

5 World Commission on Environment and Development, *Our Common Future* (Oxford: Oxford University Press, 1987).

6 Wayne Grady, *Toronto the Wild: Field Notes of an Urban Naturalist* (Toronto: MacFarlane, Walter and Ross, 1995), 2.

7 Grady, *Toronto the Wild*, 2–3.

8 Grady, *Toronto the Wild*, 3.

9 Grady, *Toronto the Wild*, 5, 8.

10 Grady, *Toronto the Wild*, 8.

11 Grady, *Toronto the Wild*, 12.

12 Witold Rybczysnki, *City Life* (New York: HarperCollins, 1995), 35.

13 For multiple case studies, see, for example, Christopher Duerkson and Cara Snyder, *Nature-Friendly Communities: Habitat Protection and Land Use Planning* (Washington: Island Press, 2005).

14 Quoted in Robert Roy Britt, 'The New Nature: Cities as Designer Ecosystems,' *LiveScience*, 10 January 2004, at http://www.livescience.com/environment/050110_designer_ecosystem.html (accessed 13 September 2008).

15 Cf. Benton-Short and Short, *Cities and Nature*, chapter 7, 'Urban Ecology.'

16 Alexander Stille, 'Wild Cities: It's a Jungle Out There,' *New York Times*, 23 November 2002.

17 Comments by Steven E. Clemants, vice-president for science at the Brooklyn Botanic Garden, cited in Stille, 'Wild Cities.'

18 For more discussion on some of these alternatives, see Benton-Short and Short, *Cities and Nature*, chapter 12.

19 See Benton-Short and Short, *Cities and Nature*, 224–6.

20 For more information, see http://www.smartgrowth.ca/home_e.html.

21 For more information, see http://www.smartgrowth.on.ca.

22 See Ken Brooks, design leader, HOK Architects, 'Future City: Inspired by Biology,' presented to the Green Building Festival, 4th Annual Conference and Expo, 9–10 September 2008, at the Toronto Congress Centre, Canada.

23 Cf. Andres Duany, Elizabeth Plater-Zyberk, and Jeff Speck, *Suburban Nation: The Rise of Sprawl and the Decline of the American Dream* (New York: Farrar Straus and Giroux, 2001).

24 For more information, see http://www.aalborgplus10.dk/media/key_documents_2001_english_ final_09–1-2003.doc.

25 Carl Honoré, *National Post*, cited in http://www.strans.org/slowlink.html (accessed 13 September 2008).

26 Honoré, *National Post*, cited in http://www.strans.org/slowlink.html (accessed 13 September 2008).

27 For more information about the TRCA, see http://www.trca.on.ca.

28 See http://www.toronto.ca/livegreen/ for more information.

29 See Robert Kirkman, *Skeptical Environmentalism: The Limits of Philosophy and Science* (Bloomington: Indiana University Press, 2002), chapter 1, 'The Nature of Nature,' where he correctly points out the dangers of defending inequities of capitalism under a Darwinian interpretation of evolution as being part of 'nature's plan.' Kirkman also refers to other examples where religious conservatives argue of the 'unnatural' character of homosexuality, using that justification for prejudice and hatred.

30 Lowenthal reminds us that it is, after all, only non-virgins who produce more virgins! See David Lowenthal, 'Daniel Boone Is Dead,' in *Natural History*, American Geographical Society (August–September 1968). Cited in Michael Hough, *City Form and Natural Process* (New York: Routledge, 1984, 1989), 19.

31 Robert Elliot, 'Faking Nature,' in *Environmental Ethics*, ed. Robert Elliot, 82.

32 Kirkman, *Skeptical Environmentalism*, 47.

33 Aldo Leopold, *A Sand County Almanac* (Oxford: Oxford University Press, 1949), 224–5.

34 For an interesting discussion of this issue, see Joseph Des Jardins, *Environmental Ethics: An Introduction to Environmental Philosophy* (Belmont, CA: Wadsworth Publishing Company, 1993), chapter 9.

35 An issue of the journal of the International Association for Environmental Philosophy is dedicated to exploring these kinds of issues. See *Call to Earth* 3, 1 (March 2002).

36 Phil Macnaghten and John Urry, *Contested Natures* (Thousand Oaks, CA: Sage Publications, 1998), 1.

37 Macnaghten and Urry, *Contested Natures*, 1.

38 Macnaghten and Urry, *Contested Natures*, 1.

39 Macnaghten and Urry, *Contested Natures*, 2.

40 Macnaghten and Urry, *Contested Natures*, 2.

41 David W. Kidner, 'Fabricating Nature: A Critique of the Social Construction of Nature,' *Environmental Ethics* 22 (2000): 339–57.

42 Eileen Crist, 'Against the Social Construction of Nature and Wilderness,' *Environmental Ethics* 26 (2004): 5–24.

43 For additional papers in this area, see, for example, N. Evernden, *The Social Creation of Nature* (Toronto: University of Toronto Press, 1992); K. Soper, *What Is Nature?* (Oxford: Blackwell, 1995); A. Peterson, 'Environmental Ethics and the Social Construction of Nature,' *Environmental Ethics*, 21 (1999): 339–57; B. Braun and N. Castree, eds., *Social Nature: Theory, Practice, Politics* (Oxford: Blackwell, 2001); A. Franklin, *Nature and Social Theory* (London: Sage, 2002); Klaus Eder, *The Social Construction of Nature: A Sociology of Ecological Enlightenment* (London: Sage, 1996).

44 See http://philpapers.org/surveys/results.pl for full results.

45 Adrian Ivakhiv, 'Toward a Multicultural Ecology,' *Organization and Environment* 15,. 4 (2002): 389–409.

46 Ivakhiv, 'Toward a Multicultural Ecology,' 392.

47 Ivakhiv, 'Toward a Multicultural Ecology,' 392.

48 Ivakhiv, 'Toward a Multicultural Ecology,' 401.

49 B. Latour, *We Have Never Been Modern* (Cambridge, MA: Harvard University Press, 1993), 104.

50 Holmes Rolston III, 'Natural and Unnatural; Wild and Cultural,' *Western North American Naturalist* 61, 3 (2001): 275.

51 Rolston, 'Natural and Unnatural,' 268.

52 Rolston, 'Natural and Unnatural,' 272.

53 For more about how phenomenology opens up reflection on the relationship between humans and the world in which they are implaced, see Ingrid Leman Stefanovic, *Safeguarding Our Common Future: Rethinking Sustainable Development* (Albany: State University of New York Press, 2000).

54 Martin Heidegger, 'Building Dwelling Thinking,' in *Poetry, Language, Thought*, trans. Albert Hofstadter (New York: Harper and Row, 1971), 147.

55 This theme of ontological implacement is brilliantly explored by authors such as Edward Casey, in *Getting Back into Place: Toward a Renewed Understanding of the Place-World* (Bloomington and Indianapolis: Indiana University Press, 1993); Robert Mugerauer, *Interpretations on Behalf of Place* (Albany: State University of New York Press, 1994); and J.E. Malpas, *Place and Experience: A Philosophical Topography* (Cambridge: Cambridge University Press, 1999).

56 Cited in Gaston Bachelard, *The Poetics of Space*, trans. Maria Jolas (Boston: Beacon Press, 1969), 137.

57 Doxiadis was the founder of the Athens Centre of Ekistics and the World Society for Ekistics, as well as the *Ekistics* journal of the study of human settlements. See his *Ekistics: An Introduction to the Science of Human Settlements* (New York: Oxford University Press, 1968).

58 C.A. Doxiadis and J.G. Papaioannou, *Ecumenopolis: The Inevitable City of the Future* (Athens: Athens Centre for Ekistics, 1974).

59 See Ingrid Leman Stefanovic, *Safeguarding Our Common Future*.

60 Christopher Alexander, 'A City Is Not a Tree,' in *Human Identity in the Urban Environment*, ed. Gwen Bell and Jacqueline Tyrwhitt (New York: Penguin Books, 1972), 401.

61 Alexander, 'A City Is Not a Tree,' 427.

62 David Seamon, 'Place, Belonging and Environmental Humility: The Experience of the "Teched" as Portrayed by American Novelist and Agrarian

Reformer, Louis Bromfield,' in *Writing the Land: John Burroughs and His Legacy*, ed. Daniel G. Payne (Newcastle, UK: Cambridge Scholars Publishing, 2008), 158–73. See also David Seamon and Robert Mugerauer's seminal edited work in this area, *Dwelling, Place and Environment: Toward a Phenomenology of Person and World* (New York: Columbia University Press, 1989).

63 Seamon, 'Place, Belonging and Environmental Humility,' 159.

64 David Seamon, 'Place, Placelessness, Insideness, and Outsideness in John Sayles' *Sunshine State*,' *Aether: The Journal of Media Geography* 3 (June 2008): 4.

65 Ronald H. Brady, 'The Idea in Nature: Rereading Goethe's Organics,' in *Goethe's Way of Science: A Phenomenology of Nature*, ed. David Seamon and Arthur Zajonc (Albany: State University of New York Press, 1998), 97.

66 See Christopher Alexander, *A Pattern Language: Towns, Buildings, Construction* (New York: Oxford University Press, 1977) and *The Phenomenon of Life: Nature of Order, Book 1: An Essay on the Art of Building and the Nature of the Universe* (Berkeley, CA: Center for Environmental Structure, 2004).

67 Bill Hillier and J. Hanson, *The Social Logic of Space* (Cambridge, UK: Cambridge University Press, 1984).

68 Mark Sagoff, 'Genetic Engineering and the Concept of the Natural,' in Morton Winston and Ralph Edelbach, eds., *Society, Ethics and Technology*, 2nd edition (Belmont, CA: Wadsworth, 2003), 292.

69 Martin Heidegger, 'On the Essence and Concept of *Physis* in Aristotle's Physics B, I,' in *Pathmarks*, ed. William McNeill (Cambridge: Cambridge University Press, 1998), 183.

70 Elliot, 'Faking Nature.'

71 Martin Heidegger, *An Introduction to Metaphysics*, trans. Ralph Manheim (New York: Doubleday, 1959), 85–6.

72 Heidegger, 'On the Essence and Concept of *Physis* in Aristotle's Physics B, I,' 230.

73 Rolston, 'Natural and Unnatural,' 275.

74 Jarmo Jalava, 'Taboo of the Sacred,' *Alternatives* 34, 1 (2008): 20.

75 Jalava, 'Taboo of the Sacred,' 20.

76 Kirkman, *Skeptical Environmentalism*, 46.

77 Wade Sikorski, 'Building Wilderness,' chapter 2 in *In the Nature of Things: Language, Politics and the Environment*, ed. Jane Bennett and William Chaloupka (Minneapolis: University of Minnesota Press, 1993), 24.

78 Sikorski, 'Building Wilderness,' 29.

79 Lynn White, Jr, 'The Historical Roots of Our Ecological Crisis,' *Science* 155 (March 1967): 1203–7.

80 Sikorski, 'Building Wilderness,' 29.
81 Heidegger, 'Building Dwelling Thinking,' 149ff.
82 Heidegger, 'Building Dwelling Thinking,' 149.
83 Heidegger, 'Building Dwelling Thinking,' 149.
84 Some Scandinavian cities heat their sidewalks with building exhaust, in order to accommodate bicycle ridership during the winter months. In North American cities, we resort to polluting cars and leave our bicycles behind.
85 Heidegger, 'Building Dwelling Thinking,' 150.
86 Heidegger, 'Building Dwelling Thinking,' 150.
87 For a discussion of the meaning of originative thinking, see Ingrid Leman Stefanovic, *Safeguarding Our Common Future.*

2 Can Cities Be Both Natural and Successful? Reflections Grounding Two Apparently Oxymoronic Aspirations

W.S.K. CAMERON

This book envisions the 'natural city' – but is this not an oxymoron? After all, the city has been the explicit antitype of nature ever since Rousseau and his Romantic heirs voiced their alienation from the urban birthplaces of the Industrial Revolution. An implicit opposition between city and country, between cultivated and wild, and between civilized and pagan[1] has architecturally embodied foundations as old as the city walls that fell at the ancient battle of Jericho. Moreover, one oxymoron tumbles into another when one adds to the designation 'natural city' the aspiration to 'success.' Cities have been successful in many ways, but the famously successful cities – the most populous, the most developed, the most luxurious, and, also, inevitably, the most squalid – have achieved their remarkable industrial, financial, and cultural productivity at the cost of correspondingly intense demands on the natural world.

In this chapter, I will address these two apparent oxymorons by taking up three critical categories: 'success,' 'the city,' and 'natural.' Though I cannot follow Nietzsche's reasoning to its end, here I do think we need a transvaluation of values, for our current interpretations of these concepts offer only the promise of sickness and eventual death. In his stunningly subtitled *Twilight of the Idols: or, How to Do Philosophy with a Hammer*, Nietzsche invites his contemporaries to tap the idols of his age with a tuning hammer to see how they resound. There can be little doubt that the idols of our age produce cacophony: the question is whether and how we can retune them so that their constructive interference will not smash human culture – not to mention the natural world – over the coming century. Having briefly reviewed a few ways in which we must transvalue our ideals of urban success, I turn to the temptation to deconstruct cities as part of a return to a less dense, more pastoral ideal. Taking a cue from Jacques Ellul, I will argue that cities must not be destroyed, but redeemed – and, to this end, we must reflect on the possibility of developing a new, more organic model of the relation between cities and the ground on which they stand. The 'natural city' is not only possible, it *must* succeed – but this will require a creative reconsideration of what we mean by all three critical terms: success, nature, and the city.

Deconstructing 'Success'

Of the three critical ideas we will examine, the most obvious candidate for transvaluation is the concept of 'success.' Environmentalists have known for half a century that what looks like success on one scale portends disaster from another, more comprehensive view. Pick your favourite example: Aldo Leopold's discovery that killing top-level predators leaves herbivores to over-reproduce and devastate entire ecosystems; Rachel Carson's warning that DDT's success in killing malaria-carrying mosquitoes would soon herald a bird-free 'silent spring'; or Garrett Hardin's rattling conclusion that open access to common resources – a fundamental assumption of both liberal politics and capitalist economics since the seventeenth century – leads inevitably to the destruction of those resources.[2] More recently, Herman Daly has argued that the default index of economic success – a growing gross domestic product (GDP) – is ecologically treacherous, since it ignores the value of natural capital and natural services. Worse, what the index *does* count often falls in the wrong column.[3] The GDP merely tabulates the total value of all domestically produced goods, regardless of whether the producers are domestic or foreign firms. By its criteria, the best use we could make of any particular parcel of land is almost invariably to produce throwaway widgets, since these – unlike a park that we merely enjoy – must be produced, transported, marketed, sold through various middlemen, and eventually disposed of, and each of these stages adds to the GDP. Indeed, if, having made really expensive and dangerous throwaways, such as nuclear bombs, we produced a superfund cleanup site, we would have made a far greater contribution to the GDP than virtually any other alternative. A rising GDP is taken to indicate 'economic good times'; just as often, however, it documents growing misery.[4]

Some have suggested abandoning the GDP for other, broader indices of social health, such as the 'Genuine Progress Index,' pioneered in Nova Scotia,[5] or the American 'Index of Social Health.'[6] Such efforts are always controversial, since they presume contestable value judgments about green space, convenience, security, predictability, social networks, and privacy. But even if they could give only rough indications of social progress, they would at least acknowledge more of the relevant factors, and constrain the GDP's tendency to count liabilities as assets. What success index would be appropriate for the 'natural city'?

Among a variety of contenders, some are clearly relevant. The current buzzword 'sustainability' offers a convenient shorthand: we must take into account at least the use of resources for immediate consumption, including food, water, transportation, and environmental control (e.g., housing and heating); resources used for the production of durable goods, including both consumption costs (as a function of energy efficiency) and product life-cycle analysis; and resource costs against natural capital, in the form of both non-renewable resources and finite pollution sinks. Cities must forge tools, in short, for assessing and then reducing their ecological footprint.

But if that is the direction in which we are headed, why not go further? Cities have always had a disproportionate impact on the planet. If organic food is good, but non-organic grub grown locally and available in season may be better,[7] and if telecommuting knowledge-workers and the development of boutique production processes make possible a more diffuse distribution of people, shouldn't we simply abandon our cities? Is it not now possible, as the Romantics first aspired to do, to reverse the historical drift of people to cities in favour of a less dense, quasi-pastoral model? At the very least, this model is an attractively easy sell: the massive move of the middle class to the suburbs in postwar North America reflected the powerful appeal of green country, even if that green existed only in well-manicured but ecologically disastrous lawns dotted with exotic trees and shrubs. The question is whether this ex-urban ideal is really green. This brings us to the next two of our title concepts, which have been opposed for virtually all of written history: nature and the city.

Nature versus the City

The contrast between nature and the city is so familiar that it easily eludes reflection.[8] Before I challenge it, let us remind ourselves of its powerful appeal on a variety of fronts:

(a) *Ecologically*, cities are not natural: they constitute sites of egregiously imbalanced exchange, i.e., the exploitation of nature. Nor is this an accident, since

(b) Cities are not *anthropologically* natural, either: we have only had villages, let alone cities, for about 8,000 years – less than a tenth of the time that humans have existed in our current form.

(c) Thus, it can be no surprise that cities are not *economically* natural, in their causes or in their effects. Self-sufficient village economies have been the norm over vast expanses of time and space; cities, on the contrary, required regional political powers to set up and defend the administrative, cultural, and religious headquarters from which they could establish special rights to trade and taxation; administer the collection, banking, and distribution of food and water; and police trade routes among urban centres. These practices attracted a progressively more disproportionate share of producers and consumers.

Yet, if cities are not economically natural in their causes, they are even less natural in their effects, since the fine-grained division of labour that they encourage makes possible a thorough alienation from the bodily processes that connect us with the natural world: the growing, gathering, slaughtering, and preparation of food, for instance; the collection of water for drinking, watering, and washing that has historically demanded (and in many cultures still demands) enormous human effort; and the completion of the cycle of self- and other-production through the efficient management of waste.

(d) Finally, we do not experience cities *phenomenologically* as natural. One of the most vivid images of this point comes from my graduate school years in the Bronx, where a friend overheard local youths talking about 'falling on the floor.' This was not a remarkable phrase until one realized that these kids were talking about something that had happened *outside*. Falling on 'the floor' outside: initially an odd-sounding idiom, but hardly a surprising one given that virtually all of the South Bronx is covered in walk-up apartments, concrete sidewalks, and asphalt roads. These in turn cover water mains, sewer lines, electrical conduits, heating ducts, and (sometimes) subways and associated underground walkways to a depth of 10 to 50 or more feet (3 to 15 or more metres). In this urban environment, there really appeared to be no ground, just 'floor.'

Nature versus the Suburbs

Yet despite the obvious truth captured in the opposition between city and nature – one so familiar it appears to demand no further thought – we must challenge the adequacy of this old trope. Above, I recalled the Romantic pastoral ideal that played an essential role in selling the suburbs, but that ideal is now obviously self-defeating, for the following reasons:

(a) Suburbs virtually always involve paving conveniently flat but scarce arable land – the same land that supplied the initial growth of the urban core, and in many cases, especially in Canada, the most productive land available. This, in turn, both increases the alienation of urban and suburban residents from the country, and commits them to the ecologically inefficient and politically risky long-distance transportation of food.

(b) Suburbs sustain the illusion of living 'closer to nature' – but only temporarily, until the next two or three developments further afield hem in earlier outliers among the congestion and pollution of city life. The Bronx was once a suburb, too.

(c) Suburbs impose tremendous costs in low-volume, ecologically inefficient private transportation to buildings inefficiently heated and cooled due to their high ratios of external wall to living space and served by expensive, because so widely spread, systems of water and power distribution, and sewage and solid waste recovery.

(d) And while suburbs typically feature a monoculture of Kentucky blue grass broken up by exotic and sometimes invasive show species, neither of which provide adequate cover or forage for native birds, bugs, and small mammals, cities sometimes provide – admittedly, often by accident – refuges and remnant lands where native species flourish below the radar of urban redevelopers. The New York Botanical Garden, located in the middle of the Bronx, contains an old-growth forest, a gem unequalled in many more remote and wilder-looking second-growth areas upstate. A recent Public Broadcasting Service (PBS) documentary noted that the best examples of oak savannahs, wetlands, and prairie in Illinois are *within* the nine million–strong metropolis of Chicago.[9] Outside the city, everything was ploughed under to make way for monocultures of soy and corn.

(e) Finally, environmentalists cannot win the necessary political battles by appealing only to a parochial aesthetic interest in wild areas while ignoring the surburban environments where many live, and the urban environments that others simply cannot escape. Alliances linking ecological concerns with the interests of the urban poor have recently grown under the call for environmental justice – a natural enough alliance, once reframed. As Jerome Ringo – a former petrochemical worker from Louisiana's 'Cancer Alley' and the first African American to head a major U.S. environmental organization – notes, 'for poor people, issues like ozone depletion have not been a priority, compared with next month's rent. But I tell people in Cancer Alley, what good is next month's rent if you're dying from cancer?'[10] Yet if contemporary environmentalists insist – surely rightly – on adding an interest in the city to older concerns for wilderness areas, we leave the old contrast intact. And that is a problem, because it suggests a kind of ideal that is unattainable in the cities and suburbs where the vast majority of us live. A few of us – academics in summer, computer programmers, direct-mail envelope stuffers, and telemarketers – really can move our work outside the city, but the rich networks of interconnection needed to maintain our complex economy and to serve human needs efficiently simply cannot function without areas of high density. Accepting the unthought contrast between nature and the city means being torn between the ideals we cherish and the places we actually live.

A Theological Compass Suggesting a New Heading: Jacques Ellul on the City

The contrast between city and country has long had theological as well as philosophical overtones. Recall the ancient contrast between civilized and pagan (valorizing the former), and the Romantic contrast between tame and wild (valorizing the latter). Here I pause to offer a more recent theological spin. You may not share, as I do, Jacques Ellul's core theological convictions, but reflecting on them sent this philosopher in a new direction that I hope may prove edifying.

Ellul highlights the historical complexity of the notion of the city in the Jewish and Christian scriptures. The story starts in a garden, of course – the Garden of Eden – though the crisis of sin (in the Christian interpretation) immediately results in permanent exile. The main thread of the subsequent narrative focuses on a line of patriarchs and matriarchs forming a temporally extended kinship group, but a series of mostly negative allusions to cities begins right away. Having been cursed to wander east of Eden, Abel's brother and murderer, Cain, founds there the first city, named after his son Enoch. The account of Nimrod[11] associates cities with the ugly realities of war; after the Flood, Noah's children aspire to build their city around a tower threatening to stretch up to heaven. Already here – just 11 chapters into Genesis – the city appears as the ultimate symbol of hubris, and the romantics among us may relish the dispersal that follows the confusion of tongues. Later we meet Abraham – the common father of faith for Jews, Christians, and Muslims – living in the city of Ur. Yet he follows God by *leaving* that city for a pastoral life in the promised land; his cousin Lot eventually flees the cursed city of Sodom; and Moses grows up in the palaces of imperial Egypt, but first encounters God, and later brings his people to meet God, in the wilderness. The typology appears clear and consistent: we lost the Garden of Eden, and now continue to choose cities to our destruction. But the biblical arc does not stop there. Though people were first blessed with life in a garden, fell into cities, and then sought redemption by way of journeys through the wilderness, both Jewish and Christian typologies see the final redemption as embodied in a new Jerusalem. This is not, to be sure, Augustine's City of Man, but it is the divinely redeemed *City* of God.[12]

To some, these stories will appear to be no more than metaphors, but the shared Wisdom literature of the Jewish and Christian traditions points me in an interesting direction. In a planet with a population of more than six billion, we cannot return to some real or imagined rural past – even in Canada, Australia, or the United States, let alone the more densely populated parts of the world. Ecologically catastrophic as cities have been, the contemporary challenge is not to renounce them, but to redeem them.

Towards the Natural City

How can we overcome the contrast – one as old as written history – between 'nature' and 'the city'? To this huge project, I can make only a few brief contributions here. Let me begin by recalling that odd Bronx idiom identifying the ground with the floor. What, after all, is a floor, and how does it connect us to the earth from which we came, and to which we will all return? In contemporary houses, floors are not – as in many traditional dwellings – the ground, but rather what separates us from the ground. Does this offer a clue?

I will return to this point below, but first, I must introduce an idea that dramatically recontextualized my grasp of environmental problems when I first heard it many years ago. Why do we face a colossal environmental crisis now? Part of the problem is population: there are far more of us than ever before, and we exert a correspondingly greater pressure on the natural world. But that quantitative change, a function of declining mortality, was itself the effect of a qualitative change brought about by a series of prior successes. The aspiration to power had been implicit in the modern project ever since René Descartes promoted his method as the foundation of a practical science that would make us 'lords and masters of nature.'[13] Yet the last 50 years have witnessed unprecedented successes by relying on materials that have never existed in the natural world, and thus have no place in organic and inorganic cycles of composition and decomposition. Reflect, for a moment, on the amazing powers of plastic. Want to keep something – organic or inorganic, solid, liquid, or gas – in or out virtually permanently? At higher temperatures plastic melts, and at normal environmental temperatures it does eventually break down over time under sunlight, but virtually no plant, insect, or animal will ingest and metabolize it.[14] No wonder one study found pieces of plastic outweighing plankton by a ratio of six to one in the mid-Pacific.[15] The great power of modern materials comes at an ecological cost: by resisting breakdown, they become virtually immortal as trash.

Now, back to floors. We build floors, buildings, and ultimately cities with a pervasive goal – permanence – sought by a pervasive means – impermeability.

Naturally, both goal and means have had a legitimate appeal. Take permanence: Ferdinand Braudel's magisterial history of capitalism reports that in the pre-modern era, most investments in capital equipment lasted no more than five to six years, whereupon they needed to be replaced.[16] This represents an enormous investment of human and natural capital, all dedicated not to reinventing, but continually to remaking, the wheel. The development of modern iron alloys such as steel and stainless steel has made a huge difference to our economy, and thus to our lives. Yet despite huge leaps in the longevity of our capital investments, permanence remains well out of our reach, as a ride on an older highway or a look at an old car quickly reveals.

Moreover, our Sisyphean aspiration to permanence attempts to master the universal solvent, water, by means of another Sisyphean aspiration – *impermeability*. Again, impermeability is obviously useful: it is comfortable to have buildings sufficiently tightly designed to keep out water, drafts, and most bugs.[17] Yet adopting this means to achieve our goal of permanence not only cuts us off from the cycles of the natural world, but creates temptations and new problems. For example:

(a) Fools can build cities in defiance of natural limitations where other fools – like me – will move, because impermeable dams and canals bring water from hundreds of miles away. In Los Angeles, 10 million people live in an area with water resources sufficient for a few hundred thousand.

(b) It gets worse: in the water-starved American Southwest, the run-off from acre upon acre of impermeable structures and roads immediately transmogrifies life-giving rain into waste water, i.e., sewage.

(c) Moreover, the impermeability of modern materials resists breakdown. Thus, ironically, the only permanence we really achieve is the landfill. No kidding: a study of American landfills initiated at the University of Arizona showed that 40 per cent or more of their space was filled with paper, grass clippings, and old vegetables – i.e., with things that were theoretically biodegradable. Perhaps because the impermeable things buried on top had effectively made the landfills anaerobic environments, researchers found carrots discarded five and six decades ago that still looked like carrots.[18] I have focused on our defiance of the water cycle, but I could just as well have taken up a variety of others: cycles of temperature, of wind, of sun and shade, and of the organic input of food and output of waste.[19]

What Might All This Mean, Practically Speaking?

My question for the would-be natural city is whether we can relinquish the impulse to defy natural cycles – an impossible goal, after all, that must rely on self-defeating means – in favour of the effort to reconnect floor and ground. We must, in other words, reintegrate buildings and their support systems into natural cycles so that those cycles not only exist under and over and around the city, but are suffused throughout it. For the last four centuries, city planners and engineers have envisaged the city as a machine sustained by discrete sewer, water, transit, and electrical systems. This machine metaphor presupposes the relative independence of the city from its natural context; it is conceived as separate and self-sufficient, i.e., as an automaton. What would happen if we began to conceive the city as an organism in continual exchange with its environment, an organism striving – like natural organisms – for a life-sustaining homeostasis? That such a reorientation of thinking is possible is evident in the following, more concrete examples.

First, rather than simply overpowering local cycles of light and temperature through high-energy illumination and climate control systems, we can model new buildings on the experimental houses, office buildings, and even factories where natural cycles of light, air circulation, and heat transfer have been integrated through design techniques deploying passive and active solar heating, light wells and conduits, ventilation systems, and heat exchangers. The Mobbs's family house in

Sydney, Australia, incorporates even more radical techniques, capturing all rain that falls on the house for drinking water, washing water, and irrigation, and treating all waste water and most domestic waste on-site using techniques originally designed for composting toilets. All this in an ordinary townhouse lot![20]

Second, cities need lungs as well as skin and kidneys, and people must connect to nature not only outside but within the natural city. We North Americans must thus rethink our love of the house with its lawn in light of the older European model of dense developments with easy access to urban parks. One of the most livable places I have ever spent time was also one of the densest – Bonn, Germany. One could walk around the entire downtown serving a city of 350,000 – and I do mean virtually every street, with a babe in a sling and pushing a toddler in a stroller – in about 1.5 hours, and one could escape the city for nearby forests after a 10- to 15-minute ride by bus or train. Here – unlike Los Angeles, where I live now – one needed no car to get away. Indeed, city parks can provide surprisingly rich experiences of nature. One of the best places to see birds during their annual migrations up and down the east coast is Manhattan's Central Park. Why? Look at Manhattan from the air: the grey of a vast megalopolis, and then a jewel of green. For a bird – and for those who appreciate them – there is no question where to drop in.

Third, we must start building houses, offices, factories, and even more ambitious public works knowing that all of them are mortal. Of course, some will stand the test of time and find advocates for their preservation, but most buildings will eventually be knocked down. If we built with an eye to their deconstruction and reuse, we could destream much of the 20 per cent of urban solid waste directly attributable to building demolition, and reuse some portion of a building's lifetime energy use – up to 40 per cent, depending on the building's environment[21] – that goes into its construction. This may be a blue-sky idea now, but European manufacturers are already designing cars and computers with recycling in mind, so it is clearly not impossible in principle.

Can we incorporate nature into the city, and the city into nature? Of course we can – but it will demand determination, effective zoning, and revised building codes, along with incentives such as enlightened taxation and a new look at our accounting.[22] We will not get there all at once. But having slammed Los Angeles a few times in this chapter, I will now offer it as a model. Los Angeles has had a long series of building codes over the last hundred years, mostly because they are continually revised with the knowledge gained after each significant earthquake. Newer buildings, consequently, are as safe as one can find in earthquake zones anywhere in the world. The toilet exchange program pioneered by long-time Los Angeles city councilwoman Ruth Galanter has replaced millions of old toilets with new, low-flow models, thereby saving millions of gallons of water each year. Rebate programs offered by the Los Angeles Department of Water and Power have made the early adoption of efficient dishwashers, washing machines, and dryers accessible to many. These seem to me to be some of the best ways to push for progress: pragmatically, concretely, incrementally, and persistently. Regulation need not strangle innovation if governments set high targets while allowing flexibility in determining the means to achieve them. Cities have always been loci of disproportionate environmental impact. But just for that reason, we do well to focus on them: positive changes there will have a disproportionate impact as strong as the problems they resolve have historically had. If we reimagine what we mean by our terms, the 'natural city' can be – indeed, must be – a success. All we need to set off towards that goal is the intelligence to acknowledge what is already being done well, and the courage to demand its broader implementation.

NOTES

1 The ordinary sense of the word 'pagan' as heathen derives from the classical Latin *paganus* – of or belonging to the country (Oxford English Dictionary). Christianity spread first from city to city, and in the post-Constantinian era, orthodoxy could best be enforced there, so the link between country and heterodoxy was a natural one.

2 I've refined Hardin's view here: he actually makes the more general claim that freedom in conjunction with individual ownership leads inevitably to what he famously calls the 'tragedy of the commons.' For his view and for the respects in which I think that this view must be modified, see his 'The Tragedy of the Commons,' *Science* 162 (1968): 1243–8, and my 'Can We Afford the Tough Love of Liberals? A Deflationary Look at Garrett Hardin's Lifeboat Ethic,' *Environmental Philosophy* 2 (2005): 30–43.

3 Herman E. Daly, 'Moving to a Steady-State Economy,' in *Beyond Growth: The Economics of Sustainable Development* (Boston: Beacon Press, 1996). Technically, Daly thematizes problems with the gross national product or GNP – the primary economic measure used in the United States until a few years ago, since replaced by the more broadly used GDP. The differences

between these two indices of economic growth are relatively minor, and both are blind to the problems Daly identifies.

4 Imagine the commercial possibilities of the popular personal finance management software program Quicken, if it so egregiously counted obvious liabilities as assets.

5 For information about this project, start with its homepage: www.gpiatlantic.org. The project is now being developed on a more ambitious scale as the Canadian Index of Wellbeing, described at http://www.ciw.ca/en/Home.aspx.

6 A U.S. version with much the same inspiration, the 'Index of Social Health,' has been developed by Marc Miringoff and his colleagues at Fordham's Graduate Campus in Tarrytown, NY. See their statement of purpose in Marc L. Miringoff, 'Toward a National Standard of Social Health: The Need for Progress in Social Indicators,' *American Journal of Orthopsychiatry* 65, 4 (1994): 462–7. Recent reports may be ordered through their homepage at: http://www.fordham.edu.

7 I borrow the epithet 'grub' and the advice from the book by Anna Lappé and Bryant Terry, *Grub: Ideas for an Urban Organic Kitchen* (New York: Tarcher/Penguin, 2006).

8 Some may worry that the terms 'nature' and 'city' as used below evade precise definition, not only because cities commonly fade into much less dense suburbs, widely spaced industrial parks, and intensively farmed land before breaking up into something approaching 'nature,' but also because cities sometimes contain large, relatively 'natural' parks. Conceded. My point, indeed, is to initiate a much-needed process of clarification that begins from the realization that the inherited contrast must be rethought.

9 I owe this point to the documentary *Chicago: City of the Big Shoulders*, part of the recent series *Edens Lost and Found*, available from PBS Video (along with much supplementary material) through its homepage, http://www.edenslostandfound.org.

10 Ringo is chairman of the board of the National Wildlife Federation, the largest environmental organization in the UnitedStates. The quote comes from Mark Hertsgaard's article 'Brave New Enviros,' in *The Nation*, 25 July 2006, and available online at http://www.alternet.org/story/39183 (accessed 4 May 2008).

11 The grandson of Cain by Cain's cursed son, Ham.

12 Some might say that the cities to which I point in Genesis would barely qualify as towns now. True enough, though even at that size they already appear dysfunctional. More remarkably still, the redemption of cities

appears most clearly in eschatological literature like St John's Book of Revelation – i.e., in a book written by and for people who knew first-century Jerusalem and who stood in the cold shadow of imperial Rome. These were much closer to what we would recognize as cities, and that makes the hope not just for their redemption, but of our redemption *through* them, all the more stunning.

13 René Descartes, *Discourse on the Method*, in *The Philosophical Writings of Descartes, Vol. I*, trans. John Cottingham, Robert Stoothoff, and Dugald Murdoch (Cambridge: Cambridge University Press, 1985), 142–3.

14 I have seen trail markers on the Appalachian Trail that have been badly chewed by porcupines – only they know why – but if chewing somehow soothed their teeth, I am sure they were under no illusions that they had found food.

15 Research by Algalita reported by Lee Peterson in 'Here's Hoping Someone Gets a Message on Some Bottles,' in *The Daily Breeze*, 13 May 2006, downloaded from http://www.dailybreeze.com/news/articles/2797626.html (accessed 15 May 2006).

16 Braudel cites a remarkable study by Simon Kuznets: 'If most equipment lasted no more than five or six years, if most land improvement had to be maintained by continuous rebuilding amounting to something like a fifth of the total value per year, and if most buildings were destroyed at a rate cumulating to fairly complete destruction from 25 to 50 years, then there was little that could be classified as durable capital ... The whole concept of fixed capital may be a unique product of the modern economic epoch and of modern technology.' See Ferdinand Braudel's *The Wheels of Commerce*, vol. 2 of *Civilization and Capitalism: 15th to 18th Century*, trans. Siân Reynolds (New York: Harper Collins, 1983), 247.

17 Of course, no one can design a building that keeps out cockroaches.

18 See W.L. Rathje, 'The Archaeology of Us,' in C. Ciegelski, ed., *Encyclopedia Britannica's Yearbook of Science and the Future: 1997* (New York: Encyclopedia Britannica, 1996), 158–77, available online at: http://metamedia.stanford.edu:3455/Symmetry/174 (accessed 4 May 2008). For a fuller study, see William L. Rathje and Cullen Murphy, *Rubbish! The Archaeology of Garbage* (New York: HarperPerennial, 1993).

19 According to Ivan Illich, pre-Revolutionary Paris was self-sufficient in vegetable production due to the remarkable yield of household gardens fertilized by human waste. See his *H2O and the Waters of Forgetfulness: Reflections on the Historicity of Stuff* (Dallas: Dallas Institute of Humanities and Culture, 1985).

20 See more details in Nicholas Low, Brendan Gleeson, Ray Green, and Darko

Radovi, *The Green City: Sustainable Homes, Sustainable Suburbs* (New York: Routledge, 2005), 45–50.

21 See Low, Gleeson, Green, and Radovi, eds., *The Green City*, 229, note 18. At the first reading of this chapter, someone observed that the proportion of a building's lifetime energy use spent in construction is likely much lower in Canada, where winters are cold and heating costs high. Whatever the proportion, however, the embodied energy is surely better reused than wasted.

22 A quick example: in *The Green City*, the authors point out that we do not normally consider the huge fixed-cost liabilities imposed by the construction of streets and the broad distribution of city utilities (e.g., water, sewer, power, and solid waste recovery) and services (e.g., fire, ambulance, police, and communications) when assessing the economic viability of suburbs, while on the other hand we insist that public transit systems must make a profit (151–3). If we acknowledged the saved infrastructure costs of building denser neighbourhoods, couldn't we credit that against the cost of providing bus or train service priced favourably to serve those areas, thus encouraging both residence and public transit ridership there?

3 The 'Gruing' of Cities

FRANK CUNNINGHAM

'Grue' is defined as 'the colour that is green until some unspecified time after which it is blue.' The concept figures in the philosophy of induction, since it exposes a limit to the reliability of expectations based on experience: observations supporting a belief that something is green equally support its being grue.

Thoroughgoing philosophical sceptics aver that for all we can know, everything is like grue, thus casting doubt on the reliability of all our empirical beliefs. Setting aside this radical deployment of the concept, one can sort things according to how grue-like they are. The more uniformly things change and the more their features cohere in law-like and hence predictable ways, the less like grue they are.[1]

Cities, however, are in the grue-like category. This is not to say that unifying models are not available in urban theory. Kevin Lynch identified five: an organism, an economic engine, a communication network, a system of linked decisions, and an arena of conflict.[2] But the point is exactly that there are five of them, each with different and, one might add, notoriously unreliable predictive or policy-supporting powers. The grueness of cities also helps to explain why it is so difficult to find more than vague and incomplete definitions of the term 'city' and why urban planning confronts not just practical and political impediments, but theoretical and ideological ones as well.

To say that cities are grue-like is to say that in addition to being diverse and complex – that is, consisting of many elements located within interacting demographic, economic, cultural, infrastructural, political, juridical, and other domains – they are subject to sometimes rapid change and in directions that defy long-range prediction. Hypotheses that isolate types of events within one of the domains as independent variables driving changes in the character of the other domains seem always to fail, despite the elegance (or clumsiness) and enthusiasm with which they are propounded. This is part of the idea that the late and greatly missed urban writer and activist Jane Jacobs expressed in her character-ization of cities as 'problems in organized complexity.'[3] This feature of cities presents a challenge to any project for introducing environmental sustainability into urban planning and comportment.

The core organizing concept of environmentalism, I take it, is *ecosys-tematicity*. Both recognition of the nature of challenges to environmental sustainability and strategies to meet these challenges crossed a thresh-old when environmental concern ceased to be predicated on piecemeal conservationist or protectionist measures. Instead, all aspects of natural and built environments were viewed as integrated parts of an interac-tive whole, in which the parts have the potential to be either mutually supportive or mutually destructive.[4]

The problem – or, more grandly put, problematic – of urban environ-mentalism is that programs for enhancing environmental sustainability depend upon holistic, ecosystemic understanding that calls for long-range and widely integrated policies. Cities, if they are indeed grue-like, do not lend themselves to such understanding or policies.

Let me be clear about this claim. It is not that cities cannot or should not prominently figure in environmental perspectives. The 1992 study of the Toronto waterfront, *Regeneration*, was groundbreaking in its approach to the problem of rejuvenating the city's waterfront precise-ly in situating Toronto within the ecosystem stretching from the Oak Ridges Moraine to Lake Ontario, Niagara to Oshawa, and including both natural and built aspects of this system as well as its sociological, political, cultural, and economic dimensions.[5] The problem with imple-menting *Regeneration*'s recommendations was and, through subsequent proposals, continues to be that the city does not lend itself to the sort of whole-scale planning called for by an ecosystemic perspective. This problem is, to be sure, exacerbated by messy federal/municipal rela-tions with respect to waterfront authority, the machinations of vested interests, unwieldy bureaucracy, and petty political manoeuvring. But even absent these things, the problem poses a severe challenge to ecosystemically informed, overarching planning. The root reason is that situating the city within a thoroughly integrated long-range plan would require a detailed vision of its nature and shape into an indefi-nite future.

Well, one might ask, why not formulate such a vision? This is the orientation sometimes called utopian, though the name is a misnomer. Unlike utopian schemes, which literally exist nowhere, urban utopians at least from the time of Ebenezer Howard and (drawing on the explicit utopian, Charles Fourier) le Corbusier tried and, to a certain extent, succeeded in putting their ideals into practice. Indeed, each integrated a green, if not ecosystemic, element into his vision: Corbusier's (violated) prescription that his phalansteric 'machines for living' be surrounded by ample green space, and, of course, Howard's garden cities.[6]

Time did not treat the visions of Corbusier and Howard well. Marseilles grew to engulf Corbusier's showcase *L'Unité d'Habitation*, and not a few of the housing projects inspired by him ended up as vertical slums. Garden cities turned into suburban developments, usurping farmland and sucking populations out of inner cities. At the same time, utterly unplanned urban growth has led to its own disasters. Left to the mercies of unconstrained development, cities have found themselves denuded of public spaces, urban expressways have displaced pedestrian life and polluted the air, waterways have been paved over, neighbourhoods homogenized or eradicated, and so on, in an all too well known list. Thus the problematic tension between what may be labelled environmental holism and urban incrementalism reduplicates itself with urbanism.

Markets and Democracy

In form (and, as will be seen, also in substance) the urbanism/environmentalism problematic mirrors those in two other realms. In the world viewed economically, the limits of centralized planification are now universally recognized. But at the same time, with the exception of those regions of the world where neo-conservative ideologues hold political sway, the destructiveness of unbridled markets is also generally recognized.

The analogue of free markets and incrementalism in the realm of democratic politics is self-interested voting and interest-group competition of the sort held up by theorists in the traditions of Joseph Schumpeter and the neo-Hobbesist interest group school as the essence of democracy. Against this view stand theorists such as J.S. Mill, John Dewey, and the Civic Republicans (among many others), who view it as crucial for a persisting democracy that citizens and elected leaders temper a propensity to further their individual interests by looking to the commonweal in supporting and carrying out political policy.[7] This is the analogue of holistic, ecosystemic thinking.

I wish now to suggest that solutions proposed and, to varying extents, implemented in these economic and political realms offer clues to ways of addressing the urban environmental problematic just described.

In economic practices associated with social democracy or Keynesian regulated capitalism, parameters are put in place marking domains insulated from free-market activity or placing constraints on market activities insofar as they impact upon provision of public goods. In addition, of course, to effective enforcement of the resulting regulations, successful pursuit of this strategy depends on flexibility in their deployment, where this means relocating market constraints in accord with changing circumstances and allowing for exceptions when intrusion of market forces into the delivery of public goods demonstrably serves or subverts the latter. Skill is required in these exercises, and those charged with the task must be trusted not to revert to bureaucratic planification or to serve private interests, thus implicating the political problematic.

Unless the practice of democracy is to be no more than self-interested power politics, citizens, elected leaders, and civil servants must all be possessed of a culture of civic virtue. Such motivation is not properly described as altruism; indeed, pure altruism on the part of either voters or elected officials would make democratic politics impossible. Voters would have nothing to vote for (like the three friends ordering lunch at a restaurant, each telling the waiter to bring whatever each of the others orders), and leaders would be pure populists (all things to all people and hence nothing to any of them).

Rather, civic virtue involves including among one's political priorities a commitment to policies that promote or preserve goods for the body politic as a whole – that is, that enable those bound together in the community of fate of common living and working circumstances and subject to the same governing authority to pursue their various life goals without destructive conflict and, as far as possible, in satisfying ways. Civic virtue does not eliminate conflict, not just because it is sometimes (indeed, often) only hypocritically proclaimed, but because there is a lot of room for difference of opinion over what policies are in fact in the public interest. What marks civically virtuous citizens or leaders is that, faced with such difference, they are sincerely prepared to abandon a policy if persuaded that it is out of accord with the demands of the public good.

Boundaries

Referring to the ways that urban architectural designs might address the diversity of spaces in cities, and with reference to social, economic, and cultural divisions within them, Richard Sennett draws a useful distinction between boundaries and walls.[8] Each serves the essential function in a city of demarcating spaces – residential, commercial, industrial, recreational, public and private, and so on – but there is a major difference between their modes of demarcation. Unlike walls, boundaries are permeable and shiftable.

Both walls and boundaries define spaces appropriate for unique uses and, in each case, these uses could change through time. But walls impede felicitous interactions with adjoining spaces. The configuration and precise locations of boundaries allow for experimental change, while walls are either permanent or require whole-scale destruction. In these ways, boundaries are both confining and enabling, while walls are primarily just confining. (No doubt many of us have experienced a micro-example of the distinction when a neighbour erects a solid wall along a shared property line. If fences as boundaries make good neighbours, as walls they make bad neighbourhoods.)

Boundaries are analogous to economic parameters. In terms of the problematic addressed in this chapter, their permeability and shiftability recognize the unpredictably fluctuating nature of urban life and functions, while their definitions of spaces permit environmentally sensitive planning. Depending on how they are implemented and how supple their administration, the Province of Ontario's recent Greenbelt legislation and its Places to Grow regulations to direct urban growth could function as boundaries in the required way.[9] Their success could have the important environmental effects of preserving green spaces and curtailing urban sprawl. The desire of some developers or landowners wishing to make large profits from the sale of land will no doubt be thwarted, and the dream of some for houses on large tracts of land curtailed. Yet city growth within the established boundaries, including negotiated shifts in boundaries where this does not impede the aim of preventing sprawl, need not create insurmountable 'problems of organized complexity.'

The urban environmental possibilities of the Greenbelt and Places to Grow initiatives require relevant agents to harbour appropriate values as well. If municipalities or private owners of currently green land looked only to local and short-term advantage, or if exemptions became political currency rather than adjustments consonant with the plans' intents, it is doubtful that the plans could realize their potentials. This brings us to the theme of civic virtue.

Civic Virtue

Aside from agreement that civic virtue involves giving precedence to public goods, political philosophers have advanced a variety of candidates for what the core virtues are. Without entering into these debates, let me suggest that, with respect to cities, at least two virtues are crucial: *concern* and *tolerance*. These are derived from consideration of features of the grue-like nature of cities.

One thing that makes cities both vibrant and in flux is their extraordinary demographic diversity: by class, by profession, by ethnicity, and in accord with proclivities across a wide range of styles of life – alternative religious commitments (or secular rejection thereof), sexual orientation, modes of child rearing, cultural tastes, forms of recreation, and so on. Unlike villages, in most if not all daily interactions, urban citizens are anonymous to one another in a way decried by some, who see this as a source of anomie, but celebrated by others, such as Georg Simmel or Walter Benjamin, who saw anonymity as potentially liberating.[10] In such a society, family, friendship ties, or tradition cannot be counted on to ensure that people will look out for one another when needed or that the civilities of daily interaction will be sustained. It is for these reasons that a culture of mutual concern is vital to city life. Similarly, it is because some of the diversities within cities involve beliefs and modes of life not shared across a population, and sometimes incurring mutual disapproval, that a culture of toleration is important.[11]

With respect to urban environmentalism, I now wish to follow the environmental pragmatist Andrew Light by adding a third core urban virtue: *trusteeship*.[12] From at least the writings of environmental pioneers such as Aldo Leopold to the present, and cutting across different environmental philosophies (as, for example, the anthropocentrism/biocentrism divide), there has been near unanimity that environmental sustainability requires people to see themselves in a relation of stewardship to the natural world. A culture including a similar orientation towards the institutions, built structures, and natural prerequisites, enclaves, and settings of cities is likewise to be encouraged. In the next part of the chapter, I shall advance claims about the *nature of*, the *justi-*

fication for, and the *prospects for realizing* a civic culture that includes a stance of trusteeship.

Nature

Civic trusteeship involves taking responsibility for the preservation of public places such as parks (whether directly, as in a neighbourhood park committee, or indirectly, by supporting elected officials for whom this is a priority). It means caring for one's domicile with an eye to the life of future inhabitants. Building projects and architectural design from a standpoint of trusteeship are informed by an understanding of the open-ended and changing futures of cities (their grueness) and hence are undertaken in such a way as to keep future uses and transformations as open as possible. Infrastructural support and future maintenance costs are built into planning and budgeting for development. Civic trusteeship centrally includes an environmental component. If alternative futures for a city are to be protected, then so must its natural environment. Future options are obviously limited by poisoned water or air, by the unavailability of local farm produce or natural places for recreation.

Justification

One candidate to justify promotion of the virtue of urban environmental trusteeship links up with a common argument appealing to Richard Florida's thesis about cities and 'creative classes.'[13] His perspective is often employed to wrest funding from higher levels of government. This is the argument that in order for cities to be globally competitive, they must attract dynamic business leaders and skilled employees, who will gravitate to vital cities. Without entirely dismissing the argument (whatever works), I do not think it a good one to motivate an ethic of trusteeship. Such an ethic, in the first place, should apply to citizens of any city, not just of one that sees itself as a potential 'alpha' global competitor. Further, the argument is better suited to justify short-term mega-projects and to appeal to governments and moneyed elites than to motivate a multitude of ongoing, often local and unpublicized exercises of trusteeship by urban citizens at large.

Turning to more philosophical justifications, perhaps foundational ethical theory will suffice. One might adopt a biocentric ethic and argue that a general moral obligation to the natural world (human and otherwise) carries with it an obligation to promote urban environmentalism, which, in turn, requires trusteeship. Or, from an anthropocentric orientation, an ethical theory supporting the claim that those in the present generation have moral obligations to future generations (utilitarianism is the most straightforward supporting theory) might be made to work in the same way.[14]

While I wish urban philosophers well in taking such tacks, the approach to justification of urban trusteeship suggested here is of a somewhat different order – not exactly ethically foundationist and, though anthropocentric, not, I think, in a way that sets its prescriptions against those of biocentrism, at least as far as promoting urban environmental sustainability goes.[15] It hearkens to the grandfather of virtue theory, Aristotle. For him, the virtues were habits, action in accord with which was requisite for 'happiness.' Happiness, for Aristotle, was definitive of a meaningful life. Such a life involves people developing their proper potentials to the fullest. Since some potentials – such as to inflict pain on others or to ravage the earth – ought not to be encouraged, a way to identify worthwhile life activities is needed. Aristotle himself expanded on the list of virtues embedded in the conventions of his time – courage, prudence, temperance, justice – for this purpose.

Most, if not all, subsequent philosophers have (like Aristotle) been loath to rely on tradition (or on it alone) to identify appropriate virtues, and they adopt a variety of strategies to find an alternative. The theorist I shall draw on is C.B. Macpherson. He offered an open-ended list of 'truly human powers' – the capacities for aesthetic creation, contemplation, friendship and love, religious experience, moral judgment and action, rational understanding – identified by reference neither to tradition nor to a foundational ethical theory, but to the formal property that successful realization of the potentials by some people need not be at the expense of their realization by others. One is not in a zero-sum game with respect to the development of human potentials.[16]

Or rather, one *need* not be in this game. Acquiring knowledge requires education, and nurturing friendship requires free time. In a world of limited and unevenly distributed resources, it may happen that for some to receive adequate education or free time requires others to pay taxes for public education, which they balk at doing, or, again reluctantly, provide employees with sufficient salaries so that they need not work more than one job or so they receive paid time off. Macpherson's claim is that these conflicts are not inherent to the potentials themselves, but derive from constraints subject to removal by appropriate social and economic policies. The virtue of concern referred to earlier enters as one motive for removal of the constraints, provided that substantial numbers of citizens – and, hence, the public policies they support – are motivated by concern for adequate resource distribution.

The goal projected by Macpherson (no doubt a goal the full realization of which could be approached only asymptotically) is a world where everyone can lead a meaningful life in something like an Aristotelian sense. Theorists of ethics disagree about whether or how the moral desirability of such a world requires justification. For the purpose of addressing the urban environmental problematic, I do not think one needs to enter these debates. It suffices to show, rather, that in such a world – for whatever reasons it is ultimately valued – progress towards environmental sustainability, which recognizes the unique nature of cities, would be facilitated.

To demand approaching urban projects and problems in an attitude of trusteeship is not to enjoin collective subscription to one particular urban (or, indeed, natural-environmental) vision. Rather, individuals with different visions or with aims that fall short of grand visions are asked to pursue these things with an eye to maintaining options for future urban citizens.

Being diverse, there is no guarantee that the visions and aims will always converge on common actions, but when they do not, issues of collective problem solving will be posed. If such exercises are themselves guided by the virtue of trusteeship, along with concern and tolerance, they will at least have these shared values as benchmarks in negotiating differences. If, in addition, each understands the importance of border creation instead of wall construction, this should also allow for the preservation of both present and future diversity by not creating built forms, infrastructures, civic plans, and institutions that are difficult to adjust or dismantle.

As for environmental preservation, it should be obvious that exercise of the all too often exhibited human potential for environmental destruction fails Macpherson's test for being a 'truly human' component of a meaningful life. Humans are, after all, themselves animals. As such, humans are continuous with and dependent on their natural environment. Destructive behaviour towards nature on the part of some people can only put severe constraints (in the limiting case, death) on the ability of other people to develop their own potentials.

This observation does not by itself suggest how to address situations when available resources (both natural and created and equitably distributed or not) are insufficient to provide everyone with the means of developing their proper potentials, given overall consumption demands. One of Macpherson's reactions is to claim that the resulting shortfall of resources is artificial. It derives from what he saw as a consumerist thirst for consumption far beyond what is required for a meaningful life as viewed by Aristotle, who referred to the drive in question as the pathological state of *pleonexia*.[17] Contrary to depictions of what he labelled 'possessive individualism' as an ineradicable feature of human nature, Macpherson argued that a thirst for indefinite private consumption was an effect, rather than a cause, of life in a competitive market society.

The nub of the pleonexic problem for Macpherson is that people regard their own and other people's powers as private property. In fact, the powers are mainly some combination of genetic inheritance and the products of socialization and education, themselves the issues of historically accumulated knowledge, habits, and institutions. The alternative to 'self-ownership' with respect to people's talents is that people are their trustees. If I am the trustee of my powers, with obligations to employ them in a way that is beneficial to others (as to myself), it follows that I am also the trustee of those resources required for the development and deployment of these powers. To the extent that these resources include elements of my natural environment – as surely they do – I am also their trustee.

Realism

The examples of planning and design in terms of boundaries instead of walls illustrates that this orientation is realistic. Many political leaders, urban planners, and urban architects, as well as ordinary citizens and some entrepreneurs, already adopt this orientation. The realism of urban dwellers adopting trusteeship roles needs more defence. Notwithstanding the misgivings expressed earlier about utopian urban planning, it must be allowed that a certain measure of visionary, if not exactly utopian, entreaty is unavoidable in thinking about urban environmentalism. The alternative is either foolish complacency or debilitating despair. Still, if no discernible paths towards realization of the goal in question – a general culture of trusteeship – could be identified, then, according to the arguments of this chapter, prospects for urban environmentalism would indeed be bleak.

Recent surveys of some U.S. cities report two sets of pertinent findings. One is that public support for sustainable urban planning is the strongest in cities with relative lack of industry and with populations of older people.[18] Another finding is that, from a menu of potential outcomes of urban planning, citizens consistently place 'livability of the built environment' as their top priority.[19] The authors of the latter report, Philip Berke and Maria Conroy, find it distressing that the livability priority tops 'harmony with nature,' 'freedom from pollution,' and other directly environmentalist values, just as Kent Portney, the author of the other report, sees it as challenging that cities with industry and younger populations are not equally supportive of urban sustainability. No doubt these are causes for concern, but, at the same time, the reported findings hold out hope for the possibility of a culture of urban environmental trusteeship.

If some people, older or otherwise, can support environmentally sustainable urban planning (a presumption of the first-mentioned report), then a stance of environmental stewardship cannot be inimical to human nature per se. It might be pointed out as well that a value of trusteeship is not entirely foreign to other than older people. Parents exhibit this value when they make sacrifices in the interests of the future lives of their children. That the presence of industry in a city inhibits environmental planning suggests that people confront a trade-off between economic and environmental concerns. But the problem admits of possible, if demanding, confrontation, for example, in the way that some European countries have combined technological innovation and regulation to promote green development. It is not difficult to demonstrate that livability requires environmental sustainability. If people highly value the former, it becomes a matter of education to link the two – again, a challenging but not impossible task.

The observation about industrial cities harks back to the earlier discussion of economics and politics, now considered substantively. Scott Campbell situates the problematic here being addressed in what he calls the 'planning triangle' of environmental protection, economic development, and social equity. Echoing the views of many pessimists, he describes how these three goals can work against each other, but unlike the pessimists, he also sees ways that they can be mutually supportive.[20]

He thus depicts a spiral situation. We have too many examples of political/economic/environmental spirals moving in downward directions. If there is the possibility of economic development, equitable and democratic city planning, and environmental sustainability mutually supporting one another, there is no reason, in principle, that they could not spiral upward instead. Attitudes of urban-environmental trusteeship are required, but also nourished and strengthened, in such a process.

Finally, one element of the grue-like nature of cities related to the virtue of concern suggests another ground for optimism, namely, the anonymity of cities. In one way, the anonymity of city life makes people's thinking of themselves as trustees for those things that enhance city life more tenuous than when they are acting for people known to them, such as their children. But at the same time, once inculcated, a trusteeship stance is richer, precisely because of urban anonymity. As the future of a city held in trust becomes more distant from the present, it is increasingly anonymously populated. Of the two components of the beneficiaries of a culture of urban-environmental trusteeship – that they exist in the future, and that they are anonymous to the trustee – the latter is already present in the case of cities.

Agency

This chapter has inquired after conditions conducive to the promotion of urban environmentalism in the face of differences between the natural and the urban-built environments: that is, between ecosystematicity and grueness. The central hypothesis of the chapter is that a combination of urban development that shuns walls in favour of borders and that includes a civic culture of trusteeship is suited to this task.

A dimension of the question not so far addressed is that of agency. *Who* is to promote the recommended virtues and border-sensitive orientation? Researchers, elected officials, civil servants, community pillars, and media folk are all potential educators, as, of course, are teachers or apprentice teachers. Urban planners, political leaders, and urban architects can teach by example. The planner, councillor, or mayor who acts only to aggrandize a local constituency (or him- or herself) and who erects divisive and inflexible walls sets a bad example, as does the developer who looks only to profit or the architect who acts as a hired gun for a client, no matter how irresponsible the latter's charge, or just to gain notoriety by creating startling edifices.

Contrary comportment for all these categories of urban citizens is not hard to describe. The more practitioners and educators there are exhibiting such comportment, the more hopeful the prospect that urban grue will be green.

NOTES

1 The reason that these features are evidence against grueness is that they substantiate a hypothesis that something is structured in a way that militates against the sort of sudden and dramatic change that marks grue-like entities. Such a hypothesis is strengthened if it is derived from a coherent and independently empirically supported theory about the structure in question. (The thoroughgoing sceptical position set aside in the chapter sees a regress problem, since putatively empirical support would also confront gruish logical possibilities.)

2 Kevin Lynch, *A Theory of Good City Form* (Cambridge, MA: MIT Press, 1981), 328–42.

3 Jane Jacobs, *The Death and Life of Great American Cities* (New York: Random House, 1961), 433.

4 The notion of ecosystematicity is the starting place of all streams of post-conservationist approaches to environmentalism, whether of the 'deep' and biocentric approach or the 'social-ecological' anthropocentric one. An originating publication of the former approach is Arne Naess's 'The Shallow and the Deep, Long-Range Ecological Movement,' *Inquiry* 16 (Spring 1973): 95–100, and of the latter approach, Murray Bookchin's *Our Synthetic Environment* (New York: Colphon, 1974).

5 David Crombie et al., *Regeneration: Toronto's Waterfront and the Sustainable City*, Report on the Royal Commission of the Future of the Toronto Waterfront (Queen's Printer of Ontario, 1992).

6 Ebenezer Howard, *Garden Cities of Tomorrow* [1902] (Cambridge, MA: MIT Press, 1965); Le Corbusier, *The City of Tomorrow and Its Planning* [1929] (London: Architectural Press, 1971). Howard's *Garden Cities of Tomorrow* is also treated in Stephen Bede Scharper's chapter in part II of this volume.

7 I survey these and other approaches to democracy in my *Democratic Theory: A Critical Introduction* (London: Routledge, 2002).

8 Richard Sennett, *The Conscience of the Eye: The Design and Social Life of Cities* (New York: Norton, 1990), 190ff.

9 The Greenbelt legislation protects some lands around urban areas from development. The Places to Grow legislation prohibits municipalities from expanding into new suburbs unless they have achieved specified living/working densities within their existing borders. To access the legislation, use www.gov.on.ca, then search for Greenbelt Act 2005 and scroll to the act; see also www.placestogrow.ca.

10 See Georg Simmel's 'The Metropolis and Mental Life,' written in 1903, reproduced in *The Sociology of Georg Simmel*, ed. Kurt Wolff (New York:

Free Press, 1964), 409–24. The theme of anonymity (that which makes cities safe for the *flâneur*) is a central one in Walter Benjamin's *Pariser Passagen*, written between 1928 and 1930, in English translation as *The Arcades Project* (Cambridge, MA: Harvard University Press, 1999).

11 I develop this topic in 'Cities: A Philosophical Inquiry,' Centre for Urban and Community Studies Research Bulletin 39, University of Toronto, September 2007. This Centre was the forerunner of the University's Cities Centre. The paper is available at: http://individual.ca/frankcunningham.

12 Andrew Light sees stewardship as the central value required for 'ecological citizenship' in cities. 'Urban Ecological Citizenship,' *Journal of Social Philosophy* 34, 2 (Spring 2002): 44–63, at 58.

13 Richard L. Florida, *The Rise of the Creative Class* (New York: Basic Books, 2002). The notion of the 'global city' is also critically examined by Hilary Cunningham in part III of this volume.

14 Dale Jamieson examines several arguments to justify stewardship, specifically regarding the preservation of urban landmarks. Finding flaws especially in those that appeal to obligations to future (or past) generations, he settles on the argument that landmarks embody 'common wisdom' and are therefore more likely to provide present and future generations with the conditions for a 'higher quality of life than anything we may produce.' *Morality's Progress* (Oxford: Oxford University Press, 2002), 276.

15 The criterion of compossible potential development appealed to below could be fully compatible with biocentrism only if the potentials of all living things were included, as, perhaps, the teleological biocentrist Paul Taylor would have it. *Respect for Nature: A Theory of Environmental Ethics* (Princeton: Princeton University Press, 1986). Otherwise, deployment of the criterion with respect to urban environmentalism would be mute on such topics as vegetarianism or animal experimentation and hence in potential conflict with biocentrism.

16 C.B. Macpherson, *Democratic Theory: Essays in Retrieval* (Oxford: Oxford University Press, 1973), 4.

17 Aristotle, *Nicomachean Ethics,* book 5: 1130a. See Bernard Hodgson's deployment of this concept in 'On Economic Men Bearing Gifts and Playing Fair,' in *The Invisible Hand and the Common Good*, ed. Hodgson (Berlin: Springer, 2004), 279–98.

18 Kent E. Portney, 'Taking Sustainable Cities Seriously: A Comparative Analysis of Twenty-four US Cities,' *Local Environment* 7, 4 (2002): 363–80.

19 Philip R. Berke and Maria Manta Conroy, 'Are We Planning for Sustainable Development? An Evaluation of 30 Comprehensive Plans,' *American Planning Journal* 66, 1 (Winter 2000): 21–33.

20 Scott Campbell, 'Planning: Green Cities, Growing Cities, Just Cities? Urban Planning and the Contradictions of Sustainable Development,' in *The Earthscan Reader in Sustainable Cities*, ed. David Sitterhwaite (London: Earthscan Publications, 1999), 251–73. An example of a pessimist on this matter is Kai Lee, who sees little hope for urban sustainability either in the poor cities, in virtue of their very poverty, or in rich cities, due to the extravagant consumerism of their inhabitants. 'Urban Sustainability and the Limits of Classical Environmentalism,' *Environment and Urbanization* 18, 1 (2006): 9–22.

4 'My Streets Are My Ideas of Imagination': Literature and the Theme of the Natural City

PETER TIMMERMAN

The simple message of this chapter is this: one main obstacle to the spread of the 'natural city' is the fact that the Western cultural tradition has consistently seen the city and nature (often 'the country') in moral and mutually exclusionary categories. Seldom, and mostly in occasional metaphoric usage only, were nature and city brought together. Only very recently have 'nature in the city' themes emerged, signalling something of a shift or breaking down of these categories; this breaking down derives, in part, from a few significant moments in late Romanticism. The strength and continuing cultural influence of the earlier categorical divide is, I argue, one of the great obstacles to the project of 'the natural city.'[1]

Given the power of this long-standing tradition and its influence, what follows is an attempt to explore the theme of the 'natural city' in the main Western literary tradition, even though the theme hardly exists per se; perhaps this chapter is designed in hope as a starting point for future explorations. It is impossible to do more than sketch some of the elements that contributed to the theme, by way of triangulation from the separate themes of the city and nature. For want of space, I have chosen to focus more on the city. I provide a brief look at a few touchstone texts in the tradition as a way of introducing the topic. Certain critics, including David T. Herbert, have argued that the city itself is a minor theme in the Western tradition.[2] That is the case only because they begin too late, usually in the aforementioned late Romantic period, by which time the 'polarities' of nature and city have been reversed, and only nature appears to be valued positively.

However, Northrop Frye and others[3] have pointed out that culturally, for most of the Western tradition (and most Eastern traditions), the

Figure 4.1. Ancient Western cosmology (after Frye and others).

Heaven: Rational order = God, Cosmos, Stars, Sky, Father, Male

Lower heaven: Serving order = Gods, Angels, Priests, Kings, Cities

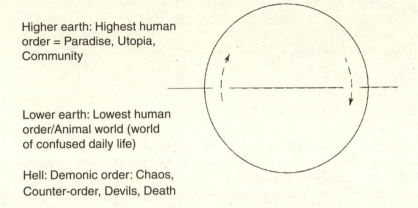

Higher earth: Highest human order = Paradise, Utopia, Community

Lower earth: Lowest human order/Animal world (world of confused daily life)

Hell: Demonic order: Chaos, Counter-order, Devils, Death

city has been the positive focus of expectation and the locus of human endeavour – the culmination of necessary order and reason. The city (see figure 4.1 for a generalized image of the traditional Western structure from roughly 500 CE to 1750 CE) is where humanity is supposed to be at its peak on earth – the city on the hill, if you like.

The city is reason embodied: where nature in the city appears, it is tamed and ordered – the ornamental garden, the park, the zoo. The city is constantly contrasted with the wild world of natural chaos out of which the city struggles to be constructed; the triumph of construction is the glorification of the city over chaotic nature. Between these two poles one can ambiguously find 'the country,' the agricultural or pastoral zones where tensions between city and nature play out in many different ways, from the bucolic peasant and shepherd to the aristocratic manor house and the suburban tract home, as characterized in exemplary fashion by Raymond Williams in *The Country and the City*. Williams points out:

> Clearly ideas of the country and the city have specific contents and histories, but just as clearly, at times they are forms of isolation and identification of more general processes. People have often said 'the city' when they meant capitalism or bureaucracy or centralized power, while 'the country'

... has meant everything from independence to deprivation, and from the powers of an active imagination to a form of release from consciousness.[4]

To clarify this interplay of specificity and generality through cultural history, my approach in the first part of what follows is twofold: to set out some main thematic approaches to the city, primarily in classic Western literary texts from the beginnings of the tradition to today, and to lay the groundwork for extracting from this review a set of possible 'natural city' themes. In the second, shorter part of the chapter, I look briefly and more generally at these themes, which proponents of 'the natural city' might wish to consider when creating a more focused future literature about the natural city as a preferred way of life. The first theme is that of the city as a 'naturalish' organism, often portrayed as a natural expression of humankind: just as bees make hives, so people make cities. A second theme, deriving from the agricultural and pastoral traditions, plays with the tensions between the natural and the artificial that tilt mostly towards the city. Yet, particularly as Romanticism develops, these tensions begin to tilt the other way: suburbia is its most familiar expression. Third, and following on the second, is the theme of the attempt by those raised in nature or the country to make sense of the emergent phenomenon of the city. Fourth, and from the urban side, is the appearance of the wild in the city, reminding city dwellers of the world beyond. Fifth, and to complete a kind of cycle, is the theme of the descent of the city back into that nature from which it sprang.

Part I: Historic Themes of City/Nature

The Ancient City: From Gilgamesh to the City of God

The first major literary text in any tradition is *The Epic of Gilgamesh*. It immediately puts in place, thanks to the physical Sumerian situation (cities dependent on very well organized irrigation and agriculture), the basic theme of the glorious city, as represented by Gilgamesh the hero, versus the wild, represented by Enkidu, the wild man tamed. The taming of the wild brings new powers to Gilgamesh. He and Enkidu are able to destroy the protective god of the forests of Lebanon, thus enabling the trees in the forest to be felled to help build more of the city:

He slew the ogre, the forest's guardian,
at whose yell were sundered the peaks of Sirion and Lebanon,

... the mountains did quake ... all the hillsides did tremble ...
He discovered the secret abode of the gods,
Gilgamesh felling the trees, Enkidu choosing the timber.[5]

At the end of Gilgamesh's search for the meaning of life and death, he and the ferryman, Ur-shanabi, who has ferried him to Hell and back, return to the city of Uruk. Gilgamesh sees that the city is his true monument:

'O Ur-shanabi, climb Uruk's wall and walk back and forth!
Survey its foundations, admire the brickwork!
Were its bricks not fired in an oven?
Did the Seven Sages not lay its foundations?
A square mile is city, a square mile date-grove, a square mile is
clay-pit, half a square mile is the temple of Ishtar:
Three square miles and a half is Uruk's expanse!'[6]

Gilgamesh's world is one of terrible gods, uncontrolled powers, physical dangers, and Death at the end: the city is a deliberate act against all that. What nature it contains – parks, gardens, date-groves – are triumphant symbols of nature under control.

This deliberate act of city building is championed throughout the ancient world, and to the present day, owing in part, of course, to the hegemonic fact that most writers have been city people. Opposition to the city as a phenomenon is discernible early on in the counter-proposition that it is among farmers and the like that virtue, non-corruption, and ease away from the bustle of urban life are to be found. Around this counter-proposition will gather most of the elements that establish the later pastoral, anti-urban, and rural traditions.

The urban life is nowhere more celebrated than in classic Greek literature, centred on the *polis* (city). Right at the beginning of the tradition, Homer often speaks of the 'sacred city' of Troy, and of the sanctity of the act of founding cities and building foundations and walls: these are in many ways embodiments of divinity, and each city has its protective god or goddess.

Yet even here there are complications. For instance, in Plato's *Phaedrus*, one of the most important and beautiful dialogues, the dialogue begins with a walk outside the walls of the city:

Socrates: 'Upon my word, a delightful resting place, with this tall spreading plane, and a lovely shade from the high branches of the *agnos* ... And as crowning delight the grass, thick enough on a gentle slope to rest your head on most comfortably. In fact, my dear Phaedrus, you have been the stranger's perfect guide.'

Phaedrus: 'Whereas you, my excellent friend, strike me as the oddest of men. Anyone would take you, as you say, for a stranger being shown the country by a guide instead of a native – never leaving town to cross the frontier nor even, I believe, so much as setting foot outside the walls.'

Socrates: 'You must forgive me, dear friend; I'm a lover of learning, and trees and open country won't teach me anything, whereas men in the town do.'[7]

This repudiation of the countryside in favour of the city is balanced at the very end of the dialogue by the fact that Socrates offers a prayer to the divinities of the countryside in which he has been ensconced for many hours:

Socrates: 'Dear Pan, and all ye other gods that dwell in this place, grant that I may become fair within, and such outward things as I have may not war against the spirit within me.'[8]

City and country are seen here as elements of a common universe, with different gods, different tasks. Nevertheless, this pastoral spot is ambiguously natural, for it is cultured in its own way: it is not wilderness, and it is not farmland. It is the civilized pastoral, of which much will also be made later. Moreover, one must always keep in mind that while the rhetoric of city versus country was strong, Athens (for example) was quite small; given that its main protective 'wall' was the Acropolis, the rest of the city was permeated with countryside in ways that aren't often reflected in the literary texts.

While the Greeks focused on the city for much of their literary background, and some philosophical speculation, in the Western tradition the theme of the sheer glorification of the city is Roman, in part because Rome the city is synecdoche for Rome the empire. The critical moment in the Roman tradition was the founding of the city of Rome, and it is in Virgil's *Aeneid* that the founding of cities becomes the hero's task and life work. The *Aeneid* draws on Homer's epics, the *Iliad* and *Odyssey*, rewriting the epic journey of Odysseus after the fall of Troy so as to

create a new epic journey and hero (Aeneas) whose end is the building of a new Troy (Rome). To rebuild Troy somewhere else is a theme
that provides the basis not only for the *Aeneid*, but for many other later
stories and proposed epics. (Virtually hundreds of towns and cities in
the Middle Ages created legends about their supposed Trojan origins.)
The launch of this theme in the *Aeneid* takes place at the moment when
Aeneas, the hero, a shipwrecked refugee from Troy, suddenly reaches the top of a ridge and stumbles upon the building of the new city
of Carthage, home to Queen Dido. Among the multiple ironies of the
scene is the fact that Carthage will eventually become Rome's deadliest
enemy. Aeneas witnesses, with a growing sense of guilt, how another
people are hard at work on their future:

> Soon climbing a long ridge that gave a view
> Down over the city and facing towers.
> Aeneas found, where lately huts had been,
> Marvelous buildings, gateways, cobbled ways,
> And din of wagons. There the Tyrians
> Were hard at work: laying course for walls,
> Rolling up stones to build the citadel,
> While others picked out building sites and plowed
> A boundary furrow. Laws were being enacted,
> Magistrates and a sacred senate chosen.
> Here men were dredging harbours, there they laid
> The deep foundation of a theatre,
> And quarried massive pillars to enhance
> The future stage – as bees in early summer
> In sunlight in the flowering fields
> Hum at their work, and bring along the young
> Full grown to beehood; as they cram their combs
> With honey, brimming all the cells with nectar,
> Or take newcomers' plunder, or like troops
> Alerted, drive away the lazy drones,
> And labour thrives and sweet thyme scents the honey.
> Aeneas said: 'How fortunate these are
> Whose city walls are rising here and now!'[9]

This crucial passage, which will echo down the whole Western tradition, sketches out the physical and social elements of a city, inter-
twines them – they require each other to make a full community – and,

through the extended metaphor of the bees and the hives, suggests that city building is the natural human activity. It is what human beings do. For Virgil in particular, who also wrote *Georgics* – books on farming – in which the bee metaphor reappears, this is his way of describing 'the natural city.'

Virgil's heroic city succumbed to later realities in the Roman world, of which Juvenal's *Satires* are the darkest expression. But doubts about the city can also be found, if only obliquely, in poems by Horace extolling the rustic life, and complaints in various pastoral poems about the lot of the peasant in a world of fast-talking, deal-making Romans. For instance, Juvenal's 'Satire III' is a complaint from someone who is about to abandon Rome for the countryside (Cumae) because, as he says, 'there is no room in this city for the decent professions.'[10] 'I'd prefer a barren island to down-town Rome.'[11] The city is full of frauds and liars and pimps. The Satire is made particularly dark because of its setting. Juvenal borrows the pastoral scene already described from Plato's *Phaedrus*, but this time the grotto is 'modernized beyond recognition'[12] and

> each tree's under orders to pay rent to the city,
> The Muses have been evicted … [13]

Fires, burglaries, muggings – these are all enumerated by the departing urbanite:

> Who fears, or ever feared, the collapse of his house in cool
> Praeneste, or rural Gabii, or Tivoli perched on its hillside,
> Or Volsinii, nestling amid its woodland ridges? But here
> We inhabit a city largely shored up with gimcrack
> Stays and props: that's how our landlords avoid slippage.[14]

The theme of the corrupt city reaches its apotheosis in St Augustine's *City of God*, wherein he turns the satires of Rome against the whole of Roman culture. Augustine's text is a response to the accusation that the new worship of the Christian God, as opposed to the traditional gods of Rome, was responsible for the increasing vulnerabilities of the late Roman Empire. Augustine counters not just with a series of historical vignettes about the barbarities and corruptions of Rome (and its gods) from its earliest days, but with the creation of a counter-city to the earthly city of Rome: the City of God. This counter-city reveals by contrast the failures of the earthly city, and its necessary replacement in the future by the heavenly city. The setting up of these two polar opposites is traceable to the biblical suspicion of Babylon, the city of the Israelite captivity. But Augustine begins well before that, with Cain, son of Adam, murderer of Abel:

> Cain, we know, became the father of Enoch, and founded a city in his name. This was the earthly city, of course, the city which is not just a pilgrim in this world, but rests satisfied with its temporal peace and felicity ... Enoch ... means 'dedication' for the earthly city is dedicated here, where it is founded, since it has here the end of its purpose and aspiration.[15]

Eventually,

> Not to spend time over a multitude of detail, the city of Rome was founded to be a kind of second Babylon, the daughter, as it were, of the former Babylon. It was God's design to conquer the world through her, to unite the world into the single community of the Roman commonwealth and the Roman laws, and so to impose peace throughout its length and breadth.[16]

God's design (as St Augustine goes on to paint in great detail) was to incubate the City of God within the earthly city: historically, so there would be a reasonably peaceful Roman empire through which Christianity could spread more easily; theologically, because in every earthly city there are hidden members of the City of God – the church, the body of Christ.

The political nature of the City of God is perhaps most noticeable in the fact that nowhere does St Augustine refer to Jerusalem, the city that was traditionally opposed to Babylon. By this time, Jerusalem was a ruined shell of its former self, and notorious throughout the Roman Empire as a seat of rebellion.

This is perhaps the place to make the point that the Heavenly City (which St Augustine does refer to generically) was also traditionally seen to be the goal during and after the end of time. The gradual replacement of the city as end point in common mythology by something less urban and more 'paradisal' is an interesting historical dynamic, partly due to the slow rise of more positive views of the natural world, but also due to the slightly awkward question about whether the Garden of Eden at the beginning of biblical history would be part of the redemptive space after history came to an end. It is interesting that Dante, in his later *Divine Comedy* (circa 1320), is careful to orchestrate, in the 'Purgatorio,' the return of the Garden of Eden. In Dante's work, it is located in Purgatory as the jumping-off point for the movement upward into 'Paradiso' (which is, in Dante, not a city at all, but a vast cosmic rosette).

Perhaps because of his bitter lifelong experience with medieval Italian cities, Dante consigns the one city that appears in the *Divine Comedy* to Hell. Dante and Virgil, his guide, are temporarily stopped at the gates of the city of Dis, whose walls encircle the lower depths of Hell. The city is the home of traitors and other infernal beings. Among the elements of the city, Dante notes,

'Master, already I distinctly discern its mosques there within the valley, red as if they had come out of the fire.'[17]

The inhabitants of the city refuse to allow Dante to enter: it requires the descent of one of God's angels to force the city gates open. As in this little vignette, Dante throughout casts the city as a place of conflict, endless grudges, and unholiness – not unlike his own city of Florence. It is as he circles within the precincts of this desperate city that Dante learns of his future banishment from Florence, and hears, many times, of the unrepentant hatred of factions of Florentines for each other, even after death. We get glimpses of the notorious evolution of the medieval city as a 'free space,' where the emerging bourgeoisie is not subject to prince or church, and is therefore dangerous by definition.

From the City of Dis to London

As mentioned, the *locus classicus* for a discussion of the evolving role of the country and the city in sixteenth-, seventeenth-, and eighteenth-century literature in English (and related forms in French) is Raymond Williams's *The Country and the City*. Williams sketches the economic basis for a literature that harks back to the Roman Augustan period, with its glorifications of a rural nobility whose sources of revenue include both extensive land holdings and (underplayed) connections to urban wealth. Themes from Juvenal and Horace return, as in this stanza from the English Renaissance playwright and poet Ben Jonson's poem to Sir Robert Wroth, who had a country estate north of London:

How blest art thou, canst love the country, Wroth,
Whether by choice, or fate, or both;

And, though so near the city and the court,
Art ta'en with neither's vice nor sport;
That, at great times, are no ambitious guest
Of sheriff's dinner or mayor's feast,
Nor com'st to view the better cloth of state,
The richer hangings, or crown-plate,
Nor throng'st, when masquing is, to have a sight
Of the short bravery of the night,
To view the jewels, stuffs, the pains, the wit
There wasted, some not paid for yet;
But canst at home in thy securer rest
Live, with un-bought provision blest ...[18]

The country house, with its commanding – literally – views over the surrounding countryside, appears throughout this period, in literature ranging from Sir John Denham's 1642 poem 'Cooper's Hill' to Henry Fielding's 1749 novel *Tom Jones*. The true nobleman brings disordered Nature into order, reinstating a sort of pastoral paradise, reinforced by the mutual interplay between the stately home and the cultivated landscape of garden vista and rustic park.

Out of this mix comes the one 'natural city' poem of the period (and one of the singular examples before our time): Edmund Waller's 'On St. James's Park' (1686). When Charles II gained the throne in 1660, one of his projects was the transformation of St James's Park in the centre of London along the lines of some of Louis XIV's gardens in France (Charles had spent time in France in exile). Much of this park was designed to be quite artificial. It included a tree-lined avenue – the Mall – down which Charles could play 'pall mall,' a form of croquet. Waller, however, emphasizes a British naturalness to the park:

Near this my Muse, what most delights her, sees
A living gallery of aged trees;
Bold sons of earth, that thrust their arms so high,
As if once more they would invade the sky.
In such green palaces the first kings reigned,
Slept in their shades, and angels entertained;
With such old counsellors they did advise,
And by frequenting sacred groves, grew wise.
Free from the impediments of light and noise,
Man, thus retired, his nobler thought employs.[19]

Here Waller draws on the theme of ancient tribal wisdom ('green palaces') to flip the polarities between city and country: the country is where nobler thought is possible. Of course, in this case, the country is a park in the middle of the city. And, as already mentioned, this arrangement can reinforce the image of the powerful ruler, one who is able to subdue nature so much as to bring it into the city. One of Charles's St James's Park projects was to divert part of the Thames River to make a lake. Waller picks up this point, and in his own fashion, slightly subverts it:

> The sea, which always served his empire, now
> Pays tribute to our Prince's pleasure too.
> Of famous cities we the founders know;
> But rivers, old as seas, to which they go
> Are nature's bounty; tis of more renown
> To make a river than to build a town.[20]

Charles rules both sea and river.

Contrary in many ways to Charles II and all his works was John Milton. With Milton, who was suspicious of kings and their projects, the theme of the unnaturally contrived city becomes stronger and stronger. Milton draws on Virgil, St Augustine, and Dante in his portrayal of the city of Hell. In Book I of *Paradise Lost*, the pseudo-king Satan and his devils create their anti-city, Pandemonium in Hell, as opposed to the Pantheon in Heaven. To do this, they first must rape the Earth, driven by Mammon, who was dazzled in Heaven by the gold-paved streets:

> Men also, and by his suggestion taught,
> Ransacked the centre, and with impious hands
> Rifled the bowels of their mother earth
> For treasures better hid.[21]

They use the gold and other minerals to build Pandemonium, which is a combination of all the unnatural cities of heresy, myth, and story:

> Not Babilon,
> Nor great Alcairo such magnificence
> Equalled in all their glories to enshrine
> Belus or Serapis their gods, or seat
> Their kings, when Egypt with Assyria strove
> In wealth and luxury.[22]

The city they build also bears an uncomfortable resemblance to the Catholic Rome in the seventeenth century, which Milton, a Protestant, had visited as a young man. This connection links back to St Augustine's denunciation of the pagan Rome, and poetically argues that Catholic Rome has strayed so far from its early Christian roots that it is indistinguishable from pagan Rome at its height. One of Milton's great themes is that all Western culture before Christ was a pagan deformation of what was to come (and Catholicism is a Christian deformation in turn). So, after the building of Pandemonium (also reminiscent of Aeneas's first view of Carthage), the demons swarm to meet in the domed quasi-cathedral court of Satan. Suddenly, and almost inevitably, we are treated to a demonic return of Virgil's urban bees:

> Thick swarmed, both on the ground and in the air,
> Brushed with the hiss of rustling wings. As bees
> In spring time, when the sun with Taurus rides,
> Pour forth their populous youth about the hive
> In clusters; they among fresh dews and flowers
> Fly to and from, or on the smoothed plank,
> The suburb of their straw-built citadel,
> New rubbed with balm, expatiate and confer
> Their state affairs.[23]

From Milton's demonic city, it is but a short step to the Romantic city of night, beginning with Blake's eighteenth-century London:

> I wander through each chartered street,
> Near where the chartered Thames doth flow,
> And mark in every face I meet,
> Marks of weakness, marks of woe ...[24]

Here, London is a 'charter' city, but its chartering spreads out to capture the river, and the 'chartered streets' are the equivalent of prison bars for its alienated citizens, now merely some of a string of passersby. For Romantic poets such as Blake, the city has metastasized, and has become some kind of new machine, alienated from nature and alienating all who live in it. This point is underlined in the horrific visions of the newly industrializing cities such as Manchester.[25] While Milton's Pandemonium launched this theme in its modern variant, it was William Wordsworth who captured the tone of the shift in Book VII of his autobiographical *Prelude*. In this chapter, the young man from the countryside is suddenly plunged into the madness of London:

> Rise up, thou monstrous ant-hill on the plain
> Of a too busy world! Before me flow,
> Thou endless stream of men and moving things
> …
> On strangers, of all ages; the quick dance
> Of colours, lights, and forms; the deafening din;
> The comers and the goers face to face,
> Face after face
> …
> … homeward through the thickening hubbub, where
> See, among less distinguishable shapes,
> The begging scavenger, with hat in hand …[26]

Later, reflecting on a fairground show he witnesses, Wordsworth says,

> Oh, blank confusion! true epitome
> Of what the mighty City is herself
> To thousands upon thousands of her sons,
> Living amid the same perpetual whirl
> Of trivial objects, melted and reduced
> To one identity, by differences
> That have no law, no meaning, and no end –
> Oppression, under which even highest minds
> Must labour, whence the strongest are not free.[27]

Yet, even under these conditions, Wordsworth is not lost. His foundational experiences as a child and a young man of oneness with Nature protect him even in the city:

> This did I feel, in London's vast domain.
> The Spirit of Nature was upon me there;
> The soul of Beauty and enduring Life
> Vouchsafed her inspiration, and diffused,
> Through meagre lines and colours, and the press
> Of self-destroying, transitory things,
> Composure, and ennobling Harmony.[28]

The 'Spirit of Nature' survives, even in the city. It is the great claim of Romanticism that through natural processes, one can discover or protect a deeper nature. This deeper nature is closer to the core of our being, and is protectable – and indeed should be protected for the soul's sake – in the confused life of the city.

Even as urbane a writer as Byron succumbs to this claim. His hero, Childe Harold, wandering Europe, says,

> I live not in myself, but I become
> Portion of that around me; and to me
> High mountains are a feeling, but the hum
> Of human cities torture; I can see
> Nothing to loathe in nature ... [29]

Paris and More Paris

The influence of the Romantic movement on the denigration of the city cannot be overestimated; nor can its proposed solution to the problems of urban alienation – i.e., flight into nature – as a significant contributor to, for example, the spread of urban parkland in the nineteenth century. Its further contributions to the positive re-evaluation of rural literatures, nature writing, and travel narratives are well known, and often studied.

Less considered in literary contexts is the way in which its opposite, anti-Romanticism, became a primary source for modernist literature about the city. (T.E. Hulme's pre–First World War essay 'Romanticism and Classicism' is a pivotal critical response to this source.) The arrival of this anti-Romanticism is ironically associated with Paris. Perhaps it has something to do with that quality of French urbanity that essentially means Paris. (Samuel Johnson's belief that 'When a man is tired of London, he is tired of life' has not nearly the same resonance in English culture.) Baudelaire is the primary example of an anti-Romantic, one for whom the artificial is preferable to the natural. In his essay 'In Praise of Makeup' he argues,

> It is philosophy (I mean real philosophy) and religion which order us to feed our poor invalid relatives. Nature (which is nothing but the voice of our self-interest) orders us to kill them. If you pass in review and analyse everything that is natural, all the actions and desires of the pure natural man, you will find only horrible things. All that is beautiful and noble is

the result of reason and calculation ... I am thus led to look upon adornments as one of the signs of the primitive nobility of the human soul.[30]

For Baudelaire, the essence of modern life, indeed the heroic figure of modern life, is the inhabitant of the metropolis, especially the *flâneur*, the artificial dandy wandering the streets:

> The crowd is his element, as the air is that of birds and water of fishes. His passion and profession are to become one flesh with the crowd. For the perfect *flâneur*, for the passionate spectator, it is an immense joy to set up house in the middle of the multitude, amid the ebb and flow of movement, in the midst of the fugitive and the infinite.[31]

Baudelaire's 'natural world' is the city. He says, 'Parisian life is rich in poetic and miraculous subjects. The miraculous envelops us and waters us like the atmosphere; but we do not see it.'[32]

What makes him specifically modern – and this is a theme picked up by T.S. Eliot, James Joyce, and Walter Benjamin, among others – is that not only is the city natural in its artificiality, but it is the new home of heroism. Ancient mythologies and natural forces have become ironically domesticated, naturalized in the city. In the journey to work of the average businessperson, we can see the outlines of the myth of the search for the Holy Grail. The jungle becomes 'The Jungle' (the title of a novel about Chicago by Upton Sinclair). Some of this thematic shrinking is a modernist devotion to the ironic (e.g., Leopold Bloom as Odysseus in James Joyce's novel *Ulysses*), a commentary on the shrivelling of the human to the level of the rest of the crowd. But some of it is a warning that the forces that have created the modern city are the demented result of the usurpation of real nature by urban domination, and they threaten to lurch out of control.

One critical aspect of the modernist view of the city is the way in which the city comes to pervade, and represent, the world itself. Williams notes, 'For the city is not only, in this vision, a form of modern life; it is the physical embodiment of a decisive modern consciousness.'[33]

A significant example of this point is provided by William Carlos Williams's epic poem *Paterson*, which is not only about the life, history, and geography of the New Jersey city, but, as Williams says at the beginning of his Author's Note,

> *Paterson* is a long poem in four parts – that a man in himself is a city,

beginning, seeking, achieving, and concluding his life in ways in which the various aspects of a city may embody – if imaginatively conceived – any city, all the details of which may be made to voice his most intimate convictions.[34]

In Paterson, as in Joyce's Dublin, or Eliot's London, we have achieved a kind of apotheosis of the city, for good and bad. It is the world and the self: nothing is really outside the reach of its realm.

This form of the 'natural city' – the city as the only true nature there is – is perhaps a good place to conclude this somewhat breathless review of the tradition. One capstone figure, already mentioned, might be Walter Benjamin. Benjamin is in many ways the 'natural historian' of the modern city. For Benjamin, the myth-layered history of the city (Paris, Moscow, Berlin, Rome) is a kind of geology of failed impulses towards utopia: fossilized dreams of future possibilities that only barely got off the ground. If we look about us, we can see in the older structures around us – expressways, skyscrapers, monuments – moments when these structures embodied the future: for example, the expressway as the dream of cars swooping at high speeds through high-tech cities. The role of the 'natural historian' is to resurrect these myths and fossils, and present them to us in a way that they no longer have any hold over us. Then we can move on from the failed categories of the civic past.[35]

Part II: Themes for the Natural City

In this regard, and in this concluding second part of the chapter, I want to review several of the themes (fossils or not) that have appeared here and there in various guises in the literature of nature and the city.

The first recurring theme is that of the city as a 'naturalish' organism: just as bees make hives, so people make cities. As we have seen, this theme is based on the idea that the construction of cities is an expression of the true goal of humanity, which is to aspire towards more reason, defined in part as the domination of nature – 'nature' here meaning not just wild nature, but the lower nature of our own selves. This act of supposed civic heroism is foundational to many ways of thinking about the city, especially in countries (such as Canada) where the natural world upon Europeans' arrival appeared to be forbidding and unforgiving. Trees and other natural elements were allowed into these cities as trophies of conquest or as abject slaves. They were to be kept under control within the city: the lawn was not to be allowed to go wild, for the unkempt lawn was the outward expression of the unkempt person, a symbol of the failure of the owner to understand the goals of urban life.

The second theme, deriving from the agricultural and pastoral traditions, plays with the tensions between the natural and the artificial that tilt mostly towards the city. Yet, particularly as Romanticism develops, these tensions begin to tilt the other way. The relaxation of the city towards the suburb is the fullest expression of this idea. Here, each person is allowed to have his or her own plot of land, neither working farm nor urban park. The setting is pastoral in the sense of deliberately useless, a place of retreat and recovery from the stresses of urban life.

Third, and building on the second, is the theme of the attempts by those raised in nature or the country to make sense of the emergent phenomenon of the city, and its shadowy influence on the surrounding countryside. We might call this the imaginative footprint of the city. Regional literatures of many kinds (deriving, many of them, from Thomas Hardy and D.H. Lawrence) are drawn or repelled like magnets by the prospect of the city. Endless variations on this theme exist, ranging from the young naive man or woman who goes to the city and returns sadder and sometimes wiser, to the refugee from the urban realm seeking a new and simpler life.

Fourth, from the urban side, is the dramatic appearance of the wild in the city, reminding city dwellers of the world beyond. Sometimes this appearance is purely a form of poetic imagination struck by a sudden epiphany, as in Ezra Pound's 'In a Station of the Metro':

> The apparition of these faces in the crowd;
> Petals on a wet, black bough.[36]

A more contemporary set of poetic parallels is imagined in Di Brandt's poem 'Zone: le Detroit,' where the 'glorious tree splendour' of autumn on city streets is likened to the 'queens on Church Street' (Toronto) who also preside over ordinary rush-hour traffic.[37]

Apparitions of nature in the city come in different forms. For instance, they are often associated with sudden glimpses of the sky, or the heroic struggles of lone flowers peeking up through sidewalks. Or, as in Betty Smith's 1943 novel *A Tree Grows in Brooklyn*, nature in the city is associated with an ailanthus or plane tree, a robust city survivor that provides the sole aesthetic pleasure to be found in the barren streets and alleys.

The metaphor of the sky glimpsed above the metropolis, again to be found initially in Baudelaire, is associated with a momentary vision of a landscape that is larger than, and sometimes seen as untouched by, the dirty warrens of the city. One looks up from the tight streetscape to the vast sky above. This suggests not only that there are natural worlds beyond the city, but that the city is a prison from which one can escape only in moments and glimpses, as an imprisoned man looks out through the tiny barred window of his cell.

Related to this point is what I call 'intensive wilderness.' Intensive wilderness is the attempt to experience on a micro-level scale in the city some of the same pleasures others can find only in vast expanses of untouched wilderness. The obvious examples are Japanese: the aesthetic of a tight focus on a tiny plot of exquisitely managed green or flower or even rock garden. But urban gardens on whatever scale are saturated with this aesthetic in various forms: the deliberate tight focus on a natural creature or landscape surrounded by man-made artifacts.

Finally, and appropriately, a somewhat contemporary theme, though with deep literary roots, is the dream (or nightmare) of the collapse of the city in ruins, ruins that are slowly reclaimed by nature. This is quite an old image, drawn particularly from the quasi-Gothic obsession with the ruins of Rome and destroyed medieval churches. In paintings from the eighteenth century (Salvator Rosa and others), travellers sit on broken columns and consider, in a melancholy mood, the transitoriness of life as symbolized in the remnants of the glories of the past. At the end of the nineteenth century, this view became entwined with images of the Mayan ruins deep in the Central American jungles, and has now become a cliché of apocalyptic frissons in movies and novels. It received a structural jolt in the twentieth century, beginning with the visions of H.G. Wells, and reinforced by the urban experiences of the Second World War, when the idea arose that the city itself might be seen as a target, first of German (or other) bombers, and then as the ground zero of atomic attack. At the beginning of the twenty-first century, we have added to these images ecological collapse, another version of the end of life as we know it, and wonder if the natural world would be better off without our presence. *The World without Us* (2007), Alan Weisman's exploration of what would happen to cities if human beings disappeared, is only one recent version of this scenario. Apart from everything else, this theme reminds us that the city is constantly under 'threat' from nature, that nature must be managed and controlled if the city is not to go under. Again the eco-apocalyptic question is raised: is the end of the city a good thing or a bad thing? Returning to Raymond Williams's analysis, this is a metaphor for the question of whether the alienation of the city from nature is the precursor of humans' elimination from nature's realm.

As can be seen from this brief review, it is obvious that there is no simple way of characterizing 'the natural city' from a literary or cultural perspective. The long history is saturated with oppositions and ironies, infiltrations and repulsions. Nevertheless, I would conclude by arguing that both the Romantic approach and its opposites are serious obstacles in the path of a twenty-first-century renegotiation of the roles of nature and city. What we lack at the moment is what Waller, in 'On St. James's Park,' called 'green palaces.' There is still no strong sense that the true measure of human reason is an accommodation to, and learning from, natural systems, and that these natural systems, and nature in general, can be a contribution to the redesign and rebuilding of more appropriate cities. There is still a visceral, culturally laden resistance to the naturalization of the urban, which, as I have tried to show, has a long pedigree, rooted in, among other things, the shadow of other binary oppositions (e.g., body/mind) that have outlived whatever usefulness (if any) they may once have had. But I hope I have also shown that there are possibilities in that culture as well.

In her poem 'City Psalm,' Denise Levertov reminds us, in Blakean terms, that the possibilities of vision are everywhere, including the city – 'I saw Paradise in the dust of the street'[38] – and literature reminds us in the end that we are as much threatened by fossilized categories as we are by fossil fuels. In the ancient Chinese Daoist work the *Chuang-Tzu*, a Chinese philosopher famously dreams one night that he is a butterfly, and from that moment on, is never quite sure that he is not a butterfly dreaming he is a Chinese philosopher. The point of the story is not that he is one or the other, struggling with Cartesian might and main to determine which one is the truth; the point is that by not making a definitive choice between them, by keeping things aloft, fluttering, he rejoices in the possibilities inherent in being both at once – as do we in dealing with the natural city.

NOTES

1 The quotation in the title is from William Blake, 'Jerusalem,' ch. 2, plate 34, line 31, in *The Complete Poetry and Prose of William Blake*, ed. David V. Erdman (Berkeley and Los Angeles: University of California Press, 1981 and 2008), 180.

2 David T. Herbert, 'Imaginative Literature and the City,' in *The Spirit and Power of Place, National Geographical Journal of India* 40, pts.1–4 (1994): 269–78.

3 See Peter Timmerman, 'Literature and the Environment,' in *The Encyclopaedia of Global Environmental Change*, vol. 4 (London: John Wiley and Sons, 2002).

4 Raymond Williams, *The Country and the City* (Oxford: Oxford University Press, 1975), 291.

5 *The Epic of Gilgamesh*, ed. and trans. Andrew George (London: Penguin Books, 1999).

6 *The Epic of Gilgamesh*.

7 Plato, 'Phaedrus,' trans. R. Hackforth, in *The Collected Dialogues of Plato*, ed. Edith Hamilton and Huntington Cairns (Princeton: Princeton University Press, Bollingen Series LXXI, 1963), 25.

8 Plato, *Phaedrus*, 279.

9 Virgil, *The Aeneid*, trans. Robert Fitzgerald (New York: Vintage Books, 1983), lines 574–96.

10 Juvenal, 'Satire III,' in *The Sixteen Satires*, trans. Peter Green (Harmondsworth: Penguin Books, 1998), line 21.

11 Juvenal, 'Satire III,' line 5.

12 Juvenal, 'Satire III,' line 18.

13 Juvenal, 'Satire III,' lines 15–16.

14 Juvenal, 'Satire III,' lines 190–4.

15 Augustine, *The City of God*, ed. and trans. Henry Bettenson (Harmondsworth: Penguin Books, 1972), Book XV, chapter 17.

16 Augustine, *The City of God*, Book XVIII, chapter 22.

17 Dante Alighieri, *Divine Comedy*, Canto VIII, 70–3 (Los Angeles: IndoEuropean Publishing, 2010).

18 Ben Jonson, 'To Sir Robert Wroth,' in *Ben Jonson and the Cavalier Poets*, ed. Hugh Maclean (New York: W.W. Norton, 1974), lines 1–14.

19 Edmund Waller, 'On St. James's Park,' *The Poems of Edmund Waller* (Chiswick: College House 1822), 138, lines 67–73.

20 Waller, 'On St. James's Park,' lines 7–11.

21 John Milton, 'Paradise Lost,' in *The Poems of Milton*, ed. John Carey and Alaistair Fowler (London: Longmans, 1968), Book I, 685–8.

22 Milton, 'Paradise Lost,' Book I, 717–22.

23 Milton, 'Paradise Lost,' Book I, 767–75.

24 William Blake, 'London,' in *Poetry and Prose of William Blake*, ed. Geoffrey Keynes (London: Nonesuch, 1967), lines 1–4.

25 See, for example, Friedrich Engels, *The Condition of the Working Class in England*, ed. David McClellan (London: Oxford World Classics, 1993).

26 William Wordsworth *The Prelude: A Parallel Text* (Harmondsworth: Penguin Books, 1971), Book VII, 149–213. I am quoting from the 1850 version.

27 Wordsworth, *The Prelude*, Book VII, lines 722–30.

28 Wordsworth, *The Prelude*, Book VII, lines 765–71.

29 Lord Byron, 'Childe Harold's Pilgrimage' (USA: Feather Trail Press, 2009), Canto III, 680–4.

30 Charles Baudelaire, 'In Praise of Makeup,' in *Les Fleurs du Mal* (Flowers of Evil), ed. and trans. Wallace Fowlie (New York: Bantam Books, 1963), 201.

31 Baudelaire, *The Painter of Modern Life and Other Essays,* trans. Jonathan Mayne (New York: Da Capo Press, 1986), 9.

32 Baudelaire, 'The Heroism of Modern Life,' in *Les Fleurs du Mal*, 171.

33 Raymond Williams, *The Country and the City*, 239.

34 William Carlos Williams, *Paterson* (New York: New Directors Books, 1992.).

35 Graeme Gilloch, *Myth and Metropolis: Walter Benjamin and the City* (Cambridge: Polity Press, 1996).

36 Ezra Pound, 'In a Station of the Metro' in *Selected Poems of Ezra Pound* (New York: New Directions Books, 1956).

37 Di Brandt, 'Zone: le Détroit,' in *Now You Care* (Toronto: Coach House Books, 2003), 4.

38 See http://lightandstorm.wordpress.com/2008/01/30/city-psalm/ (accessed 30 May 2011).

PART TWO

From the Stars to the Street:
Cosmological Perspectives

For peoples, generally, their story of the universe and the human role within the universe is their primary source of intelligibility and value ... Our story not only interprets the past, it also guides and inspires our shaping of the future.

– Thomas Berry

While cosmology, as an academic discipline, is often housed within physics and astronomy, where the provenance and progression of the universe is charted and explored, it also finds a home in philosophy and religious studies, where the role or the purpose of the human within the universe's unfolding is an added dimension for reflection.

It is less common, however, to find cosmology as a feature of urban planning and urban design programs. The contributions in this section help address such a lacuna, showing the historical and pragmatic importance of cosmological concerns for sustainable and equitable urban living.

Stephen Bede Scharper attempts to root the concept of the natural city within both a biotic and cosmic context. After reviewing sundry historical and theoretical attempts to integrate nature and city in the modern period, Scharper introduces the 'land ethic' of Aldo Leopold and the 'new cosmology' of Thomas Berry, showing how these might enhance and deepen the framing of the natural city.

Bruce V. Foltz provides a thoughtful and incisive historical look at Constantinople, the modern-day city of Istanbul, which originally was known as the Greek colony of Byzantium. He shows how Constantinople was conceived and designed not simply as a seat of imperial power, but as a 'bridge between heaven and earth.' He explores the complex interplay of human society, non-human nature, and urban living within a Byzantine theological world view, and raises the question, through the reading assistance of modern phenomenology, of whether a 'natural city' and a 'holy city' are indeed one and the same.

Vincent Shen fruitfully probes the role of Asian understandings of the interpenetration of the human, nature, and the city. Through a concise yet comprehensive overview of the many-layered meaning of the Dao, with its cosmological as well as its discourse dimensions, Shen, in creative dialogue with Martin Heidegger and Maurice Merleau-Ponty, offers a rich and ultimately hopeful vista of the natural city as a place which can possibly, ultimately, embody the spiritual, societal, and pragmatic aspects of a just and ecologically vital urban landscape.

Kenneth Maly also utilizes Western notions of 'nature' as well as Asian traditions, particularly Buddhism, in envisioning what cosmological implications pertain to the natural city. Helpfully delineating a Western posture of 'control' over nature and 'disdain' for the 'primitive,' Maly observes the promising move away from such a posture in contemporary environmental thought, and constructively embraces several key insights from engaged Buddhism to provide a more humble and integrative role for the urbanizing human within the larger life trajectory.

All of these contributions thankfully unpack the deeper, often unexamined and at times recessed cosmological underpinnings of urban planning, and help illumine the many ties that bind civic and cosmic concerns within the envisioning of the natural city.

5 From Community to Communion: The Natural City in Biotic and Cosmological Perspective

STEPHEN BEDE SCHARPER

A thing is right when it tends to preserve the integrity, stability and beauty of the biotic community.

– Aldo Leopold

The universe is a communion of subjects, not a collection of objects.

– Thomas Berry

The above epigraphs might appear incongruous for a reflection on urban environmentalism. After all, Aldo Leopold (1887–1948), who provided the foundation for wildlife ecology and intellectual grist for deep ecology, is not known for his writings on the urban condition. And Thomas Berry (1914–2009), cultural historian and 'geologian,' has focused on the 'new cosmology' and the awesome wonder of the expanding universe more than on the ecology of cities. Yet both of these environmental pathfinders, with their profound insights into the intricately integrated community of life, proffer insights at once incisive and challenging for those seeking environmental integrity within an urban context.

In this chapter, I wish to reflect upon the implications of Leopold's 'land ethic' as well as Thomas Berry's idea of a universal 'communion of subjects' for the notion of ecological integrity within cities. As the ecological consequences of sprawling and increasingly poverty-stricken urban spaces are addressed with more frequency in literature on 'sustainability,' there are signs that a significant ethical transformation concerning human relationships with the natural world is emerging in the process. The natural city concept is, in a sense, part of this 'evolution of ethics,' to borrow Aldo Leopold's term, and holds the potential of bringing together pragmatic, ontological, and cosmological issues in cogent ways as it attempts to imagine a new way of being urban in the world.

Town and Country

The town and country, urban-rural divide is arguably the most nettlesome Gordian knot in urban environmental thinking, and may be as old as the first human settlements. This diremption is perhaps as dust-strewn as the ancient remains of Athens, when persons began to build and inhabit the polis and distinguish themselves from the cosmos. As theorist Raymond Williams has shown in his rich literary account of this nature-city divide, from the pastoral vistas of Virgil's *Eclogues* (37 BCE) through D.H. Lawrence's dichotomy of mine and farm in *Sons and Lovers* (1913), this separation has been solidified not only in the literary imagination, but in the economic, cultural, and political practice of the West in both uplifting and oppressive ways.[1] In probing this literature through a lens profoundly critical of industrial capitalism, yet with a deep-seated, almost visceral appreciation of its urban achievements, Williams unearths the social background to many of our assumed nostrums concerning the separation of not only town and country, but also many other concomitant dualisms, such as city dweller and peasant, metropole and backwater, enlightened and benighted. He writes:

> On the country has gathered the idea of a natural way of life: of peace, innocence, and simple virtue. On the city has gathered the idea of an achieved centre: of learning, communication, light. Powerful hostile associations have also developed: on the city as a place of noise, worldliness, and ambition; on the country as a place of backwardness, ignorance, limitation. A contrast between country and city, as fundamental ways of life, reaches back into classical times.[2]

Williams highlights the varied complexities behind such assumed dichotomies, and explores how the nature of both city and country was profoundly altered by industrialization, a transformation portrayed in novels such as Richard Llewellyn's 1939 work, *How Green Was My Valley*, a poignant story of ecological and family disintegration in an industrial mining village in Wales.

It was just such a gulf between town and country as it emerged through the advent of industrialization that early visionaries of urban planning, such as Ebenezer Howard, strove to bridge in their early city schemas. In his 1898 classic, *Garden Cities of Tomorrow*, Howard attempted to fuse town and country into a unique amalgam, using the metaphor of the 'three magnets': 'town,' 'country,' and 'town-country.' The latter, he averred, blended the best of both realities. In Howard's gaze, this urban vision was nuptial in nature: 'Town and country *must be married* and out of this joyous union will spring a new hope, a new life, a new civilization.'[3]

For Howard, marital bliss became the utopian template of sustainability; he hoped to create a 'garden city' that consummated such a union of rural and urban life. His efforts met with some pragmatic success, leading to the creation of the Garden Cities Association and his own involvement in the development of the towns of Letchworth (1911) and Welwyn (1928) outside of London, based on his precepts.[4]

Building on Howard's hoped-for town-country marriage in the wake of the rapid industrialization of urban areas, the dynamic social critic and urban theorist Lewis Mumford also sought a deeper interconnection between urban and rural life. In *The Culture of Cities*, he states, 'City is a fact in nature, like a cave, a run of mackerel, or an ant heap. But it is also a conscious work of art.'[5] Like Scottish urban critic Patrick Geddes, Mumford was interested in furthering Howard's notion of the 'garden city' as a response to the underside of industrialized urban living: overcrowding, poor sanitation, pollution, and accompanying public health concerns.[6] For Mumford, cities, as both organic realities and sites of human artistic expression, were a type of societal artistry, and had to move beyond both the 'will to power' and the 'will to profit.' Such proclivities, in his estimation, led to wide social and economic imbalances, and yielded fulsome slums and ghettos, which he describes as 'crystallization of chaos' and forms of 'social derangement.' Mumford's comments on the newly industrial urban landscape reveal an almost plaintive, nostalgic tone:

> The new cities grew up without the benefit of coherent social knowledge or orderly social effort; they lacked the useful urban folkways of the Middle Ages or the confident esthetic command of the Baroque period: indeed, a seventeenth-century Dutch peasant, in his little village, knew more about the art of living in communities than a nineteenth-century municipal councilor in London or Berlin.[7]

The task of the urban planner and indeed all 'artists' of the urban canvas, Mumford claimed, must be to reject a 'stale cult of death,' such as the architects of both German and Italian fascism had produced, and erect instead a 'cult of life.' (Here, interestingly, Mumford echoes the ancient Hebrew exhortation: 'Let the heavens and the earth listen, that they may be witnesses against you. I have placed before you life and death, blessing and curse, therefore choose life, so that you and your descendants may live' [Deuteronomy 30:19–20].)

Deeper in the twentieth century, Scottish-born urban theorist Ian L. McHarg also attempted to reconstitute the city within nature. His influential work, *Design with Nature* (1969), sold a quarter of a million copies, and has been credited, along with Rachel Carson's *Silent Spring* (1962), with helping to foster the modern environmental movement.[8] By encouraging architects, urban planners, and municipal policy makers to integrate the natural world more systematically within their planning, McHarg sounded a tocsin over the emerging urban sprawl and its odious social and ecological consequences.[9]

Noting the disturbing shift from cities to metropolitan areas in North America, McHarg chastised suburban planners for failing to see that 'a subdivision is not a community,' nudging them to take detailed ecological inventories involving floodplains, marshes, aquifers, and woodlands before breaking ground for new development.

In anticipation of what would become standardized environmental assessments and impact statements, he exhorts:

Let us ask the land where are the best sites ... In the quest for survival, success and fulfillment, the ecological view offers an invaluable insight. It shows the way for the man who would be the enzyme of the biosphere – its steward, enhancing the creative fit of man-environment, realizing man's design of nature.[10]

The Environmental Movement Meets the City

As the tide of environmental concern began to rise during the 1960s and early 1970s, it began to spill over into North American governmental legislation, urban planning, and social policy, leading to new environmental approaches in a wide array of areas, including architecture, energy, housing, social equity, land restoration, economic development, transportation, policy formation, governance, and myriad others.

Such developments highlighted the dearth of serious environmental consideration that had marked the erection of modern cities. Stephen M. Wheeler and Timothy Beatley succinctly survey this 'de-natured' legacy:

> Although landscape architects and park designers have long sought to bring nature into cities, this need was often ignored by developers and the nascent city planning profession in the nineteenth and twentieth centuries. Engineers and developers filled in or paved over streams, wetlands, and shorelines to make way for urban expansion. Highways or railroad lines cut many cities off from their waterfronts. Hills were leveled and native vegetation removed. Landowners plotted lots and built roads without considering the implications for wildlife, native plant species, or human recreation. With the advent of central heating, electric lighting, air conditioning, long-distance food transport, or huge dams and pipelines bringing water from hundreds of miles away, urban residents became well insulated from nature in all its forms, and even from the limitations of climate and local geography.[11]

Cities had become *de facto* monuments to modern humanity's self-understanding as 'master' and 'conqueror' of nature, a stance that envisioned nature as separate from the human, serving the human project as both booty to be exploited and backdrop to be decorated with human desires.

Among those championing a deeper understanding of the foundational relationships between cities and nature emerging out of the environmental movement was Anne Whiston Spirn, professor of architecture at the University of Pennsylvania. Her 1984 book, *The Granite Garden*, argued that cities should be viewed as something wholly within, rather than beyond or above, the natural world. Building on the insights of both Mumford and McHarg, Spirn began to view the omnipresence of nature within city limits:

> Nature pervades the city, forging bonds between the city and the air, earth, water, and living organisms within and around it ... The city must be recognized as part of nature and designed accordingly. The city, the suburbs, and the countryside must be viewed as a single, evolving system within nature, as must every individual park and building within that larger whole.[12]

Spirn's innovative work on community, albeit a managed one, was continued in the work of Peter Calthorpe, Andres Duany, Elizabeth Plater-Zyberk, and other founders of 'new urbanism,' which can be viewed as fostering sustainable living by creating smaller, pedestrian-friendly, and resource-efficient living spaces.[13] For example, reflecting the utopian aspirations of Mumford and McHarg, urban designer Peter Calthorpe wrote about the new urbanist vision in his 1993 book, *The Next American Metropolis: Ecology, Community, and the American Dream*, which he describes as 'a search for a paradigm that combines the utopian ideal of an integrated and heterogeneous community with the realities of our time – the imperatives of ecology, equity, technology, and the relentless force of inertia ... Quite simply, we need towns rather than sprawl.'[14]

Ecological integration, in short, has become a *sine qua non* of theoretical reflections on how ideal cities should be both envisioned and organized. Yet, the nature of that integration, its underlying understanding of the place of the human within not only the biotic community but also the unfolding cosmos, remains at times unexplored in such urban projections and planning. Although McHarg, Mumford, Spirn, and the new urbanists were constructively and creatively moving away from the nature–urban divide, their work remained problematic in its depiction of the human. While seeking to more deeply commingle the human and the natural in their cityscapes, and eschew the noxious elements of sprawl and suburbanization, these theorists still depicted the human as 'gardener,' 'steward,' manager, or town builder. While these are assuredly welcome advances over notions of the human as conqueror, overlord, and domineering master, they nonetheless imply a controlling, supervisory, and, by extension, superior vantage point for the human in relation to the overall ecosystem of urban areas. At a philosophical level, they also appear to embrace the modern or Enlightenment anthropocentric subject at the centre of reality. Consequently, they appear able to relate to the natural world only as something other than, or less than, human. This modern subject remains circumscribed in terms of its ethical relationships with the natural world. It stands largely as an independent, rather than as a wholly contingent, self, and does not acknowledge the fact that a mountain, watershed, or wolf may not approve of its actions. While this paradigm can assist the human in becoming a better manager, a more benevolent steward, or a more sensitive gardener, and can facilitate a critical perspective on its own epistemological lineage, it ultimately cannot incorporate or acknowledge, in either ecological or ethical terms, its integral relationship with non-human nature.

It is here that the thought of environmental theorist Aldo Leopold marks both an ontological and an epistemological watershed. Leopold's 'land ethic' – briefly defined, as indicated by the chapter's epigraph, as the maintenance of 'the integrity, stability, and beauty of the biotic community' – challenges not simply the town and country divide, but the modern split between human and non-human nature. This ethic questions not only the cultural and historical dimensions of this divide, but also its ethical premises by positing the existence of a deep inter-relationship between humans and non-humans through the concept of the biotic community. Ecology and ethics walk hand in hand, as it were, throughout Leopold's philosophical writings, which intimate that there is not only an ecological, but also an ethical, web of life. Such a radical co-penetration of the human and non-human is what in part renders his work so groundbreaking (or, more aptly, given his accent on the energy circuit of dirt, soil revealing).

Aldo Leopold: 'Thinking Like a Mountain' in the Concrete Jungle

After three decades of working assiduously in the area of game management and wildlife ecology with various U.S. governmental agencies, including vigorous leadership in state-sponsored wolf eradication programs, Aldo Leopold came to a sobering conclusion. Upon seeing, year after year, wolfless lands spawn burgeoning deer herds that first denuded wildlands and subsequently succumbed to starvation, Leopold had a type of metanoia. He began to discern that the purpose of conservation lay not in protecting or promoting individual animals, such as deer, by eliminating predators and thus producing a 'shootable surplus.' Rather, taking an ecosystem approach, he viewed conservation more as a labour of 'preserving health' rather than 'managing game,' recognizing the inherent value and vitality of ecosystems and thus attempting to support 'the widest possible realm in which natural processes might seek their own equilibrium.'[15]

Sitting down to pen his essay 'Thinking Like a Mountain' in April 1944, Leopold recounts a key experience that served as a catalyst for his altered conservation approach. Recalling his experience as a government slayer of wolves, which he at one time referred to as 'varmints,' Leopold speaks of another reality that might not deem such killing an optimal idea:

> In those days we had never heard of passing up a chance to kill a wolf. In a second we were pumping lead into the pack, but with more excitement

than accuracy; how to aim a steep downhill shot is always confusing. When our rifles were empty, the old wolf was down, and a pup was dragging a leg into impassable side-rocks. We reached the old wolf in time to watch a fierce green fire dying in her eyes. I realized then, and have known ever since, that there was something new to me in those eyes – something known only to her and to the mountain. I was young then, and full of trigger-itch; I thought that because fewer wolves meant more deer, that no wolves would mean hunters' paradise. But after seeing the green fire die, I sensed that neither the wolf nor the mountain agreed with such a view.[16]

The 'green fire' of the fading wolf helped give rise to the intimation that both wolf and mountain had notions about wildlife management that didn't involve brutal eradication of species. 'Green fire' and 'thinking like a mountain' thus became cogent metaphors for Leopold's emerging ecological ethic and his speculations concerning a potential agency, an alternative wisdom tradition, as it were, existing within non-human nature. The cozy thinking of a commodity-based, comfort zone economy, which perceives the natural world as merely an instrument to human ease, is questioned, for Leopold, by the wolf's howl, heard by the mountain but rarely by humans:

> We all strive for safety, prosperity, comfort, long life, and dullness. The deer strives with his supple legs, the cowman with trap and poison, the statesman with pen, the most of us with machines, votes, and dollars, but it all comes to the same thing: peace in our time. A measure of success in this is all well enough, and perhaps is a requisite to objective thinking, but too much safety seems to yield only danger in the long run. Perhaps this is behind Thoreau's dictum: 'In wildness is the salvation of the world.' Perhaps this is the hidden meaning in the howl of the wolf, long known among mountains, but seldom perceived among men.[17]

Leopold, who had at one time embodied all the traits of the master, professional nature manager, now saw his role, and indeed that of the human species as a whole, not as conqueror and director, but as just 'plain member and citizen' of the biotic community. This became, for him, the basis of a 'land ethic' and changed the role of *Homo sapiens* from conqueror of the land-community to plain member and citizen of it. Leopold continues:

> It implies respect for his fellow-members, and also respect for the com-

munity as such. In human history, we have learned (I hope) that the conqueror role is eventually self-defeating. Why? Because it is implicit in such a role that the conqueror knows, *ex cathedra*, just what makes the community clock tick, and just what and who is valuable, and what and who is worthless, in community life. It always turns out that he knows neither, and this is why his conquests eventually defeat themselves.[18]

At the heart of Leopold's biotic approach is the recognition that, in conquest, there is always eventual defeat – thus, the human, as plain citizen, seeks not to master the natural world, but to inhabit it as a responsible, participatory member. The human, like any citizen in a democracy, might assume a special leadership role for a time within the biotic community, yet such a temporal service role would ultimately be for the benefit of the larger community and the common good, not for personal gain.

For Leopold, the extension of human ethics to embrace the 'integrity, stability, and beauty of the biotic community' is a logical step in the evolution of ethics. Part of this evolution includes the incorporation of an affective dimension to environmental ethical discourse, encouraging the development of an 'ecological conscience' that engenders 'love, respect, and admiration for the land.'[19] This sense of beauty in nature, and deep admiration for its mysteries, is not ancillary, but constitutive of Leopold's land ethic. Thus, both wildlife policy and urban planning, if bereft of this 'love, respect, and admiration for the land,' are perhaps for Leopold not only flawed, but also potentially baleful, leading to the continued destruction of the planet. The inclusion of both compassion and admiration into an environmental ethic is singular. It creates not only a realignment of nature and the human, but also a profoundly different interrelationship grounded upon ecological interdependency and a moral disposition of love, respect, and admiration. The paradigm shift Leopold inaugurates is as much about transforming philosophical understandings of the human subject as it is about traversing the traditional town-country divide.

Thomas Berry: From Biotic Community to Communal Intersubjectivity

Certain philosophical and cosmological implications of Aldo Leopold's ethic have been picked up and placed in a universal context by cultural historian and Roman Catholic priest Thomas Berry. Upon his retirement from Fordham University, Berry established in 1970 the Riverdale Centre for Religious Research in New York, and became chief architect of the 'new cosmology,' which addresses current ecological challenges by exploring the role of the human within the larger unfolding of the universe. He views the human as deeply enmeshed not only in the biotic community, but also within the universe itself. For him, the Enlightenment subject is broadened via increased ecological awareness and recent discoveries concerning the mysteries of an unfolding, dynamic universe, confirming by his lights that we dwell not only in a terrestrial biotic community of interrelationships, but also within a cosmic communion of intersubjectivities. Berry thus provides innovative directions for ontology, cosmology, and the place of the human within an increasingly urbanized landscape.

With his emphasis on the community-based aspect of life, as well as a profound sense of beauty and the need for admiration of the natural world, Berry views our present ecological moment as a distinctive geological juncture, the closing of the Cenozoic period and the beginning of an as yet unnamed period:

> What is happening in our times is not just another historical transition or simply another cultural change. The devastation of the planet that we are bringing about is negating some hundreds of millions, even billions, of years of past development on the earth. This is a most momentous period of change, a change unparalleled in the four and a half billion years of earth history.[20]

To help nourish the cultural and psychic energy needed to respond to such seismic changes, Berry advocates a deepened awareness of the awesome beauty of the natural world, from a mountain meadow blanketed with flowers to a star-strewn summer sky. Deeply influenced by Jesuit paleontologist and theologian Pierre Teilhard de Chardin, Berry claims that there is a psychic-spiritual dimension to all reality, and that the emerging, expanding universe holds a place for human consciousness as one locus in which the universe, in a sense, reflects upon itself. Building on Leopold's notion of the dying wolf's 'green fire' and the mountain 'thinking,' Berry represents a call away from a commoditized world view of consumerism and an invitation into a deeper communion, an intersubjectivity, with all of creation. For him, the universe is indeed a 'communion of subjects' to be in deep relationship with, rather than a 'collection of objects' to be bought, sold, used, and discarded.[21]

For Berry, the stakes are high: 'The human community and the natural world will go into the future as a single sacred community or we will both perish in the desert.'[22]

Like Leopold, Berry sees the severe limitations of human efforts to manage or control nature. Yet he also sees human inclinations and spontaneities as part of nature, leading to a nuanced understating of the human vocation:

> What we need, what we are ultimately groping toward, is the sensitivity required to understand and respond to the psychic energies deep in the very structure of reality itself. Our knowledge and control of the environment is not absolute knowledge or absolute control. It is a cooperative understanding and response to forces ... If responded to properly with our new knowledge and new competencies, these forces will find their integral expression in the ... new ecological age. To assist in bringing this about is the present task of the human community.[23]

Community, Communion, and Cosmology: Implications for the Natural City

As I have briefly outlined, the overcoming of the divide between rural and urban has been a perduring task for much of Western history, but, beginning with modern industrialization and continuing though our present ecological moment, has been offering new insights and opportunities for addressing this dichotomy. The natural city concept is one such approach.

The thought of Leopold and Berry represents, in a sense, an epistemological shift in dealing with both urban and environmental concerns. Just as the Cartesian self-reflective subject framed the early modern period, and the Kantian subject and its inability to perceive absolute knowledge marked part of the Enlightenment, Leopold, Berry, and the environmental movement represent the human as the biotic or cosmological subject, pointing towards a new ontology spurred by our current ecological moment.

Whereas the modern subject is reflected in modern cities built as glorious edifices to the achievements of captains of industry and masters of nature, and the postmodern subject speaks of a protean self constantly remaking its identity and its environment in new and creative ways, Leopold and Berry are speaking of something different: a biotic and cosmic subject. This subject brings wolves and mountains, meadows and stars into a context of multiple subjectivities along with that of the human, providing perhaps a new epistemological pathway into the problem of urban sustainability.

Their insights, by positing a more integrative and humble role for the human, and by probing a deeper understanding of the nature of biotic community and cosmic communion in a collective intersubjectivity with all matter, offer the prospect of the city itself as a new aperture onto the cosmos. Cities are indeed biotic communities, whether they are recognized as such or not, and perhaps constitute a fundamental modality by which we as humans connect with the cosmos. Leopold's land ethic, therefore, is not just for wilderness areas and national parks, but for densely urban sites as well. Just as gravity applies beyond the edges of a city, so too does the biotic community extend beyond designated wilderness areas.

While the idea of a natural city retains a utopian dimension, it also, in light of our present ecological moment, perhaps offers a new critical interface, one that places certain avenues of analysis, including biotic and cosmological analysis, into conversation. As the work of McHarg, Mumford, Spirn, and even the new urbanists intimates, but perhaps does not fully articulate, if urban planning is to remain vital, it must move away from a human-centred, or 'anthropotic,' orientation, if you will, where green architecture, more parks, and energy-efficient buildings are merely enhancements for the prime inhabitants, i.e., the humans. In contrast, in a 'biotic' orientation, the reigning urban ethic is one that privileges the integrity, beauty, and stability of the urban community, in communion with all the subjects that dwell within and beyond city limits.

Just as, for Leopold, the human is 'plain member and citizen' of the biotic community, for Berry, the universe is primary, and the human secondary, to the unfolding of creation. When certain philosophical and geographical constructs striving for sustainability, however well meaning, continue to place the human at the centre of both the city and the cosmos, they run the risk of furthering the ultimately self-defeating and death-dealing role of the human as master and conqueror.

Moreover, we run the risk of diminishing our capacity not only to cultivate a love, respect, and admiration for the land, as Leopold urges, but also to develop a sense of awe and joyful celebration when we gaze upon the night sky, or witness the delight of a child running down a grassy hill. By continuing to choose an 'anthropotic' rather than a biotic and cosmic perspective, do we risk losing a sense of love, respect, and admiration for the land and for each other? Psychologist and *Tikkun* magazine founder Michael Lerner reflects upon this prospect in his influential book *The Politics of Meaning: Restoring Hope and Possibility in an Age of Cynicism* (1996), wherein he delineates the 'destructive ways in which people find meaning' amid the alienation and loneliness of 'market societies.'[24] To counter such alienation, Lerner proposes shifting society's dominant discourse 'from one of selfishness and cynicism to one of idealism and caring' – engaging in a political project to create societies that support 'love and intimacy, friendship and community, ethical sensitivity and spiritual awareness' while encouraging people 'to relate to the world and to one another in awe and joy.'[25]

Lerner's 'progressive politics of meaning' is in part a pragmatic, political expression of Leopold's affective ethic and Berry's call to cosmic wonderment. All three thinkers, in a sense, view our ecological and social challenges not simply as serious impediments, but as unique opportunities to develop deeper, more loving, more joyful, and ultimately more life-yielding personal, societal, ecological, and even cosmological relationships.

In reflecting on our present moment, and the choices it places in front of the human community as a whole, Berry invites the human community to what he calls the 'great work' of our time: the task of 'befriending,' rather than besieging, the earth.

> All indications suggest that we are, in a sense, a chosen group, a chosen generation ... We did not ask to be here at this time ... Some of the prophets, when asked to undertake certain missions, said, 'Don't choose me. That's too much for me.' God says, 'You are going anyway.' We are not asked whether we wish to live at this particular time. We are here. The inescapable is before us.[26]

As the challenges of climate change, global poverty, and rapid urbanization deepen, the project of envisioning sustainable urban settlements becomes increasingly compelling. As I have attempted to show, the environmental movement has engendered a tremendous array of fruitful reflection on ecologically fertile ways in which humans can live in urban community, and the sundry roles humans can adopt in such a quest: gardener (Mumford and Spirn), steward (McHarg), or town builder (Calthorpe).[27]

With the challenging ontological and cosmological implications of Leopold and Berry's thought, persons involved in urban planning and environmental concerns are invited to view the human community as members as well as plain, self-reflecting citizens of both the biotic and cosmic communities. They are encouraged to regard themselves as human agents amid a variety of non-human subjects, induced to move with humility, respect, love, awe, and admiration in a participatory, non-masterly role with the rest of creation. It is a daunting yet bracing challenge to bring such a role to the visioning and building of the natural city, but this remains one of the most pressing and promising tasks of our time.

NOTES

1 Raymond Williams, *The Country and the City* (New York: Oxford University Press, 1973).

2 Williams, *The Country and the City*, 1.

3 Ebenezer Howard, *Garden Cities of To-morrow* (1898; Cambridge, MA: MIT Press, 1965), 8.

4 Stephen M. Wheeler and Timothy Beatley, eds., *The Sustainable Urban Development Reader* (London: Routledge, 2004), 279.

5 Lewis Mumford, *The Culture of Cities* (New York: Harcourt, 1938), 5.

6 Wheeler and Beatley, eds., *The Sustainable Urban Development Reader*, 7.

7 Mumford, *The Culture of Cities*, 8.

8 Ian L. McHarg, *Design with Nature* (New York: Doubleday, 1969).

9 Wheeler and Beatley, eds., *The Sustainable Urban Development Reader*, 35.

10 McHarg, *Design with Nature*, 197.

11 Wheeler and Beatley, eds., *The Sustainable Urban Development Reader*, 113.

12 Anne Whiston Spirn, *The Granite Garden* (New York: Basic Books, 1984), xi, 5.

13 This movement has been faulted, however, for insufficient attention to affordable housing, non-incorporation of green design, architecture, and landscape techniques, and selecting sites, such as Duany's Seaside, outside of pre-existing urban areas (Wheeler and Beatley, eds., *The Sustainable Urban Development Reader*, 74).

14 Peter Calthorpe, quoted in Wheeler and Beatley, eds., 76.

15 Susan Flader, *Thinking Like a Mountain: Aldo Leopold and the Evolution of an Ecological Attitude toward Deer, Wolves and Forests* (Columbia: University of Missouri Press, 1974), 32.

16 Aldo Leopold, 'Thinking Like a Mountain,' in *A Sand County Almanac: And Sketches Here and There* (New York: Oxford University Press, 1948), 139.

17 Leopold, 'Thinking Like a Mountain,' 141.

18 Leopold, 'The Land Ethic,' in *A Sand County Almanac*, 240.

19 Leopold, 'The Land Ethic,' 261.

20 Thomas Berry, *Befriending the Earth: Toward a Theology of Reconciliation between Humans and the Earth* (Mystic, CT: Twenty Third Publications, 1991), 51.

21 Berry, *Befriending the Earth*, 73.

22 Berry, *Befriending the Earth*, 35.

23 Berry, *The Dream of the Earth* (San Francisco: Sierra Club Books, 1988), 48–9.

24 Michael Lerner, *The Politics of Meaning: Restoring Hope and Possibility in an Age of Cynicism* (Redwood City, CA: Addison-Wesley, 1996), 58.

25 Lerner, *The Politics of Meaning*, 59.

26 Berry, *Befriending the Earth*, 132.

27 While Spirn seems closest among the urban voices surveyed to Leopold's notion of a biotic community, she still uses the modern language of mastery in relationship to the natural ecosystem, noting that cities 'have mostly neglected and rarely exploited the natural forces within them,' and that the 'social value of nature must be recognized and its power harnessed, rather than resisted. Nature in a city,' she argues, 'must be cultivated, like a garden, rather than ignored or subdued' (Spirn, *The Granite Garden*, 87). Although signalling a major advance over ecologically pernicious urban attitudes, Spirn nevertheless seems to view the human as land manager – a benevolent cultivating gardener, to be sure, but one who still 'exploits' and 'harnesses' nature for his or her own benefit. (I am speaking here strictly of Spirn's 1984 text, and not her later writings.) This is a different understanding from Leopold's view of the human as 'just plain citizen' within the biotic community, and an even further cry from Henry David Thoreau's insight that 'in wildness is the preservation of the world.'

6 Sailing to Byzantium: Nature and City in the Greek East

BRUCE V. FOLTZ

> The beauty of the city is not as heretofore scattered over it in patches, but covers the whole area like a robe woven to the fringe. The city gleams with gold and porphyry ... Were Constantine to see the city he founded ... he would find it fair, not with apparent but with real beauty.[1]
> – Themistius, fourth-century Byzantine orator

I

Constantinople. *Constantinopolis. Nova Roma*: 'the polis founded by Constantine as the New Rome.' First known as the Greek colony of Byzantium, it had been settled by residents of ancient Megara, a faraway city on the Isthmus of Corinth, the narrow land bridge between Attica and the Peloponnese. Spanning both Europe and Asia, Byzantium – Constantinople, modern-day Istanbul – has always served as a bridge between these two great continents of the ancient world, a double-headed eagle looking simultaneously east and west. And this was indeed the principal reason for its selection as the New Rome, the imperial capital for what by the fourth century had become as much an Asian as a European empire. That, and to be a bridge between heaven and earth, a city to do what Old Rome never could: to embody and set to work the ontological bridge between the visible and the invisible at which both occidental philosophy and oriental religion had, in their own ways, and to varying degrees, already arrived.

Naturally, it has always been a land of waters that would separate. Waters of the Bosporos. Waters of the Sea of Marmara – the Sea of Marble. Waters of the Golden Horn. Three waters, everywhere visible, and often audible, ready to isolate its sectors and perhaps to swamp, and overwhelm, the putative city itself in waters and seas. These are not just nearby. They surround and embrace the city, as if to immerse it, inundate it. The city is built down into the very waters themselves, and it everywhere rises up from them.

Civically, it is – on the contrary – a land of bridges. Its bridging and conjoining character is its primary civic feature. Its unity and coherence as a city is a function of human *technē*: both the human art that joins the terrestrial element to the circuit of the city, and the human art that joins the terrestrial with the celestial, the visible with the invisible, the secular with the sacred.

'Therefore I have sailed the seas and come,' sings the poet, 'to the holy city of Byzantium.' Crossing the waters to the holy city, he hopes to find 'sages standing in God's holy fire as in the *gold mosaic* of a wall.' William Butler Yeats's 'Sailing to Byzantium' unfolds with images of golden artifacts and golden artisans, and even golden nature! Gold-smiths and hammered gold. Golden boughs and golden birds. In his prose work entitled *A Vision*, Yeats envisions golden Byzantium as the bridge city, the unifying city, the integral city, reflecting that

> … in early Byzantium, [as] maybe never before or since in recorded his-
> tory, religious, aesthetic and practical life were one, that architect and artif-
> icers … spoke to the multitude and the few alike. The painter, the mosaic
> worker, the worker in gold and silver, the illuminator of sacred books,
> were almost impersonal, almost perhaps without the consciousness of
> individual design, absorbed in their subject-matter and … the vision of a
> whole people.[2]

He goes on to imagine that had he really sailed to the Byzantium of Justinian the Great, he would have found 'in some little wine-shop some philosophical worker in mosaic who could answer all my ques-tions, the supernatural descending nearer to him than to Plotinus even.' Unity of the religious, the aesthetic, and the practical. Unity of the human, the natural, and the supernatural. The ever-attracting lustre of gold, and the mosaic composite of golden fragments that have been drawn together into one.

Finally, in his Preface to the 1893 edition of *The Works of William Blake*, Yeats reflects that

> In Imagination only we find a Human Faculty that touches nature at one

side, and spirit on the other. Imagination may be described as that which is sent bringing spirit to nature, entering into nature, and seemingly losing its spirit, that nature being revealed as symbol may lose the power to delude.[3]

It is thus no longer in Byzantium itself – undone in 1453, as the last act of the genuine decline and fall of the Roman Empire – that we can find the 'natural city': the city that would bridge the organic world, the world of the artisan, and the spiritual world, unifying spirit and nature, nature and super-nature. The poet seems to suggest that we can now find the natural city only in the imagination. The bridge – for the modernist poet – is now an interior, and even a psychological function.

Was Constantinople, 'the holy city,' in fact 'the natural city' as well? Let us listen closely to the report of envoys who sailed to Byzantium in the tenth century. Travelling the earth in search of the religion best suited to unify the Russian people, the emissaries of Prince Vladimir of Kiev finally reached Constantinople. Their report back to him became decisive, and it is quoted in every history of Russia:

> Then we went to [Byzantium], and the Greeks led us to the edifices where they worship their God, and we knew not whether we were in heaven or on earth. For on earth there is no such splendor or such beauty, and we are at a loss how to describe it. We only know that God dwells there among men, and their service is fairer than the ceremonies of other nations. For we cannot forget that beauty. Every man, after tasting something sweet, is afterwards unwilling to accept that which is bitter.[4]

As in the poetic narratives of Yeats, in this historic account, too, we find earth and heaven, the visible and the invisible, joined together by means of beauty. But this is not the beauty of nature left in a raw or wild or pristine state. It is that of nature rendered beautiful through *technē*, through human art and artifice: through the art of the architect and poet and iconographer, of ritual and liturgy, and, indeed, through the art of the goldsmith. The beauty that bridges, joins together, and unifies – the beauty that renders possible the seeming paradox of the natural city – this beauty itself comes about not through nature, but through production, through what the Greek language spoken in Byzantium called *pōeisis*.

II

These portrayals of Byzantium find deep resonance in the aesthetic thought of Martin Heidegger, which can help articulate their coherence. In Heidegger's thought, the dark self-closure of earth is thought in contrast both to the openness of what he calls 'world' as well as to the manifest measure of the heavens. The work of art, then, is understood as 'setting-forth' the earth, allowing it to be seen in its earthliness, even as it brings the earthly into the dynamic unity of a world. (And what work of art, we may ask, sets forth the earth more dynamically and dramatically – and sets to work a world more effectively – than the Hagia Sophia, the 'Great Church' of Constantinople?) Beauty, in turn, can be seen as the revealing or unconcealing of *physis*, nature regarded as what comes forth of its own accord.[5] Moreover, because *physis* or 'nature' is not just one region of beings, but rather is everywhere emergent in all that is, to reveal this all-present self-emergence through beauty is at the same time to reveal the unity through which beings as a whole join together and cohere. 'Beauty,' Heidegger maintains, 'is the original unifying One.'[6] Nor is this a simple or abstract unity. Because it is 'all-presence,' beauty is that captivating, *enrapturing* unity that 'lets one opposite come to presence in its opposite.'[7] (A unity, we may add, that allows the captivating conjoining of visible and invisible, the human and divine, the celestial and terrestrial, sacred and secular, nature and the city.) Finally, Heidegger sees this integral and healing unity disclosed by the arts in their 'poetic' character as itself being a revealing of what he calls 'the holy.' He characterizes the latter, in turn, as the necessary element for humans to encounter the divine, and thus for the authentic poetic task – the task of art itself – to be possible. Perhaps, then, rather than being incidental to its character as 'natural city,' the fact that Constantinople was singularly founded *as* a sacred city – as a city that would be the pre-eminent bridge between earth and heaven, and vice versa – would serve as the very precondition for its singular power to unify nature and humanity as well. The natural city, then, would at the same time be, in the words of Yeats, 'the holy city.' Byzantium is not only the New Rome: it is also the New Jerusalem – as its residents, in fact, understood it to be.

But we must ask once again, was Byzantium – not just the city of Constantinople, but the inhabited empire itself – in some distinctive and even definitive sense really 'the natural city'? What we have considered so far, from the poetic vision of Yeats to the captivated, enraptured report of the Russian emissaries, is surely suggestive, but it is hardly conclusive. And indeed, there is a body of opinion and scholarship that would argue just the contrary: that rather than being 'the natural city,' Byzantium represented instead the historical-cultural beginning of the unnatural city.

III

The field of Byzantine Studies is in its early stages, still far from overcoming 1,200 years of Western prejudice and provincialism in understanding not just Eastern Christendom, but European history as a whole..The entire period of Late Antiquity – the years from 250 to 800, during which Byzantium took shape and first flourished – has been seen almost exclusively through the prism of the 'Dark Ages' undergone in Western Europe after the fall of the First Rome. Eastern Christendom, too, has been viewed from the perspective of the Latin Church that was born out of those dark times. Seen in this way, Byzantine Christianity becomes merely a mystically oriented aberration from the Latin norm, and Byzantium as a whole a curious, rococo remnant, somehow persisting out on the margins. It is hardly surprising, then, that few of those who have thought historically about nature and city have been free from this parochialism. The architectural historian Vincent Scully – who is in other respects without peer for his lifelong study of the relation between nature and the city – does only slightly better than most. Examining his otherwise excellent narrative will sharpen our understanding of Byzantium as the natural city.

In his book *Architecture: The Natural and the Manmade*, Scully presents the fruit of a life's work: a magisterial history of architecture tracing the alienation of the city and nature, from the ancient Egyptians, Minoans, and meso-Americans to its sad end with the inhumanity of modernist architecture and the frivolity of the postmodern school. Scully sees two tendencies at play in the relation between our buildings and the natural environment around them. One sees the city as part of the landscape, and seeks in its architecture to imitate and intensify surrounding nature, to invoke its deities and indeed to aid and assist them. His favoured example is the great pyramid (the 'Temple of the Moon') at Teotihuacán, which Scully sees as mimetically presenting the spirit of the mountain that serves as its background. And in doing so, it evokes – and invokes – the water goddess to bring down the needed water from the earthly heights. (He passes lightly over the fact that all too often, as was certainly the case with the Aztecs, this kind of primal identification with nature has simultaneously entailed human sacrifice to hungry deities as well.)[8] In the second tendency, literally invented by the ancient Greeks, the city stands up against nature, confronts it, raises up human – and, eventually, abstract and geometrical – forms to master and control it. At a certain point, this mastery reaches a point of totalization, in which the world is brought indoors – that is, the interior environment of the buildings becomes the primary element, a world unto itself to replace the natural environment. This latter step, Scully argues, is taken first of all in the Pantheon of Rome, whose dome is conceived as a planetarium, but even more decisively in the great temple, the Hagia Sophia of Constantinople. He sees its circular dome over a square floor plan as the triumph of Pythagorean abstraction – and human control – over the very cosmos itself, and finds that its vastness impresses the visitor with a sense that the building is a world unto itself, subduing and interiorizing the natural world outside.[9]

In part, Scully's analysis simply repeats the time-honoured cliché: a world that is old and tired, and that has lost its nerve, now retreats inward – into stoicism and neoplatonism and ultimately into the interior, psychological recesses of Christianity. The Western world begins to waken during the Renaissance and look 'outside' to the world of nature, while the Christian East never does, remaining dreamily entranced in mysticism. Yet this doesn't quite work for Scully, since the very tendencies he thinks begin in Byzantium in fact proceed more definitively in the West: from the Gothic cathedrals and their interior spaces oriented so decisively heavenward, away from the earth, to the abstract interiorized buildings of the International Style in the twentieth century. But in another sense, Scully occupies solid ground here. His polarity of confrontation and abstraction versus imitation and identification is parallel to Nietzsche's contrast of the Apollonian and the Dionysian, Wilhelm Wörringer's contrast of abstraction and empathy, and indeed Heidegger's notion of a conflict between earth and world.[10] Such a tension, it seems, may be an irreducible element of the human condition. It is the thesis of the present chapter, then, that rather than initiating a decisive fissure between these two tendencies, Byzantium – as the consummation of ancient thought and spirituality – instead presents in an exemplary manner nothing less than a successful resolution of the conflict between them. To see how and why this is the case, however, will require a brief consideration of Byzantine philosophy and theology.

IV

All of the great world religions address themselves to some (perhaps one) great, intractable Problem. For Hinduism, it is the veil of Maya or illusion – endemic to, and generative of, the very universe itself. For Buddhism, it is Suffering – not just human suffering, but suffering of cosmic proportions – brought about by clinging and grasping. And for Christianity, it is the Fall. But for Byzantine Christianity, and for the Christianity of Late Antiquity generally prior to Charlemagne, the Fall is a disorder of the whole cosmos, of nature as well as humanity. Redemption, then, must in all these traditions have the same cosmic dimensions: a restoration of humanity and nature alike to their prelapsarian condition, transfiguring both, and returning them to their paradisiacal state. In that blessed state, according to the Byzantine vision, human beings would exercise, as they had once before, a cosmic priesthood, apprehending and consecrating the divine presence not only in one another, but in the world as a whole: in every ray of light and each fallen leaf. The eternal *Logos*, through which the cosmos was created, can once again be apprehended within the inherent *logoi* of all creation, because that same *Logos* entered creation, became material and earthly, precisely to restore this lost unity of heaven and earth. And this allows human beings to once again realize their inherent divinity as images of God. (Byzantine theology calls this process *theosis*, and it is summarized in the celebrated formula of Athanasios: 'God became man in order that man might become God.') Humanity can thus resume the cosmic priesthood for which purpose it was created: to be that being through which the divine image within all creation becomes fully realized, the nodal point through which creation apprehends and consecrates its own inner divinity. .

Humanity and nature are retrieved from opposition and confrontation, because both are restored to unity with the *Logos* from whom they commonly derive their own being. Because heaven has come down to earth, earth and heaven are now essentially reunited – a theology that underlies all Byzantine art, but which is most characteristically embodied in the art form of the icon. Here, in the icon, the terrestrial is infused with the celestial. The icon, properly understood, is not a representation, but a presentation – not a *Vorstellung*, but a *Darstellung* – of the invisible by means of the visible, a temporal epiphany of the eternal, a visible window upon the invisible. (Latin theology, in contrast, properly begins with the *Libri Carolini*, in which Charlemagne's court theologians – responding to the Second Nicene Council, which had vindicated the icon from the accusations of the iconoclasts – rejected this theophanous character of the icon, insisting instead on the jurisdictional separation of earth from heaven, and substituting the discursivity of allegory and instruction for the noetic immediacy of iconic experience.)[11] The background, the very element, of every icon is gold: the inner radiance of the divine energies. That Byzantium is the golden city, that its icons and murals and mosaics radiate with gold, that its ceremonial vessels and reliquaries and garments and gateways are golden, that the pages of its illuminated books shimmer with gold, that its very flag features its double-headed eagle against a golden background simply articulates the Byzantine vision: a restoration of all creation to its divine roots, which can be seen to radiate and well up from deep within the earth itself. It is the golden glow of the pristine dawn of creation shining within the city. But glimpsing the Byzantine flag, which still flies over Mount Athos on the Halchidiki Peninsula of Macedonia, let us return to the ancient city itself.

V

Hagia Sophia. The Great Church of the Divine Wisdom. The Divine Wisdom is the eternal *Logos*, seen as shaping the cosmos and holding it together. It is thus also the inner *logos* of each being that, when fully realized, joins it to the whole in a love that must be understood ontologically. St Maximos the Confessor, Byzantium's greatest philosopher and theologian, states this powerfully: 'the unspeakable and prodigious fire hidden in the essence of things, as in the [burning] bush, is the fire of divine love and the dazzling brilliance of his beauty inside every thing.'[12] The Great Church of the Divine Wisdom, then, itself serves to bring together all the elements of the cosmos in a transfigured form, making manifest the inner glow of their divine beauty.

Contrary to Scully's Westernized interpretation, the Great Church – like all authentic Byzantine temples – serves not to transport the worshipper to heaven, as the Gothic temple would do, or to replace the natural and earthly with an abstract, Platonized heaven, or even less with a psychologized 'inner' space. Rather, it serves to join together heaven and earth, to be the ontological bridge between them. The great dome, originally lined with solid gold, still seems to float weightlessly above, as if suspended from heaven or borne by seraphic orders. It is heaven itself, but brought down to earth and joined with it. The

Divine Liturgy, for whose sake the church is built, dramatically enacts the joining of heaven and earth: the drama is a progressive interaction and eventual communion of the heavenly (the sacred space and the celebrants in the sanctuary, behind the chancel or iconostasis) and the earthly sphere of the nave, towards whom the icons face, offering the vision of heaven. The rounded apse, deep within the sanctuary, is the cave of Bethlehem, the hollow of earth in which God first assented to become visible. The supporting arches 'mark the cardinal directions of space, [and] its piers and pavements the mountains and plains of earth.'[13] According to Justinian's contemporary Procopius, the cathedral's 'marvelous' and 'indescribable beauty' was enhanced by the rich hues of the precious stones in the galleries and arcades:

> one might imagine that one has chanced upon a meadow in full bloom. For one would surely marvel at the purple hue of some, the green of others, at those on which the crimson blooms, at those that flash with white, at those, too, which Nature [*Physis*], like a painter, has varied with the most contrasting colors.[14]

This observation was echoed by a contemporary poet known as Paul the Silentiary, who saw the use of coloured marble on the floors and walls as a painting in stone that presented a gathering of twelve kinds of 'marble meadows' from the far corners of the earth.[15] And all of this is *oriented*, as is every Byzantine church – that is, it faces the golden glow of the rising sun in the orient, or east.

This could not be further removed from Scully's claim of an abstract, Pythagorean space. Rather, it is much more evidentially mimetic than the meso-American pyramids or the Green Corn Dance of the Taos Pueblo, which Scully valorizes. Yet this *mimesis* evokes not dark gods, hungry for human blood, but a deity inhering deeply within nature – indeed, a transcendent god become earthly – who nourishes the faithful with his own blood, at the consummation of the Liturgy, under the golden dome of heaven. The Apollonian moment of form and structure, in turn, is not imposed from outside – as a human or mathematized mastery of nature – nor realized as confrontation, but as a restoration of the paradisiacal elements of nature's innermost *logoi*. Aesthetically, it is – in the classical terms revived by Hölderlin and Nietzsche, and in a most unexpected way – a marriage of Dionysios and Apollo.

Much has been made of the desacralization of the earth that some claim to have taken place during the early Christian era. This notion

forms the basis of Max Weber's influential concept of the disenchant-
ment of nature. Yet this view, as well, sees matters only through Lati-
nized lenses. Long before the rise of Carolingian theology in the West,
nature is seen and experienced as iconic, as the visible window upon
the invisible. The Byzantine temples and liturgies and holy things set
this iconic and noetic relation to nature into play. But it is not just that
nature as a whole acquires a new kind of sacred character. It does so
locally as well, with regard to specific places. Writing in the Harvard
University *Guide to the Postclassical World*, Béatrice Caseau describes
a much more complex understanding than the usual view of 'sacred
landscapes.' Rather than a generalized, pagan sense that nature was
somehow sacred, she describes a rich ebb and flow of sacralization,
desacralization, and resacralization of specific places in relation to specific deities as peoples and religions migrated and changed. The Christian desacralization was thus a normal part of this process, although
accompanied by a new kind of sacralization of place.[16]

Princeton historian Peter Brown has richly documented this process,
describing how through holy relics – and, much more importantly, in
the East, through the life and death of holy men and women, monastics
and saints and holy fools – 'paradise itself came to ooze into the world.'

> Nature itself was redeemed … The countryside found its voice again …
> in an ancient and spiritual vernacular, of the presence of the saints. Water
> became holy again. The hoof-print of his donkey could be seen beside a
> healing spring, which St. Martin had caused to gush forth from the earth
> … They brought down from heaven to earth a touch of the unshackled,
> vegetable energy of God's own paradise.[17]

But not only does the ascetic, the holy person of God, sanctify the natural environment through serving as a vehicle of the divine energies:
he sanctifies the inhabited places as well. In the Byzantine world of the
Christian East, Brown continues, the most important conceptual polarity was not that between city and countryside, but rather between the
'world' and the 'desert' – and of course 'desert' in the Orthodox East
soon came to refer not literally to the arid expanses of Egypt, Palestine,
and Syria, but just as much to the Caves of Kiev and the wild forests
of the Russian *taiga* or the aerial heights above the North Syrian High-
lands. The life of the ascetic who can inhabit the wild places of the earth
that are usually seen as uninhabitable is angelic, in contrast to those
more timid and conventional Christians, the *kosmikoi*, who remain 'of

the world.' Such ascetic figures, spiritual athletes themselves, become the most important apertures of all, through which holiness and grace become tangible 'in' the world as such, and thus in both the city and the country. Two of the great and exemplary ascetics of early Byzantium were St Symeon the Stylite, and his precocious successor, Symeon the Younger (521–592), who as a boy set out for the mountains above Antioch. This younger Symeon was believed to have played with mountain lions, calling them 'kitty.' Settled on a high mountaintop, yet still accessible to pilgrims from Antioch and elsewhere, Symeon was believed to have brought back to earth, in his own lifetime, the sweet smell of Paradise, and a hint of Adam's innocent mastery of the animal kingdom.[18]

Those same sorts of wonderful stories that have been told surrounding St Francis of Assisi and his empathetic relation to animals and nature – virtually peerless in the Latin West, and extolled by Scully as noble exceptions to the usual relation to nature in Western Christianity – have been regularly observed and recounted innumerable times in the Byzantine East, from the Desert Fathers and Mothers of fourth-century Egypt to the holy hermits of the Russian *taiga* in the nineteenth. Indeed, they are experienced and retold today about not a few of those several thousands of monks still living on Mount Athos, the Holy Mountain. This last, and perhaps greatest, Byzantine holy city – the remote, and nearly forgotten, monastic republic – juts out some 20 miles (32 km) into the Aegean, while preserving intact the religion and culture and sensibilities of Byzantium. Nature on Athos, as visitors invariably report, is indeed holy. Its dozens of cities – monastic communities hanging on cliffsides and clinging to shorelines, merging imperceptibly into the landscape – are strikingly integrated with the natural environment: holy people living close to the land, gathering their sustenance gently and humbly from a landscape that has been sanctified for a millennium. The natural city is resolutely resisting the European Union's insistence that it divest itself of its own 'nature' to be 'opened up' for mass tourism. For those fortunate enough to have visited and lingered here, it is the strongest evidence of all that ancient Byzantium was, and may remain for us today, in an exemplary way, the profoundly natural city. But for those, too, who have paused perceptively in any one of hundreds of traditional Greek villages – hugging some sea cliff or nestled in a fertile valley – the natural city of the Byzantines is still alive, if more immediately threatened by modernity and the seductions of European affluence. The novelist Alexandros Papadiamandis, sometimes characterized as Greece's Dostoevsky, has tenderly articulated this ancient village life in a way that constantly shows the subtle bridging of heaven and earth, of secular and sacred, of *physis* and *polis*, in the midst of everyday encounters.[19] And it may even be sometimes glimpsed in the bustle of Greek cities, as a hurried pedestrian suddenly stops to light a candle before an icon at one of Thessaloniki's scores of sidewalk shrines, or as a Vespa rider routinely crosses herself while passing in front of St Demetrius Cathedral, itself one of the glories of Byzantine architecture.

Whether we regard these glimpses merely nostalgically, as vanishing traces of an archaic past, or rather ponder them more seriously as clues for learning how to build cities that would themselves once again be fully natural – even as we recall Heidegger's insight that learning to build requires learning to once again dwell ... as mortals, upon the earth and beneath the heavens, and in the light of the holy – may be decisive for us.[20] For although there are lessons here that can also be learned in the solitary serenity of a Zen garden in Kyoto – or while looking out contemplatively from the Mount of Olives, across the Kidron Valley, upon the Temple Mount in Jerusalem – Byzantium may nevertheless remain for us in the West the exemplary bridge between the secular and the sacred, the temporal and the eternal, between the visible and the invisible: the once and future natural city.

NOTES

1 Jane Taylor, *Imperial Istanbul: A Traveller's Guide* (London: I.B. Tauris, 1998), 14.

2 W.B. Yeats, *A Vision* (New York: Macmillan, 1961), 279f.

3 W.B. Yeats, Preface, *The Works of William Blake: Poetic, Symbolic, and Critical*, ed. with Lithographs of the Illustrated Prophetic Books and a Memoir and Interpretation by E.J. Ellis and W.B. Yeats, 3 vols. (London: Quaritch, 1893).

4 G.P. Fedotov, *The Russian Religious Mind. Vol. I: Kievan Christianity: The 10th to the 13th Centuries* (New York: Harper and Brothers, 1960), 372.

5 Martin Heidegger, *Elucidations of Hölderlin's Poetry*, trans. Keith Hoeller (Amherst, NY: Humanity Books, 2000), 185.

6 Heidegger, *Elucidations of Hölderlin's Poetry*, 156.

7 Heidegger, *Elucidations of Hölderlin's Poetry*, 76.

8 Vincent Scully, *Architecture: The Natural and the Manmade* (New York: St Martin's Press, 1999), 6ff.

9 Scully, *Architecture*, 99–121.

10 See Nietzsche's *Birth of Tragedy*, Wörringer's *Abstraction and Empathy*, and Heidegger's *Origin of the Work of Art*.
11 See the article by H. Liebeschütz on 'Frankish Criticism of Byzantine Theories of Art,' in *The Cambridge History of Later Greek and Early Medieval Philosophy*, ed. A.H. Armstrong (Cambridge: Cambridge University Press, 1970), 565–75.
12 St Maximos the Confessor, *Ambigua*, PG 91, 1148C, in Paul Evdokimov, *The Art of the Icon: A Theology of Beauty*, trans. Fr Steven Bigham (Redondo Beach, CA: Oakwood Publications, 1990), 12.
13 Christopher Tadgell, *Imperial Space: Rome, Constantinople and the Early Church* (London: Ellipsis, 1998), 214.
14 W. Eugene Kleinbauer, *Saint Sophia at Constantinople: Singulariter in Mundo*, Frederic Lindley Morgan Chair of Architectural Design Monograph No. 5 (Louisville, KY: Allen R. Hite Art Institute, 1999), 40.
15 Kleinbauer, *Saint Sophia at Constantinople*, 40.
16 Béatrice Caseau, 'Sacred Landscapes,' in G.W. Bowerstocck, Peter Brown, and Oleg Grabar, eds., *Late Antiquity: A Guide to the Postclassical World* (Cambridge, MA: Harvard University Press, 1999), 21ff.
17 Peter Brown, *The Rise of Western Christendom: Triumph and Diversity*, 2nd ed. (Malden, MA: Blackwell Publishing, 2003), 164.
18 Brown, *The Rise of Western Christendom*, 172ff.
19 Alexandros Papadiamandis, *The Boundless Garden: Selected Short Stories*, vol. 1 (Limni, Evia, Greece: Denise Harvey [Publisher], 2007)
20 See Heidegger's essay 'Building Dwelling Thinking,' in Martin Heidegger, *Poetry, Language, Thought*, trans. Albert Hofstadter (New York: Harper and Row, 1971), 141 passim. See also Bruce V. Foltz, *Inhabiting the Earth: Heidegger, Environmental Ethics, and the Metaphysics of Nature* (Englewood, NJ: Humanities Press, 1995), 154 passim.

7 Dao in the City

VINCENT SHEN

Dichterisch wohnt der Mensch.

– Hölderlin

Chaque perception expresse dans mon voyage à travers Paris – les cafés, les visages de gens, les peupliers des quais, les tournants de la Seine – est découpée dans l'être total de Paris, ne fait que confirmer un certain style ou un certain sens de Paris.

– Merleau-Ponty

Human Desire on the Way

The city is a relatively well structured complex of gathering in which human beings realize their desire/existence with intensive communication and complicated infrastructure. Here, the term 'existence,' as distinct from the onto-factological concept of 'being,' refers to 'human existence' – though without any hint of exclusiveness from, but rather extendable to, human relation with the rest of nature and realm of beings. By 'human existence,' I mean the whole process of constructing a world of meaningfulness by an individual or a collectivity in the spatio-temporal context. For me, the infrastructures in the city – such as streets, transportation, schools, markets, administrative centres, parks and gardens, churches and temples – are there to structuralize the life-world.[1] These infrastructures make it possible for people to go outside of themselves to meet many others or, more properly speaking, 'strangers,' as Georg Simmel calls them, and to cultivate themselves so as to form a meaningful lifeworld for all.[2]

Simply put, human life is an unceasing process of self-extension by way of 'strangification' as well as self-awareness by way of reflection. I use the neologism 'strangification,' or *waitui* 外推 in Chinese, to denote the act by which one goes outside of oneself to many others, from familiarity to strangeness, from one's own to strangers. On the other hand, people also need to spend time alone for the purpose of self-awareness and self-reflection, even if they naturally and inevitably live with many others and communicate with many others. (I use the term 'many others' or sometimes 'multiple others' to replace the term 'the other,' used by Jacques Lacan, Emmanuel Levinas, Jacques Derrida, and Giles Deleuze. For me, 'the other' is a mere philosophical abstraction. In no moment of our life are we facing purely and simply 'the other.' We are all born into many others and grow up among many others. It is better for a life of sanity that we humans keep in mind the existence of many others and our relation with them. This is true everywhere, including the countryside and the city, on the mountain and at the sea. However, it is particularly true for human life in the city, which is full of many others and strangers.)

Chinese philosophy always recognizes that self-reflection without strangification results in the shadow of self-enclosure, while strangification without self-awareness results in self-alienation. Great Chinese philosophers always suggest, even in different terms, that strangification or *waitui* is the most crucial process in human existence. This process unendingly extends from oneself to the family, to the community, to the state, to all under heaven, and even to the whole universe. However, strangification without self-awareness is doomed to lead to a loss of self among many external things, somewhat like the Daoist Master Zhuangzi's description of Huishi, who was 'chasing after myriad things without returning to himself.'[3]

Strangification is also emphasized by great Confucians, such as Mencius, who puts emphasis on *tui* (extension or strangification) in saying, 'One who extends his bounty can bring peace to the Four Seas; one who does not cannot bring peace even to his own family. There is just one thing in which the ancients greatly surpassed others, and that is the way they extended what they did.'[4] On the other hand, Mencius also speaks of 'returning to one's mind,' 'unfolding one's heart,' and 'knowing one's own self-nature.' He says, 'A human being who can fully unfold his own heart would know well his own self-nature. He who knows well his own self-nature will be able to understand Heaven.'[5] Indeed, Mencius has articulated well the dynamic tension between strangification and self-awareness.

I would say that human existence, as a process of constructing a world of meaningfulness, is indeed constituted of an endless dialectical process of strangification and self-reflection. Strangification starts from within one's own immanent energy to go beyond towards many others, while the return to one's most sincere and authentic self proceeds always by way of self-reflection and self-awareness, moving inward, into one's self. The city is a complex hub of human existence in which multiple forms of lives and directions of existence converge in diverse, complicated networks, in which human beings always look for meaningfulness by way of strangification, from immanence to transcendence, from self-transcendence to border-crossing, in order to extend unceasingly their own existence, with an increasing degree of self-understanding, self-awareness, and self-transparency.

As I see it, there is an undetermined dynamic energy in search of meaningfulness in human desire, which transcends any particular form of realization. This is the original energy by which human beings could attain transcendence from immanence, not as an idealist process of spiritual adventure, but as an incarnated energy originated from a body-based desire that develops upwards and more fully, integrating the mental and the spiritual. Basically, this search for meaningfulness starts with our desire in our lived body (*corps vécu*). The access of the body to different forms of representation – non-linguistic in the beginning stage, then linguistic in the following stages, first oral, then written – is our first step towards a meaningful life. It prepares us for our later appropriation of higher and finer forms of language, such as the cultural, the scientific, and the spiritual. In phenomenology, one's own body is considered the locus of one's desire, the field in which appears the unconscious yet active energy towards meaningfulness. In Merleau-Ponty's term, the *corps propre*, one's own body, is the mode of existence of human desire. Desire appears in one's body and expresses itself through the movement of the body.[6] Starting from one's body, one extends to the social dimension of co-construction of a meaningful life, even to the cosmic dimension of human existence.

Dao as the Way

Dao is the Way of nature and, therefore, also the way of that particular nature in us: that is, our desire starting from our body to its eventual expansion to the universe. I tend to see the city as a complex structure of human gathering that is the realization and hub of human desires. The city is a gathering of desires, and Dao is the Way or, better, the waying of myriad things including human desire, the most natural thing in us. Still, Dao has deeper meaning and prospect than the image of a pathway. It is true that, etymologically speaking, the Chinese character *Dao* (道) is composed of two components. The first, 首, signifies a human head, a practice that probably originated in imaging the visage of divinities. The second, 辶, signifies the act of running or walking along.[7] Together, they signify a pathway or a way for people with a thinking head to walk upon or to go along, with a way out. Therefore, taking the image of the way as metaphor, Dao is related to the road we walk on, the pathways that connect one village to another, that link village to city, or city to city, and the roads and streets on which we move our body in the city. It means a way on which we could work out a direction and a way out. This image of a way is very suggestive for understanding the meaning of Dao, though Dao never limits itself only to the idea of a physical way. We understand Dao more broadly also as a way out of human desire, a way of life, the way for a society, the way of a civilization, the way for a people's future, and so on. As Heidegger says, it is improper to represent the Dao as a physical way, as the distance relating two loci. However, Dao might be the Way that puts everything on the way, or way-making. Heidegger says, 'Way-making understood in this sense no longer means to move something up or down a path that is already there. It means to bring the way ... forth first of all, and thus to be the way.'[8] The way reveals to us more than the way itself. Basically, the Dao is wherein our body and mind can seek a direction for meaningful existence. Dao is the way-making of desire.

Second, when used as a verb, *Dao* means also 'to direct,' 'to guide,' and 'to say,' 'to tell,' or 'to be told of.' The implicit sense of 'guiding' and 'directing' could be extended to mean principle, reason, or even method, closely related to the concept of the way that we developed previously. On the other hand, the sense of 'saying' and 'telling' could be extended to mean discourse, speech, and even theory. But these later meanings, so important for the Greek concept of *logos* and for Western philosophy in general, are less important for Laozi and Chinese philosophy. That is why the first chapter of the received version of the *Laozi* says, 'Dao could be told of, yet the Dao told is not the constant Dao.'[9] That which is told of is already a constructed reality by human language, not the Reality Itself.

Third, 'Dao' also means the law of becoming or law of nature. In Chinese cosmology, *Dao*, especially in the term *Tian Dao* (Heavenly Dao), means laws or patterns of nature, revealing itself in both its structural and its dynamic perspectives. The structural pattern says all things are structurally constituted of components different from yet complementary to each other, such as being and non-being, *yin* and *yang*, movement and rest, weak and strong. The dynamic pattern says that once a state of affairs is developed to the extreme limit in the process of change, then it will naturally move to its opposite state of affairs. The patterns of nature are to be shown in the natural part of the city, not only through the sky above the city, the earth under the city, the mountains and hills surrounding the city, the river(s) across the city, but also the parks and gardens in the city. These serve not only as the lungs of the city, but also as the locus in which the patterns and rhythm of nature are to be revealed to citizens in the city.

In pushing the meaning of Dao to its most speculative level, it becomes not only the way followed by all things and persons, but also the Way Itself, the Origin of all things and the Ultimate Reality. *Dao* means the Origin that gives birth to all things. The process of giving birth to all things by the Origin is its self-manifestation through a process of differentiation and complexification. As Laozi says, 'The Dao gave birth to One. One gave birth to two. Two gave birth to three. Three gave birth to all things.'[10]

Different doctrines of Ultimate Reality have been given in different accounts of Chinese philosophical schools. In Confucianism, this could be Heaven, or *ren* (humanity), or *cheng* (sincerity). In Buddhism, the Ultimate Reality could be the Emptiness, or, in order not to limit one's self to the emptiness, the Emptying of emptiness, or the Mind in Tiantai Buddhism and Chan Buddhism. In Daoism, it is the Dao, the ever self-manifesting Act of Existence, that is the Reality Itself. All that is said about the Dao is but a Constructed Reality, and Constructed Reality is not and never could be the Reality Itself. Here is the paradox revealed by Daoist philosophy: on the one hand, one should say 'Dao' in order to express it; however, once said, it becomes a Constructed Reality and not the Reality Itself and, therefore, should always be deconstructed. In order to keep one's mind open to the Reality Itself, all human constructions should be ready for further deconstruction.

Streets in the City and Trees along the Streets

We walk in the city. We walk from home to work, to school, to see friends, to go for dinner, or just for an outing. We walk along the street, under the trees. We walk in the park. We walk home. On this level, the way is the course of connection and direction on which we move to arrive somewhere. On the way, streets extend from one place to another. The Way is that which puts people on the way, the way that ways. The way-making of the Way basically relates to the movement of our body. Body movement is the simplest way of developing and fulfilling our act of strangification and self-awareness.

In the everyday lifeworld, I experience a tension creative of meaning between the original intimacy and the otherness of my body. The intimacy of my body means that I am my body, or at least my body is intimately related to my self and is an authentic part of my self. It is on this level, and only on this level, that it is legitimate to say, as religious Daoist texts did, that *Dao* is my self and my self is my own body.[11] On the other hand, the otherness of my body manifests itself through the fact that my body is also different from my self, resistant to my will and, basically, open to others in the world. The desire in my body always signifies many others; as Lacan says, 'the unconscious is the discourse of the Other,' and 'the desire of man is the desire of the Other.'[12] However, for me, this act of signifying many others is a positive and creative act, not to be conceived negatively, as Lacan did. In real life, my body, as the locus of origination and effectuation of desire, is always signifying multiple others in its basic movement, and thereby begins a project of meaningful life always going beyond any particular desired object, beyond any desired desire.

As I see it, body movement synthesizes and goes beyond this tension between intimacy and otherness of my body and is thereby productive of meaning. In this sense, we can understand the origin of meaning in the movement of body. Desire, as the original project of meaning, is first immersed in the body dynamism and body movement. Body movement, when elaborated by different non-linguistic forms, such as gestures, sounds, or pictures, attains its first moment of meaningfulness. This is also the first step of the meaning project by which our desire becomes intelligible, or, if you like, the first outlet of our desire towards meaningfulness.

In body movement, there is always a certain direction. We understand that people, in their everyday life, have directionality in their body movement, as Heidegger said. For him, the spatiality of being-in-the world consists first in 'the characters of de-distancing and directionality.'[13] Heidegger would put de-distancing as the first experience we have in our movement in the space:

We use the expression of de-distancing in an active and transitive sense. It means a constitution of being of Dasein of which de-distancing something, putting it away, is only a definite factical mode. De-distancing means making distance disappear, making the being at a distance of something disappear, bringing it near. Dasein is essentially de-distancing.[14]

On the other hand, Heidegger says that being-in-the-world's spatiality consists also in its directionality. 'As being-in which de-distances, Dasein has at the same time the character of directionality. Every bringing near has always taken a direction in a region beforehand from which what is de-distanced approaches so that it can be discovered with regards to its place.'[15] And it is because Dasein is directional that signs are needed to give direction:

in the being-in the-world of Dasein itself, the need for 'signs' is already present. As useful things, signs take over the giving of directions in a way that is explicit and easily handled. They explicitly keep the circumspectively used region open, the actual whereto of belonging, going, bringing, fetching. If Dasein is, it always has directing and de-distancing, its discovered region.[16]

I should say that the pair of terms 'de-distancing' and 'directionality' is well put as the phenomenological characterization of the way, or the street, rather than that of spatiality in general. It is especially well conceived as characterizing streets in the city, where signs are everywhere, giving a concrete sense of directionality and de-distancing. Certainly, in the countryside, or on the mountain, or in the forest, we still have certain kinds of roads, such as a *horzweg* or a sentinel, although usually signs appear only rarely. Freedom in nature allows people to find their own way by familiarity in a region, since everything seems to be nearby, with a sense of closeness, even with a sense of intimacy. However, in the city, where the environment is more a kind of constructed reality, signs are overwhelmingly present to give guidance to strangers, or people looking for efficiency without being able to get into a sense of nearness or closeness, not to say intimacy.

I agree with Heidegger that, in the city, those roads and streets, boulevards and avenues, are concretization of directionality and de-distancing, with all kinds of technological devices and transportational assistance. However, I do not agree with Heidegger's claim that de-distancing arises before directionality. For me, it is because our existence has a directionality that we begin to de-distance and know how to de-distance. This means that I would put directionality before de-distancing. Human beings are directional in the sense that we are dynamically related to one another. It is because we are being-with, relational, being-together with many others that we are directional. For Heidegger, de-distancing comes from being-with: 'The circumspect de-distancing of everyday Dasein discovers the being-in-itself of the true world, of being with which Dasein as existing is always already together.'[17] In fact, it is because we are in the ontological situation of being-with, existing in a dynamic ontology of relation, that we are directed to one another, that we desire many others, that we dialogue with and take action on one another. This is to say that we are directional because we are relational, and we create or constitute a meaningful world by way of directing ourselves towards many others. Because we are directional, we are always in the process of de-distancing, getting closer to one another by means of making the distance disappear.

Under this philosophical idea, in our everyday life, the trees alongside the streets, being the component of nature on the street, serve also as the directional signs to our movement on the streets. Trees on the streets usually are the first things that amaze visitors with green leaves and solid trunks on the ground that remind people that there is earth in the city. For Maurice Merleau-Ponty, as shown in the quotation at the beginning of this chapter, it was on account of the poplar trees on the piers alongside the river, and the turnings of the Seine as he walked along, that Paris impressed him as a city and brought him the meaning of Paris as a whole.[18] In many old Chinese cities, weeping willows, standing on both sides of the streets, inspired romantic poems; more modern cities, such as Shanghai, Nanjing, and Wuhan, are populated with London plane trees – or, as they are often called, French planes, because of the fact that they were first introduced and planted in the French Concession of Shanghai. These trees are harmonious with city buildings. It is part of the everyday lives of common people to live under their cover.

Along the streets, along highways or roads connecting cities or villages, alongside the streets in the parks, on school campuses, beside temples, within communities, these trees stand against the wind: their shade covers people with cool spaces, their green stands firmly on earth, inspiring people with their rootedness in nature. These trees have the function of purifying the air, reviving the oxygen and cleaning the dusty air, while accommodating the local weather, cooling down the heat island and increasing the relative humidity. They can reduce the noise that adds to environmental stress, and can replace machine noises by the more natural symphonies of woods and animals living in them. They increase the security of driving by serving as signs, indicating the street lines and diffusing dazzling lights, not to mention helping the health of citizens by enhancing the negative ions and spreading phytoncid in the air. They not only render the city green and beautiful, in the jungle of concrete buildings, but they are also full of historical and cultural inspirations and interpretations that constitute a precious part of a city's collective memory.

Dao as Discourse and Discourses in the City

As we saw earlier, *Dao* also means 'to say,' 'to speak,' or 'to discourse,' as in the second use of *Dao* in this saying of Laozi's: 'Dao could be told, but the Dao told is not the constant Dao.' This understanding shows a negative view of language and discourse in Daoist philosophy. Discourse, once pronounced, must be hushed; words, once written, must be erased, because the Ultimate Reality is never to be disclosed as such by any human language.

This is quite different from Confucian philosophy, which believes positively in the expressive function of language and the rectification of names so as to fit reality. Confucius said, 'The use of language is simply a matter of expressing one's intents.'[19] Also, he emphasized the learning of elegant language, to enhance one's ability of expression. 'If you do not learn the *Book of Poetry*, you will not be able to say things properly.'[20] Learning language and expressing ideas well are therefore a Confucian concern to be implemented in education. On the other hand, correction of names is to be implemented through political process:

> If names are not rectified, then language will not be in accord with truth. If language is not in accord with truth, then things cannot be accomplished. If things cannot be accomplished, then ceremonies and music will not flourish. If ceremonies and music do not flourish, then punishments will not be just. If punishment is not just, then the people will not know how to move hand and foot.[21]

For me, the city is a place of discourse or, better, a locus of many discourses in competition, in conflict, and, sometimes, in harmony. A city offers specific places for different kinds of discourse, such as the school system, from primary to middle school, to high school, to colleges and universities. Here is where languages and discourses of various kinds are learned, developed, created, and pronounced. People come to the city for these purposes. In fact, learning language and discourses is most important for the development of human desire for meaningfulness. As Wittgenstein says, different language games correspond to different lifeforms. Our appropriation of a language gives us access to the lifeform correspondingly implied in that language. From the time of our childhood, we appropriated a certain language, through the generosity of some significant others taking the initiative to talk to us, and thereby open us to a world of meaningfulness. Once we are grown up, we learn by appropriating different kinds of language – scientific, cultural, or that of everyday life. Most sophisticated forms of language – such as those of science, technology, history, arts, rites, social and cultural studies – are learned at various levels of school. By appropriating different forms of languages, we are allowed to enter into different worlds and thereby enrich the construction of our own world. The process of growth for us is not merely a physiological fact or educational progress, it is indeed a process of existential extension by the dialectic interaction between meaning construction and self-transcendence. This process thereby integrates both the inside and the outside, strangification and self-awareness, in the process of language appropriation, creation, and expression.

By learning artistic languages and performance, mostly through formal as well as informal education, our body movement is beautified and thereby becomes elegant and cultured. In fact, all forms of art have their origin in the dynamics of body movement and the desire of meaningfulness. Through diverse forms of intelligible representation, such as sounds, pictures, and gestures, the project of meaning in our desire is specified. The movement of the body through intelligible forms is the common origin of music, dancing, and performing arts. In this sense, body movement, especially body movement as elaborated by visual forms, sounds, or gestures, transforms into the intelligible dynamism of our desire, insofar as it embodies our energy towards meaning as ways to work out intelligible representations. In all countries or cultural groups of the world, I see different kinds of music, dancing, drawing and painting, performance arts, and even the art of making films – which synthesizes image, music, and body movement in presenting images moving in time so as to tell stories of different kinds – as 'inducers of desire.' These art forms articulate and thereby determine our desire for meaning in particular images, sounds, and gestures, or their combination/synthesis in a storytelling configuration. In a certain sense, they determine, articulate, and give a particular direction to our desire for meaningfulness. Places in the city – schools, opera houses, music halls, museums, cinemas, theatres, private homes, and public spaces – are all places in which we have access to these diverse forms of artistic language.

In the unending process of training, cultivation, and promotion of the human soul towards ever-higher levels of meaningfulness, education itself could be seen as a process of development and cultivation of human knowledge, culture, and desire. It always strives towards the 'better,' always moves beyond the border, always looks for higher perfection. The city is also the place, or indeed it contains a lot of places, for political discourses and economic or market discourses. Parliament, the town hall, and marketplaces everywhere remind us of these most secular functions of the city. We could say that these are the crucial functions of the city, or that they make the city function. Nevertheless, we understand also that, even if our desire for meaningfulness might be directed to and fixed upon the power of domination and the possession of more money, the energy and dynamism of this desire go much deeper. The unconscious fixation upon power and money could hinder the dynamism of desire of meaningfulness, thereby causing mental illness. The openness and determination to further unfolding of meaningfulness, on the other hand, is the way to sanity.

Indeed, a city is always the forum of political and economic discourses, the arena for the struggle for power and money, and therefore the place where people greedy for power and money tend towards self-enclosure in selfishness and struggle. Yet the city should not be seen as a pit of human selfish desires; nor should money and power be blamed for people falling into a sickness of soul. On the contrary, money could be seen as a system of publicly recognizable symbols representing certain exchangeable conventional values in a social community. Power, especially political power, is the institutionalized capacity to realize individual and collective subjectivity by the mobilization and organization of resources in view of a particular direction of realizing one's collective historicity. The selfish struggle for power and money and their abuses lead to violence. But the view that political power can lead to the realization of one's genuine historicity, and that money can lead to the exchange of conventional values, means that both contain the possibility to go beyond domination, violence, and selfish possession, and move towards communication and co-construction of a meaningful world for everyone. All possibilities of self-transcendence and further strangification are also best implemented in the place that we call 'city.'

Cosmic Patterns Revealed through Parks and Gardens in and near the City

In Chinese cosmology, *Dao*, especially in the term *Tian Dao* (Heavenly Dao), means cosmic patterns or laws of nature. Daoist wisdom shows that nature follows laws or patterns that have their structural, dynamic, and teleological perspectives. The structural pattern of nature says that all things are structurally constituted of elements that are different yet complementary, such as being and non-being, *yin* and *yang*, movement and rest, weak and strong, straight and winding. The dynamic pattern says that once a state of affairs is developed to the extreme limit in the process of change, it will naturally move to its opposite state of affairs, such as movement into rest or vice versa. On the level of cosmic teleology, all things return to the Dao at the end of their existence by way of death or passing away; that which was given birth always must pass away and return to its origin. All things, as begotten by the Dao, which is their origin, have to return to the Dao also as their final end. Therefore, corresponding to the process of differentiation, there is the process of conversion. Laozi said, 'All things come into being, and I see thereby their return. All things flourish, but each one returns to its origin. This returning to its origin means tranquility. It is called returning to its destiny. To return to destiny is called the constant.'[22]

The fundamental principle of nature is best synthesized by Laozi's saying that 'Reversion is the action of the Dao.'[23] Here, reversion has two connected meanings: one means opposition, reversal, while the other means returning, conversion. This differs, therefore, from the principle of causality in Western philosophy, which presupposes the before/after linear temporal scheme in structuring the precedent phenomenon and the consequent phenomenon with a kind of determinist necessity. In contrast, Laozi's principle of nature is based on the dialectical movement of opposing elements and their mutual interaction as fundamental to all natural phenomena. We read in the *Laozi*, for example, texts such as these:

> Being and non-being generate each other; the simple and the difficult complement each other; the long and the short compensate each other; the high and the low incline towards each other; the tones and the melodies constitute harmony one with another; and the earlier and the later follow one another.[24]

The heavy is the root of the light; The tranquil is the ruler of the hasty.[25]

Opposing yet complementing, differentiating yet unifying, distancing yet co-belonging, these structural and dynamic contrasts are constitutive of Laozi's fundamental principle of nature.

For the Chinese mind, these patterns are revealed to human beings in the city by virtue of the presence of nature in the city: by the sky above, by mountains, hills, rivers, valleys, ravines, forests, and by the change of weather and seasons, but mostly through the gardens and parks in residential neighbourhoods that are therefore part of people's everyday urban life. Parks and gardens are the spaces in which citizens have direct contact with nature in their daily lives. Both in China and in the West, private gardens in the past were enjoyed only by people of power or wealth (or both) whose aesthetic appreciation of nature and its patterns was preserved in their own residence. With the rise of modernization and democratization, the private luxury of gardens led to the emergence of parks for the use of common citizens, although those parks remained susceptible to diverse kinds of control: for instance, the notorious sign announcing 'Dogs and Chinese Not Admitted' at the entrance to the Huangpu Park in Shanghai in the late nineteenth and early twentieth centuries.[26]

Indeed, parks are essential to the public, cultural life of a city. Many historical monuments are located in parks, and cultural events take place there. In parks, one finds all kinds of reminders of the collective memory of the local community and even of broader reflections of national or humanist values. Also, parks and gardens are seen as the lungs of the city. They contribute enormously to rendering the city green, to purifying the air, and to the process of exchange of material energy between human constructs and nature. Parks and gardens respond to the need of communication between human beings and nature, and human beings with many other human beings, including strangers in the city. Plants specific to the area and local cultural histories are revealed in the parks and gardens to all citizens of the city. Among all these functions, the most important is the citizens' experience with nature, and their understanding of the patterns of nature, inspiring life's meaningfulness in their body movement and communication process in the parks and gardens.

Take the example of Chinese gardens under the inspiration of Chinese philosophy and aesthetics, specifically focusing on the contrast and dynamism of being and non-being, *yin* and *yang*, movement and rest, which are always core to people's experience in parks and gardens. If we take water as *yin*, as quietude, as calm, as mirror reflections of things as they are, then hills are *yang*, challenges to human effort to climb upon, a goal to overcome, featuring a mounting object on the earth. The change of seasons is seen in these gardens. Spring makes everything tender and green; summer brings all trees and flowers to exuberance and prosperity; autumn renders all vegetable life mature and ready for harvest while the leaves start to fall; and winter sees the foliage disappear, giving all citizens the most intuitive experience of things changing from being to non-being, and again from non-being to being.

Usually, the Chinese mind prefers the idea of comprehending movement in rest or quietude, and the rest or quietude in the dynamics of movement. After a period of movement, one is led to calm and quietude, and after a period of rest, one is invited again to move on. Water invites human meditation, flowers attract butterflies, mountain rocks invite mists, and tracks seduce always more tentative adventures. In cities that are naturally endowed with hills, rivers, lakes, and ponds, there are more possibilities for miraculous design to transform the city into a huge garden, or a city with many beautiful gardens.

Indeed, the fact that there is no motion without rest, and no rest without motion, is revealed both in natural phenomena and in human constructs. To a person sitting in a pavilion, the racing clouds and flowing water, the flying birds and falling petals are all in motion; to a sailing boat or a strolling person, the hills, rocks, trees, and woods are all at a standstill. Fish swimming leisurely in calm water are an example of the interaction of motion and repose; beauty naturally results. Here we understand the Chinese wisdom that myriad things, when looked at with quietude, will be left each to their own being.

Sometimes the straight way from one spot to another is indeed the most direct and short, as proved by geometry. Nevertheless, in parks and gardens, the winding and the straight exist with each other and coexist naturally and with ease. Indeed, in the parks and gardens, winding bridges, paths, and corridors were originally intended to facilitate communication between places. All kinds of curving paths were meant to bring to the sight of people in promenade in the gardens and parks a variety of pleasant scenery, thus rendering the walks on the paths more interesting and revealing the unexpected. It is, in some ways, better for the roads in the garden or parks to be winding rather than straight.

Among the hills and forests, narrow paths and trails should predominate over main roads, to allow for numerous spots of seclusion, so visitors may scatter all over the area. People need to look for their own favourite retreats where they can linger, listening to flowing springs, taking short rests on the rocks, or lapsing into a contemplative mood and giving play to their imaginations and poetic impulses.

The changing presence of clouds and waters, flowers and trees, waters and rocks, and the sound of wind going through trees, of the murmuring of water, the singing of birds and barking of dogs, the fragrance of grass, flowers, trees, and earth, so penetrating and so convincing for human sensibility, both sensational and spiritual – all these bring people to transcendent imagination and poetic sentiments, creating thereby a sense of infinite space within a limited area. To create a taste of the infinite from finite space: this is the essence of designing a park or garden in the city. Why? Because here, in the parks and gardens, people in the city can have a limited experience of nature in the city. Here in the parks and gardens, people can see the charm of nature, and expect also, if you like, to be seen by nature. Here people's minds come most spontaneously, and therefore most naturally, to their own self, in mutual enrichment with nature, which is the most natural way to conduct strangification, and to get back to one's own self in the act of self-reflection.

The City and the Ultimate Reality

When we come to the question of the ultimate dimension of existence, the city has a deeper meaning. The gathering of so many desires in a well-structured space and their different orientations and destinies is astonishing when we ponder it philosophically. So many bodies move in the city, so many souls seek meaning in their lives, with the rhythmic dialectics of strangification and self-reflection, familiarity and strangeness, immanence and transcendence. The energy – both individual and collective, emerging and vanishing and re-emerging unceasingly in various times and spaces – is imbued with some common origins and targets some ideals dreamed of in individual and collective imaginations.

Because of this utopian, imaginative, and dreaming function, a city – as visible in its streets, architectures, trees and parks, and in particular in its sacred places, such as churches, temples, and shrines – reveals to us an invisible city, at least in terms of human beings' affectivity and preconceptual awareness. An invisible city as the fulfilment of all of the deepest human desires, somewhere in the always retreating and there-fore inaccessible horizon, exists always in human existential expecta-tions. There, the visible city could be metamorphosed into an invisible city through the mediation of human affectivity, revealing the totality of human existence. That is why Hölderin is able to say that 'poetically man dwells.'[27]

In the city, we have our lives of joyfulness, sadness, anger, melan-choly, ambition, anxiety, effort, repression, exuberance, calculation, decisions – whole lives, both intellectual and affective, forming person-alities and relations with many others. All things considered, it is in the city that we have the joy of existence, in particular the spiritual joy of seeing all things as beautiful, good, true, and holy. Eventually, we have the hope of that which is announced now only in a vague promise, where the search for our existential origin and finality could eventually converge: i.e., the encounter with the Ultimate Reality supposed to be the origin and the final end of our life, or, more precisely, of our desires.

That is why the city is also a place full of religious presence of all kinds. In all religions, there is always the supposition of an Ultimate Reality, such as God for Christianity and other forms of monotheism, *tian* or Heaven for Confucianism, Dao for Daoism, Buddha or the Mind or Emptiness for Buddhism. Ultimate Reality is revealed to people in the diversity of their religious experiences. This is usually expressed as the revealing of the sacred, or hierophany, as Mircea Eliade called it.[28] People may experience the sacred in churches, in temples, in syna-gogues; they may also experience it on the mountain, under the sky; they may experience it in the presence of a Great power, or that of the Origin, that of the true being of all things, or when sensing the tran-scendent. A magnificent waterfall, an immense tree, a powerful animal, or an amazing mass of rock always fills us with a sense of awe in the presence of a great power or a terrible strength of life. An ancestral hall or temple, or even a solidly grounded root of a huge tree, shows us always a sense of the origin. Even in the city, under a night sky, we still have access to what Kant describes as 'the starry sky above me and the inner moral principles within my heart.' For Chinese common people, the manifestation of lucky and unlucky omens (*jixiong* 吉凶) in the temple or in the act of divination is a manifestation of the holy and the Ultimate Reality.

The memory of the city of our childhood or our hometown always brings us to the origin, always in our heart and our imagination. We recall the most cherished memory of all our beloved, of all those who, from our childhood, so generously talked to us and allowed us thereby to learn our first language, to build up a meaningful life, and to orient our desire accordingly. They stirred up in us the first original generosity to go outside of our self-enclosure to many others.

The Original/Ultimate, even experienced profoundly each in its own way for those who live in the city, is still unfathomable and, therefore, hidden. There is an unceasing interplay between transcendence and immanence, strangification and self-reflection, for not only is everything imbued inherently with the Dao, but also everything manifests the Dao and becomes thereby a concrete and particular manifestation of the Dao.

The Dao, while unfathomable, exists also in myriad things. All natural phenomena, all orientations of human desire, all cultural values, and all social and historical processes are but occasions for the manifestation of the Dao, the meaningfulness of their existence consisting always in the manifestation of Dao and marching towards Dao. Even if Laozi ever attributed some characteristics to Dao – such as the undifferentiated whole, inaudible, invisible, independent, immutable, pervasive, ceaseless, great, acting everywhere, far-reaching, and cyclical or spiral – nevertheless, all these are given reluctantly. The unfathomability of the Dao tells us that all we can say of it is the 'il y a,' which points silently, poetically, and eloquently to the Way. Martin Heidegger says,

> This unknown-familiar something, all this pointing of Saying to what is quick and stirring within it, is to all present and absent beings as that first break of dawn with which the changing cycle of day and night first begins to be possible; it is the earliest and most ancient at once. We can do no more than name it, because it will not be discussed, for it is the region of all places, of all time-space-horizons ... It yields the opening of the clearing in which present beings can persist and from which absent beings can depart while keeping their persistence in the withdrawal.[29]

So, Dao is manifesting itself in Saying, yet still unfathomable. The city is visible and we live in it, yet it is still invisible and bringing us beyond. Human desire is always craving and longing to determine itself in the desired desire. Still, the desiring desire is moving on, insatiably, infinitely, and unfathomably, to a destiny that is beyond all borders.

NOTES

1 I use the term 'lifeworld' (*Lebenswelt*) in Husserl's sense (Vincent Shen, 'Annäherung an das taoistische Verständnis von Wissenschaft. Die Episte-

mologie des Lao Tses und Tschuang Tses,' in *Grenzziehungen zum Konstruktiven Realismus*, ed. F. Wallner, J. Schimmer, and M. Costazza [Vienna: WUV Universitätsverlag, 1993]), as well as its interpretation by Jürgen Habermas as the correlate and background of communicative action (Habermas, *The Theory of Communicative Action*, vol. 1, *Reason and the Rationalization of Society*, trans. Thomas McCarthy [Boston: Beacon Press, 1984], 70–1).

2 Georg Simmel, *On Individuality and Social Forms: Selected Writings*, ed. Donald N. Levine (Chicago: University of Chicago Press, 1971), 143–9.

3 Zhuangzi, *Zhuangzi Jishi* 莊子集釋 (*Collected Commentaries on the Zhuangzi*), ed. Guo Qingfan, reprinted edition (Taipei: World Books, 1982), 408.

4 Mencius, *Mencius*, in *Sishu Zhangju Jizhu* 四書章句集注 (Collected Commentaries in Chapters and Sentences of the Four Books), reprinted edition (Beijing: Zhonghua Bookstore, 1983), 209; *Mencius*, trans. D.C. Lau (New York: Penguin, 1970), 57.

5 Mencius, *Mencius*, 349. My translation.

6 As Paul Ricoeur says, 'le mode d'être du corps, en tant qu'il n'est ni représentation en moi, ni chose hors du moi, est le modèle ontique pour tout inconscient conceivable. Ce n'est pas la détermination vitale du corps, mais l'ambiguité de son mode d'être qui est exemplaire. Un sens qui existe, c'est un sens qui est pris dans un corps, c'est un comportment signifiant.' Paul Ricoeur, *De l'interpretation. Essai sur Freud* (Paris: Éditions du Seuil, 1965), 372.

7 Xü Shen, *Shuowen Jiezi* 說文解字 (Explication and Analysis of Chinese Words), reprinted edition (Taipei: Yi-wen, 1966), 76.

8 Martin Heidegger, *Being and Time*, trans. J. Macquarrie and E. Robinson (New York: SCM Press, 1962), 130.

9 Laozi, *Laozi Sizhong*, 老子四種, *Four Versions of the Laozi*, reprinted edition (Taipei: Da An Press, 1999), 1.

10 Laozi, *Laozi Sizhong*, 37.

11 As could be seen in the Daoist texts such as *Xiang Er Commentary on the Laozi* (*Laozi Xian Er Zhu*; see chapters 4, 13, 21, 25, 29) and the *Middle Scripture of Laozi* (Laozi Zhong Jing; see chapters 39, 12, 44). See Baotian Gu and Zhongli Zhang, *Xinyi Laozi Xian Er Zhu* 新譯老子想爾注, *Xiang Er Commentary on the Laozi: A New Translation* (Taipei: Sanmin, 1997), 4–29; and Daozang, *Laozi Zhong Jing* 老子中經, *Middle Scripture of Laozi*, in the *Zhengtong Daozang*, vol. 37, reprinted edition (Taipei: Xinwenfeng Bookstore, 1985), 302–14.

12 Jacques Lacan, *Écrits* (Paris: Éditions du Seuil, 1966), 814.

13 Heidegger, *Being and Time*, 97.

14 Heidegger, *Being and Time*, 97.

15 Heidegger, *Being and Time*, 100.

16 Heidegger, *Being and Time*, 100–1.

17 Heidegger, *Being and Time*, 99.

18 Maurice Merleau-Ponty, *Phénoménologie de la perception* (Paris: Gallimard, 1945), 325.

19 Confucius, *Lunyu* 論語 (the *Analects*), in *Sishu Zhangju Jizhu* 四書章句集注, *Collected Commentaries in Chapters and Sentences of the Four Books*, reprinted edition (Beijing: Zhonghua Bookstore, 1983). My translation.

20 Confucius, *Lunyu*, 173. My translation.

21 Confucius, *Lunyu*, 142. From *A Source Book in Chinese Philosophy*, trans. Wing-tsit Chan (Princeton: Princeton University Press, 1973), 40.

22 Laozi, *Laozi Sizhong*, 13.

23 Laozi, *Laozi Sizhong*, 35.

24 Laozi, *Laozi Sizhong*, 2.

25 Laozi, *Laozi Sizhong*, 23.

26 A recent discussion of this sign can be read in Robert Bickers and Jeffrey Wasserstrom, 'Shanghai's "Dogs and Chinese Not Admitted" Sign: Legend, History and Contemporary Symbol,' *China Quarterly* no. 142 (June 1995): 444–66.

27 '*Dichterisch wohnt der Mensch*,' quoted from Martin Heidegger, *Poetry, Language, Thought* (New York: Perennial Classics, 2001), 211.

28 The term 'hierophany' comes from hiero (meaning 'sacred') and -phany (meaning 'manifestation'). It is used by Mircea Eliade when he writes, 'To designate the act of manifestation of the sacred, we have proposed the term hierophany. It is a fitting term, because it does not imply anything further; it expresses no more than is implicit in its etymological content, i.e., that something sacred shows itself to us.' Mircea Eliade, *The Sacred and the Profane: The Nature of Religion*, trans. Willard R. Trask (New York: Harcourt Brace Jovanovich, 1959), 11.

29 Martin Heidegger, *On the Way to Language*, trans. Peter D. Hertz (San Francisco: Harper and Row, 1982), 127.

8 Biocracy in the City: A Contemporary Buddhist Practice

KENNETH MALY

There is an ancient mythos being told these days, more and more. By mythos I do not mean story, narrative, myth, saga, or tale – although bits and pieces of some of those words might fit. Rather, by mythos I mean a saying that manifests from what is both 'real' and 'not real' – or what is simultaneously not real and not not-real: in the space or gap between real and not real, it says the truth. Another way to say this: mythos 'tells a tale' or 'says a saga' about – or, better yet, *from* – what is in its non-transparency, that withdrawing dynamic that sustains.

In his own story or mythos, Black Elk says the following: I do not know whether what I tell here is real or not; but if you think about it, you know that it is true. I invite your mind to proceed in this mode. Here is one version of this mythos:

The Mythos of Life Emergent

Once upon a time, a long time ago, when humans and non-humans still spoke the same language – or at least still understood one another's languaging – there were bio-human communities where humans lived in their world by being in constant contact with energy and its dynamic. The human community was ruled by Life. All beings, humans as well, lived in movement and change, everything was possible, circling in seasons. They listened to the natural world and heard what it said.

There was a rich understanding and enactment of interdependence of all living beings, where things like the wind and water and air were living parts of that interbeing. The bio- or eco-dynamic held up and sustained the way things were and were known. All things and all beings were in a dynamic emergence, always open to and moving within the possible.

In this time-space, the natural world made demands on all these beings, in order to maintain what it gave to them. In turn, all living beings, including humans, paid attention to these demands and respected what they called for – either because their direct experience gave them awareness that this is the truth of things, or because their survival depended on this attention.

The Shift

A new story emerged, one of humans and ego-subjectivity engaging in controlling the natural. Humans saw themselves as the epicentre. Humans started seeing the universe as having a single, even linear, destiny. They began to take nature and the earth as a system of mechanical parts, a physical reality that is objectifiable, a fixed reality. Nature became subservient to human desire, and humans ignored the demands that natural design makes. Technologies were developed in accord with these shifted assumptions, and humans developed an immense confidence in such technologies – confidence even that their technology would save them from any ecological disaster or destruction. Any problem had an exclusively human answer.

Humans were no longer committed to the earth for their well-being and sustenance. Even though the earth and nature remained vital to their survival, humans thought and acted as if this were not true. The practice was dysfunctional, but many people – especially those in political and economic power – simply did not see this.

The big word for humans was *control*. Always have it, never lose it, make it the centrepiece of all lifestyles. Things – both those things humanly made and naturally occurring things – no longer emerge as things that gather what is, that enact what is their own; rather, things are reduced to disposables, items that are non-earth-generated and have no lastingness, no staying power as things, but rather are intended for disposability. Not to become one's own, but to be disposed of.

There developed a certain disdain for things 'primitive,' as if they were less-than. But this disdain hides a resentment that lies not so dormant in the dominating culture; for no longer living fully in the present, in the ongoing emergence as the way things are, this dominating culture created its own illusion of security. And it was always fearful of losing this security. It grabbed for control (although this was an illusion) and let fear be one of its primary motivators.

This way of being in the world sees itself as very logical and rational, even as it is itself a constructed world, one that relies for its being on what is precisely not rational, on its own mythos. Both the dominance of reason and the drive for security bled the people's hearts of bliss, openness to change, and emergent life lived fully.

The Newly Emerging Mythos

In recent times a new story is welling up, one of human dwelling as earth-dwelling, with awareness. Here the mythos returns to honouring the limits of growth and the limits of cognition – to a reverence for what humans do not and cannot know. Here the non-physical energies manifest more in the dynamic movement in space than the particulate substances as seen in the mechanical world view.

Now the natural is engagingly thought as an ongoing process of unfolding and emergence. Humans and non-humans *are* what is natural, in a non-duality. The way things are, in nature and in earth, does not involve a transcendent being or even just a 'spiritual' quality, but something that is not limited to the physical, the quantifiable, the tangible. Even scientists have taken to calling this a dynamic of 'consciousness' – or, as Buddhists would say, belonging to 'mind.'

In this newly emerging mythos, the natural is again taken to be coherent and inherent in its suchness, to have its own excellence, not needing any being or any power from the 'outside' to give it meaning or dignity. This suchness or intrinsic dignity of earth includes human participation, but humans do not control or define or dominate. In this self-inherence there is always variety and diversity. Mirrored in what biologists call biodiversity, this articulation of what is own to each living being is part and parcel of all living beings. Diversity on all levels – social, cultural, genetic, natural – is celebrated. All these unique beings are always intimately within and a part of the larger biotic community. All things are imbued with spontaneities, acting and responding to what is their 'own,' each in its own niche, as well as emerging and acting within the biotic community of which each is a part.

Knowing this, humans act accordingly. Humans are not 'on' the earth, but 'in and of' the earth. It is amazing what a difference this difference makes. There is radiance, not only from the sun! Now humans look to earth itself for their paradigm. Nature has always taught humans much, but in this recently emerging mythos, the natural becomes the 'own' of the way things are. Named variously as nature's patterns, ecological design, or natural law, this is a teaching from earth. Earth is now the teacher, without the dualism of 'us versus them' or the dichotomy of 'nature versus humans.' Humans are part of earth, and the whole is contained in every part. Non-dualistically, the earth as a whole is manifest in each natural being, just as 'earth' does not exist separately from those beings that are 'in' it.

Rather than seeing themselves as in control, both in definition and in action, humans now know themselves to be actively participating in the unfolding of nature/earth, to be aware and present to the sustaining dynamic of earth. Humans now know the self-inherence and self-unfolding and self-renewing of the natural world – how things are in their 'ownness,' in what is own to them – as that in which humans take part but which is not of human design.

All of this is about the invisibles of the sensuous in their awareness and adaptivity and in humans' awareness and active owning the invisibles while being enowned by and from them. Emergent, unfolding life. Within the life-enhancing tension of the back-and-forth movement within, among, and encompassing all things, nature and earth manifest in and as emergent life, with the earth-human dynamic in its non-duality. The 'forces of nature' are once again celebrated, nature that is never complete or static – passing beyond … into possibility.

So, let us pause here, before turning to Buddhism. In the end, the mythos of Life Emergent is one of possibility. But how is this newly emergent mythos, in our time, different from the originary mythos *before* the shift, as just described? And how is it the same mythos? Today's context is surely different, as are the working paradigms in which the newly emergent mythos is unfolding. At the same time, it taps into the ancient and elemental in striking ways. The newly emergent mythos sees possibility, even as it is ensconced in inherited traditions, values, constructs, interpretations. What is important is the turning that takes place in the interaction between the way things are naturally and how human awareness experiences and thinks the mythos.

Turning to Buddhism

This mythos, in its most recent turning, moves within the same dynamic as Buddhism. Or: This mythos mirrors Buddhism in its teachings and practice. Or: Some core notions and practices of Buddhism invite us to clarify and deepen our place in the emerging mythos of biocracy in the city. This word *biocracy* comes from the writings of Thomas Berry and Brian Swimme. *Bio-* from the Greek word for 'life'; *-cracy* from the Greek word *krateo*, for 'ruling.' 'Democracy' says that the people rule; 'biocracy' says that life rules. Taking this one step further, the Greek verb *krateo* means 'to rule' or 'to hold sway' – to have the power, to be the sustaining force. Biocracy says that life holds sway and has the power for sustaining. From democracy to biocracy is the move from a people-only holding sway to the larger earth-life community holding sway. These Buddhist teachings are of a piece with this mythos of Life Emergent.

Dare we take time to be with and meditate on this mythos, when 'all is crumbling around us'? Dare we pause in the challenging work of 'saving the earth' and 'stopping the destruction'? There is so much devastation and species extinction and so much to be done and so much intricacy in all of this. It becomes overwhelming, and it seems irresponsible to stop and ponder the emerging mythos. We have no choice but to 'do it' and to do the best we can.

But how to do it? What I offer here is meant to *go along with* the necessary and most useful actions for ecosystems and healthy cities – not a replacement paradigm. It is meant to enrich us as we continue the great work of earth whole-making. It is meant to offer a perspective and a practice to go along with and sustain environmental action and policy. Think of it as a freshening up.

The path to this emerging mythos and its connection to Buddhist practice in the city goes something like this:

1. Since Buddha and Buddhism are primarily oriented to liberation and enlightenment – or development of mind as such – they do not thematize the human–nature relationship.

2. In a sense they did not need to up until now, since the Buddhist world view and practice were within awareness of a non-dualistic permeation of humans and nature. One could also say that the world at that time was in synchronicity with nature and thus would not have thematized it.

3. We can carefully and lightly tease an environmental philosophy out of Buddhist teachings by sharpening our grasp of how it looks at non-human life forms.

4. BUT: If we look more at sustainability, we are in luck! Because the image of sustainability is at the core of Buddhist teachings on how humans are to comport themselves regarding all life forms.

5. Sentient beings are to be preserved and not harmed, (a) since they all have Buddha-nature and (b) since within the bodhisattva promise is the core notion of compassion, i.e., realization that we are all connected and thus your degradation is my degradation. Sentient beings include plants and ecosystems, for this suchness that we spoke of earlier, the Buddha-nature, or *tathagata* (different names that 'say the same'), pervades and fills the 'hearts and minds' of all beings – trees and ecosystems thus all have Buddha-nature. So, in practice, Buddhism is about

sustainability, even if neither sustainability nor environmental ethics/ philosophy were ever thematized.

6. Now we turn to the city. We turn to engaged Buddhism, working buddhistically for sustainable living, for dwelling richly and fully in human-earth community, e.g., cities.

Buddhist Ecology as Implicate

Ecology and environmental ethics as we know them are not part of the Buddhist world view. There is no word in Sanskrit, Tibetan, or Pali for 'environment' or 'ecology.' It is well nigh impossible to find an explicit ecology or environmental ethic in either the classical texts of Buddhism or in the traditional Buddhist cultures.

This does not mean that ecological wisdom is not implicit in much of Buddhist teaching. Along with the directive of 'not taking life,' the core Buddhist teaching of benefiting all sentient beings fits here. One would have a hard time not including all forms of life in this directive.

It is still true that Buddhist teaching and practice focus on liberation, the removal of suffering, enlightenment, and the potential of mind's development. In this context, the 'normal' Western mind usually assumes two things. One, this 'mind' belongs only to humans – although there are some intuitive indications otherwise. (For example, Tibetan Buddhism makes very refined and subtle distinctions of 'mind': *sem*, the 'mind' or 'sentience' that pertains to all beings; *yid*, the cognitive, discursive 'mind,' which Westerners stress and essentialize; *shepa*, the ordinary awareness of 'mind,' the mind that is naked awareness of what is here and now, in front of us; and *rigpa*, 'mind' as awareness as such – awareness awareness. Do any or all of these qualities of mind belong to non-humans?)

The second thing that the 'normal' Western mind usually assumes is that Buddhism is not officially or explicitly concerned with the environment. Thus Buddhist teachings are seen as *implications* in Buddhism for ecology.

What emerges does so from within conditions that bring it about. Never in isolation; isolation is illusion. Compassion. Interdependence. Impermanence, decay as natural, change. The unhurried rhythms of the natural. The path of liberation is for all beings with Buddha-nature, for sure including animals ... and what about trees and ecosystems, or the 'land'? This 'open' question may call for reverence in the face of our not-knowing.

The word 'nature' in Buddhist literature means (a) the world –

including non-humans, in non-dual interbeing; (b) the way things are – as in the universe, the way things are, how things all together are; and (c) the 'total field' system, with its enmeshment in the big, connected cosmos of humans, animals, and gods. The English word *nature* comes from the Latin *natura*, which was the Latin translation of the Greek word *physis*: the self-unfolding, birthing, life emergent. The Japanese have a word for this same phenomenon: *shi-zen*, what is such unfolding, of itself; or *jinen*, 'made to become so by itself,' coming into its own, in its own way, 'ownly.' *Nature, natura, physis, shi-zen, jinen*: the together of things, life, earth, always including humans, in emergent life.

Gathering these several threads, the phenomenon of nature is about dynamic changing. This includes the five laws of the physical (of seasons), the biological (of seeds and planting), the psychological (of personalities), the 'moral' (of doing what is own to one, what is one's truth), and the all-encompassing 'causal' law (the one that wraps them all, the recognition that everything is 'caused,' i.e., emerges from within conditions and is thus impermanent and changing).

Sustainability

There is a sense in which the word and notion of sustainability and sustainable living names the kind of work that is called for in the mythos of Life Emergent – and might be the key to the resonance of Buddhism within the mythos. But it is imperative that we know clearly how the word gets used in today's language. Sustainability has three levels:

(a) Economic
   - maintain level of resources
   - protect commodities
   - replace what you take from resources
   - replace as fast as you use

(b) Human survival/quality of human life
   - meet survival needs and
   - give humans means to a 'better life' (quality)

(c) Interactive balance of ecosystem
   - bio- and cultural diversity
   - ecological interactions
   - human responsibility for active participation in (not control of) healthy human–non-human communities

It is on this last level of sustainability that Buddhism resonates; it is here that Buddhism and ecological thinking get enmeshed.

Buddhist Practice

With no god or transcendent being, we humans have the responsibility and are held accountable. Open minds. Knowing interbeing. Simplicity and moderation, along with and responding to the natural cycle of life. When we humans stand up, we see that it is we who begin to bring about the change that the newly emerging mythos calls for. Loving-kindness, compassion, sympathetic joy, equanimity (not more important than anyone else, human or otherwise).

Human community cultures as well as diverse ecosystems are manifestations of mind; they mirror what is most 'own' to compassion: namely, the experience that every being is connected, that the way things are is in non-separation. This experience makes contact with the deep mind of peoples and sentient beings of all times and places.

Within Buddhist practice, humans recognize that they are embedded and enmeshed in the natural, Indra's net. This awareness transforms environmental practice, from one of a separate ego, knowing in some fashion of its moral duty to other separate beings – standing somehow outside of that which it is 'saving' or otherwise working for – to a sense of an 'ecological self' that is synergistically and 'ownly' connected to all of the natural. This transformation leaves behind duty and morality and engages in spontaneous responsible action based on awareness of non-dualism, of being part of the whole and the whole's being part of one's own unique being. With Buddhism, ecological thinking moves beyond altruism (and the accompanying sense of duty, morality, and sacrifice) to spontaneous and joyful action for earth and the earth–human community based on the wisdom of compassion (and the bodhisattva heart that generates this connection-awareness).

In principle, a Buddhist practice would not 'escape from' the world in ecological need. Rather, it will enrich and deepen the human involvement with earth in these two ways: that is, beyond self-identity to an ecological self, and beyond moralism to spontaneous joyful action that enowns humans. (Heidegger's notion of 'thinking as thanking' comes to mind here. Spontaneity and joyfulness bring with them gratitude: being grateful in the engaged thinking/thanking. Thankful for the awareness and for the beauty liberates mind from fear, anger, and resentment, and embraces spontaneous joyful action.)

A Buddhist practice will actively and spontaneously respond to the conditions that manifest in front of the mind – in the same way as all interdependent phenomena simply manifest the exciting and complex set of conditions that make them up. It is in this sense that a rainbow is as real or not real as a bicycle is real or not real. The rainbow is not solid, but it is there, made up of parts that have combined to manifest this phenomenon. Buddhist practice is of the same mould. Being non-dual (interconnected), non-self-identical (non-egoic, enmeshed self), and impermanent (dynamic, changing, non-substance), the Buddhist environmental practitioner stays present to the phenomenon that is in front, becomes a part of the conditions that brought about the event, and takes action in this same freedom.

Life emergent exists only in context, depending on the conditions that bring it about and in line with the mutual intermeshing of earth and of things of earth as one and including humans. In this deep interbeing, specific beings are called to be-with mutually, rather than obstructingly. The world is seen as a field of complementarity and affordance to one another, rather than as filled with beings competing and dominating. The earth is seen as one dynamic of interplay, rather than the arena for survival of the fittest in the competition that we call natural selection. And humans, within their own way of being, are actively participating in the renewal of life emergent and the recovery of earth.

Buddhist practice has already benefited ecological thinking with its dynamic within interrelatedness of the whole earth, its manifesting within particular beings or ecological (now in the biological sense) niches, and its informing environmental responsibility and action in a way that undoes the separation as well as the moralistic conscience. It is this same interconnectedness and the bodhisattva dynamic that works for earth and earth beings who are *not* human – this same dynamic works for humans in their function within human community: that is, within the city.

Dwelling Buddhistically-Sustainably in the City

Recognizing the intricate complexity of the web of the universe, the web of life emergent, we also recognize that we cannot separate ourselves from the other, humans from earth. This vast web of things and the necessary interpenetration of everything draw us to our humility. And in this humility we ask: How do we dwell sustainably in the city?

If it is true that classical Buddhism does not explicitly talk about environmental ethics, it is probably even more the case that Buddhism does not explicitly deal with sustainability in the city. Clearly, cities as we know and live them did not exist in Buddha's time. Granting that there may have been some rather large urban settlements at that time, human community took place as 'pockets' in a mostly humanly uninhabited earth. Today, humanly uninhabited earth exists as 'pockets' in a mostly humanly inhabited planet.

If Buddhism is not indifferent to destruction of life, and if Buddhism is open to the changes that happen in specific places and times, and if Buddhism has underlying principles for engaging where one is, then how would Buddhism teach 'dwelling sustainably in the city'?

Humans are part of the earth, part of the land. In order to know this land, humans are in a place, a bioregion. In order to live and work in a bioregion, humans come together and a community is created. Perhaps Buddhist principles of compassion, interdependence, equanimity, and restraining from harming were focused on the individual and mind development, liberation from suffering and enlightenment – all for the sake of happiness, which all humans seek. But this was never in isolation from the principle of benefiting all sentient beings. So, given that today's environmental responsibility calls for community involvement and collective work, how will these principles get expressed in this contemporary situation? How do mindfulness training and developing the mind and practising equanimity serve the 'natural city'?

One might say that the conditions that have come together, such that there are urban centres of human-earth community, are not stagnant. Thus they are always open to new possibility. Buddhism would not replace the dynamic of the community in its possibility; rather, Buddhism provides a perspective and practice that makes sense within the context of the urban community. The sangha – formerly and classically thought, perhaps, as the community in which the individuals practised mindfulness training and mind development – now becomes a practice in its own. Practising 'community' takes place within the ecological complex of human-earth community. Ecological sustainability takes its measure from – as well as serves – the local community, the community in place.

The community is central to the sangha, which includes trees and water. One might speak of the 'watershed sangha.'

This awareness leads to some general and then some specific possibilities for dwelling buddhistically-sustainably in the city, that is, living in terms of sangha-community (in both the narrow and the broader sense of 'sangha') in one's bioregion of the city. Generally, possibilities include working with and depending on one's neighbours; reverence for the natural as it emerges within the city; valuing eco-justice as a practice of including all humans and the natural within the human-earth community; looking for the Buddha-nature in one's urban dwelling space; becoming aware of one's habitat or dwelling place as within a given watershed; increasing one's awareness of the seasons and of the flora/fauna that belong to one's bioregional watershed.

Specifically, possibilities include practising an architecture that is sensitive to urban-earth design; building open/public spaces for dwelling humanly-earthly; developing and supporting locally nurtured economics (small businesses that are rooted in neighbourhoods, community banks, a local exchange and trading system); living a materially simpler life (more complex in 'nature,' more simple as defined by consumption); responsible food purchasing (buying local, buying organic, eating lower on the food chain, community-supported agriculture).

Working with Delight

City life, as well as any Buddhist lifestyle, calls for a spontaneity and joy and excitement that offset the non-Buddhist moralism that dominates in the Judeo-Christian world view – even for atheists! Rather than viewing things and the world in the black-and-white model of 'right and wrong,' to be dealt with morally from out of the 'fixed self-identity' of the individual, judged by one's inner voice of 'conscience,' Buddhist principles offer pregnant possibilities to biocracy in the city: the 'isness' of what happens when certain conditions come together, the excitement that emerges when there is nothing to hold together or hold firm (the bliss of impermanence), and the possible that always sits at the edge of change.

I would like to close by reaching for a word that does not dominate in Western environmental literature, although it is not totally absent (John Seed, Joanna Macy, Dolores LaChapelle): delight. Whether it is William Blake's 'Energy is Eternal Delight' or Gary Snyder's 'Delight is the innocent joy arising ... from the mutually-embracing, shining / single world beyond all discrimination / or opposites' – and whether the delight is in the whole human-earth community or just in the personal experience of the individual – the world or universe is viewed as a radiant, interdependent world-earth, joyful and spontaneous when experienced non-dualistically.

In utter delight, engaged thinking becomes a rich part of the mythos of life emergent, as it emerges and is practised in the urban cityscape.

PART THREE

Expanding Our Collective Horizons: Societal Implications

The oldest task in human history: to live on a piece of land without spoiling it.

– Aldo Leopold

Aldo Leopold's pithy apothegm of sustainable living has complex ecological and societal implications, as the contributors to this section make clear.

Social-cultural anthropologist Hilary Cunningham constructively shows how rapid urbanization has been accompanied by a rising gap between the haves and have-nots within urban centres. Building on the work of urban theorists Saskia Sassen, David Harvey, and others, Cunningham looks at the notion of the 'global city,' which often promotes 'world-class' status while eschewing issues of capital, social justice, and environmental degradation. Cunningham concludes that the natural city, if it sees poverty, ecology, and urban life in a constitutive continuum, might provide an antidote to such gleaming but deeply flawed urban dreams.

Richard Oddie explores the fascinating but often overlooked world of 'acoustic ecology.' Building on the pioneering work of R. Murray Schafer, Oddie creatively demonstrates that such an approach entails far more than simply acknowledging 'noise pollution,' and proffers the prospect of new paths of research into urban space and design. By taking urban soundscape seriously, Oddie suggests, we might find additional tools, insights, and stratagems as we attempt to erect more equitable and sustainable cities.

Employing the non-dualistic, non-anthropocentric tenets of ecofeminism, Trish Glazebrook develops an original designation – 'cityzenry' – pertaining to city dwellers rather than others in the nation-state, and begins to draw the contours of a non-essentializing ethic of urban care. Noting that cities are shared ecosystems in which nature and civilization are not necessarily in opposition, Glazebrook provides illuminating case studies of urban citizens taking responsibility for urban flora and fauna through education, policy, and praxis, and provides a vision of what such engagement would look like within the context of the natural city framework.

Process thinker John B. Cobb, Jr, contrasts an 'ecological' notion of sustainability with an 'economistic' understanding, and provides a prophetic call for adoption of the former. Providing an insightful critique of our petroleum-based economy, Cobb, whose observations were first shared with a Chinese audience, reflects on the rapid industrialization of China. He uses the work of Paolo Soleri and David Orr, among others, to suggest a compelling alternative ecological view for cities, not only in China, but around the world.

The difficulties of urbanization in newly industrialized nations are also explored by anthropologist Shubhra Gururani. Using the high-tech, call centre–based 'cyborg' city of Gurgaon, India, as a case study, Gururani provides a useful schema of development models in cities of the global South. Building on the work of Bruno Latour and Donna Haraway, Gururani examines the hybridization of the urban and natural landscapes in such neo-liberal urban developments. She also explores the notion of 'metropolitan nature,' insightfully intimating that the destructive tendencies of such urban spaces of the new globalized economy are symptomatic of a consumption-based, deleterious world view.

All of the contributors in this section delineate the underlying nexus that unites ecology, political economy, culture, and urbanization, providing choice insights into possible contours and directions for the natural city.

9 Gated Ecologies and 'Possible Urban Worlds': From the Global City to the Natural City

HILARY CUNNINGHAM

Introduction: The Urban-Ecology-Poverty Nexus

Recently, a group of undergraduate students in my course on ecology, poverty, and urbanization gave a presentation on Lagos – a megacity of 11 million inhabitants and the former capital of the Federal Republic of Nigeria. Lagos is a city that has been in the news of late, owing to its alarming and phenomenal rate of urbanization. In 1990, Lagos's population was just over 4 million. In 2005 it reached 10 million and by 2015 it is expected to reach 18 million. Not surprisingly, this rate of growth has put an insupportable pressure on the city's infrastructure, resulting in human suffering on an almost unimaginable scale. Lagos's environmental ills (in evidence perhaps most acutely in its erratic water and energy supply, disastrous waste management, wholly inadequate public transportation system, and housing crisis) have been compounded by its troubling colonial history as well as its position within the global economy as West Africa's premier seaport and industrial centre. Several decades of military rule, World Bank Structural Adjustment programs, foreign control of oil production, and ineffective privatization measures have severely compromised Lagos's urban identity, and indeed its very future as a viable place to live.

Yet, despite its enormous population, Lagos has no functional mass transit system. Indeed, the first slide the presenters showed us brought home the sheer magnitude of the obstacles facing any program designed to improve the city's human and environmental future. The first image depicted an attempted light rail transit project, implemented by the city to decrease traffic congestion and air pollution. The slide showed several rail cars inhabited not by commuters, but by squatters. While the failure of this particular project was probably due to a variety of factors, clearly Lagos's massive homelessness and desperate poverty were primary among them. Needless to say, this light rail system never managed to get on track, revealing that issues of ecological sustainability in cities cannot be addressed over the lives and realities of the urban poor.

This image of a failed public transportation project, although eloquent in and of itself about sustainability in cities such as Lagos, is also paradigmatic of much broader demographic trends that form an important backdrop to any discussion of a 'natural city.' The first of these trends has been the tremendous shift in human settlement patterns over the past hundred years. In 1900, only about 10 per cent of the world's population lived in cities. Today, that figure has reached nearly 50 per cent. Over the next 15 years, it is predicted, nearly two-thirds of the world's population will live in urban areas. As urban guru Mike Davis has noted in his *Planet of Slums*:

> The earth has urbanized even faster than originally predicted by the Club of Rome in its notoriously Malthusian 1972 report, *Limits to Growth*. In 1950 there were 86 cities in the world with a population over one million; today there are 400, and by 2015, there will be at least 550. Cities, indeed, have absorbed nearly two-thirds of the global population explosion since 1950 and are currently growing by a million babies and migrants each week. The present urban population (3.2 billion) is larger than the total population of the world in 1960. The global countryside, meanwhile, has reached its maximum population (3.2 billion) and will begin to shrink after 2020. As a result, cities will account for *all* future world population growth, which is expected to peak at about 10 billion in 2050.[1]

In light of these demographic trends, one can safely conclude, along with urban geographer David Harvey, that the past hundred years has indeed been '*the* century of urbanization.'[2]

Yet a second distinguishing characteristic of the late twentieth century brings us to the political and economic processes that have so moulded contemporary urban life and lifestyles. While cities across the globe have experienced various permutations of these processes, industrialization, colonization, development, and globalization have profoundly shaped not only the urban built environment, but also the complex and myriad inequalities that characterize cities as well as the 'countrysides' to which they are connected. Currently, over half the world's population is impoverished. The gap between the 20 richest countries and 20 poorest countries has doubled over the last 40 years. As a result, the income of the world's richest 1 per cent is now equal to that of the poorest 57 per cent. Moreover, it is women who remain the poorest of the poor. Representing 70 per cent of those who live in absolute poverty, women labour for two-thirds of the world's total working hours, produce almost half the world's food, and yet have earnings of only 10 per cent of the world's gross income.

As urban scholar Janice Perlman notes, these broader global trends in poverty reveal a distinctively urban quality. It is the impoverished communities living in the 'informal city' (i.e., the parts of cities consisting of squatter, clandestine, and provisional settlements) that are growing. They now account for 40 per cent of the total urban population in countries of the global South. Even this is a conservative estimate; many place it closer to 70 per cent.[3] Like Lagos, these communities typically lack clean water, sanitation services, public transportation, and adequate housing. Many residents live in chronic fear of eviction.[4] It is not surprising that these areas are also the stigmatized and marginalized zones of the city where poverty and 'the poor' are read as dangerous, undesirable, and, in many cases, 'disposable.' The late twentieth century, then, has also borne witness to pervasive and acute poverty, most of which is on the increase in cities.[5]

These two trends – global urbanization and global impoverishment – are thus likely to remain salient features of cities in the future. Although most of the world's poor continue to be largely rural,[6] human settlement trends suggest that poverty in cities will continue to expand, particularly as high rates of land displacement and migration into urban job markets persist. Cities, then, are becoming not only the principal centres of human activity and production, but also sites of increasing poverty and economic segregation. Indeed, the bulk of projected urban population growth (95 per cent) will occur in the developing world.[7] Cities such as Lagos are thus becoming more the rule than the exception for most of the world's urban dwellers. The proliferation of megacities (cities with populations of around 10 million) and hypercities (cities with populations of 20 million or more)[8] will continue to have the compounded problems associated with poverty – as will many smaller urban centres that are absorbing rural populations displaced by market reforms.

Environmentally, this urban portrait is hardly salutary. Poor city dwellers disproportionately suffer from the direct effects of contaminated water, infested housing, flooding, and pollution from industrial production. Corrupt governments, aid strategies that do not address the needs and aspirations of local communities, and ideologies that pit environmental concerns against economic prosperity obstruct more equitable environmental policies in many cities.[9] Moreover, these congested cities are principal sources of greenhouse gases and water pollution, both of which have far-reaching and devastating consequences for communities connected through weather circuits and water systems. Very few of us – perhaps none of us – will escape the consequences of overcrowded, polluted, and polluting cities mired in deepening patterns of segregation and inequity.

Thus when we speak of a 'natural city' at the beginning of the twenty-first century, it must come out of a context – indeed, a nexus – in which poverty, ecology, and urban life exist in critical interrelationship. What kinds of urban worlds are possible or desirable in light of these trends? What kinds of cities can we hope for and help to build? Clearly there can be no 'natural city' outside the context of a 'natural globe' in which the larger trends and interconnections that I outline above are taken seriously and, one could argue, foundationally.

The City and 'Gated Ecologies'

The questions posed above suggest that any discussion of a 'natural city' must engage deeply with the economic, political, and cultural processes that have helped to shape contemporary cities, urban life, and the landscapes of inequality that continue to characterize them. At the core of such an engagement is an acknowledgment that there is nothing 'unnatural' about cities themselves, and that cities are inherently socio-ecological processes and as such do not stand in distinction from or in opposition to 'nature.'[10] Thus, a re-envisioning of the city is not simply a question of realigning 'town' and 'countryside' to produce more sustainable living spaces. It entails a deeper 're-naturalizing' of urban theory (to borrow a phrase from Heynen, Kaika, and Swyngedouw)[11] – that is, a new way of thinking about how forms of 'the urban' and 'the natural' are constitutive of particular social orders.

The expansion and deepening of poverty in the late twentieth and early twenty-first centuries therefore posits two central challenges for a 'natural city.' The first, as the above suggests, involves seriously addressing the role of contemporary capitalist processes in shaping cities and delineating how these processes create particular forms of urban-nature configurations.[12] The second challenge involves critiquing dominant and hegemonic visions of cities that do not give issues of political-economic and cultural marginalization a central place – both in terms of their conceptualizations of city life itself, and in their proposed solutions to environmental issues. Both of these challenges suggest that any discussion of a 'natural city' must be situated firmly within a broader critique of contemporary models of the 'urban' and 'nature,' which demands that we pay special attention to the visions of cities that tend to avoid and obfuscate the systemic inequalities experienced by the vast majority of urban dwellers.

While cities are themselves complex and diverse entities, and while poverty rates differ greatly among countries, among regions, among cities, and within cities themselves, it is nevertheless useful to think about the poverty-ecology-urban nexus broadly and to probe the kinds of ideas and values that currently dominate conceptions of cities and shape their futures. The need to do so now, however, is perhaps even more urgent, especially as various cities explore, adopt, and experiment with different sustainability models. Certain visions of the city will 'green' the urban environment in particular ways; some of these will inevitably reproduce (and may even enhance) existing class, ethnic, and gendered divisions. Certain paradigms of cities, then, run the risk of generating 'gated ecologies' in which the wealthier residents of cities not only enjoy socio-economic benefits, but also selectively reap the advantages of clean water, adequate sanitation, beautiful parks, and environmentally friendly buildings and products from within enclaves of privilege.

If one of the tasks of formulating the natural city, then, is to engage critically with both the values and the structures shaping contemporary urban forms, which models of 'the city' should be a focus of critique? While many contemporary visions of 'the city' are likely to find themselves at odds with the urban-ecology-poverty nexus outlined above, foremost among these, I would suggest, is the 'world city.'

Although the world city model has deeper roots in postwar urban theory, it became the 'poster city' of late twentieth-century capitalism under conditions of globalization. Beginning in the late 1980s, politicians, urban theorists, and urban planners enamoured of the 'world city' model began to refer more frequently to these kinds of cities as 'global cities' – i.e., cities that had emerged as 'premier' world destinations and important 'nodes' in the swirling world of global capital, culture, and technology. Among many political geographers, however, global cities were viewed much more critically. Consequently, these scholars have analysed the world city model more along the lines of how neo-liberal forms of capitalism have created a hierarchy of cities in which a handful are considered to be 'on' the global map, while the majority are rendered 'off.'[13] Below I explore these two different approaches to the city, with an eye to underscoring how the 'natural city' might be different from a world cities model and yet productively engage with many of the insights emerging from critical urban geography and its assessment of the global city.

The Global City as a Critical Concept

Few cities escaped the transformations that were stimulated by the economic restructuring crisis of the 1970s – a period when industrialization rapidly shifted to a more flexible, globalized system of production. By the 1980s, however, the contradictory effects of the new global economy were visible in many North American and European cities. In many cases, cities saw a deepening decline of their once industrialized cores, while a smaller number experienced new forms of urban dynamism around the concentration of financial and information/technology services. It was in this context that many urban scholars began to rethink the ways in which cities were viewed, particularly in terms of the nation-state as an organizing framework. As a result, cities began to be reconceived in terms of their relationship to the globalizing economy. Urbanists such as Saskia Sassen, David Harvey, and Manuel Castells developed an analysis in which cities were treated as entities embedded in an emerging global economy and as linked to new forms of capital accumulation. Urban centres, then, under global economic conditions, were deeply affected and shaped by these processes, and surfaced as important locations for global commodity chains and market networks.[14]

Some scholars, building on the theme of 'globalization,' began to develop a research agenda around what was named the 'global city,' and started to focus on cities that had become important nodes of capital management in expanding global economic networks. Cities such as London, Paris, Frankfurt, and Amsterdam in Western Europe; New York, Los Angeles, Chicago, and Toronto in North America; and Tokyo, Hong Kong, and Singapore in Asia became premier global cities, achieving the status of so-called command centres of capital and finance in the global economy. These 'newly industrialized districts of transnational management and control' – as Jennifer Robinson has called them – became (and remain) powerful players on the global stage, representing not only potent concentrations of wealth and financial influence, but also new models of the urban. The turn to the global city or the world city, then, set new precedents for understanding ourselves as an urbanizing society.

While some cities sought (and a few achieved) urban ascendancy on the global stage, other cities, such as Lagos, Nairobi, Mumbai, Lima, Rio de Janeiro, Jakarta, Cairo, and Manila, were also 'globalizing' and rapidly becoming centres of severe poverty and ecological degradation. In the 1990s, urban scholars noted that the rise of the global city was deeply connected to processes of uneven development and exclusion – both among cities and within city neighbourhoods. As Saskia Sassen argued, for example, the increasing geographical dispersal of production stimulated an equally intense centralization of financial command and control in certain cities. This had profound effects on both the spatialization of cities and the kinds of values that came to dominate forms of urban governance. In many cases, urban space underwent a form of restructuring in which transnational capital and finance clustered in dense corporate corridors, often stimulating speculative real estate booms and the gentrification of poor and working-class neighbourhoods. Residential displacement, through escalating real estate prices, thus became a signal feature of life in the global city as local housing markets catered to the tastes and pocketbooks of the upwardly mobile.[15]

Additionally, others documented transformations in what might be called the social fabric of cities, whereby intensifying forms of inequality and social segregation took root and transformed cities into not so much the 1960s 'doughnut' form of inner-city decay surrounded by suburban affluence, but rather a 'complex checkerboard of segregated and protected wealth in an urban soup of equally segregated impoverishment and decay.'[16] Saskia Sassen and John Friedmann[17] linked this pattern to a central effect of the globalizing economy, or what they termed the creation of a 'dualized urban labour market' in which a small segment of the population working in the prosperous financial and knowledge-based sectors earned high wages while a larger mass of workers remained employed in menial and low-paying jobs. The latter group lived in the less desirable parts of the city – both economically and environmentally.

Branding the City as 'Global'

While the critical approaches from urban geography tended to underscore the ways in which global cities were implicated in the structural processes that produced and intensified patterns of social inequality, more celebratory versions of the global city, as intimated earlier, took a very different direction. As globalization became a leading ideology about urbanization, it began to affect the ways in which many planners, politicians, and developers viewed, organized, and governed cities.

In positive versions of the global city, for example, urban space was seen principally as commercialized space. Certain understandings of the social were promoted, while others (such as the notion of a public or a commons) were devalued. 'World-class' thus became a symbol of global capitalism; it came to connote a place with an exciting, viable relation to the world economy. According to the more sanguine version of the global city, it became a place where successful, on-the-move people (who were themselves real players in the global economy) could live and enjoy the fruits of a consumer-oriented cosmopolitanism. It became a city where the 'successful' could expect to find the best art, the best cuisine, the best and the brightest universities (with cutting-edge research agendas that were competitive in the 'global knowledge industry'). Consequently, cities, especially those that aspired to join the ranks of the 'big four' global cities (London, New York, Paris, and Tokyo), came to image and represent themselves in terms of their relation to global markets and aspire to the standards of international prominence and importance.

Although definitions of global or world-class cities varied, in 1998 the Globalization and World Cities Study Group and Network (GaWC) produced an influential list of criteria and city rankings. Started in Loughborough University's Geography Department, United Kingdom, GaWC's early research suggested that a 'global city' designation meant that a city had to have international 'name recognition' (i.e., it had to be successfully 'branded') and possess the following features: (1) the presence of large financial institutions (such as corporate headquarters) as well as businesses that service them (e.g., legal and accounting firms); (2) an advanced communications infrastructure as well as several large and important media outlets; (3) a large metropolitan area typically consisting of several million inhabitants; (4) world-famous cultural institutions (especially art galleries and other collections); (5) a dynamic cosmopolitan cultural scene; (6) expansive shopping districts (as well as entertainment and restaurant complexes); (7) advanced transportation systems, including freeways and public transit; (8) a large international airport; (9) influence and participation in world events (e.g., through hosting forums or summits); and (10) the capacity to host large international sporting events (such as the Olympics).[18]

An important aspect, however, of the global or world-class city model has been the implementation of urban policies and practices that have, in many cases, intensified urban poverty. Thus, while the absence of ecological criteria in the foregoing list is striking, so too is any mention of poverty reduction measures. Urban governments seeking global status were encouraged to 'restructure' their economies in order to make them 'more competitive' in (and thus more attractive to) the global marketplace. Such an approach resulted in, for example, the downsizing of government infrastructure (often resulting in massive layoffs), the reducing or eliminating of government subsidies and services (particularly in the areas of health care and education), and the privatizing of state-owned aspects of the economy, to name a few.

It is perhaps not surprising, then, that in connection with efforts to become a world-class city, attitudes towards and interpretations of 'the poor' have been largely transformed, so that even in contemporary discussions, dominant discourses on poverty frequently portray the economically disadvantaged in terms of personal moralities.[19] Consequently, highly racialized and gendered debates (reminiscent of the nineteenth century) revolving around the 'deserving' and 'undeserving' poor have re-entered the mainstream and have profoundly shaped policies around the delivery of social services. As social theorist and critic Henry Giroux has observed, this behaviour has effected a 'murdering of the social,' in which communities are left with a set of policies aimed not at alleviating but *containing* the undesirable aspects of social life, including the poor. The prevalence of gated communities, especially but not exclusively in world-class cities, is a further aspect of this kind of urbanism and is indicative of the linkages being forged between containment and the criminalization of poverty.[20] The moralizing discourses of the deserving poor have thus underscored poverty as an individual problem to be solved by programs that are aimed at personal ethical transformation. While there may be many kinds of agencies involved in situations of poverty, it certainly seems unconscionable to suggest that people mired in deep poverty, suffering from chronically poor health, and experiencing the unavailability of a decent livelihood could change their impoverished circumstances if only they tried hard enough or if government-supported incentives were removed and replaced by market conditions. The world-class city, however, is unlikely to dwell upon such statements and seems ill equipped to address the environmental consequences of the globe's burgeoning urban inequalities.

But perhaps most relevant to the discussion here is a critique of the world city model as a nature-urban configuration – something that urban geographers in particular have begun to do in a variety of forums. While space constraints prevent a full discussion of the rich analytical insights that these scholars provide,[21] many of them point to the fact that although many so-called world/global cities are embracing 'ecology' as an urban problem, few do so in a way that adequately addresses urban poverty. As Gene Desfor and Roger Keil note in their discussion of environmental policies in Toronto and Los Angeles,[22] the model that has often come to dominate approaches to environmental issues among policy makers in these (and aspiring) global cities has been drawn from *ecological modernization*, with its emphasis on market-driven solutions, 'experts' who will act on behalf of 'everyone,' and a penchant for 'win-win' scenarios in which economic growth continues apace but within sustainable 'limits.' Like David Harvey, writing over 15 years earlier in *Nature Justice and the Geography of Difference*, Desfor and Keil's work points to the ways in which such approaches sideline issues of social inequality, since they do not engage in any sustained and serious way with the structural aspects of poverty, social marginalization, and the unjust distribution of environmental degradation.

Conclusion: Getting Poverty and Ecology 'on Track'

How is the natural city a different kind of space and place from the global city? Can it be built using the critical lens offered through the original work of urban geography on the global city and yet eschew the world-class city's indifference to the urban-ecology-poverty nexus?

Against the backdrop of global poverty and massive urbanization, the natural city, in attempting to address ecological despoliation through an urban lens, is challenged to become a more just 'social ecology' – one that takes poverty, social justice, and human sustainability as integral environmental concerns. The natural city can thus provide an antidote to the neo-liberal, neo-Darwinian 'world-class' aspiration of current world/global cities. Building on the insight that human settlements are not aberrations but 'natural' and 'natured' extensions of the human project, and that cities can be shaped into ecologically sanguine spaces, the natural city concept has the potential to offer us a welcome countervailing paradigm to the neo-liberal global city, which is mysteriously and allegedly shaped by the invisible (but heavy) hand of the marketplace and to which governmental, economic, and environmental stratagems must all pay homage and show obeisance. If natural cities are to become a dominant and fruitful way of thinking about urbanization, ultimately they cannot be discussed outside the salient political and economic trends structuring life in contemporary cities. Further, if we are going to talk about the natural city as an urban paradigm, then it appears that we will have to look critically at other dominant and hegemonic paradigms of 'the city,' especially those in which poverty and social inequality have suffered an 'unnatural' normalization.

As this brief overview suggests, the natural city cannot simply leap over social and economic questions to a sustainable urban space. Rather, it must trudge through the muddy ravines of poverty, social inequality, racism, and other forms of discrimination, along the way asking the question of how 'the social' is being articulated in the quest for a naturalized urban landscape. As the squatters in Lagos's occupied rail cars reveal, the natural city will remain a mirage rather than a reality as long as poverty alleviation and environmental protection run on different tracks.

NOTES

1 Mike Davis, 'Planet of Slums,' *New Left Review* 26 (March–April 2004): 5.
2 David Harvey, *Justice, Nature and the Geography of Difference* (**Malden, MA: Blackwell Publishers** 1996), 403.
3 The 2003 UN-Habitat publication *The Challenge of Slums: Global Report on Human Settlements* estimated that people who live in slums represented 78.2 per cent of the urban population of least developed countries.
4 Janice Perlman and Molly O'Meara Sheehan, 'Fighting Poverty and Environmental Justice in Cities,' in *World Watch Institute: State of The World 2007: Our Urban Future* (New York: W.W. Norton and Company, 2007), 172.
5 Jeremy Seabrook, *The No Nonsense Guide to World Poverty* (Oxford: Verso, 2003).
6 *UN World Resources Report*, 2005.
7 Global Urban Observatory, *Slums of the World: The Face of Urban Poverty in the New Millennium* (New York: United Nations Human Settlements Program, 2003), 10.
8 Jakarta, Dhaka, Karachi, Mumbai, Shanghai, Lagos.
9 Perlman and Sheehan, 'Fighting Poverty and Environmental Justice in Cities.'
10 See William Cronon, *Changes in the Land: Indians, Colonists and the Ecology of New England* (New York: Hill and Wang, 1983).
11 Nik Heynen, Marie Kaika, and Erik Swyngedouw, eds., *In the Nature of*

Cities: Urban Political Ecology and the Politics of Urban Metabolism (New York: Routledge, 2006).

12 See David Harvey, *Social Justice and the City* (London: Edward Arnold, 1973) and *Justice, Nature and the Geography of Difference*; Ira Katznelson, *Marxism and the City* (Oxford: Oxford University Press, 1993); Neil Smith, *The New Urban Frontier: Gentrification and the Revanchist City* (New York: Routledge, 1996).

13 Jennifer Robinson, 'Global and World Cities; A View from Off the Map,' *International Journal of Urban and Regional Research* 26, 3 (2002): 531–54.

14 See also M.P. Smith, *Transnational Urbanism: Locating Globalization* (Malden, MA: Blackwell Publishers, 2000).

15 Sharon Zukin, *Landscapes of Power: From Detroit to Disneyland* (Berkeley: University of California Press, 1991); Smith, *Transnational Urbanism*.

16 Harvey, *Justice, Nature and the Geography of Difference*, 405.

17 See John Friedmann, 'The World City Hypothesis,' *Development and Change* 17 (1986): 69–83 and Saskia Sassen, 'Locating Cities on Global Circuits,' *Environment and Urbanization* 14, 1 (2002): 13–30.

18 For a more updated profile of these features and the criteria for ranking, see Globalization and World Cities Research Network: http://www.lboro.ac.uk/gawc/ (accessed 20 January 2010).

19 See Michael B. Katz, *The Undeserving Poor: From the War on Poverty to the War on Welfare* (New York: Pantheon Books, 1989); and Judith Goode and Jeff Maskovsky, eds., *The New Poverty Studies: The Ethnography of Power, Politics and Impoverished People in the United States* (New York: New York University Press, 2001).

20 Setha M. Low and Denise Lawrence-Zúñiga, eds., *The Anthropology of Space and Place: Locating Culture* (Malden, MA: Blackwell, 2003). One result that we are perhaps experiencing in connection with this and in a post-9/11 context is the rise of what might be called security landscapes in which the gate, and not the public commons, articulates the primary sense of 'the social' in global cities.

21 See, in particular, Nik Heynen, James McCarthy, Scott Prudham, and Paul Robbins, eds., *Neoliberal Environments: False Promises and Unnatural Consequences* (New York: Routledge, 2007); and Heynen, Kaika, and Swyngedouw, eds., *In the Nature of Cities*.

22 Gene Desfor and Roger Keil, *Nature and the City: Making Environmental Policy in Toronto and Los Angeles* (Tucson: University of Arizona Press, 2004).

10 Other Voices: Acoustic Ecology and Urban Soundscapes

RICHARD ODDIE

Now I will do nothing but listen,
To accrue what I hear into this song, to let sounds contribute toward it.
I hear bravuras of birds, bustle of growing wheat, gossip of flames,
clack of sticks cooking my meals,
I hear the sound I love, the sound of the human voice,
I hear all sounds running together, combined, fused or following,
Sounds of the city and sounds out of the city, sounds of the day and night[1]
  – Walt Whitman, 'Song of Myself'

In an age characterized by its restless activity, relentless productivity, and unprecedented volume, it may seem quaint or idealistic to advocate a slower pace of life and the development of one's capacity to listen sensitively, rather than speak forcefully. Yet, this is perhaps the fundamental ethical message of environmentalism – to stop and listen to the world around us, and to respond to the imperative for change that can be heard beneath the surface noise of our present existence. Surely, in order to live a life that is socially and ecologically responsible, we must begin by learning to listen to the other voices that surround us. I am referring not to the familiar drone and chatter of our dominant speakers, with their loudspeakers, satellites, and sound bites, but to the voices of those others, human and non-human, who are marginalized, neglected, and poisoned by socially and ecologically harmful practices. Mindful listening, then, is not simply an aesthetic practice that brings us closer to our surroundings, but an ethical practice that allows the voice of the other to speak to us without interruption, to provoke a genuine response in us.

The aesthetic and ethical dimensions of listening are pervasive themes in acoustic ecology, a relatively obscure field of study initiated by the Canadian composer R. Murray Schafer in the early 1970s. Acoustic ecology explores the relationships between sound, environment, and society primarily from a phenomenological perspective, drawing our attention to the ways in which the acoustic environment or 'soundscape' shapes our experiences and understanding of the world. There are strong parallels between acoustic ecology and the field of environmental phenomenology that has been built upon the philosophical foundations laid by Martin Heidegger, among others. Both acoustic ecology and environmental phenomenology recognize a mutual interdependence between human experience and the surrounding environment, demonstrating how self and world interpenetrate one another. Both fields also provide a critique of modern society, undermining the dominant view of environment as material resource and commodity. Schafer shares Heidegger's concern about the radically individualistic and anthropocentric values of the modern world. His work can also be seen as an attempt to provoke a critical rethinking of the relationship between humanity and technology. In his essay 'Radical Radio,' Schafer describes his position in terms that clearly evoke the spirit of the Heideggerean critique: 'Let the phenomena of the world speak for themselves, in their own time, without the human always at the centre, twisting, exploiting and misusing the events of the world for private advantage.'[2]

Particularly in this critical mode, acoustic ecology and environmental phenomenology have both tended to emphasize the positive qualities of wilderness spaces and rural environments, while representing urban environments as manifestations of the negative qualities associated with industrialization, mechanization, and modernity. Schafer, for example, places particular emphasis on the ways in which urban environments encourage a loss of connection with the non-human world, silencing non-human voices beneath the din of modern technology. This anti-urban view can of course be found within much environmental thought and writing, but is increasingly being challenged by volumes such as this one that urge us to consider urbanization as the product of interdependent social and biophysical processes rather than as the antithesis of nature. In the pages that follow, I argue that acoustic ecology opens up new avenues for understanding the city as a socio-ecological hybrid, provided that we think beyond the divisions between culture and nature suggested by some of the more influential writings on this subject.

The Musicality of the World and the Noise of the City

During the late 1960s, concerned by what he perceived as a growing insensitivity to sound, accompanied by the proliferation of loud, obtrusive forms of technology, R. Murray Schafer began studying and writing about noise pollution within the broader context of the relationship between sound and society.[3] In the effort to promote greater public sensitivity to this issue, he proposed that we consider our acoustic environment or 'soundscape' as a musical composition to which we necessarily contribute and for which we must take responsibility. His writings on 'soundscape analysis' propose various methods for studying the perceptual and symbolic qualities of acoustic phenomena. This initial work led to the formation of the World Soundscape Project at Simon Fraser University, where Schafer was employed as a professor of communications studies. In collaboration with a group of his colleagues and students, Schafer began to conduct a detailed study of acoustic environments within the city of Vancouver, the results of which were documented with a booklet and two vinyl recordings in 1973.[4] This study, the first of its kind, has inspired numerous other soundscape projects over the last decades, ranging from strict documentation of a given environment to more artistic endeavours that use location recordings as inspiration and source material.

Based on this project, along with related sound studies in Canada and Europe, Schafer and company developed the notion of 'soundscape design,' calling upon 'scientists, social scientists and artists' to assist in the development of principles and techniques that could improve 'the social, psychological and aesthetic quality of the acoustic environment.'[5] Schafer championed this cause in his influential book *The Tuning of the World*, which explores the relationship between sound and society throughout history, focusing particularly upon the contrasting features of pre-industrial and post-industrial soundscapes.[6] His writing illuminates the link between the acoustic environment and personal and cultural identity, making use of numerous examples and anecdotes from the past and present. Within this text, Schafer also introduced a new terminology that had been developed during the World Soundscape Project, allowing one to more accurately distinguish and classify sounds on the basis of their prominence, frequency, and significance within a given soundscape. For example, 'soundmarks' refer to unique sounds that characterize a particular community, while 'keynotes' designate the dominant background sounds that often go unnoticed, such as the sounds of automobile traffic and computer systems within the modern city.

The Tuning of the World draws our attention to the dominance of the visual modality within modern culture, engaging in a critique of our fascination with speed, power, and the visually spectacular. Schafer describes 'visual culture' as a society obsessed by the desire to discover the unseen and expose the concealed, engaging in a relentless search for knowledge and control in the name of human progress. The fetishism of the visual and the gradual deterioration of our ability to listen to our surroundings are linked in his writing with urban environments, evoking a familiar critique of cities as places that encourage individuation and estrangement from the non-human world. Schafer suggests that the cluttered 'lo-fi' quality of the modern urban soundscape reflects and promotes insensitivity to one's surroundings and the natural rhythms of life. Whereas the 'hi-fi' soundscape of natural and rural areas is said to be characterized by its depth, clarity, and balance, allowing each sound to be heard distinctly, the urban soundscape is dominated by the monotonous, low-frequency sounds of modern technology, creating a 'sound wall' in which individual sounds are often distorted or obscured entirely. Schafer argues that this shrinkage of the individual's range of hearing and the blurring of distinct sounds into a narrow frequency range diminishes one's sensitivity to one's surrounding environment. In the 'hi-fi' soundscape, one's sense of place is shaped by aural information about the environment; this information can be heard over a great distance. However, in the city, the constant presence of excessively loud sounds diminishes our capacity to distinguish individual sounds and the meanings they convey. Indeed, the average sound level of urban environments reportedly doubled from 1982 to 2002.[7] On a busy street, the roar of traffic may be so loud that we cannot even hear our own footsteps, let alone the voices of others around us. Schafer contends that this diminished sonic awareness contributes to the isolation and self-absorption that he associates with urban life. In this environment, ambient sound easily becomes 'noise,' a meaningless irritant to be blocked out by earplugs or personal stereos.

Complementary to the ecologist's efforts to preserve and restore the biodiversity of ecosystems, the acoustic ecologist advocates the preservation and restoration of diverse and informative acoustic environments. Encouraging the development of greater sensitivity to the sounds around us, acoustic ecology aims to foster a deeper awareness of the social and psychological significance of sound. To this end,

Schafer and others have suggested various 'ear cleaning' techniques designed to develop one's listening skills.[8] The most simple of these is to take a walk with the mouth closed and the mind still, focusing exclusively upon the sounds that one hears. A notebook and tape recorder are often used to document the 'soundwalk,' so that one can later analyse the context and significance of the sounds. This can be a surprisingly revealing experience because, when one listens carefully and attentively, one begins to notice the presence and complexity of sounds that were previously taken for granted. This practice of 'deep listening'[9] provides the foundation for a number of contemporary artists who use sound recordings as raw material, creating audio compositions that explore the aesthetic and social significance of acoustic space.

Schafer notes that sound is increasingly used to consciously shape the atmosphere of private and public spaces in the city, from the living room to the waiting room. We are now able to amplify and broadcast subtle sounds across massive distances, and digital recording and production technology allows us to radically modify and recombine sounds with increasing sophistication. During the past century, the distinctions between music and environmental sound have blurred, leading to the discovery of the musicality of ambient sound, the recognition of music as an inherently spatial art form, and the conception of music-as-environment. Schafer argues that music now often serves as an acoustic backdrop for urban life, an ever-present accompaniment to our everyday routines, whereas, in the past, music was used to designate a break in that routine, such as a celebration or ceremony. While driving and working, we listen to music and news on the radio. While shopping, we are surrounded by the syrupy strains of Muzak. While relaxing, we immerse ourselves in the sounds of the dance club, the concert hall, the cinema, or the home theatre. Schafer claims that sound often functions as an 'audioanalgesic' in the modern city, preventing the relative stillness that is necessary for reflection.[10] In a world of constant activity and noise, silence is frequently associated with boredom and disconnection from life, while the dissociating effects of modern technology, exemplified by the virtual worlds of the television and the computer, are often overlooked or ignored. Schafer and others argue that the undynamic and excessive soundscape of urban life encourages a fear of silence – or, rather, a fear of the other voices, the buried dreams, desires, and concerns that may arise in moments of silence.

Soundscape studies demonstrate how the unique character or atmosphere of a place, be it a suburban home, a city street, or a rural marsh, is greatly determined by acoustic phenomena. Sound orients us in space, reflecting and revealing to us the physical and social features of the surrounding environment. We also know that sound is implicated in the basic functioning of the body, contributing to our sense of balance and constituting the perceptual 'ground' of conscious awareness. Indeed, the world disclosed to us through hearing is very different from that which is given to us by the eye. Visual awareness extends forward, in one direction, revealing a world of independent objects with clearly discernible boundaries, the majority of which are stable and persistent. Visual space is thus easily divided, measured, and represented. In contrast, aural awareness reveals a world of dynamic, transient, and indeterminate events that surround the listener, endlessly moving into and out of existence from a multitude of directions. The aural world is a world in flux – omnidirectional, unbounded, and difficult to divide, measure, or represent. Schafer contends,

> The territorial conquest of space by sound is the expression of visual rather than aural thinking. Sound is then used to demark property like a fence or wall … Not only does the notion of bounded shape give us our physical sciences (which are concerned with weights and measures), but it also contributes to the establishment of private property and by extension to the private diary and the private bank account. Once the bounding line becomes a strong perceptual distinction, the whole world begins to take on the appearance of a succession of spaces waiting to be filled with subjects or shattered by vectors.[11]

'Aural culture,' according to Schafer, is characterized by cooperation rather than competition, displaying a general lack of concern for the accumulation of personal wealth, and related notions of progress and development. Schafer suggests that genuine listening, particularly within a 'visual culture' such as ours, can foster a more receptive attitude to the world that is free of the desire to impose absolute boundaries, be they conceptual or physical, upon the phenomena of one's experience. For the acoustic ecologist, mindful listening can be an act of engagement with the world that temporarily suspends the boundaries between the self and the other, the perceiver and the perceived. Listening becomes a metaphor for thinking, representing a more inclusive and respectful awareness of the world. To listen attentively, one must be silent, stilling the voice and the chatter of the mind in order to allow other voices to speak.

These ideas have provided inspiration for many sound artists who have put them into practice by documenting various acoustic environments and/or using location recordings to create sound compositions that aim to convey a sense of place or raise questions about the relationship between place, identity, and environment. Sound artist Hildegaard Westerkamp, another prominent participant in the World Soundscape Project, regards this process of listening, recording, and composing with environmental sound as a means of exploring, articulating, and celebrating the unique characteristics of a place. She maintains that the responsible sound artist is one who is mindful of the original context of her recordings, preserving this context in an exploration of the sounds and their personal, social, and/or environmental significance. The creation of soundscape compositions, based upon the phenomenological study of a particular locality, is understood as an artistic practice that can deepen our understanding and appreciation of our surroundings. For Westerkamp, this is a way of resisting the cultural homogenization brought about by economic globalization, which threatens to efface our 'sense of place' – our sense of belonging to a place that is grounded in the unique features and relationships within our environment.[12] Like poetry, this approach to sound art aims to provoke the development of greater sensitivity to one's surroundings, uncovering the beauty and complexity of the familiar. Listening and composing with sound can become a form of poetic expression that draws us nearer, in the sense of concerned and meaningful involvement, to the local environment.

Acoustic Ecology and Urban Environments

Barry Truax, one of the original members of the World Soundscape Project, describes the mediating role that sound plays between the individual and the environment as a process of 'acoustic communication' – an 'information exchange' in which our awareness of and orientation to our surroundings are shaped by the soundscape, just as we in turn shape that acoustic environment through our daily activities.[13] By exploring the unique manner in which sound contributes to our personal and cultural sense of identity, we can provide a more comprehensive account of the reciprocity between human existence and environment. This recognition of the significance of sound, and the complexity of contextual meaning that it conveys, draws our attention to the visual bias of environmental studies, encouraging geographers, urban planners, and ecologists alike to consider sound as an integral component of both natural and built environments.

Beyond this descriptive moment, acoustic ecology also advocates the preservation and improvement of soundscapes. Unique acoustic phenomena that contribute to the particular character of a place must be preserved if its inhabitants wish to preserve that character. This preservation requires that much more thought be given to dramatic changes in the acoustic environment, and encourages including the public in the making of such decisions. Similarly, acoustic ecology promotes the improvement of the local soundscape, asking us to look beyond the question of mere noise abatement when considering the acoustic qualities of the built environment. Rather than simply attempting to block out the unwanted 'noise' of the urban environment, we should consider ways in which to enhance our acoustic spaces, actively working towards the creation of more diverse, informative, and harmonious soundscapes. Again, such considerations must be based upon the knowledge of how members of the local community perceive their acoustic environments, determining which sounds they find pleasing or otherwise significant.

Within the realm of urban environmental planning and policy, the impact of the ideas introduced by acoustic ecology has largely been confined to noise abatement measures. Indeed, noise-level standards have been set in many cities, and noise abatement has become an essential part of large-scale infrastructure and development project planning, particularly for roadways and airports. These efforts are supported and encouraged by citizen organizations that are dedicated to limiting or eliminating the excessive 'noise pollution' generated by vehicles, outdoor appliances, and stereos.

Another major focus in acoustic ecology has been the recording and preservation of endangered sounds, including the sounds of threatened animal species, ecosystems, human settlements, and cultures. More recently, there has been a flourishing of new publications and events exploring the relationship between sound, space, and human behaviour.[14] However, the writings of Schafer and other advocates of acoustic ecology suggest a humanistic framework for urban design that goes further, foregrounding the need for public participation and cultural sensitivity in the *collective* recomposition of urban soundscapes. For acoustic ecology, what is at stake in the deterioration of the modern urban soundscape is nothing less than our very humanity. Schafer writes,

When, as today, environmental sound reaches such proportions that human vocal sounds are masked or overwhelmed, we have produced an inhuman environment. When sounds are forced on the ear which may endanger it physically or debilitate it psychologically, we have produced an inhuman environment.[15]

How, then, might acoustic ecology contribute to the creation of more humane urban environments? I identify four avenues for inquiry and action here. First, acoustic ecology has much to contribute to the study of urban environments within more established disciplines, including urban geography, sociology, political science, and environmental studies. By encouraging consideration of the vital role that sound plays in shaping our understanding and use of urban environments, acoustic ecology can open up new lines of research in these fields and contribute to a more comprehensive understanding of urban space.

Recent work in urban political ecology seems particularly amenable to such considerations as it encourages us to view the city as a complex hybrid of interwoven social and biophysical relationships, produced through flows of matter, energy, ideas, money, and symbols.[16] This approach to urban research reveals the city as the product of interconnected networks or 'city-nature formations'[17] that extend beyond the familiar conceptual and physical boundaries of the urban. Thinking outside the limits of rigid categorical distinctions between society and nature, urban and rural, and global and local, cities appear as significant nodal points or concentrations in these networks rather than as distinct and discrete entities. Recent work in this field has explored the role that discursive and visual representations of urban nature play within conflicts over the course of urban development.[18] This approach could fruitfully be expanded to consider how contested processes of urbanization are influenced by the amplification or silencing of different voices: human and non-human.

Reciprocally, acoustic ecology would greatly benefit from a stronger engagement with social scientific research. As Henrik Karlsson has noted, this field has 'been dominated by aesthetic-artistic rather than social-scientific attitudes and this has impeded a development of theory and methodology.'[19] I believe that it is this focus on aesthetics, art, and ethics that makes acoustic ecology so compelling as a tool for exploring the relationship between place and identity, but agree with Karlsson that closer engagement with social science research on sound, space, and environment would greatly expand the horizons of acoustic ecology by encouraging dialogue and debate over goals and methodologies. This would also open up some of the basic principles of the field, rooted in the writings of Schafer, to more critical scrutiny. How tenable, for example, is Schafer's distinction between hi-fi 'natural' soundscapes and the degraded lo-fi soundscapes of the city? Are these generalizations useful and can they be sustained in the light of analysis of the varying qualities of urban soundscapes, or more detailed analysis of the actual sound preferences of urban dwellers?

This brings me to a third avenue for acoustic ecology research and action – further inquiry into the sound environments that citizens value, why they value them, and how they are connected to particular place-based identities. From the early work of the World Soundscape Project, this has been a strong emphasis in acoustic ecology, but Schafer's categorical distinctions between hi-fi and lo-fi soundscapes have been unhelpful for interpreting the results of such studies, insofar as they presume that urban acoustic environments are inherently offensive and oppressive. Furthermore, there has been a tendency to focus on the elimination of unwanted noise within urban environments, rather than to identify and enhance valued sounds and acoustic qualities.

Finally, little attention has yet been paid to creating effective mechanisms for integrating public valuations of urban soundscapes into planning processes.[20] As Ursula Franklin has noted, we continue to witness the 'privatization of the soundscape' as the acoustic environments of public spaces remain outside the realm of democratic control. In Franklin's words,

> ... the soundscape has become increasingly polluted by the private use of sound in the manipulative dimension of setting and programming moods and conditions. There is a desperate need to be aware of this, and to be aware of it in terms of the collectivity rather than only in terms of individual needs ... Just as we feel we have the right to walk down the street without being physically assaulted by people, preferably without being visually assaulted by ugly outdoor advertising, we also have the right not to be assaulted by sound, and in particular, not to be assaulted by sound that is there solely for the purpose of profit.[21]

Franklin encourages us to recognize the urban soundscape as a crucial part of our environment, vital to the health and well-being of living things, and, as such, as something over which the public should have control. What is needed, then, is not only enhanced sensitivity to the

acoustic dimensions of urban life, but also effective means of collectively creating the kind of urban environments we desire and deserve. This
is, of course, by no means a simple task, and forces acoustic ecology
to engage more directly with timely debates over the theory and practice of democratic governance and environmental citizenship. Furthermore, as both Ursula Franklin and Henrik Karlsson suggest, it requires
more serious consideration of the political and economic impediments
to advancing democratic control over the urban soundscape and urban
environments more broadly.

This brings us back to one of the most compelling aspects of acoustic
ecology: its emphasis on listening to other voices. This ethics of listening is vital to the struggle to create more ecologically harmonious and
socially just cities. Acoustic ecology has long advocated the need for
urban life to open itself up to the non-human voices that are silenced
or obscured by the solipsistic din of modern technologies. Numerous
sound installations and recordings have pursued this theme, ranging
from profound works that challenge our understanding of the boundaries between humanity and nature to the now ubiquitous cliché of ambient 'relaxation' soundtracks featuring the sounds of whales, birdsong,
or babbling streams. More recently, sound artists have been exploring
the interaction of human and non-human life within the city, and the
blurring of boundaries between nature and culture, through sound. For
example, *Buildings (New York)*, a recent work by the renowned sound
artist Francisco Lopez, uses location recordings from the infrastructural
networks of the city to create a sound world of seemingly organic origins, drawing attention to the biophysical processes that sustain the
city while challenging conceptual divisions between nature and the
urban, and between organic and synthetic. The Los Angeles–based
artist collective Ultra-Red focuses attention on marginalized human
voices, using location recordings from a wide variety of urban spaces,
ranging from office buildings to sweatshops to large public protests,
to explore themes of resistance to poverty, cultural and socio-economic exclusion, environmental injustice, and other forms of oppression
within the contemporary city. Another example is provided by Darren
Copeland's *Toronto Sound Mosaic*, which combines archival research,
location recordings, and interviews with local citizens to create a socio-
ecological history of the city in sound.

These kinds of projects point us towards an urban acoustic ecology
that moves beyond the familiar and misguided division between natural perfection and urban degradation to consider the urban soundscape

as a space of potential for creating more equitable and sustainable cities. Combined with, but not subsumed by, a stronger engagement with relevant research in other fields of urban and environmental research, and a stronger commitment to the creation of positive urban soundscapes through community organizing and democratic participation, acoustic ecology has much to contribute as a tool for better understanding urbanization as a product of interconnected social and biophysical processes and as a means of raising public awareness and engaging citizens in reflection and action.

NOTES

1 R. Murray Schafer uses a modified version of this quote to introduce his most famous book, *The Tuning of the World* (New York: Alfred A. Knopf, 1977). I use it here to introduce an effort to reconsider and expand his approach to urban soundscapes.

2 R. Murray Schafer, 'Radical Radio,' in *Sound by Artists*, ed. Dan Lander and Micah Lexier (Toronto: Art Metropole, 1990), 214.

3 Schafer's early writings include *Ear Cleaning* (Toronto: Berandol Music, 1967), *The New Soundscape* (Vienna: Universal Editions, 1969), and *The Book of Noise* (Wellington, New Zealand: Price Milburn, 1970).

4 R. Murray Schafer, ed., *The Vancouver Soundscape* (Vancouver: ARC Publications, 1978).

5 Barry Truax, ed., *Handbook for Acoustic Ecology* (Vancouver: ARC Publications, 1978), 5.

6 Schafer, *The Tuning of the World*. This text was republished as *The Soundscape* (Rochester, NY: Destiny Books, 1994).

7 Detlev Ispen, 'The Urban Nightingale or Some Theoretical Considerations about Sound and Noise,' in *Soundscape Studies and Methods* (Helsinki: Finnish Society for Ethnomusicology, 2002).

8 In addition to *The Tuning of the World* and *Ear Cleaning*, see *A Sound Education: 100 Exercises in Listening and Sound* (Indian River, ON: Arcana Editions, 1992).

9 'Deep listening' is a phrase coined by composer Pauline Oliveros, whose theories of sound and 'sonic awareness' have much in common with acoustic ecology, albeit with a more explicit focus on ethics and spirituality.

10 Schafer, *The Tuning of the World*, 96.

11 R. Murray Schafer, 'Acoustic Space,' in *Dwelling, Place and Environment: Towards a Phenomenology of Person and World*, ed. David Seamon and Robert Mugerauer (Dordrecht, Netherlands: Martinus Nijhoff, 1985), 92.

12 Hildegard Westerkamp, 'The Local and Global Language of Environmental Sound,' paper presented at the 'Sound Escape' conference on acoustic ecology at Trent University, Peterborough, Ontario, Canada, 28 June–2 July 2000. This essay can be accessed from the website of the World Forum for Acoustic Ecology: http://interact.uoregon.edu/MediaLit/wfae/home/ (accessed 18 October 2008).

13 Barry Truax, *Acoustic Communication* (Norwood, NJ: Ablex Publishing. 1984).

14 See, for example, Steve Roden and Brandon LaBelle, *Site of Sound: Of Architecture and the Ear* (Santa Monica, CA: Smart Art Press, 1999); Peter Grueneisen, *Soundspace: Architecture for Sound and Vision* (Basel: Birkhauser, 2003); *In the Place of Sound: Architecture, Music, Acoustics*, ed. Colin Ripley, Marco Polo, and Arthur Wrigglesworth (Newcastle: Cambridge Scholars Publishing, 2007).

15 Schafer, *The Tuning of the World*, 207.

16 See, for example, Erik Swyngedouw, *Social Power and the Urbanization of Water: Flows of Power* (Oxford: Oxford University Press, 2004); Maria Kaika, *City of Flows: Nature, Modernity and the City* (New York: Routledge, 2005); and *In the Nature of Cities: Urban Political Ecology and the Politics of Urban Metabolism*, ed. Nik Heynen, Maria Kaika, and Erik Swyngedouw (London: Routledge, 2006).

17 Steve Hinchliffe, 'Cities and Natures: Intimate Strangers,' in *Unsettling Cities: Movement / Settlement*, ed. John Allen, Doreen Massey, and Don Pryke (London: Routledge/Open University, 1999).

18 See, for example, Matthew Gandy, *Concrete and Clay: Reworking Nature in New York* (Cambridge, MA: MIT Press, 2002); Gene Desfor and Roger Keil, *Nature and the City: Making Environmental Policy in Toronto and Los Angeles* (Tucson: University of Arizona Press, 2004); and Kaika, *City of Flows*.

19 Henrik Karlsson, 'The Acoustic Environment as a Public Domain,' *Soundscape: The Journal of Acoustic Ecology* 1, 2 (Winter 2000): 10–13.

20 A recent notable exception is the Positive Soundscapes project, which has brought together researchers from a number of disciplines and universities in the United Kingdom 'to acknowledge the relevance of positive soundscapes, to move away from a focus on negative noise, and to identify a means whereby the concept of positive soundscapes can effectively be incorporated into planning.' For more information, visit http://www.positivesoundscapes.org/ (accessed 18 October 2008).

21 Ursula Franklin, 'Silence and the Notion of the Commons,' *Soundscape: The Journal of Acoustic Ecology* 1, 2 (Winter 2000): 14–17.

11 Ecofeminist 'Cityzenry'

TRISH GLAZEBROOK

The United Nations Population Division predicted that 2007 would be the first year in which more people lived in cities than in the country. Cities occupy just 2 per cent of the Earth's land surface, but consume 75 per cent of resources used each year. London, for example, requires an area 125 times its size to supply the resources it uses. Cities also generate clouds of greenhouse gases, billions of tons of solid waste, and significant volumes of toxic effluents.[1] Functional eco-management of the planet thus requires more than wilderness preservation. Greening the contemporary city is necessary if the human presence on the planet is to be sustainable. This chapter argues from an ecofeminist perspective that sustainable city dwelling, if achievable at all, is most promising through ecological literacy and participatory policy.

The approach is ecofeminist in several ways. First, it connects specific environmental theories with a feminist theoretical framework. For example, it combines both the widespread environmentalist belief that non-human entities warrant moral consideration and the deep ecologist's refusal to reduce nature to its instrumental value with a feminist ethics of care. Moreover, the analysis accepts the relational autonomist argument from feminist bioethics that human identity and experience are determined more by relationships than by atomistic individualism, but extends this thesis beyond relations between people to relations with cohabitant species and the city itself. Relational autonomists further recognize that oppressive or restrictive situations always also provide the conditions for autonomy that make resistance possible, so they undermine privileging of perspective, or at least demand its justification. This chapter argues similarly that since people are always already acting in ways that determine their experience of city dwelling, they

can consciously and purposefully resist the degradation of urban living conditions, and that it is in their best interests to do so in ways that
do not privilege humans over others who share the city-space. Second,
then, the approach is ecofeminist because it denies anthropocentrist
assumptions of human superiority and authority over nature. Third,
the analysis rejects other forms of authority by arguing anarchistically
that functional eco-city dwelling begins with the everyday experience
of embodied living, consistent with feminist philosophies of embodiment in contrast to the traditional philosophical preference for abstract
and universal truths. The city dweller is not a passive occupier of city-
space so much as an active participant in and contributor to a city's
ecosystem, for which people can take responsibility in their roles as
inhabitants, corporate actors, or policy makers. Finally, social ecologists
and environmental justice theorists have documented well the fact that
environmental problems are deeply entangled with social issues. This
chapter is grounded in the ecofeminist belief that human justice issues
and ecological challenges cannot be resolved independently. Democratic, co-operative approaches to problem-solving, achieved through
ecological literacy and education of and by city dwellers, promote
autonomy so that cityzens themselves can enact a functional ecological
footprint while improving their quality of life.

The terms 'cityzen' and 'cityzenry' are used to distinguish city dwelling from membership in the nation-state. The paradigmatic state citizen is the wage earner who makes the state possible through revenue
contribution in the form of taxes. Cityzens are also economic units,
and cityzenry is embedded in state citizenry. Concerning resource consumption, for example, the state may build the dam, but the city often
manages delivery of and revenue collection for the electricity the dam
provides. Power can also be managed by private corporations, but the
for-profit structure of corporate culture can compromise principles of
distributive justice and other goals, such as sustainability. In 1998 and
1999, for example, the dangers of a deregulated power industry became
clear in California: power shortages that forced prices to skyrocket,
with disproportionately severe consequences for the already disadvantaged, were a direct consequence of market manipulation.[2] To live in
a city is to be embedded in an infrastructure that has various levels of
organization, both corporate and governmental. In a world economy
dominated by multi- and transnational corporations, membership in
the nation-state has less impact on the lived experience of cityzens than
does their participation in capitalist economies of production and con-

sumption. This may be less true in nation-states such as Canada and northern European countries that have socialized medicine and strong social welfare programs, but it remains the case that the city dweller's experiential context is determined in large part by institutions other than the state.

Thus cities are embedded in the nation-state, but cityzenry is distinct from citizenry. In particular, participation in the state lends itself to construal in terms of public/private dualism. Feminists have shown that this distinction is inadequate for understanding lived experience, particularly in the case of women, whose consignment to the private realm has obscured analysis of their labour and political function. Cities are especially challenging to the public/private distinction. They provide the immediate living space of the quotidian for a large part of a country's population, and are a context in which public participation and private decision making are inseparably linked. Despite political gains such as the right to vote, persistent widespread gender inequities even in developed nations maintain women's status as second-class citizens, while also perpetuating their role and function as the actors who reproduce the daily living conditions of human experience. That is to say, female cityzens make daily decisions about things such as resource consumption that have substantial environmental impact, yet they remain marginalized as citizens – their relational autonomy as cityzens cannot be adequately conceived in terms of their citizenship. Furthermore, the citizen is an abstract entity in ways that the cityzen is not. For the cityzen, the character of embodied living is determined directly by the conditions of city dwelling: it is the city that first and foremost constitutes the space of lived experience. Given that ecologically functional human living depends in large part on making cities sustainable, the distinction between citizenry and cityzenry is particularly significant for environmental issues.

Cities are varied spaces, both urban and suburban. Environmental challenges that can face inner-city dwellers (e.g., congestion, concentrations of pollutants, and aging, heavily used infrastructure) are significantly different from those that face suburban dwellers (e.g., sprawl, privately owned green-space management, and waste-facility siting). Factors such as class and income level, consumption patterns and habits (e.g., big-box park versus pedestrian shopping), and access to recreational spaces can also vary dramatically between inner-city and suburban dwellers. Suburban cityzens often, albeit diurnally, share inner-city spaces, while inner-cityzens may not have the need or resources to access the suburbs regularly. Freedom to escape the congestion, pollution, and degraded living conditions that can characterize urban centres is a class privilege that constructs poor consumption patterns, while disadvantaged, inner-city inhabitants face the different challenge of finding economically viable sustainable options in their daily living patterns. Where inner-city neighbourhoods have been 'yuppified' or cleaned up so they are desirable places to live, the least privileged are usually obliged to move elsewhere in response to rising rents. Thus a central difficulty for ecologically sound city dwelling is equitable management of environmental issues with respect to such diversely constituted cityzenry.

A consensus is emerging among planners and policy makers that the two main principles for greening cities are increasing recycling and reducing car use. London, for example, uses annually 1 billion tons of clean water, 2.4 million tons of food, 2.2 million tons of paper, 40 million tons of oxygen, 20 million tons of fuel, 360,000 tons of glass, 2.1 million tons of plastics, 1.2 million tons of lumber, 2 million tons of cement, and 36 million tons of bricks, blocks, sand, and tarmac, but recycles only 18 per cent of its waste.[3] It produces 60 million tons of carbon dioxide, 400,000 tons of sulphur dioxide, 280,000 tons of nitrogen oxides, 4 million tons of household waste, 11.4 million tons of industrial and demolition waste, and 7.5 million tons of wet sewage sludge annually.[4] Recycling can cut consumption and manage waste production, while reducing car use will decrease both resource consumption and the production of greenhouse gases and other pollutants. But how are these principles to be enacted when transportation issues, for example, affect particular segments of city populations differently? If higher-density urban housing arrangements might address the transportation issue in part, they also lead to the heat island effect, and conflict with people's conceptions of pleasant living, which entails access to more natural green spaces. What is called for is a new vision of citizenry, in which ecologically literate cityzens themselves contribute to planning processes and support implementation.

Towards that vision, the strategy of this chapter is first to break down the idea that nature and civilization are oppositional categories, and, second, to provide evidence that cities are ecosystems shared by many species, with attention to both the risks and the benefits of eco-city dwelling for cohabitant species. Finally, praxical and policy approaches are examined for better eco-city dwelling: that is, ecocityzenry that is healthier and more conducive to human, non-human, and environmental well-being. The conclusion drawn is that functional eco-city life requires collaborative participation between policy makers and ecologically literate human cityzens who are guided and motivated by an ethic of care towards themselves, human and non-human others, and the ecosystems that are their home. This conclusion is both anarchistic and policy oriented, but is shown nonetheless to be surprisingly internally consistent.

Nature versus Civilization

The idea that 'nature' and 'civilization' are oppositional terms remains pervasive. Cities are human constructs that interrupt, intervene in, and appropriate natural processes for the benefit of their human inhabitants. They open spaces for human beings to set the terms and conditions of their lifeworld. The weather, for example, is of little concern to the cityzen: patterns of mobility and the daily reproduction of the material conditions of living are rarely affected, even in severe climates. Distribution systems allow cityzens to ignore the seasonality of produce. Grasses and trees are cultivated in landscape design; homeowners might even decide to preserve an undeveloped part of their yard to take advantage of the ornamental value of wildness. Nature is thus pushed back and restrained, and reintroduced in controlled and chosen ways. The city experience includes, for its privileged members, taking a recreational break on weekends, or other such designated holiday (i.e., non–wage exchanged) time, by 'getting back to nature' in a park or wilderness preserve.

This conception of the city has a long history and impressive pedigree. In part, it is a hangover from nineteenth-century Romanticism, in which nature and civilization figure as irreducible categories incapable of even dialectical resolution. Several even older intellectual strands interweave in its support. First, the city entails an ideology of technology that goes back as far as Aristotle: artifacts are definitively distinct from natural entities, and production entails the appropriation of material from the natural order. As a result, nature is reduced to its instrumental value and subject to human ends. This Aristotelian anthropocentrism was exacerbated by subsequent Judeo-Christian belief in which the human being is fundamentally distinct from and privileged over the natural order. The rise of modern science from out of this ideological context further entrenched attitudes in which nature appears as nothing more than material standing by for appropriation to human ends. Francis Bacon promised precisely that science can master nature to improve the human condition. Newton's ontology, in which nature is reduced to bodies in motion subject to forces, displaced any natural teleology that might interfere with the human project of appropriating nature to human ends. Thus compounded, layers of anthropocentrism and materialism together promote the idea that cities are human constructions in which nature is held at bay. Much contemporary environmental philosophy, particularly wilderness ethics, likewise calls for a return to nature, and thereby reinvests strongly in the distinction between nature and human projects of dwelling.

Yet the anthropocentrist and materialist foundations of the distinction between nature and civilization readily crumble, even under superficial scrutiny. Humans are animals, and embodiment entails natural processes. At a recent conference, a speaker who urged the audience to 'get back to nature' was quickly challenged: when had he left? He had been seen eating breakfast. People continue to perform such bodily routines as eating and sleeping, and still get sick, despite technological intervention. HIV/AIDS and the H5N1 virus (avian flu) are evidence both that the human being remains squarely in the natural order, and that nature itself consists not in inert material, but in constantly evolving processes and life forms. Even the Aristotelian legacy is a misinterpretation, or at least a short-sighted appropriation. Aristotle himself notes that 'owing to the fact of [an artifact's] being composed of earth or stone or some mixture of substances, it incidentally has within itself the principles of change which inhere primarily in these materials.'[5] That is to say, production does not free an artifact from natural processes. Aristotle cites Antiphon:

> If a man buried a bedstead and the sap in it took force and threw out a shoot, it would be a tree and not a bedstead that came up, since the artificial arrangement of the material by the craftsman is merely an incident that has occurred to it, whereas its essential and natural quality is to be found in that which persists continuously throughout such experiences.[6]

Nature is not raw matter, but self-directed process, and technological appropriation does not remove material from the natural order. Even if the source-entity is killed, the material is still subject to rot and decay. Thus technology is at best a borrowing, albeit often murderous, and human projects remain entangled within natural processes. The relation between technology and nature is analogous to the eggbeater move in water polo: the swimmer moves the legs quickly and strongly in opposite and overlapping circles that raise the torso above the water. The swimmer does not leave the water; on the contrary, the water supports the swimmer and makes the move possible. Likewise, production is a temporary interruption of natural process. Nature makes production possible, but is not left behind when technology takes over. Rather, all human constructs sink back into the home they have never left. Technology is as deeply embedded in natural process as Ozymandias in Shelley's sonnet.

There is, then, a significant difference between technology and nature. As Aristotle understood it, nature grows itself, while artifacts require human production. But the relation is one of embeddedness rather than separation or opposition. Cities are built environments, but they are environments nonetheless.

Cities as Shared Ecosystems

Giving up a conceptual separation of civilization from nature promotes new possibilities for urban dwelling. Recognition that cities are ecosystems can lead to constructive assessment of eco-city life that grounds sustainable urban planning. The Baltimore Ecosystem Study is a groundbreaking program that conceives of the city in just this way.[7] It is an interdisciplinary project of biological, physical, and social scientists in large part motivated by the fact that, despite the plethora of research available on natural ecosystems, very little data has been collected concerning urban ecosystems. As is typical of cities, Baltimore has a varying population with changing densities, and abandoned land at its centre coupled with suburban sprawl. The study uses watershed function as a basis for understanding the reciprocal interactions of the social, biophysical, and built environments. Its focal questions address the flow of energy and matter through the system, the effect of spatial structures and socio-economic factors on ecosystem function, and the ways in which residents can use understanding the city as an ecological system to improve their lives and the quality of their environment. Specific research includes ecological experiments testing the role of exotic species and the effect of neighbourhood revitalization on ecosystem processes. The study functions as a long-term test of whether ecological literacy among citizens can promote ecologically sound practices.

Certainly, ecological literacy can overcome some of the prejudices that city dwellers have about the species with which they share the city.

In Austin, Texas, for example, reconstruction of the downtown Congress Avenue bridge in 1980 unexpectedly made it a perfect roost for the 1.5 million Mexican free-tailed bats that migrate each year to roosting sites in the southwest United States. At first, locals were horrified, and petitioned to have the bats eradicated. In response, Bat Conservation International pointed out that the bats consume up to 15 tons of insects each night. Once they became aware of the bats' function in their urban ecosystem, locals quickly became friendlier towards the bats. Now more than 100,000 people visit the site each year to watch the bats emerge at dusk, generating tourism revenue of about $10 million U.S. annually.[8]

On the other side of the globe, bats took up residence in the Royal Melbourne Botanic Gardens (RMBG). Some 30,000 grey-headed flying foxes fly up to 60 kilometres from the city each night to feed. Bat guano is a concern in a botanical garden that contains rare species of plants, so in April 2001, the RMBG began shooting the bats. In an attempt to forestall public reaction, its director, Dr Phillip Moors, refused to release details of how the operation would proceed or how many bats would be culled.[9] On 15 June, an agreement was reached between the RMBG, the Humane Society for Animal Welfare (HSAW), and other environmental groups. Lawrence Pope, president of the HSAW, noted a hope that 'understanding and education rather than killing and vilification will now occupy the minds of the MBG management.'[10] In the case of Austin, environmental groups were able to raise ecological literacy of locals, but the RMBG case shows that citizen education of policy makers can also be called for. Moreover, policy makers can learn that locals are stakeholders who deserve a voice in policy. Both examples show, however, that the best educators are in fact eco-cityzens, whether their role is simply local inhabitant or policy maker. That is to say, cityzens who take responsibility for urban ecology can educate each other about technical, scientific aspects of ecological management, and also move both public and policy perception away from 'pest' to 'functional member of the local ecosystem.' Eco-educated cityzens teach policy makers, who can promote education of more cityzens in a positive dialectic. Both citizens and policy makers who support dialogue make constructive resolution of eco-challenges possible.

It is not always the case, however, that tolerance is the outcome of education. Some non-human city dwellers are simply not good to have around. Education allows for intelligent discrimination between non-human city dwellers with whom to share the urban space, and leads to humane and effective planning for dealing with species that will never be welcomed. Rats, for example, are uninvited citizens that pose a public health concern as well as having a negative economic and aesthetic impact. Their presence is, however, an indication of poor human practices, especially concerning food and food waste, that promote their thriving. Rats are highly adaptable, and their mobility through a variety of media, ability to access food, and reproductive success make them hard to control. Cities are congested, and the number of restaurants and snack bars collected in close proximity causes a proliferation of refuse, often kept in plastic bags overnight on the street while awaiting pickup. Bruce Colvin, a global rat specialist, notes that urban environments are so well suited for rats that it seems 'we're inadvertently doing wildlife management for the rats as if they were an endangered species.'[11] Cars are cozy places to sleep, and aging sewer systems provide loose bricks in which rats love to make their home while living off the sewage. In advising the city of Boston during construction of the Central Artery Tunnel Project, Colvin argued that poisoning efforts are wasted unless enough is known about the rats' habits and preferences to make targeting effective. Uninformed, widespread poisoning is akin to farming insofar as the farmer establishes optimal growing conditions each year by privileging the crop over other plants. Harvesting also contributes to this process by preventing overgrowth of the crop that would compromise its health. Likewise, wiping out a large part of the rat population through poisoning simply improves conditions for the subsequent population by making for less competition over food and living space. It turned out that rats prefer older, brick sewers less than 60 centimetres in diameter. Mapping their movement through the system made poisoning strategies more effective. Placing poisoned bait in reservoirs just prior to seasonal breeding nipped the problem in the bud. Also, rats like to inhabit areas with thick shrubs, low-hanging trees, and needle evergreens. An effective control strategy was to ask people to trim their shrubbery. Furthermore, co-ordination of city departments managing garbage collection, sanitation, sewers, and urban planning was necessary, but municipal efforts succeeded only with the participatory co-operation of local businesses and neighbourhood organizations. Rather than simply chasing rats and trying to kill them, participatory urban management was the key to rodent control in Boston. And it is more humane. Rats are unwanted cohabitants, but eco-cityzens can take responsibility for behaviours that promote rodent thriving instead of reproducing inhumane and ineffective practices. Participatory management of the rat problem in Boston demonstrates that policy and its implementation are more successful when cityzens are informed and actively involved.

Other species are increasingly drawn to urban contexts. In British cities, foxes are now common, and in southern California, bighorn sheep leave the mountains to feed on suburban lawns. Raccoons are common in 49 U.S. states. They like to live in attics and under mobile homes and decks, where they have easy access to garbage, bird feeders, and pet food bowls. Some species of birds do well in cities around the globe, again because people provide easily accessed food sources and comfortable living spaces. Gulls and pigeons have never been averse to urban dwelling, but there is also a variety of newcomers. Canada geese nest on roofs and balconies in Vancouver. Rainbow lorikeets that disappeared from Melbourne in the 1920s have recently returned. Sixteen pairs of peregrine falcons, which traditionally prefer lonely sea cliffs and open country, are now raising their young in the heart of Manhattan. Monk parakeets, the most abundant naturalized parakeet in the United States, build their nests on utility poles and in trees. Ring-necked parakeets, first spotted in Kent in 1969, have moved into London, where, according to the latest count, 10,000 of these birds now live.[12]

Not all the news is good, however. Conflicts between cohabitants arise. Angry great-tailed grackles that built nests in magnolia trees outside the county hall in Houston, Texas, respond to perceived threats to their young by dive-bombing pedestrians.[13] Conservationists in London are concerned that indigenous woodpeckers and other hole-nesting birds may not be able to compete with the ring-necked parakeets.[14] Furthermore, cities can function as ecological traps. Lawn-chewing bighorn sheep near Palm Springs, California, are exposed to trichostrongyle, a parasitic nematode that makes them vulnerable to pathogens and reduces their likelihood of raising healthy young. Cooper's hawks nest earlier and lay more eggs in Tucson, Arizona, than they do in the nearby countryside. Yet the nestling mortality rate is over 50 per cent in the city, compared to less than 5 per cent in rural areas, because the hawks contract trichomoniasis from the pigeons and doves in their urban diet.[15] The city population is not in decline, as more continue to move in from the countryside. The city thus functions as a trap in which the promise of easy food and comfortable nesting lures birds to their demise. City-dwelling species also have to deal with predation issues. The long-term assumption has been that cities provide safe-nesting zones in which birds are freed from their usual predators. A recent study suggests, however, that nest predation is higher in cities, where birds must contend with cats, magpies, crows, rats, and people.[16] Some species are in decline, and though problems such as disease and predation clearly take their toll, the actual reasons why are often unknown.

For example, London used to host a population of tens of thousands of house sparrows. In Kensington Gardens alone, there were 2,600 in 1925, but only 855 in 1948, and as few as 8 in 2000.[17] Given that sparrows nest in deciduous bushes, it seemed likely that the changing urban environment was affecting their nesting sites. In an attempt to combat crime and make inhabitants feel safer, deciduous bushes, which provide cover for would-be assailants, had been removed from parks. Rather than continue to discover such unanticipated impact of urban planning on species populations after the fact, it would seem prudent to gather data so that decisions can be made knowingly. Thus the British Trust for Ornithology began the London Bird Project, and the Royal Society for the Protection of Birds has implemented the London House Sparrow Project. These are survey programs in which community members participate in gathering data. Such projects have several benefits. First, they promote biodiversity in the city by raising alarms and mobilizing response concerning declining species. Second, they raise citizen awareness. Those who participate in such projects learn to identify species they see, and become more familiar with their habits. People who understand the threat their cat poses to birds, for example, may be more likely to keep the cat indoors at night, when feline rapaciousness is at its peak. Informed gardeners can better share the space by understanding which practices encourage pests and which support more desirable cohabitants. Third, they increase the ecological literacy of policy makers, while revealing citizen interest in and support of species care and protection. Thus, urban leaders are more likely to support initiatives that cost money but protect species that are given short shrift in changing urban landscapes. In the case of the sparrow, for example, installing nest boxes and feeders in urban gardens can compensate for the loss of deciduous trees.

Eco-cityzenry thus begins with the insight that cities do not separate human beings from nature or remove them from ecosystem membership. A city is a relational context in which the human experience is deeply entangled with the experience of cohabitant species. Cities are complex ecosystems that function within larger ecosystems in the same way that a forest or river can be part of a mountain or prairie ecosystem.

Eco-City Planning

Once policy makers understand that city spaces are shared habitat, the whole process of learning to be better neighbours to cohabitant species is accelerated. An approach that considers urban space more broadly than in terms of its human function manifests a praxical ethic of care towards cohabitant species. For example, swifts migrate every year from sub-Saharan Africa to roost under European eaves. As buildings are reroofed using new designs and materials, swifts are finding fewer places to roost and their numbers are declining. In the Netherlands and Switzerland, legislation has been introduced that requires architects and developers to incorporate nesting places for swifts; the conservation group Concern for Swifts is likewise campaigning for nest boxes to be fitted under the eaves of new and renovated public and industrial buildings in Britain.[18] In London, the Thames Gateway Project is reclaiming a 60-kilometre stretch of the Thames embankment consisting of derelict sites and old docks in order to build 200,000 new homes.[19] One species' wasteland is, however, another species' haven. Just because space has become minimally useful or dysfunctional for people does not mean that it is 'empty.' The Thames 'wasteland' supports a population of black redstarts that thrive in its conditions. They will be significantly harmed by the landscaping practices typical in such developments. It will be necessary to look at which species use the space and how one can promote a sharing of space that makes cityzens better neighbours to other species and more at home in their city-space. Those who set policy or plan development projects are also cityzens of the space they manage, and can choose to be responsible eco-cityzens. Thus, eco-planners on the Thames Gateway Project recommended building 'green roofs' into the project where the redstarts can forage.

Green roofs – roofs that are partially or completely covered with soil and plants – are already popular throughout Europe. Germany is the leader, with approximately 10 per cent of its roofs having been greened, according to the PennState Center for Green Roof Research (PCGRR). Between 1989 and 1999, some 107 million square metres of green roofs were installed there. In the United States, the Atlanta and Chicago city halls have green roofs, and the Ford Corporation's River Rouge plant renovation project in Detroit incorporates 4 hectares of green space on top of the truck factory.[20] In Canada, the Vancouver Library in downtown Vancouver has a green roof.[21] The PCGRR lists reasons why green roofs are desirable: they are aesthetically pleasing; reduce the city heat island effect, carbon dioxide impact, noise, storm water runoff, and both summer air conditioning and winter heating costs; lengthen roof life; remove nitrogen pollution; and neutralize acid rain.[22] The advantages are many. Green roofs not only make for better-quality urban living and support biodiversity, but also have substantial economic returns. They provide places in which food can be grown so that cities can, at least in part, meet some of their food needs, and are excellent sites for application of composted material as a productive use of food and other wastes. There are many other ways in which cities can become greener.

Green buildings are on the increase. In 1993, Natural Resources Canada launched its C-2000 Program for Advanced Commercial Buildings. This program covers a broad range of performance criteria, including annual energy consumption of less than half that required by industry standards of good practice; minimal environmental impact; a high-quality indoor environment; adaptability; long-lived building components; and facilitation of subsequent maintenance.[23] The aim of the program is to demonstrate the feasibility of achieving a high level of energy and environmental performance. Initially, new technologies were taken to be the key to success for the program, but experience has shown that the design process itself is more important. Performance improvements come not so much from the technologies as from the thinking that assembles them into an integrated whole. Twenty-four buildings have been designed based on the C-2000 requirements, twelve of which achieved design targets and were constructed. Mountain Equipment Co-op is a Canadian company that has built three of its buildings under this program in response to the fact that building operations are responsible for approximately 30 per cent of Canada's greenhouse gas emissions, while building construction worldwide consumes 3 billion tons of raw materials annually.[24] Proper design of buildings can also combat the heat island effect by reducing the amount of direct sunlight through windows, increasing ventilation, cooling air with fountains, painting outside walls white to reduce heat absorption, and planting trees outside. Such designs cut the costs, energy use, and waste production involved in air conditioning, including waste heat usually dispersed outdoors.

What these examples show is that public institutions and corporations can contribute to functional eco-city dwelling. They are ways of greening existing cities. The Dongtan Eco-City is a different kind of example.[25] A joint project between ARUP, a British engineering firm founded on the vision of Ove Arup, and the Shanghai Industrial Investment Corporation, Dongtan is an attempt to move directly to ecological modernism without moving through traditional processes of industrialization. The city will be built on 630 hectares of Chongming Island at the mouth of the Yangtse River and connected to Shanghai by a bridge. Construction began in 2006. By 2040, the completed city should house half a million residents. Cityzens will live in six- to eight-storey naturally ventilated apartment blocks. This approach is consistent with research showing that low-rise cities are most ecologically sound, as they are dense enough to make walking feasible, but not so dense as to produce a heat island effect. Freshwater consumption will be cut by two thirds through provision of two water sources: one that is drinkable, and one of 'grey water' that mixes river water and recycled drainage water for irrigation and use in toilets. The city's waste treatment plant will convert sewage and compost into bio-gas to be used for cooking, heating, and power generation. Wind and solar power will also be used so that the city will be powered entirely by renewable sources. Cars will be allowed, but the city is not planned to make driving convenient. Thus Dongtan will be a quiet city that combines ecological viability with the social factor of pleasant living. Ma Cheng Liang, the project's director, promises that it will be a green-fringed utopia that provides new ways of living as a model for future city development elsewhere. Ken Livingstone, the former mayor of London, visited the site, announcing plans for a 1,000-home eco-development modelled on Dongtan.

There are, however, already doubts that Dongtan can live up to its promise of being the first sustainable eco-city, and worries that the vision is flawed. Zhiping Tang, deputy director of urban planning and architecture at Tongji University, argues that the planned golf course will use land that could produce food. Each cityzen's ecological footprint will be 2.2 hectares, while scientific calculations show that a sustainable ecological footprint, given equitable sharing of the world's resources among its human inhabitants, would be 1.8 hectares per person.[26] Furthermore, rural inhabitants of China have an ecological footprint of 1.6 hectares, so that those who move to Dongtan will increase their footprint. Yet the city still promises gains in sustainability for China as a whole, given that 400 million rural Chinese are expected to move into cities over the next 30 years, and that the current footprint of cityzens of Shanghai is, for example, more than four times the national average.[27] Nevertheless, since the city is a 20-minute drive to Shanghai's business district across the bridge, cityzens may rely on cars to get back and forth to the island, and it may become 'a car-dominated middle-class dormitory for Shanghai.'[28] Thus Dongtan may promote class privilege and ultimately house cityzens who can maximize desirable living conditions without adapting their expectations, practices, and consumption patterns in eco-positive ways. Ecologically progressive policy and planning are thus not in themselves enough: sustainable city dwelling also requires the active participation of committed eco-cityzens.

Moreover, the ecological literacy and concern of individual cityzens is where sustainable cities begin, for at least two further reasons. First, eco-cityzens can lobby and educate other cityzens, policy makers, and planners both to increase the number of cityzens who are ecologically minded and to promote the provision of green options for this growing body. Second, policy makers, planners, and corporate decision makers are also cityzens. Eco-cityzens in decision-making positions accelerate urban sustainability. Thus, an argument supporting policy initiatives can be anarchistic insofar as policy has its origin in the individual cityzen, at whatever various levels of city infrastructure and dwelling she or he functions. For individuality consists not in any universal and abstract property of the ego, but in the particular way each citizen functions as an embodied, living being in constant interaction and relationship with other people, with other non-human city dwellers, and with the urban ecosystem. Ecologically literate cityzens who care for each other, for cohabitant species, for the resource base that supports urban living, and for the city itself are the source and promise of sustainable cities. This is the vision of ecofeminist cityzenry.

NOTES

1 Fred Pearce, 'Ecopolis Now,' *New Scientist* 2556 (17 June 2006): 36–42, at 37.
2 Cf. Paul Krugman, *The Great Unraveling* (New York: Norton and Co., 2005), 299–325.
3 Pearce, 'Ecopolis Now,' 38.
4 Pearce, 'Ecopolis Now,' 38.
5 Aristotle, *Physics, Books I–IV*, trans. P.H. Wicksteed and F.M. Cornford (Cambridge, MA: Harvard University Press, 1929), 192b19–23.

6 Aristotle, *Physics, Books I–IV*, 193a12–17.

7 The project can be visited at http://www.beslter.org (accessed 19 May 2008).

8 See the Bat Conservation International web page at http://www.batcon. org/home/index.asp?idPage=122 (accessed 19 May 2008).

9 http://www.austrop.org.au/ghff/moors_27_03.htm (accessed 19 May 2008).

10 http://www.austrop.org.au/ghff/1st_30_june.htm (accessed 19 May 2008).

11 Diane Martindale, 'The Rat Catcher,' *New Scientist* 2275 (27 January 2001): 40–2 (an interview with Bruce Colvin).

12 These data are from Gail Vines, 'Wild in the City,' *New Scientist* 2523 (29 October 2005): 34–8.

13 http://abcnews.go.com/Technology/wireStory?id=765929 (accessed 16 June 2006).

14 James Owen, 'Feral Parrot Population Soars in U.K., Study Says,' *National Geographic News* (8 July 2004). http://news.nationalgeographic.com/ news/2004/07/0708_040708_feralparrots.html (accessed 19 May 2008).

15 C.W. Boal and R.W. Mannan, 'Nest-Site Selection by Cooper's Hawks in an Urban Environment,' *Journal of Wildlife Management* 62 (1998): 864–71.

16 Jukka Jokimäki et al., 'Evaluation of the "Safe Nesting Zone" Hypothesis across an Urban Gradient: A Multi-Scale Study,' *Ecography* 28, 1 (February 2005): 59–70.

17 The Royal Society for Protection of Birds, London House Sparrow Project. https://www.rspb.org.uk/supporting/donations/lhsp/form.asp (accessed 16 June 2006).

18 Vines, 'Wild in the City,' 37–8.

19 http://www.bgs.ac.uk/science/thamesgateway/home.html (accessed 19 May 2008).

20 http://www.post-gazette.com/pg/04317/410625.stm (accessed 19 May 2008); http://www.greenroofs.com/skygardens.htm#Sky%20Gardens (accessed 19 May 2008). Cf. http://www.mcdonoughpartners.com/ projects/fordrouge/default.asp?projID=fordrouge, the website of the architecture and community design company undertaking the renovation, William McDonough and Partners (accessed 19 May 2008).

21 http://www.greenroofs.com/projects (accessed 19 May 2008).

22 http://hortweb.cas.psu.edu/research/greenroofcenter/history.html (accessed 19 May 2008).

23 http://www.buildingsgroup.nrcan.gc.ca:80/projects/c2000_e.html (accessed 19 June 2006).

24 http://www.mec.ca/Main/content_text.jsp?FOLDER%3C%3Efolder_
    id=2534374302642651 (accessed 19 June 2006).

25 See http://www.arup.com/eastasia/project.cfm?pageid=7047 (accessed
    19 May 2008); Fred Pearce, 'Masterplan,' *New Scientist* 2556 (17 June 2006):
    43–5.

26 Pearce, 'Ecopolis Now,' 37; 'Masterplan,' 45.

27 Pearce, 'Masterplan,' 44.

28 Pearce, 'Masterplan,' 45.

12 Sustainable Urbanization

JOHN B. COBB, JR

I

All over the world, forests are disappearing and agricultural lands are eroding. Aquifers are being exhausted. Fish stocks are diminishing. Land, water, and air are being poisoned. Many species of living things are vanishing. The planet is getting warmer, resulting in increasing storms and changes in rainfall. Catastrophes loom, sometimes breaking into our own time. Those who study natural resources and the condition of the earth issue warning after warning. They tell us that long ago, humanity crossed the line into unsustainable living.

However, governments look elsewhere for guidance – primarily to economists. Economic theory has no place for resource limits. It assumes infinite supplies. Of course, economists do not mean that there is an infinite amount of petroleum in the Earth. What they mean is that as one natural resource is exhausted, technology can provide us with replacements. Obviously, this is often true. If the only shortage were petroleum, replacements would undoubtedly be found for its multiple uses as it grows more expensive. The transition would be difficult for many people, but if the economy is sufficiently healthy, economists assume, society as a whole will do well.

We have, therefore, two views of sustainability in our society. One view calls us to find ways to live within the context given us by nature, destroying as little as possible. In this view, human life adjusts to its natural context. It seeks ways to improve its condition that also benefit its natural environment. We will call this the 'ecological' understanding of sustainability.

The other view is of sustainable growth. It calls for continuing increase of economic activity, accepting the losses to the natural world that such growth entails. It is believed that this growth will be sustainable as long as there are sufficient economic resources to fund the technological research and development needed to transform the natural environment so that it will meet human needs. We will call this the 'economistic' understanding of sustainability.

This economistic vision suggests not only that we can substitute new resources for exhausted ones, but also that we can deal technologically with more fundamental scarcities. The world is losing good soil, and water for irrigation grows scarce. Accepting this as inevitable, technologists can engineer new types of plants that will grow in poor soil and with less water. As oceans become poisoned, technologists will create fish that can survive these poisons. Even human beings may have to be genetically altered to cope with a more toxic environment.

Economists long resisted taking global warming seriously. Now that they do see it as a major concern, they tend to regard its results as inevitable, and once again turn to technology to solve the problem. If ocean levels rise, people will either build dikes along extensive coastlines or learn to use the remaining land more efficiently. If the Gulf Stream ceases to warm Europe, technology will provide Europeans with new crops to grow in a colder climate. New species of animals will be bio-engineered to replace the ones that cannot adjust to climatic changes.

The economistic notion of sustainable growth can appeal to much supportive evidence. It has kept us going through many changes in our natural environment. A good example is that of insect pests and insecticides. Modern agricultural growth has been achieved by monocultures that are vulnerable to insect pests. These monocultures have required heavy use of insecticides. Insecticides kill most of the pests, but a few survive. These reproduce rapidly. New insecticides are required to kill the new insects, which have built up a resistance to the old insecticides. Thus far, technology has stayed ahead of insect mutation, but whether this trend will continue is uncertain. Herbicides provide another example of adapting to changes in the environment.

These poisons also kill many of the organisms that naturally contribute to the fertility of the land. Accordingly, there is need for more and more artificial fertilizer that has also been supplied in sufficient quantity to sustain and increase production.

At present, most of this economistic argument is based on the availability of petroleum. Nevertheless, petroleum production globally is at or near its historic peak; it will soon begin to decline in both quality and quantity.[1] Technology will be called upon to develop substitutes for insecticides and herbicides. No doubt it will have some success – by introducing genetic changes that make plants more resistant to particular pests, and by finding other ways to manufacture insecticides and herbicides.

Advocates of sustainable growth based on technological innovations are confident that technology will always stay ahead of changing threats. However, this makes the production of food more and more dependent not only on ever-new technology, but also on a social order that allows the technology to be quickly available where needed. Further, these problems must be solved by technology at the same time as the problems brought about by global warming, shortages of fresh water, and loss of topsoil confront the world. In the past, advances along one line have often caused other problems to worsen. For example, the Green Revolution required increased inputs of water and fertilizer in order to achieve its increased production. It also made grains more vulnerable to pests and diseases. The technological mindset has always focused on particular problems in some abstraction from the broader picture. To follow the economistic vision of sustainable growth, we must now be confident that, in the future, technological solutions to diverse problems will be brilliantly integrated.

My own judgment is that the economistic vision of sustainable growth is an illusion, and a profoundly dangerous one that cannot advance the development of a natural city. The longer we operate on this basis, the more the world is impoverished and the more precarious the human situation becomes. For thousands of years, healthy soils carefully tended by individual farmers have produced crops for the families that grew them, with some surplus for others. This has been a relatively sustainable system. The more we continue to husband the soil, maintain supplies of fresh water, slow climate change, and use organic methods to control insects and weeds, the more sustainable our agriculture will be. Thus, sustainability is approached not by shifting from peasant farming to agribusiness monoculture, with ever-greater applications of artificial fertilizer, insecticides, and herbicides, but by renewing reliance on nature and on human labour. This is the ecological vision of sustainability and is the condition for a natural city.

I do not want to leave the impression that, in the ecological vision, there is opposition to technological advances. The world urgently needs technological advances that lead towards sustainability. Peasant farmers need technological advances that improve their crops, enable them to survive droughts, and improve the quality of their homes. Society needs technological advances that will most efficiently bring agricultural products to local markets and preserve them while in storage. Rural society needs technological advances that will reduce the incidence of disease and bring basic medical care to all. As families and friends are separated from one another, improved technological means for communication among them are highly valued. The technology of recycling and other uses of waste products is important. There is much more to be said.

Needless to say, I understand sustainable urbanization and the natural city in ecological, not economistic, terms. From this point of view, any social order that exhausts the resources on which it depends is unsustainable. Any social order that pollutes its environment is unsustainable. The present global order is unsustainable on both counts. In many ways, U.S. society leads the way towards increasingly unsustainable resource use. A major problem in China is that it follows too closely the American lead.

II

But what I am calling 'ecological' sustainability is not simply a matter of the relation of human beings to their natural environment. Political, social, and economic considerations also interrelate with concerns about nature. A society that cannot offer its members an opportunity to support themselves cannot survive. The present global economy is actually increasing the number of persons who are excluded from economic activity within the official economy. The underground economy, partly criminal, partly simply extra-legal, is growing in much of the world. The official economy is dividing people more and more sharply into the rich and the poor within countries and between them. These trends are unsustainable.

My reflection about sustainable urbanization in China is in the context of these multiple concerns. But why direct special attention to urbanization in China? My reason for this concern is that it is now occurring, and is likely to continue occurring, at a scale and tempo never before seen in human history. This state of affairs is due partly to China's vast population, and partly to the unprecedented speed of social and economic change in China. It is my assumption that if present trends continue, hundreds of millions of people who currently reside in rural areas will be urbanized in a decade or two.

Consider, for example, what will be required if 300 million people move from the countryside to cities. (I think an even higher figure may be realistic.) This would mean that China would have to build 30 cities of 10 million each, or 300 cities of one million, or 3,000 cities of 100,000. In my opinion, a larger number of smaller cities is far preferable. Moving from a peasant farm to a city of 100,000 people that is located no more than 50 miles (80 km) away would be less disruptive to human life and family connections than the alternatives. But planning and building 3,000 cities will prove a horrendous task!

III

If Chinese cities continue to follow today's models, the unsustainability of global practices will come vividly into view all too soon. Indeed, I think it is already manifest.

I will cite only one factor in unsustainability. I have commented on the importance at this point in history of avoiding a shift to petroleum-based agriculture. Thus far, China's urban development has shared the global dependence on petroleum. China's increased demand for oil has been cited as one reason for the current spike in oil prices. If order is restored in Iraq and production there greatly increased, the price may come down somewhat. But it is public knowledge that oil is being pumped from the ground far faster than new oil fields are being discovered. Within a few years, global production will probably peak. Even if production continues to rise longer than expected, it will not rise as fast as demand, based on current practices and accelerated Chinese development of the current type. Normal market pricing will lead to a further rise in oil prices. It is safe to say that, whatever happens in the short term, oil will be much more expensive 10 years from now. It will be still more costly 20 years from now.

Economists assure us that, as the market signals scarcity, technology will make more and more efficient use of the resource. Technology will also develop alternatives. No doubt this is true. If oil were the only resource destined to become scarce, the world could make a transition to other sources of energy. However, the more rapid the transition, the more difficult it will be. Chinese cities now being built to operate on oil will pay a high price for this choice. The price signals should already warn even economistic thinkers that continuing to build cities to operate on oil is a serious mistake.

China as a whole will pay a high price for continuing to plan on the basis of an oil economy, politically as well as economically. The United States intends to control global oil production. It does so, in part, to maintain its own economy and postpone the pain of the inevitable adjustments to come. It does so also in order to secure its global hegemony. If China depends radically on oil, and the United States controls the global oil supply, China will no longer be a truly independent nation. As an American, I am distressed by this prospect. I would expect the Chinese to be even more distressed.

What is the alternative? It is complex and difficult, but not impossible. Of course, it includes efficient use of oil and development of alternatives. But these technological approaches can only go so far. Much more important is to avoid not only the development of an oil-based agriculture, but also the construction of cities dependent on oil.

Improved agricultural practices that remain labour-intensive and produce food organically, combined with prices for agricultural products that make possible a good living for peasant farmers, will slow the depopulation of the countryside. This strategy could reduce the number and size of the cities that must be built. Following the economistically driven mandates of the World Trade Organization, however, will accelerate the exodus from the countryside while making agriculture less and less sustainable. Maintaining stable communities by improving the existing system of agriculture instead of replacing it with 'modern' systems could also support the social sustainability that is eroded by rapid mass migration.

My first recommendation, therefore, is to improve life in the countryside and refuse to move from peasant production to agribusiness. However, much of the countryside is overpopulated, and there will be, and should be, continuing urbanization. This urbanization has a better chance of being sustainable, and of being a part of a sustainable China, if the flow of population from rural to urban contexts is slowed.

Increased urbanization will take two forms. No doubt much of it will occur through the expansion of present cities. However, because I think the cities of China are already too large, I would encourage aiming primarily to build new cities rather than to enlarge the present ones. A larger number of smaller cities will prove, in my view, to be more sustainable than a smaller number of larger ones.

In any case, a discussion of sustainable urbanization should consider both how to make present cities less unsustainable and how to build new cities that are, from the beginning, genuinely sustainable.

I am particularly interested in the possibility that China, facing this enormous challenge, will experiment radically with a different type of city. For decades, I have believed that the most original and important vision of what cities could be and should be is that of the American architect Paolo Soleri.[2] Soleri proposes to build architectural ecologies or 'arcologies.' An entire city would be a single building. Transportation within the city would be by elevator, escalator, moving sidewalk, and paths for walking and bicycling. Highways and city streets would be eliminated along with parking lots and filling stations. Distances within the city would be greatly reduced and access to the countryside would never be far away. All the energy of the city would be derived passively from the sun.

If Soleri is given the opportunity to build a small city somewhere in China, I believe this may be a turning point in the quest for a sustainable world. I say this not only because he points in the direction of cities that are energy self-sufficient, producing few toxic wastes or greenhouse gases. I say it because his cities will take much less land away from agricultural purposes. Further, they will encourage new forms of human community that will make possible new experiments in economic organization that guarantee to all some participation in the economic life of the city. They can reduce the hardships of poverty by making all the facilities of the city readily available to all its inhabitants. And they will make possible new forms of local self-government.

To be sure, neither Soleri nor I believe that architectural forms will solve all problems. What is needed is to get the best thinkers about community, economics, and politics to help in a comprehensive planning strategy. Ideally, several experiments should be developed soon to learn from mistakes and provide stimulus to others. Perhaps the genuinely sustainable new cities that would emerge in China would be quite different from any of the designs proposed thus far by Soleri, but the enormous value of his work is that it points forward to an entirely different conception of what cities can and should be. This is certainly an area in which China could lead the world into a new and far more promising age.

IV

Whatever breakthroughs of this kind occur, China must still deal with the problems of its present cities, which are currently not sustainable. This comment is not a criticism of China. Chinese cities are no less sustainable, I assume, than European and American ones. Bill Rees has led the way in showing that the ecological footprints of cities are enormous and still growing.[3] Modern cities developed originally when most of the world's population still lived in the countryside and could provide the goods needed by the cities. Natural resources such as coal and then oil were abundant. Pollution was a local rather than a global problem. But the relationship to the environment has now changed. This urban civilization of the petroleum age is now unsustainable.

I have given special attention to the use of oil, since the petroleum age is coming to an end. Existing cities cannot abruptly free themselves from dependence on oil. They can, however, reduce their use of oil, both by restricting their need to import energy and by substituting other forms of energy.

We now have many examples of buildings that require virtually no energy other than the heat from the sun in order to remain comfortable all year long. I am sure that Chinese architects are fully aware of this fact and are making use of many of the innovations that make it possible. I am also quite sure that much more could be done.

I am impressed by the work of David Orr at Oberlin College in Ohio. He has erected a building that produces more energy than it consumes and that is designed to require minimum-cost maintenance indefinitely.[4] Amory Lovins has constructed a building at 7,000 feet (2,100 m) in the Colorado Rockies that houses both his home and extensive office space. It is extremely well insulated and arranged to capture sunlight. As a result, it is heated entirely by passive solar energy.[5]

The policy in China should be that all new buildings must be self-sufficient in heating and cooling, as well as extremely frugal in their use of imported electricity. San Francisco recently made a city-wide effort to turn the sunlight falling on its buildings into electricity. Examples of this kind can be studied and, when appropriate, emulated.

Transporting people from home to work is another major drain on the energy supplies of a city. Not long ago, much of that transportation in China was by bicycle. Cities should be sure that they do not allow new developments to make it more difficult to return to bicycles as the major means of transportation. In general, everything should be done to discourage the ownership and use of private automobiles. Good public transportation helps. Many European cities exclude private motor transportation from the central city. Locating residences near places of work is helpful. Suburban sprawl of the sort so widespread in the United States should be prevented.

The implementation of all these policies depends on technological developments as well as political will. In the appropriation of technology, one important policy should be leapfrogging. Alongside all of the destructive aspects of contemporary technologically driven society are genuine advances that enable goals to be accomplished with far less use of natural resources. Cellphones, for example, whatever their problems, may make it possible to have the advantages of the telephone without the huge infrastructures that have been needed for this kind of communication in the past. Buildings that are self-sufficient in energy production are another example of leapfrogging over intermediate stages.

A massive example of leapfrogging is provided by the arcologies of which I have been speaking. Trends in the development of urban centres now move in the direction of arcologies. But there is no need to evolve gradually in that direction through steps that consume extreme amounts of resources. By leapfrogging over these steps, China can take the lead. Between cellphones and arcologies lie countless other examples. One might consider that certain proposals for urban economies are also a form of leapfrogging. Some excellent ideas that have been proposed have been quashed in the West by people of wealth whose interests they would have threatened. These proposals stand a much better chance of serious consideration and implementation in China.

V

Whether or not cities are built as arcologies, they are more sustainable if, together with their rural surroundings, they are relatively self-sufficient. To put the matter negatively, the more the healthy survival of a city depends on long supply lines and on decisions made by people at a distance who have no interest in the well-being of the city, the more precarious is the future of that city.

This reflection illustrates the fact that, especially in recent decades, we have been constructing a more and more unsustainable world. The world economy has been reordered so that goods are produced thousands of miles from where they are consumed. Instead of planning agriculture so that local people can be fed, huge monocultural plantations produce for export.

The economistic commitment to growth has supported this development. It may be that moves of these kinds lead to the most rapid economic growth, although I am not sure that statistics bear out this finding. But many of us do not believe that what is called 'economic growth' consistently benefits human beings. This growth is usually measured by gross domestic product (GDP), which can, and often does, rise even while the actual living conditions of most people deteriorate. There are several reasons for this result.

First, GDP is indifferent to the distribution of the income it measures. The policies employed to increase GDP are often based on the theory that wealth accumulated by the richest trickles down to the poor so that all benefit. In fact, these policies lead to an increase in the gap between rich and poor. Any 'trickle down' that takes place rarely reaches the poorest segment of society. Furthermore, concentration of wealth is typically accompanied by concentration of power. Much of this wealth and power is in the hands of foreigners who do not care what happens to local people.

Second, the GDP is unaffected by environmental deterioration. Indeed, there is a direct relation between the rise of GDP and the decline of the environment. First, extra costs incurred because of environmental decline are added to GDP. For example, if water must be transported farther and new facilities for its purification are required, these costs are added to GDP. Second, there is an obvious correlation of increased consumption and reduced resources on the one side, and increased pollution on the other. Again, nothing is subtracted from the GDP because of the loss of natural capital.

Third, the policies designed to speed economic growth as measured by GDP almost always prove destructive of human communities. People are separated from the means of production and from one another. The quality of family life declines. But healthy community is essential to sustainability. It is a profound mistake to adopt policies oriented primarily to 'economic growth' as that is measured today.

Common sense tells us that real growth must be understood in quite different ways. The question is whether the changes in the economy benefit the people, with special attention to the poorest and most vulnerable. In other words, is the society that develops sustainable? One characteristic of sustainable communities is meeting the basic needs of all its members.

The current global economy is not sustainable; the more China buys into it, the less sustainable the economy of China becomes. If new cities are built primarily to produce goods for distant countries, they will be unsustainable and will contribute to the unsustainability of the whole society. If they produce primarily to meet their own needs, they will be far more sustainable.

The goal of complete self-sufficiency, on the other hand, is undesirable. Trade can and should play an important, although minor, role. The people of the city should be able to survive without misery if the trade were ended. In other words, their basic needs should be supplied apart from trade. In that case, trade can add to the enjoyment of life without threatening its sustainability.

Trade with the countryside and with neighbouring cities should be favoured over trade with distant places. Whereas a single city provides a sufficient market to stimulate competition in the production of clothing, sports equipment, household goods, and office supplies, its demand for elevators would not suffice for a healthy market. It may be inefficient for each city to manufacture its own elevators; or, if it did so, the market would not support more than a single company. Monopoly has many negative consequences, and must be carefully controlled by government. But the results of bureaucratic control for manufacturing are often negative. If several cities manufactured elevators, it would be important that the manufacturers competed with one another without the assurance that they would be excessively favoured by the city in which they were located.

One advantage of relatively self-sufficient cities is that they could make decisions about wages and working conditions without fear that these would put their businesses at a disadvantage in competition with businesses elsewhere that paid lower wages and had inferior working conditions. Goods coming from such places should require a tax that would at least compensate for this difference. Of course, it is now very difficult to control the movement of goods into and out of a city. With an arcology, it would be easier.

VI

Let me summarize some of my basic convictions about sustainable urbanization and principles supporting a 'natural city.'

1. In an uncertain future, a city, together with its surrounding countryside, will be more sustainable if it is relatively self-sufficient. That means that it is capable of meeting its basic needs. That approach does not preclude trade with other cities and even more distant places, but the local region should not be dependent on that trade for survival.

2. Both the city and the countryside should be self-sufficient in the production of the energy that they require in order to function.

3. Smaller cities can achieve these goals better than huge ones. Arcologies could do so best of all.

4. Cities, together with their countryside, should adopt new technologies that leapfrog over wasteful ones, which are still characteristic of much of the West.

5. Cities, together with their countryside, should experiment with political and economic systems that allow maximum participation in local self-government of the people.

6. To achieve genuine sustainability, natural cities and their countryside should foster community among their people, so that none are excluded from participation and from having their basic needs met.

NOTES

1 See the Fourth Assessment Report of the Intergovernmental Panel on Climate Change (IPCC), 2007, available at http://www.ipcc.ch/publications_and_data/publications_ipcc_fourth_assessment_report_synthesis_report.htm (accessed 12 December 2008).
2 Paolo Soleri, *The Urban Ideal: Conversations with Paolo Soleri* (Berkeley, CA: Berkeley Hills Books, 2001).
3 See William E. Rees, 'Ecological Footprint and Appropriated Carrying Capacity: What Urban Economics Leaves Out,' *Environment and Urbanization* 4, 2 (1992): 121–30.
4 See David Orr, *The Nature of Design* (Oxford: Oxford University Press, 2004) and *Design on the Edge* (Cambridge, MA: MIT Press, 2006).
5 See the description of the Rocky Mountain Institute at http://www.ipcc.ch/publications_and_data/publications_ipcc_fourth_assessment_report_synthesis_report.htm (accessed 12 December 2008).

13 'Troubled Nature': Some Reflections on the Changing Nature of the Millennial City, Gurgaon, India

SHUBHRA GURURANI

Introduction

Gurgaon, also known as the Millennial City of India, is located on the outskirts of India's national capital, New Delhi. Despite its name, which means the Village of Gur, Gurgaon is not a village or, for that matter, even a city. It is certainly not a metropolis characterized by historic grandeur, cultural exuberance, or colonial trade or commerce. It is a rapidly changing city-region. Barely a few years ago, Gurgaon was a sleepy little township primarily associated with everything agrarian and rustic. Today, the story of Gurgaon is anything but rural. In 1985, Gurgaon was incorporated in the National Capital Region (NCR), and since the early 1990s, when the Indian economy was liberalized, Gurgaon's fortunes have dramatically transformed. With a heavy influx of foreign investments and the setting up of several corporate offices and call centres, present-day Gurgaon has become synonymous with glitzy towers, posh housing enclaves, corporate head offices, and fancy shopping malls. It has come to symbolize the dreams and destination of an increasingly cosmopolitan and global India.

Located 20 kilometres south of New Delhi, Gurgaon, in the state of Haryana, is one of India's prominent feeder cities and is well known globally for its state-of-the-art buildings. Until recently, Japan's Suzuki Motors, which set up a car plant in collaboration with Maruti Udyog Limited in the 1980s, in addition to a few small industries, was the most Gurgaon could boast of, but today it is a thriving urban centre. Covering a relatively small area of 2,753 square kilometres, one-third the size of Toronto, Gurgaon is currently home to half a dozen malls. Plans have been made to construct several more, along with dozens of multinational corporate offices, a large number of call centres, and countless upscale housing enclaves. Not only has Gurgaon's landscape remarkably transformed, but its population has also grown: from 57,085 inhabitants in 1971 to 1,146,090 in 1991 and is currently estimated to be 2.5 million, a number which is expected to double by 2031.

Much has palpably changed since the early 1990s – not only in the economy, but also in the social and political fabric of India, of which cities such as Gurgaon constitute an important part. There has been a critical shift from a socialist-oriented planning, housing, and infrastructure delivery to the increasingly privatized service delivery and housing development that Gurgaon exemplifies. The influx of finance capital and the post-socialist euphoria have engendered new forms of social and political imaginaries that are articulated through architectural and other consumption practices and aesthetics. At this political and economic turn, Gurgaon, among other such city-regions, has emerged as 'a key articulator in a new, regional geography of centrality, dispersal, mobility, and connectivity that expands not only to the rest of the continent but around the globe. It is the site of a high concentration of strategic resources.'[1]

In the context of significant social and spatial transformations and rapid urbanization, in this chapter I take the case of urban nature as a point of entry and present an ethnographic snapshot of how these changes have come to inform the social imaginaries[2] and politics of nature among local residents, migrant workers, and real estate developers. By focusing on the discourse and practice of urban nature in Gurgaon, I wish to explore the multiple evocations of nature as they circulate among real estate developers, local residents, and new residents, and to examine what constitutes the idea of urban nature, the understanding of environmental problems, and the politics of urban infrastructure. At a moment when it is widely acknowledged that most people in the world live in cities and that the process of urbanization is rapidly underway, particularly in the global South, these questions are important to ask. Not only do they shed light on the changing contours of nature, but they also, equally importantly, reveal the range of actors – old and new, human and non-human – who have come together in complex and unpredictable linkages to shape the urban landscape of society and nature in places like Gurgaon.

Interestingly, as the editors of this volume aptly point out, despite some recent shifts in thinking, the overarching view still seems to define 'environmental' issues as concerned with plants, animals, and untouched wilderness areas, while human settlements are usually perceived to be the domain of architects, planners, and urbanists. In Gurgaon in May 2008, in an attempt to capture the everyday understandings of urban nature in a city that is viscerally and visually being made, I engaged in discussions and conversations about 'urban nature.' In the searing heat, with temperatures reaching 45 degrees Celsius, I was faced with a challenge as soon as I began the conversation with local residents of the urban villages of Chakkarpur and Sukhrauli in Gurgaon or with migrant labourers who had come to work as factory workers, rickshaw pullers, or security guards in the last five years. At the most basic level, the challenge was how to talk about 'urban nature.' How could I describe an entity, a landscape, a place, a process, or an assemblage like nature that does not have an easy or direct cognate in Hindi, which I used in my conversations, or in Haryanavi, the local dialect, which some of the local informants spoke? Terms such as *paryavaran* (environment) and *vatavaran* (atmosphere) are used, but only in more formal circles, not in the everyday common speech of the local village residents or migrant labourers. I tried to approach the issue in different ways. After several attempts, I settled for a medley of terms, like *zar-zameen* (literally, animal-land), *hawa-paani* (air-water), *hariyali* (green or greenery). But, since Gurgaon sits on the semi-arid and rocky terrain of Aravalli Hills, the conversation was a non-starter. The most common response was 'What is there to talk here about *hawa-paani*?' A 52-year-old resident of the village of Dundahera, who had farmed in earlier years, said, 'I cannot tell you anything about *hawa-paani*; there is nothing to talk about. The land is not the same, water is not the same, air is not the same. It is *banjar* (barren) now! Everything has changed, what has not? ... I used to have many buffaloes but I sold them six years back. Where do I take them to graze? There is no grass, no greenery, no water. This is not the Gurgawan[3] I knew.' In the same vein, the villagers who continued to live in urban villages commented that 'there is no water,' 'it is just rocks,' 'there are so few animals left now,' and so on. Even though Gurgaon was always short of water, all villages had a few wells and some had small ponds, all of which have completely dried up, and it was the acute shortage of water that came to dominate the conversations. Indeed, the question of urban nature is elusive not only for residents of Gurgaon, but for scholars as well.

In social theory in general, and particularly in urban studies, nature and society are ontologically set apart and there persists a 'great divide' between them. In this chapter, I draw on the recent developments in science studies, political ecology, and postcolonial studies to bridge the analytical gap. I argue that instead of considering nature as external to the city and treating nature as a preconstituted entity that is distinct from the social, it is critical to engage meaningfully with the question of how the amalgams of social and natural are made and continue to make the *hybrids* of social-natures. By dismantling the deep dichotomy of nature and society that problematically encapsulates the idea of the city and informs the discourse of urban nature, we may consider the city as a *living* and *lively* place which is constituted of and mutually constitutes the everyday materiality and discursive dynamics of urban landscapes. The idea of dense interconnections between society and nature is not just a matter of scholarly finesse, but is of significant political import. These interconnections of social-natures highlight the complex relations of power and knowledge, through which unequal urban landscapes are produced amid intense disparities, and ever so dramatically in the times of neo-liberal hegemony. Moreover, for a country like India, where the fast pace of urbanization is unleashing new social and spatial relations, we must consider how the question of urban nature has been historically and sociologically addressed and how we need to retool our analytical framework and develop social categories that can respond to the changing context of urbanization in India and, more generally, in the global South. For instance, an exploration of the unfolding dynamics of society and nature in a city such as Gurgaon – which is neither a post-industrial city nor a developmentalist city, but, as Ashis Nandy calls it, an 'unintended' city – forces us to develop new optics and frameworks to map out the ways in which urban nature is being produced, managed, appropriated, transformed, and utilized at this historical and political juncture. Also, mapping the transformations in the nature of the city can provide useful analytical insights into new discourses and practices of capitalist production, mobility, and consumption, and can identify actors and the interactions, on different scales, that constitute the urban environment as well as its politics.

Before I discuss the case of Gurgaon, I present a brief discussion of the recent debates on the society–nature relationship in the next section, followed by a discussion of the urban question in India. The section after that presents the arguments for metropolitan nature, followed by a discussion of Gurgaon's politics of nature and then the concluding section.

Urban Social Natures

The role of nature in shaping social processes has been for too long the subject of debate in social theory. Henri Lefebvre, in his classic *The Production of Space*, wrote, 'There is nothing in history or society that does not have to be achieved and produced. "Nature" itself, as apprehended in social life by sense organs, has been modified and therefore in a sense produced.'[4] More recently, critics of science, including Bruno Latour[5] and Donna Haraway,[6] as well as contemporary scholarship in geography,[7] anthropology,[8] and science studies, have taken the discussion of the 'great divide' between nature and society further. Among post-structuralists, feminists, and environmental historians such as Cronon[9] or Worster,[10] there is a growing recognition that nature is produced relationally. What we perceive as natural is simultaneously cultural, natural, material, and discursive. Latour argues that the dichotomy between non-human and human is a product of purifying and setting apart the two domains of nature and society, which are otherwise dialectically linked and mediated by discursive, ideological, and representational practices to produce amalgams, or what he calls 'hybrids' of nature and society. His critical contribution is to show not only that hybrids bring together society and nature in countless ways, but that they are not final or stable products; hybrids, by their very construction, embody contradictions and tensions and undergo constant transformation. They proliferate and dynamically remake socio-natural reality, thereby presenting a highly dynamic and charged context of nature-society that is attentive to multiple forces and pressures that surround it. Donna Haraway, the feminist poststructuralist, writes that 'nature is figure, construction, artifact, movement, displacement. Nature cannot pre-exist its construction ... nature for us is *made*, as both fiction and fact.'[11] She argues that a careful attention to the dialectical and historically constructed relationship between nature and society demonstrates *how* 'reality' is made and allows us to see nature as a result of processes and practices that continually transform both nature and society. For her, nature, like any other entity, is foremost an embodiment of relations that can be understood in its complexity only if its diverse constituents can be traced and fleshed out.

There is a growing acceptance of the idea of socio-natures, hybrids, imbroglios, and networks in the study of agrarian environments, national parks, and conservation biology, and by the proponents of biodiversity and conservation, but the terrain of urban studies is still rooted in the fundamental dichotomy of nature and society. Erik Swyngedouw writes, 'the view that city is a process of environmental production, sustained by particular sets of socio-metabolic interactions that shape the urban in distinct, historically contingent ways – a socio-environmental process that is deeply caught up with socio-metabolic processes operating elsewhere and producing profoundly uneven socio-ecological conditions – rarely grabs the headlines.'[12] With a greater focus on housing, health, infrastructure, migration, art, or media, the engagement of urban studies with nature is limited to either a focus on urban environmental conflicts or a focus on green spaces, greenbelts, parks, and other such enclaves of green. The city, in these instances, largely appears as a backdrop, a dead space, or a resource for the enactment of human interactions, but the politics of nature is not fully integrated into it; nature is certainly not seen as constitutive of everyday social and political relations of/in the city. Simply put, city is not considered as a living place in most accounts of the urban.

Similarly, while the bulk of literature in environmental studies and environmental politics has produced rich work focused on rivers, oceans, natural reserves, forests, fish, and, more recently, climate change, it has not really taken the case of urban nature in earnest. Leaving aside some recent interventions in the field of urban political ecology, the question of urban nature and ecologies is rather under-addressed.[13]

Recently, urban geographers[14] have assessed the separation between nature and city. In an effort to collapse the great divide, they have embraced the framework of critical urban political ecology. Swyngedouw deploys the concepts of circulation and metabolism to rethink the social–nature continuum that constitutes our present times. According to him, metabolism and circulation 'embody what modernity has been and will always be about, i.e., a series of interconnected heterogeneous (human and non-human) and dynamic, but contested and contestable, processes of continuous quantitative and qualitative transformations that re-arranges humans and non-humans in new, and often unexpected, ways.'[15] Adhering to a Marxist reading of metabolism, and taking its materialist aspects seriously, Swyngedouw upholds the idea of change, transmutation, and circulation as central to the notion of metabolism and combines it with the idea of 'cyborg urbanization.'[16] Yet, in order to go beyond the framework of 'production of "urban nature"' and capture the precisely urban dynamic of society and nature as it folds and unfolds in the city, Matthew Gandy suggests the term 'metropolitan nature,' as 'it can be deployed to signal recognition of the specific ways in which cultures of nature evolved in response to the socio-economic development and technological complexity of the modern city.'[17] The idea of metropolitan nature *'encapsulates a peculiarly modern and metropolitan relationship with nature* that extends to different kinds of cultural interactions with nature as a source of leisure'[18] as well as presents a useful framework to capture the complex and intricate networks of socio-nature as they are currently being crafted. Taking the idea of metropolitan nature as a multiply mediated, inter- and intra-connected network of humans, machines, and non-human actors that attends to the specific social and material relations of our times is a productive alternative and provides a useful analytical tool to engage with the material and symbolic imbrications of society and nature and to address the non-duality of these two realms of human existence. Before I turn to a discussion of metropolitan nature in Gurgaon, I present a very brief description in the next section to situate the urban question in India.

The Urban Question in India

With over 575 million people in urban areas, India will have 41 per cent of its population living in cities and towns by 2030, from the present level of 286 million (UNDP, India Urban Poverty Report 2009). In particular, metropolitan cities such as New Delhi, Mumbai, and Bangalore have expanded dramatically. The peri-urban belt surrounding such cities has had the maximum growth in last 10 years. Cities like Gurgaon are registered to have one of the highest national urban growth rates of 44.65 per cent, almost twice that of the national average (Census of India, 2001) and will face even greater urban expansion in the coming decades. In addition to metropolitan cities and urban regions adjacent to metropolitan cities, several smaller cities, often referred to as second-tier cities, have gained ground and are growing rapidly. Like the rest of the world, India is undergoing an 'urban revolution,' which has unleashed several unknown forces and actors into the fray.

With the expansion of the urban, there is a growing academic as well as policy interest in the city. But, by and large, in the sociology of cities, I would argue that three frameworks have tended to inform the reading of the city and its nature in India: (a) developmentalist cities, (b) cities of malaise, and (c) global cities. I discuss briefly each framework below.

First is the paradigm of modernization and development, which dominated the postwar era and equated urbanization with modernization, development, and planning in the Third World. In this schema, the Third World was considered largely synonymous with the rural, backward, traditional, and underdeveloped; hence, popular and academic attention was fixated mostly on the rural as sites of nature, potential growth, change, and modernization. Cities, in the developmentalist framework, were characterized largely by their sprawling slums, shocking urban poverty, unprecedented urban growth, and chaotic planning, and came to stand as tragic reminders of modernization gone wrong. The dominant idea of cities as embodiments of urban dilemmas and environmental malaise has resulted in mainly policy-oriented literature that calls for expert intervention and identifies problems to be rectified. There is no doubt that the slums and urban poverty in such 'hyper-cities' pose a range of questions and demand scrutiny and action, but the tendency to frame the city narrowly in the developmentalist framework and to focus primarily on facilities and services, health and education delivery, transportation, and pollution has largely been prescriptive and functionalist in tone and intent. For example, Achille Mbembe and Sarah Nuttall have recently argued that the 'ways of seeing and reading contemporary African cities are still dominated by the metanarrative of urbanization, modernization, and crisis.'[19] In India, too, much like Africa, developmentalist accounts of the city 'end up mapping an urban social geography of needs, the crucial indexes of which are levels of deprivation. In the process, they underplay many other aspects of city life and city forms.'[20]

The second framework, in the case of India, but not limited to that country, is the one in which the rural is idealized as the space of authenticity, tradition, and nature, while the urban is considered primarily from the lens of malaise, negation, and evil. For example, John Stuart Mill and Henry Maine, among others, were fascinated by the village in India, arguing that it should be the site of administrative intervention and improvement. Since then, colonists, nationalists, developmentalists, and their opponents have looked up to the village as the seat of 'real' India.[21] In particular, Gandhi – as David Arnold, a British historian of colonial India, among others, has argued – harboured a special admiration for the village and regarded village India as the site of Indian authenticity and essence. Gandhi's famous statement that 'India lives in its villages' has been upheld time and again as the founding ethos of Indian nationalism, politics, and development,[22] and is prominently reflected in academic scholarship, fiction, popular media, and Bollywood. For instance, countless Bollywood films from the 1950s and

1960s evocatively capture this thematic of the city as riddled with evil, as places of violence and crime, closely reflecting the intellectual and nationalist fervour of the time; the rural, on the other hand, was the site of idyllic nature, harmony, community, and civility. The anthropology of India, with its fascination with caste, hierarchy, community, and tradition, has also been fixated for a long time on the village as the authentic site of culture and meaning. Cities were largely considered to be sites of temporary dislocations, of modernity and modernization, of migrant labour, of immoral desires, of violence and corruption. Although the cities received relatively more attention in the disciplines of sociology, economics, and planning, there, too, they have typically been framed by the discourse of social evils. Correspondingly, the Indian sociology of the city is filled with accounts of urban evils and problems – problems of housing, labour relations, poverty, crime, violence, political upheavals, and uncertainty. Clearly, the cities were viewed in opposition to the rural, and through particular optics that were significant in shaping the ways in which the space and sociality of the city came to be written.

Finally, and more recently, the optic of the global or the transnational, of flows and conjunctures, has come to frame the study of Third World cities. Acknowledging the significant transformations in the global political economy that have been unleashed by the structural adjustment programs all over the global South, and with the intention of mapping the impact of globalization on urban spaces, the focus of such studies here has been on spatial restructuring, mobility, labour migration, technology, corporate capitalism, and so on. This literature, which is largely interested in new forms of spatialization of wealth and power in such information technology–enabled cities, has focused on housing, privatization of basic services, and the power of real estate developers. The more recent work in the anthropology of cities falls into this category, and has begun to explore the social and political fabric of emerging cities. While there remains a tendency to consider Third World cities or such global cities to be 'cities under siege'[23] and to focus on the new and emerging 'problems' of global cities and assess the challenges and impossibilities of globalist aspirations,[24] there is a burgeoning interest and effort to evaluate the 'citiness' or sociality of cities in the frontiers of urban worlds, or to consider Third World cities as viable subjects of anthropological analysis.

In all these representations of the city, a thematic commonality persists. Cities are fundamentally viewed as sites of industrial production, growth, commerce, technology, and, more important, for the purpose of this chapter, as unnatural spaces, overwritten by the presence of technology, people, and things. If nature appears in the city, it is viewed either as a problem that has to be 'fixed' through techno-political mechanisms or as an entity that is outside of the social processes of the city – a specialized zone or commodity in the form of urban parks, gardens, or greenbelts upheld by middle-class environmentalists and environmentalism. Nature, in most accounts, is not seen as constitutive of cityscapes, and is certainly not constituted of or by the city. Nature is clearly external to the city. The nature-city dichotomy is far too entrenched and has deep antecedents that cannot be fruitfully traced here. But it is worth noting that the idea of the modern city as a site of evil, located in opposition to nature and harmony, is in part influenced by the evolutionist models of ecological and biological sciences, which compare societies with living organisms and treat the dynamics of urban change 'in terms of processes such as ecological succession, the metabolic transmutation of nature or even the post-industrial impetus towards putrescence and decay.'[25] Such dichotomous and exclusive readings of nature in the city not only simplify the complex social processes that produce urban natures, locally and globally, but also overlook the politics and practices of how urban natures are made and remade. Drawing on the idea of metropolitan nature, in the next section, I present a snapshot of Gurgaon and describe how the nature–society relationship is being reconstituted in familiar and unfamiliar ways.

Metropolitan Nature: The Case of the Millennial City – Gurgaon

Over the past three decades, private developers such as DLF, Ansals, and Unitech have actively changed the face of Gurgaon – especially, DLF (Delhi Lease and Finance company), the largest real estate developer in India. DLF has been buying land from farmers since the early 1970s, but much more aggressively since the 1990s. With 3,500 acres of land in Gurgaon alone, DLF has built extensive commercial, retail, and entertainment properties, including offices of General Electric, Ericsson, and Nestlé. In the housing market, too, DLF has become synonymous with 'world-class living' and luxury condominiums. One of the residential estates built by DLF has 'an 18-hole golf course designed by golfing legend Arnold Palmer.'[26] Last year it started building 'The Mall of India,' which is deemed to be one of the five biggest malls in the world, and has most recently bagged contracts to build the upcoming expressway and special economic zones (SEZ). Other developers are also active players, but DLF takes the lead.

The frenzied transformation of the city-region is, by all accounts, spectacular, and is largely welcomed by the elite and middle classes of India. Over the last decade, large numbers of middle-class families and business offices from New Delhi and adjoining areas have moved to Gurgaon. What is striking about Gurgaon's rocky and bleak landscape is that amid several construction sites and half-built buildings, all the high-rise luxury condominiums, massive shopping malls, and multiplexes have Western architecture and façades, reflecting a peculiarly modern aesthetic and urban design. For example, most of the condominium complexes in Gurgaon have Western names such as Belair, Silver Oaks, Beverly Park, Hamilton Court, Windsor Court, Florence Marvel, Garden City, Express Greens, Palm Drive, and Magnolias. They are unabashedly marketed as 'ultra-sophisticated,' 'elite,' 'elegant,' 'gated and exclusive,' and for their West-like housing and amenities.[27]

Interestingly, in this remarkable act of city-making, 'nature' is conspicuous. On the one hand, it is conspicuous by its transformation, as more and more bulldozers remake the landscape of Gurgaon, erecting towers and malls in spaces that were used for agricultural purposes not long ago. In a mere 30 years, from 1971 to 2002, the area under agriculture has gone down markedly, from 80.99 per cent to 26.50 per cent of the total, while the built-up area has increased from 8.96 per cent to 66.42 per cent.[28] On the other hand, nature is conspicuous as a ubiquitous referent of a 'good life.' The everyday discourses, images, and advertisements of housing, urban development, and leisure tap into the environmentalist sensibilities and bourgeois desires of the middle classes and evoke nature in countless ways. Developers' descriptions of 'green pastoral settings,' 'lush green surroundings,' and 'acres of green' are commonplace in Gurgaon. For example, consider the advertisement of one of the developers of Suncity Heights:

Ideally located in the heart of Suncity Township, Suncity Heights stands tall in the backdrop of picturesque Aravalli Hills and is designed to perfection for the privileged class. Suncity Heights – a condominium of luxury apartments, is a true symbol of master craftsmanship that promises genuine rewards of high living and modern lifestyle. The single factor that makes Suncity Heights a haven for the discerning lot is that it allows one to experience the height of comfort, joy, peace and luxury in a natural yet technologically advanced setting.[29]

Suncity is not alone in capturing such images of nature. Ansals – a prominent developer – states that 'Ansals as an organization can be envisaged better as a creator of man-made geographies where modern life blossoms, in active collaboration with nature.' In a context where the agrarian-natural landscape of Gurgaon has literally been trans-formed, where the Aravalli Hills have been blasted to make room for such a building boom, it is ironic that the entire real estate industry hinges on the trope of tranquillity and harmony with nature. Yet, what these representations of nature powerfully suggest is how nature is being reconfigured into a commodity that can be deployed for recrea-tion, tranquillity, or pastoral ambience for some of the residents and not others, as I describe below.

A large number of condominium complexes are indeed green and tree-lined, but outside the housing enclaves, it is a different world. This is where the majority of migrant labourers from the neighbouring states of India, who have come to work as construction workers, rickshaw pullers, security guards, drivers, and factory workers, live. A security guard who worked on a 12-hour shift in Suncity had brought his family from West Bengal recently. They lived in a tin shack on the construction site, below ground level. He paid Rs. 500 in rent for that shack. Close to 50 families lived in such temporary structures with no access to water, no electricity, and no toilets. They 'stole' water from the pipes. Another worker, Raza, a 32-year-old male, also from West Bengal, worked in a factory that made medical syringes. He said in an interview that for the last eight months he had been sharing a room with three other men. He worked six days a week, 10 to 12 hours a day, and was paid less than minimum wage. The majority of the labourers interviewed were temporarily employed and earned below minimum wage, while the permanent workers had better wages and benefits. Most had precari-ous access to housing and lived in slum-like conditions; they had poor access to water, electricity, and transportation, and certainly no other basic services, such as health care or education. In this landscape of extremes, the professional classes of Gurgaon thrive in spacious condo-miniums, with access to private water, electricity, golf courses, exclu-sive recreational clubs, private transport, and so on, while the majority live without any basic provisions. Such grave inequality underlines everyday life of Gurgaon, in which 'nature' is the constitutive actor that actively shapes the political geography of denial and deprivation.

Although, as mentioned above, it was a challenge to initiate a conversation with the local urban villagers about nature, the discussion of urban nature was relatively easy with the middle classes. Most new residents who have recently bought apartments or condominiums in Gurgaon, and who work either in Gurgaon or in New Delhi, are fluent English speakers and very conversant with the discourse of nature. For instance, in response to my question 'What do you think of the state of the environment in Gurgaon?' Latika, a 38-year-old garment exporter, said in English, 'Environment, as you know, is a problem here. There is no greenery. It is so barren, dry, and hot here. We just go to the mountains to get away and enjoy nature. Here, there is just too much pollution – air pollution, noise pollution, a serious crisis of water, and then the ongoing problem of garbage! There is hardly any place to walk or place for kids to play. We have to do everything inside the housing complexes; outside, it is still a village, very dirty and not so safe.' This sentiment was repeated by many residents of housing complexes. Like the migrant labourers and village residents, they either insisted that there was no nature in the city, no greenery, or that the 'environment' was a problem.

Environment has indeed become a problem, if recent protests by Resident Welfare Associations (RWA) and the rising number of Public Interest Litigations filed can be taken as a measure. In the last two years alone, RWAs have signed a dozen litigations and citizens have come out to protest against the unruly planning and non-existent infrastructure.[30] Just to provide a glimpse, here is one example. On 27 May 2008, 34 RWAs came together and requested the Supreme Court 'to stop proliferation of commercial complexes and save the city from "complete disaster" as unplanned development had sunk groundwater levels and created a power crisis.'[31] The residents demanded the urgent intervention of the Haryana government to ensure a constant supply of power and water. In their petition, the associations said that malls and other commercial complexes had 'adversely affected' the 'quality of life and environment' and that the situation was becoming 'more acute with each passing day.' The residents complained of '12-hour-long power cuts' and 'a trickle of water less than 30 minutes once a day in the name of water supply.'[32] On 22 September 2008, hundreds of residents of DLF Phase-I in Gurgaon came out to protest the illegal dumping of garbage in an open 60 acres of land close to residential housing.[33] Wearing masks on their faces, they complained of the unbearable stench and of the serious health risk posed by the dump. Constituted of CEOs of corporations, lawyers, academics, retired bureaucrats, and famous cricketers, the agitators took to the streets and demanded that the state and municipal authorities take immediate action. Public Interest Litigations filed earlier had yielded no results. The site was renamed *Kachra Chowk* (Garbage Square). In addition to these protests and litigations, the glaring lack of public transport, the poor conditions of roads, traffic congestion, and very poor air quality have come to raise the ire of middle-class citizens and have presented another picture of Gurgaon's troubled metropolitan nature.

Haryana Urban Development Authority (HUDA), a state body, is supposed to oversee and regulate urban development, but it has clearly not kept pace. There is no public transport, no access to public health clinics (although there are some high-end hospitals), no collection or disposal of garbage, no garbage trucks or bins, no solid or industrial waste treatment plants, no system of sewerage, and no sustainable infrastructure for water or energy. Indeed, in this context, the environment has become a problem, but in different ways for different social groups. While the middle and upper classes have private access to water, energy, health, and education, the urban poor are denied basic access to housing, health, water, energy, sanitation, and education.

Although it is beyond the scope of this chapter to present a detailed discussion of the failures of urban planning and infrastructure, the brief account of the politics of provisions and access to infrastructure in Gurgaon provides an opportunity to make some broader observations about the emergent politics of urban nature in Gurgaon, as well as in other similar cities in the global South.

First, the discussion above describes how the politics of nature is manifested through the politics of infrastructure and inequality. As nature is being reconfigured and deployed for the accumulation and production of global capital, the middle classes are able to secure access to scarce resources such as water and energy while the subaltern groups are left to languish in their meagre margins, inscribing the new cartographies of inequalities of class, place, mobility, and gender. Second, it is critical to note that with the advent of capitalist urbanization, the failed or inadequate infrastructure in the face of enthusiastic expansion of malls, entertainment complexes, SEZs, and expressways is a sign of the ambivalence of the Indian state and even its collusion with the neo-liberal capitalist regime that is increasingly answerable mostly to the middle classes. By relying on private developers, the state has fostered public-private partnerships. Yet again, it is set to serve the corporate interests but has withdrawn from its obligations to the weaker segments of society. Third, as Baviskar[34] has noted, there is a rise of 'bourgeois environmentalism,' in which the middle classes are exercising their class privilege and networks to demand a 'good life.' They are self-servingly mobilizing nature and actively working the legal and political institutions to ensure their own continued social and environmental security. But their interventions have been ad hoc, taking up issues on a case-by-case basis and not aimed at seeking any broader or regional change that could address issues of social and environmental justice and equity. Fourth, the discourse and politics of the 'problem of the environment' are embedded in the discursive binaries of city and nature, of society/nature, and persistently inform the politics of segregation, difference, and exclusion.

The problems of Gurgaon are not unique. They echo every day across cities in the global South. In fact, the questions of urban infrastructure, water and energy management, transportation, hygiene, and waste disposal have emerged as prime issues of our times. With the rapid growth of cities all over the world, these issues have become urgent.

On the other hand, the problems of Gurgaon *are* unique. They are a result of particular historical and spatial changes that have unfolded in Gurgaon at the behest of some very powerful actors who have reorganized the relationship between nature and society in significant ways and have turned the environment into a problem.

Thus, to understand the processes of urbanization currently underway, we must consider the city as being made up of an active and dynamic set of interactive processes – contested, unstable, and proliferating – of society and nature, and attend to the discursive and material politics of urban nature. The view of the city as a hybrid allows us to recognize that in the continuous process of change, new and sometimes unknown networks formed by the complex relations of power and control *produce* the problem of nature. That is, nature is not a problem, but it becomes a problem. Therefore, to understand the contexts and forces that trouble nature, it is critical that we simultaneously attend to the social and natural processes of change and uncover the local, regional, and transnational forces and processes of power that trouble nature. We must map the shifts in the socio-nature relations that have come as a result of political and economic transformations, and develop an alternative understanding of nature and society that does not treat these transformations as exclusive but as constitutionally hybrid and constitutive of nature and society. For it is not the nature of city that is in trouble. It is our society – with its new order tending towards consumption, appropriation, and accumulation – that is at a loss in dealing with social-nature.

NOTES

1 Achille Mbembe and Sarah Nuttall, 'Writing the World from an African Metropolis,' *Public Culture* 16, 3 (2004): 347-72.
2 See Charles Taylor, *Modern Social Imaginaries* (Durham, NC: Duke University Press, 2004).
3 Gurgawan is the term local residents use; Gurgaon is used by newcomers and real estate developers.
4 Henri Lefebvre, *The Production of Space*, trans. Donald Nicholson-Smith (Oxford: Blackwell, 1991), 68.
5 Bruno Latour, *We Have Never Been Modern* (London: Harvester Wheatsheaf, 1993).
6 Donna Haraway, *Simians, Cyborgs, and Women: The Reinvention of Nature* (London: Free Association Press, 1991) and 'The Promise of Monsters: A Regenerative Politics for Inappropriate/d Others,' in *Cultural Studies*, ed. Lawrence Grossberg, C. Nelson, and P. Treicher (New York: Routledge, 1992), 295–332.
7 In geography, see Bruce Braun and Noel Castree, eds., *Remaking Reality: Nature at the Millennium* (London: Routledge, 1998); David Demeritt, 'Science, Social Constructivism, and Nature,' in *Remaking Reality*, ed. Braun and Castree, 173–93; Erik Swyngedouw, 'Modernity and Hybridity: Nature, Regeneracionism, and the Production of Spanish Waterscape, 1890–1930,' *Annals of the Association of American Geographers* 89, 3 (1999): 443–65; Bruce Willems-Braun, 'Buried Epistemologies: The Politics of Nature in (Post)colonial British Columbia,' *Annals of the Association of American Geographers* 87, 1 (1997): 3–31.
8 In anthropology, see Arturo Escobar, 'After Nature: Steps to an Anti-Essentialist Political Ecology,' *Current Anthropology* 40, 1 (1999); Hugh Raffles, *In Amazonia: A Natural History* (Princeton: Princeton University Press, 2002). See also Michael Goldman and Rachel Schurman, 'Closing the "Great Divide": New Social Theory on Society and Nature,' *Annual Review of Sociology* 26 (2000): 563–84.
9 William Cronon, ed., *Uncommon Ground: Toward Reinventing Nature* (New York: W.W. Norton, 1995).
10 Donald Worster, ed., *To the Ends of the Earth: Perspectives on Modern Environ-*

mental History (New York: Cambridge University Press, 1988).

11 Haraway, *Simians, Cyborgs, and Women*, 296; emphasis in original.

12 Swyngedouw, 'Modernity and Hybridity,' 114.

13 In part, the lingering divide between city and village, country and city, rural and urban in social theory and imaginary explains why cities came to be seen as devoid of nature, while the country is overwritten by the images of nature, natural, and the essential. Raymond Williams, *The Country and the City* (New York: Oxford University Press, 1973).

14 Maria Kaika, *City of Flows: Modernity, Nature, and the City* (New York: Routledge, 2005); Maria Kaika and Erik Swyngedouw, 'Fetishizing the Modern City: The Phantasmagoria of Urban Technological Networks,' *International Journal of Urban and Regional Research* 24 (2000): 120–38; Erik Swyngedouw, 'Circulation and Metabolisms: (Hybrid) Natures and (Cyborg) Cities,' *Science as Culture* 15, 2 (2006): 105–21; Matthew Gandy, 'Cyborg Urbanization: Complexity and Monstrosity in the Contemporary City,' *International Journal of Urban and Regional Research* 29, 1 (2005): 26-49; and Matthew Gandy, 'Urban Nature and the Ecological Imaginary,' in *In the Nature of Cities: Urban Political Ecology and the Politics of Urban Metabolism*, ed. Nik Heynen, Maria Kaika, and Erik Swyngedouw (New York: Routledge, 2006); Roger Keil, 'Urban Political Ecology,' *Urban Geography* 24, 8 (2003): 120–38; Roger Keil and J. Graham, 'Reassessing Nature: Constructing Environments after Fordism,' in *Remaking Reality*, ed. Braun and Castree, 100–25.

15 Swyngedouw, 'Circulation and Metabolisms,' 106.

16 Cyborg, as used by Haraway, 'is a hybrid creature, composed of organism and machine. But, cyborgs are compounded of special kinds of machines and special kinds of organisms appropriate to the late twentieth century' (*Simians, Cyborgs, and Women*, 1).

17 Gandy, 'Urban Nature and the Ecological Imaginary,' 64.

18 Gandy, 'Urban Nature and the Ecological Imaginary,' 64. Emphasis added.

19 Mbembe and Nuttall, 'Writing the World from an African Metropolis,' 353.

20 Mbembe and Nuttall, 'Writing the World from an African Metropolis,' 358.

21 Gyan Prakash, 'The Urban Turn,' in *SARAI Reader: The Cities of Everyday Life.* http://www.sarai.net/publications/readers/02-the-cities-of-every-day-life/02urban_turn.pdf (accessed 5 November 2008).

22 In contrast to Gandhi, Nehru, the first prime minister of India, upheld the progressivist narrative of modernization and considered villages to be sites of backwardness and ignorance. In a letter to Gandhi in 1945, Nehru wrote, 'I do not understand why a village should embody truth and non-violence. A village, normally speaking, is backward intellectually and culturally and no progress can be made from a backward environment' (quoted in

Prakash, 'The Urban Turn,' 3). Prakash notes that while Nehru was largely disdainful of the village, there is some evidence that he, too, shared some of Gandhi's idealization of it. Despite Nehru's serious reservations about the ability of the village to usher in progress and modernization, he could not negate the significant differences that marked the village and the city. Importantly, an idealistic and exalted conception of village India provided a powerful moral purchase both to colonists and to nationalists to initiate improvement projects in the geography and sociality of the village.

23 Mbembe and Nuttall, 'Writing the World from an African Metropolis,' 359.
24 M. Davis, *Planet of Slums* (London: Verso, 2006).
25 Gandy, 'Urban Nature and the Ecological Imaginary,' 64.
26 Simon Robinson, 'The Real Estate Mogul Leading India's Charge,' *Time*, 2 August 2007.
27 The forces that have introduced such changes and reconfigured the power geometries of space and capital are beyond the scope of this chapter and are part of another research project.
28 Gupta and Nangia, 'Population Explosion and Land Use Changes in Gurgaon City, a Satellite of Delhi.'
29 http://news.gurgaon-properties.com/suncity-heights-gurgaon (accessed 5 November 2008).
30 Personal communication, Ram Mohan Skadia, May 2008.
31 *The Telegraph*, India, 28 May 2008, 3.
32 *The Telegraph*, India, 28 May 2008, 3.
33 http://www.expressindia.com/latest-news/No-garbage-disposal-Gurgaon-wallows-in-own-filth/325857/ (accessed 1 December 2009).
34 Amita Baviskar, 'Between Violence and Desire: Space, Power, and Identity in the Making of Metropolitan Delhi,' *International Social Science Journal* 55, 175 (2003): 89-98.

PART FOUR

Building on the Vision: Reflecting on Praxis

> The first assignment for any work on the environment is to clarify ques-
> tions … and focus emotion through the lens of logic into practical policy.
> Since the time of Socrates, that happens to be the traditional assignment of
> the discipline of philosophy.
>
> – Lisa Newton and Catherine Dillingham,
> *Watersheds: Classic Cases in Environmental Ethics*

This volume begins with philosophical reflection but, in this final section, we acknowledge that thinking must insert itself directly into social
praxis if it is to be a meaningful exercise. As Socrates situated philosophical dialogue within the *agora*, so too must our discussion about
the natural city reveal itself through the lived world.

The final section of this book begins with architect William Woodworth *Raweno:kwas*'s ancestral Mohawk reflections on the sacred lands
of Toronto, Ontario, Canada. His is a moving testimonial to the power
of place that bears witness to the fact that any natural city must respect
its roots.

David Seamon then presents us with a geography of the lived world
by drawing upon a phenomenological description of 'lively urban
places.' Seamon looks to ways in which natural cities support a sense
of place through specific design features, such as the configuration of
pathways. He also looks to Goethe's phenomenology of science to identify exercises that will help us to *see* cities in a new way. The chapter
aims to bring to light integral relationships between human beings and
their environments that foster a sense of belonging.

Architecture professor and philosopher Robert Mugerauer looks to
the way in which natural organisms interact with their environments

and identifies clues from these examples for more thoughtful urban design principles for a natural city. Drawing from evolutionary theory and empirical studies of organism-environment interactions, he points the reader towards the possibility of developing new tools for the planning and design of healthier human settlements, informed by the complex intricacies of the natural world.

Bryan W. Karney and Gaurav Kumar, who work within the field of engineering, investigate natural cities from the perspective of energy use, suggesting specific strategies for more sustainable energy management in our urban areas. The authors argue that there is a need to reduce the rift that has developed in modern, technological cities between the scale of energy use and larger-scale consequences. The chapter argues that we must find ways in which to bring the full scope and implications of energy use back into terms that are legible and meaningful on an immediate, human level.

The final chapter in the book looks to the future, focusing on children's visions of a natural city. Based on a case study of 9- to 14-year-olds living along the corridor of the Lake Ontario Waterfront Trail, the research undertaken by Sarah J. King and Ingrid Leman Stefanovic included interviews and field observations as well as the analysis of art projects, poems, and reflective essays prepared by the children. While virtually all participants emphasized the importance of integrating the natural world into urban environments, their perceptions of 'nature' were quite varied, with many relying implicitly upon strongly manicured visions of the natural environment. Some recommendations for strategies relating to education conclude the chapter.

Greek architect and planner Constantinos Doxiadis once wrote that 'cities are living organisms which are 10,000 years old and cannot be changed by magic solutions. They have to be helped to develop better, as every good physician or psychiatrist tries to help his patient. This is our great task: to build better cities.'[1] It is through a combination of thoughtful reflection – but also, as this section shows, through learning from praxis – that we can move forward towards building better natural cities.

NOTE

1 Constantinos A. Doxiadis, *Building Entopia* (Athens: Athens Publishing Centre, 1975), 56.

14 Urban Place as an Expression of the Ancestors

WILLIAM WOODWORTH *RAWENO:KWAS*

Many of us feel an inexpressible and subtle estrangement from urban places here in North America. Understanding the city in the indigenous mind can recover for each of us our profound natural relationship to place and a renewed sense of commitment to it.

As an architect, an archaeological consultant, and a person of both British and Mohawk[1] descent, born of and living on the land of my native Iroquoian Ancestors, I have learned to observe and interpret the modern city as an unconscious expression of the intentions of the Aboriginal Ancestors of its place. This naturally arising knowledge is founded in cultural and experiential forms of understanding that coincide with material evidence. All land is sacred in this understanding. Our human occupation has the capacity to participate in the sanctification of a place through the intention with which we occupy, and indeed weave and nestle ourselves into, the environmental field – earth, sky, water, air, fire – on the body of our Mother, Earth. This indigenous way of knowing finds spontaneous and compelling expression in a place named completely in the Mohawk language of my Ancestors – *Toron:to* (*dolon-do*), *Ontar:io* (*ondar-io*), *Cana:da* (*gana-da*).[2] This chapter will explore contemporary urban place as an unconscious streaming of traditional indigenous ways of knowing. *Toron:to* will be used as a demonstration of the expression of *Hotinonshon:ni*[3] forms of socio-political structure, spiritual addressing, and even prophecy.

About 100 kilometres west of *Toron:to* are the remnants of a once great political confederacy and the most comprehensive sanctuary of one of the great cultures of the planet and certainly of North America, or *Turtle Island*.[4] The Iroquois were among the first to greet the great waves of seekers and refugees from Europe.[5] I am a Mohawk *Ganiagahega* member of the Six Nations of the Grand River near Brantford, Ontario. There the people now live as refugees, some still confined to the reservation system and the Indian Act, from the original homelands in what is now upstate New York. For us and our longhouse relations (Tobacco, Petun, Erie, Neutral, and Huron) here on the north side of our sacred waters *Ontar:io*, we have had to call in our Ancestors and spirits for constant assistance in the struggle to maintain our sovereignty and identity as a distinct people in a virtual global community visited upon our homelands. I myself have some British ancestry, which I honour and respect. However, living here on the remains of my native Ancestors, I have a particular duty to them. What I have to share with you is out of respect for them, a respect that I hope can be shared by all of us one day.

We are all addressing in this book the idea of relationship in one form or another – our connection to the natural world. We humans, '*those who walk about on two legs*,' build community in a type of conversation with the natural world. The archaeological evidence reveals a vast number of settlements of my longhouse relations over the past thousand years within the contemporary boundaries of the *Toron:to* metropolitan area. Before that, our Algonquian relations, the *Anishinaabe*, lived here for 10,000 years. They, too, are still here. Since then, in a period just over 200 years, other forms of kinship have been laid down on their remains – namely, the modern city settled in vast migrations from culturally alien places, particularly, this city. My Ancestors named this place after the carcass of a great fallen tree, probably as tall as a modern 30-storey building. Resting on the forest floor, its hollowed torso served as simple shelter, a ceremonial place for the women, and then became remembered as a great landmark or 'meeting place.' The name has stayed and taken on another meaning predicted in the prophecies of our own spiritual messenger *Deganawedah*.[6]

The principal premise of this chapter is that an urban place, *Toron:to*, can continue to express the presence and even intentions of its place-specific Aboriginal Ancestors – their known material remains held in the land, recovered and recorded in modern practices of archaeology. Intangible and even improbable as this notion may seem in the dissociation that can come from migration – after all, this place is occupied principally by others who can claim an ancestral homeland elsewhere – I am here, witness to my Native relations, to help read the Aboriginal text of this urban space. Most people here now remain largely unconscious of the potential meaning of what has been built here.

First, let me share with you the salient features of our *Hotinonshon:ni* longhouse culture, which continues to inform the occupation of this place in a kind of *unconscious streaming of the Ancestors*. In our own migrations northward from among our corn-bearing relations as far south as the Mayans, the *Hotinonshon:ni* peoples found a beautiful 'nest' in the landscape and climate around a body of fresh water, which came to be held sacred. Our own spiritual messenger was born on the north shore of *Ontar:io* along the Bay of Quinte. This wise man, *Deganawedah*, took up pilgrimages first across Huronia and then in a white stone canoe, as the story is told, across the great freshwater lake and into and across what is now upstate New York. Visiting first individuals and later separate tribal communities, he convinced five strong nations to come together in a form of consensus-building democratic community. This community was contemporary with similar forms developing in Europe, although, spiritually, it was based on matrilineal lines. The important ways in which Aboriginal government informed the construction of the new North American democracies is widely acknowledged today.[7] The Great Law of Peace, as it is known, is simultaneously an integrated form of personal, communal, cultural, and spiritual consensus-building principles. We still practise these and a later form of teaching embodied in the message of Handsome Lake *Scanadar:io*[8] in the longhouses at Six Nations, where I learned. We have just two principal forms of ceremony, held with the assistance of wampum strings and belts woven of light and dark cylindrical shell beads, which are mnemonic devices for accuracy in the oral tradition. The first of these is Thanksgiving, which is carried out with the assistance of tobacco burning, and is comprised of gratitude for the many forms of Creation beginning on the earth and ending in the sky. The other, Condolence, addresses the needs of the people in loss and transition. The many forms of comforting and transference in the Condolence meet every daily situation, including encounters with strangers wandering on our lands.

My own mentor and teacher, Jake Thomas, guided me to seek my duty in a daily tobacco offering and inspired me to receive the messages held in the modern landscape of our ancestral homeland. Perhaps because I am an architect, the Ancestors communicated to me the language of the built form. They are often compassionate to those in a 'good mind.' I created a drawing to condense the architectural science of my longhouse culture.[9]

The ancient longhouse is placed in a field of the cardinal directions – east-west – under a sky field draped by the path of the Ancestors – the

Milky Way (our galaxy). It is surmounted by the star system of the seven dancing brothers – the Pleiades – by which we monitor the cycles of our ceremonies, which are built on the planting and growing seasons. We see Sky Woman falling into the vast waters of our Creation onto the turtle's back, and finally we see the animals of our clans coming out of the woods and to the door of the longhouse. Next to it is the modern longhouse, modelled on eighteenth-century colonial meeting houses of the Quakers.[10] The interiors of the ancient longhouse can still be experienced in reconstructions, where one can observe the smoke holes as sky monitors while the shifting shafts of sunlight ring the interior in a form of time-watching.[11]

With this kind of relational architecture as a model and inspiration, I began to observe the skyline of *Toron:to* in my regular tobacco offerings along the shore at what is called Ashbridge's Bay, just east of the city core.[12] What began to reveal itself to me astounded me. The shaft of the CN Tower, still one of the tallest (533.33 metres) towers on the planet, is in the form of an Aboriginal sending and receiving device, a kind of prayer staff reaching out for the aid of the unseen spirits who assist us, even unconsciously. Directly below is a circular gathering place that opens to the sky field, the great informer of the Ancestors, formerly named the SkyDome. Like a great womb, it gathers great numbers of us in a form of communal rebirth.

Toron:to has at its core seven principal tall structures innocently conceived in their simple differentiation. Each is a different form and colour gathered roughly around an axis of the six directions at the intersection of King and Bay Streets, the financial heart of the country. In the north we have a white building, the Bank of Montreal, the Aboriginal place of wisdom. In the west we have a black building, the Toronto Dominion Centre, the native home of the Ancestors who have gone before us. In the south we have a yellow building, the Royal Bank, in the place of contentment in life here on Earth. In the east we have a red building, the Bank of Nova Scotia, the place of the coming faces, the place of birth.

These are the colours in the Lakota tradition of the four directions and the four great races of the planet that were shared with us at Six Nations. They are founded deep in the earth (foundations) and reach high into the sky (skyscrapers and towers), thus completing the six directions. In the centre is a silver building, the Canadian Imperial Bank of Commerce, which stands as a mnemonic for the agreement between the *Hotinonshon:ni* and the British colonial government, rendered in a silver covenant chain, which they exchanged for our Two Row wampum.

We carry on this agreement in a silver tradition still rendered at Six Nations.

At BCE Place, the courtyard, evocative of the forest designed by Santiago Calatrava, is, in a modern form of the longhouse, oriented east-west. On either side of this great space are representations of men and women: on the south side stands a phallic tower, and on the north a building that transforms into a double-breasted tower gesturing to the sky.

Even today, Iroquoian men and women sit on either side of the longhouse. Is this mere coincidence, or a form of inevitable, irresistible, unconscious remembering – the mechanisms left to the Ancestors? This is my understanding; in my duty to them, I have conceptualized a response.

The modern occupation of the great Oak Ridges moraine watershed – including the remains of the salmon run now known as the Don River, and the great landfill of the marsh that was at its mouth – can be seen in a satellite image. This marsh was held in place by a sandbar that is still intact at the foot of Cherry Street, along the only stretch of original shoreline in the downtown core.

For me, the beginning of the answer to this call of my Aboriginal Ancestors, and the beginning of the healing of the profound rift between the indigenous and the Western mind, will come in the resumption of our traditional duties on our homeland. First among these in this process will be a greeting and ceremonial resumption of our natural relationship to those who have oppressed and forgotten us. We can remind each other of our responsibilities to this land and each other by renewing and repeating the ancient greeting ceremony that we call *At the Woods' Edge*. This form of our traditional Condolence is for those found wandering far from home and seeking a place with us on our land – a greeting that is at once descriptive, comforting, healing, and transformative. We, in essence, 'clean you up' before inviting you back to our longhouse community. Following this ceremony comes celebration in feasting and gift exchanges of all kinds, adoption, and naming.

Along this original sandbank, I have chosen an area for a developing sacred site, the setting for the ceremonies, in contemporary forms of traditional sacred architecture. A round lodge in the *Anishnabe* tradition woven among the branches of a tree will form the centrepiece. Here, models of the city through a cycle of 20,000 years – 10,000 in the past, following the receding of the glacial icefields, and 10,000 years into a projected future – will remind us of the cyclical nature of our occupation here through time. Embracing this cosmic tree space are the arms of two longhouses in the *Hotinonshon:ni* tradition, anchored by continually burning sacred fires where feasting, gift exchanges, and adoptions will accompany the ceremonies. These, in turn, are embraced by two large staghorn sumac bushes, the traditional place of teaching.[13]

The ceremonies themselves will be modelled on our cylindrical calendar, each dedicated to the greeting of peoples in their unique ancestries.

The prophecies of *Deganawedah* indicated that we would have to welcome peoples from the four directions of the four great white roots of the white pine tree to sit in consensus-building council together in a circle under its lowest branches. Under these roots, all weapons shall be buried in the spirit of peace. Our 50 chiefs will lead the council there; behind them, the clan mothers who chose them will monitor their behaviours. Today – in a developing global community led by the empowerment of women, accompanied by the sounds of tribal techno music in the nightclubs, and led by a new tribe, us, once again tattooed and pierced in their identities – we are fulfilling this vision. The epitome of it is found here at *Toron:to*.

During the depths of the economic depression of the last century, the American architect Frank Lloyd Wright conceptualized an ideal community here in North America. He named it Broadacre. Every family would have an acre of land, and could raise much of its own food. At the centre of the city, Wright placed a great round meeting place, (shown in the illustration for this volume, on the University of Toronto Press website) in model form. In the west, he placed a tall freestanding tower, the tallest built object in the city. On the drawing for the plan that accompanied his drawing, he labelled it Item 31A, and named it 'A Totem and a Beacon to the Lost Tribes of a Continent.'[14]

In May 1999, during a research visit to Taliesin West in Arizona, I met with one of Wright's apprentices, Cornelia Brierly, who travelled with the model of Broadacre City when it toured in 1935. I asked her what Wright meant by this description of the tower. She replied in a word: 'Atonement.' In his vision, Wright proposed remembering, and consciously raised what we have unconsciously replicated here in *Toron:to* as the CN Tower.

Another great American visionary, the architect Louis Kahn, said in a letter to a friend,

What was has always been.
What is has always been.
What will be has always been.[15]

I conclude with a statement from the great visionary and former Canadian prime minister, Pierre Elliott Trudeau, who said in 1982, 'I speak of a Canada where men and women of Aboriginal ancestry, of French and British heritage, of the diverse cultures of the world, demonstrate the will to share the land in peace, in justice, and with mutual respect.'[16]

It falls to us, in response to the Ancestors and to these two great men, to participate in the ongoing conversation with those who have gone on before us, and who have left us with a beautiful legacy that we are in the transformative process of conveying to the future!

Nai:wen Akwegon Skennen. Thank you. All Our Relations. Peace. As we say in our *Hotinonshon:ni* language, *onen edoh* – 'that's all I have to say at this time.'

NOTES

1 The Mohawk Nation is a part of the Iroquoian Confederacy formulated over a thousand years ago under the Great Law of Peace brought to us in forms of spiritual messenging of *Deganawedah*, or the Peacemaker. The metaphorical longhouse referred to as *Hotinonshon:ni* (people who build the longhouse) was the vast landscape of what is now New York State, from the Hudson River to the Finger Lakes. The Mohawks and Senecas were 'keepers of the eastern and western doors' respectively. The central 'fire keepers' were the Onondagas. The 'younger brothers' who lived among us were the Oneidas and the Cayugas. They are exiled today as a Confederacy at Six Nations of the Grand River, Ontario. The 'sixth nation' is the Tuscaroras, who were adopted when they were left without a homeland during colonization.

2 The colon is inserted to denote the Aboriginal intonation and will be used throughout the rest of this chapter. Toron:to can be interpreted as 'the place where great tree fell – the damp log,' Ontar:io as 'the beautiful waters – sacred,' and Cana:da as 'the village.'

3 *Hotinonshon:ni* is the native way by which Iroquoian people name themselves. It means literally 'the people who build a longhouse.'

4 The term flows from the Iroquois Creation, whereby the land is founded by a woman who falls from the sky onto the back of a turtle.

5 Cartier met Iroquoians from Stadacona (Quebec City) while exploring the Gaspé in 1534. The Beothuks, now extinct, were likely the first to be encountered by Europeans, according to Olive Dickason, *Canada's First*

Nations: A History of Founding Peoples from Earliest Times (Norman: University of Oklahoma Press, 1992).

6 *Deganawedah*, or The Peacemaker, was born at Eagle Hill in modern-day Bay of Quinte at the Mohawk community of Tyendenagea. He originated and taught our ceremonies there and brought the Wendats into a confederacy and later united the Five Nations into the Haudenosaunee Confederacy. Today, the recitation of The Great Law of Peace is told in a nine-day ceremony, which has traditionally taken place every two years. The last comprehensive speaker of The Great Law, Jacob Ezra Thomas, Cayuga Chief *Teyohonwedah*, passed on in 1998 at Six Nations of the Grand River. His last telling in English was in 1996. I participated in that ceremony and base my interpretation of The Great Law in my experience of the oral traditional he held.

7 Bruce E. Johansen, *Forgotten Founders: How the American Indian Helped Shape Democracy* (Boston: Harvard Common Press, 1982).

8 Another form of spiritual message came to the Seneca, and the other Nations of the Confederacy, in the form of the teachings of *Skanadar:io* (Handsome Lake), known today as the Code.

9 Detailed illustrations relating to this article are available on the University of Toronto Press website.

10 Handsome Lake, with the assistance of the Quakers and Jesuits, consolidated forms of practice that are still carried on in longhouse culture at Six Nations.

11 In *Ontar:io* they can be seen at Crawford Lake Conservation Area and the Kanata Village in Brantford.

12 Ashbridge's Bay is actually a modern infill project that forms a lakeside park named after the vast wetland at the mouth of the Don River, which is now itself filled in and forms the Portlands.

13 The deer is considered the animal closest to the Creator; hence, our Chiefs wear the tips of their horns on their headdresses or *gustowahs*. These act as sending and receiving devices to the spirits and the Creator. Sumac branches, which are similar to the furry staghorns, are considered to house the most potent places in which to teach.

14 Frank Lloyd Wright, *The Living City* (New York: Horizon Press, 1958).

15 Letter to Karel Mikolas, November 1973, as reproduced in Richard Saul Wurman, *What Will Be Has Always Been: The Words of Louis I. Kahn* (New York: ACCESSPress and Rizzoli, 1986).

16 Provided to me by the staff at the Canada Pavilion at Harbourfront, Toronto.

15 Seeing and Animating the City: A Phenomenological Ecology of Natural and Built Worlds

DAVID SEAMON

Ecology, both as a science and as a world view, emphasizes the study of relationships, interconnections, and environmental wholes that are different from the sum of their environmental parts.[1] 'Special qualities emerge out of interactions and collectivities,' writes intellectual historian Donald Worster in his *Nature's Economy*, a history of ecological ideas in the Western world.[2]

The central question I address here is this: What do the relationships, interconnections, and environmental wholes of ecology become in a phenomenological perspective and what might this understanding mean for examining and improving the 'natural city'?[3] To explore this question, I consider one phenomenon from the natural world – colour – and one phenomenon from the human-made world – lively urban places. I think it important to offer an example from both natural and built worlds because a 'phenomenological ecology,' as it might be called, must be responsive to all lived relationships and interconnections, examining and describing the ways that things, living forms, people, events, situations, and worlds come together to make environmental and human wholes, including cities.[4]

By lively urban places, I refer to city neighbourhoods and districts that provide easy access for pedestrians and that generate, just by being what they are, chance face-to-face encounters, sidewalk life, and a sense of taken-for-granted safety because many people are present. If, in part, one means by 'natural city' an urban environment of exuberant street life in which both 'outsiders' and 'insiders' feel comfortable and at home, then one crucial aim is an accurate understanding of lively urban places and ways, through education, design, and policy, whereby they might be created and intensified. To delineate a phenomenology of lively urban places, I turn to my own work on the bodily dimensions of environmental experience and action, especially as the lived body comes to know its everyday environment through the regularity and routine of extended time-space patterns contributing to the transformation of physical space into lived place. I also emphasize, after architectural theorist Bill Hillier, that the physical structure of place, particularly the spatial configuration of its pathways, plays a major role in establishing whether streets are well used and animated or empty and lifeless.[5] In terms of relationships, interconnections, and environmental wholes, this discussion of lively urban places indicates how a particular fit between people and world contributes to a larger environmental whole of interpersonal encounter, sociability, and place attachment.

If the natural city necessarily incorporates animated street life, it might also incorporate ways whereby the world of nature is regularly accessible to its residents and users – for example, tree-lined streets, handsomely landscaped plazas, or ready access to urban waterways. Here, I give attention to a more subtle phenomenon of the natural city – the experience of colour, which I explore through the insightful proto-phenomenology of German dramatist and poet Johann Wolfgang von Goethe (1749–1832), who devised a qualitative way of seeing and understanding that can rightly be called a phenomenology of the natural world. Most significantly for a phenomenological understanding of relationships, interconnections, and environmental wholes, Goethe's work demonstrates how light and colour involve an underlying 'belonging' seen in perceptual presence, but comprehended only through a moment of insight in which all the parts are understood together and have a fitting place. Goethe's approach to seeing intimates a style of encounter with the natural city whereby the seemingly ordinary – for example, coloured shadows cast by city streetlights – suddenly becomes vividly seen and delightful. At least for a moment, we realize the wondrous quality of the everyday urban world in which we find ourselves.

A Geography of the Lifeworld

As a geographer and environment-behaviour researcher in a department of architecture, my main teaching and research emphasis relates to the nature of environmental behaviour and experience, especially in terms of the built environment. I am interested in why places are important for people and how architecture and environmental design can be a vehicle for urban place making. These research topics became important to me when I was working on my doctorate in behavioural geography in the late 1970s. My dissertation, revised and published in 1979 as *A Geography of the Lifeworld*, focused on a wide-ranging phenomenon that I called *everyday environmental experience* – the sum total of people's first-hand involvements with their everyday places, spaces, and environments.[6] My source of experiential descriptions was *environmental experience groups*, small groups of volunteer participants who were willing to meet weekly to examine in their own daily experience such themes as movement patterns, emotions relating to place, the nature of noticing and attention, the meaning of home and at-homeness, places for things, deciding where to go when, and so forth.

Through a phenomenological explication of some 1,500 personal observations offered in these environmental experience groups, I eventually arrived at three overarching themes – *movement*, *rest*, and *encounter* – that appeared to mark the essential core of everyday environmental experience. To move towards a phenomenology of lively urban places, I summarize the book's conclusions on everyday movement. One of the first themes that came forth in the environmental experience groups was the importance of habitual movement in everyday life. Group observations suggested that, regardless of the particular environmental scale at which they happen, many movements are conducted by some preconscious impulse that guides actions without the person's need to be consciously aware of their happening.

'Body-subject' is the term that French phenomenologist Maurice Merleau-Ponty used to describe the intentional but taken-for-granted intelligence of the body.[7] 'Consciousness,' he wrote, 'is being toward the thing through the intermediary of the body. A movement is learned when the body has understood it, that is, when it has incorporated it into its "world," and to move one's body is to aim at things through it; it is to allow oneself to respond to their call.'[8]

Though Merleau-Ponty said very little about larger-scale actions of body-subject, observations from the environmental experience groups pointed to its versatility as expressed in more complex movements and behaviours extending over time and space. One such behaviour indicated by group observations is what I called *body ballet* – a set of integrated gestures, behaviours, and actions that sustains a particular task or aim: for example, preparing a meal, driving a car, doing home repair, and so forth. Also identified was what I labelled a *time-space rou-*

tine – a set of more or less habitual bodily actions that extends through a considerable portion of time – for example, a getting-up routine or a weekday going-to-lunch routine.

Most important for the phenomenon of lively urban places, group observations suggested that, in a supportive physical environment, individual body ballets and time-space routines may fuse together in a larger whole, creating an environmental dynamic that I called, after the earlier observations of urban critic Jane Jacobs, a *place ballet* – an interaction of time-space routines and body ballets rooted in space, which often becomes an important place of interpersonal and communal exchange and meaning.[9] Place ballet may occur at all manner of environmental scales – inside, outside; at the level of neighbourhood, street, public space, building interior, and so forth. A popular and well-used plaza such as New York City's Greenacre Park may be the scene of place ballet,[10] or it may be an animated stretch of city street,[11] or a weekly outdoor market,[12] or a popular café or tavern.[13] Place ballet should not be envisioned as a regimented ensemble of robot-like participants moving about in mindless precision but, rather, as a fluid environmental dynamic that allows for temporal give and take as participants are present more or less regularly, at more or less the same times. Newcomers, outsiders, and less-frequent participants may contribute to place ballet, but its foundation is some degree of environmental and temporal regularity founded in body-subject.

Spatial Configuration and Place Ballet

I next consider how qualities of the world, particularly its physical, potentially designable features, might sustain and enhance the time-space manifestations of body-subject, including place ballet. One body of work significant for addressing this question is architectural theorist Bill Hillier's theory of space syntax, which provides convincing conceptual and empirical evidence that the physical-spatial environment plays an integral part in sustaining active streets and an urban sense of place.[14]

Though Hillier's work is not phenomenological but structural and analytic, it has crucial significance phenomenologically because it demonstrates how a world's underlying spatial structure, or 'configuration,' as Hillier calls it, guides particular actions and circulations of human bodies moving through that world, and how, in turn, a self-conscious understanding of this human world/physical world intimacy might lead to environmental design and policy that supports a stronger sense of place and community.[15]

In his work, Hillier asks whether there is some 'deep structure of the city itself' that contributes to urban life.[16] He finds this deep structure in the relationship between spatial configuration and natural co-presence – that is, the way the spatial layout of pathways can informally and automatically bring people together in urban space or keep them apart: 'By its power to generate movement, spatial design creates a fundamental pattern of co-presence and co-awareness, and therefore potential encounter amongst people that is the most rudimentary form of our awareness of others.'[17] I have argued above that the lived basis for this human movement and co-presence may be in many instances the regularity of habitual bodies. Drawing on Hillier's work, we can examine how these habitual bodies do or do not make use of particular pathways, largely because of the particular spatial configuration of those pathways.

In seeking to understand the ways that pathway configuration relates to human movement, co-presence, and encounter, Hillier develops the concept of 'axial space,' which relates to linear qualities of space. Axial spaces are illustrated most perfectly by long, narrow streets, and can be represented geometrically by the maximum straight line that can be drawn through an open space before it strikes a building, wall, or some other material object. For example, the axial map for the small southern French village of Gassin, one of the first settlements that Hillier studied, is illustrated in figure 15.1.

Partly through quantitative and computer analysis, Hillier concludes that axial spaces are significant for understanding a settlement's *global* pattern – that is, the way the particular spatial configuration of a pathway fabric lays out a potential movement field that draws people together or keeps them apart.[18] 'Natural movement' is the term Hillier uses to describe the potential power of the pathway layout to automatically stymie or facilitate movement and such related environmental events as co-presence, co-awareness, informal interpersonal encounters, and animated street activity.[19]

To establish precisely the amount of natural movement that a particular pathway configuration potentially generates, Hillier introduces the concepts of 'integrated' and 'segregated' pathways. As illustrated in figure 15.2, the former is a pathway that makes itself readily accessible to many other pathways and therefore is *shallow* in relation to them. In other words, many other pathways as well as the users on

Figure 15.1. Axial map for the small French village of Gassin generated by drawing the longest possible lines through the settlement's outdoor fabric of streets, plazas, and other public spaces. From Hillier and Hanson, *The Social Logic of Space*, 91. Reprinted with the permission of Cambridge University Press.

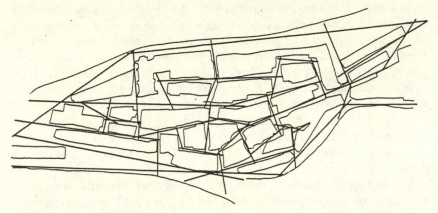

these pathways feed into this pathway; thus, it is well integrated in relation to the surrounding grid structure, and more than likely a well-used route along which many people travel. In contrast, few or no other routes feed into *segregated* pathways, which are poorly accessible and *deep* in relation to the surrounding grid. Segregated pathways typically are dead ends or elements in tree-like grids; one thinks, for example, of the 'cul-de-sac and loop' pattern of low-density, automobile-dependent suburbs, or the hierarchical circulation layouts of many modernist housing estates.

To measure and map the relative integration of all pathways in a particular pathway system, Hillier develops a quantitative procedure that he calls 'measure of integration.'[20] One product of this procedure is an integration map, like the one for Gassin in figure 15.3, which summarizes the most integrated and most segregated pathways in the village. The streets marked by solid lines depict the village's 'integration core' – those streets that have many other streets feeding into them. These streets have the highest probability of being alive with street activity, public life, and commerce. In contrast, the hatched lines identify Gassin's 'segregation core' – the streets that deflect activity away from themselves and therefore indicate pockets of quiet and seclusion that are typically residential in character.[21]

Figure 15.2. Integrated and segregated pathways. In this hypothetical street grid, street 1 is the most integrated pathway, since 10 other streets feed into it directly. On the other hand, street 3 is most segregated, since it is a dead end. Street 2 is more integrated than street 3 but less integrated than street 1. All other factors being equal (e.g., density, placement of functions, and building types), street 1 will carry the most pedestrians.

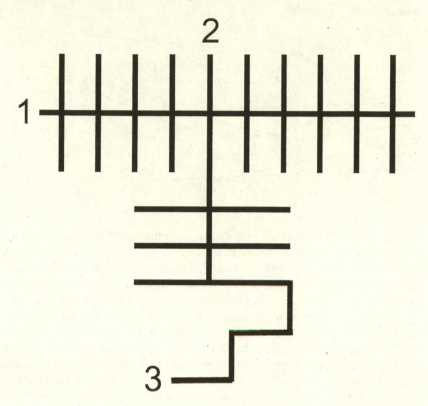

Hillier next considers whether these lines of greater and lesser integration indicate some deeper configurational structure underlying the settlement as a whole. In fact, after studying the integration and segregation cores of many settlements, both Western and non-Western, Hillier concludes that such a larger global structure exists. He calls it the 'deformed wheel' (see figure 15.3). The rim, spokes, and hub of this wheel are the pathways with high integration values (in figure 15.3, the

Figure 15.3. Gassin's 'deformed wheel.' Note that the streets of greatest integration (and thus most potential movement) are marked by the solid lines,
whose shape roughly suggests a wheel and spokes; in contrast, the hatched
lines indicate streets of greater segregation, which, overall, are residential and
between the more active thoroughfares. From Hillier and Hanson, *The Social
Logic of Space*, 117. Reprinted with the permission of Cambridge University
Press.

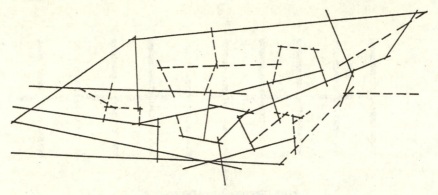

solid lines). Typically, these streets are the most used by a settlement's
residents. They are also the main entry routes, and are therefore used
by 'outsiders' – for example, a farmer bringing his produce to weekly
market or tourists exploring the settlement. Also, most of the largest
public spaces and location-dependent uses, such as shops, eateries, and
offices, are on the most integrated streets of the deformed wheel, since
these streets are the places of greatest movement.

In the interstices between the most active streets are typically found
the more segregated, less used pathways (in figure 15.3, the hatched
lines). Hillier concludes that, for many traditional settlements, the most
active areas abut the quietest areas: the places of street life, publicness,
and strangers mixing with residents are a short distance from the more
private areas used mostly by residents only. Movement and rest, activity and place, journey and dwelling, difference and locality, publicness
and home lie apart, yet together!

In regard to cities, Hillier demonstrates that most urban pathway systems have traditionally been an integrated fabric of smaller deformed
wheels (usually associated with designated neighbourhoods and districts – for example, London's Soho, Bloomsbury, or City). Their most
integrated pathways join together to shape a much larger deformed

grid that founds the dynamic of natural movement for the city as a whole.[22] '[E]ach local area,' explains Hillier, 'has its heart linked to the supergrid lines that surround it by strong integrators. These form an edge-to-centre structure in all directions, and the less-integrated areas are within the interstices formed by the structure.'[23]

Hillier is highly critical of most twentieth-century urban design and planning because it often eviscerated this relationship between local and global integration by replacing integrated pathway configurations with tree-like systems of segregated pathways. The long-term result is that these 'spatial designs create serious lacunas in natural movement,' which in turn undermines the informal sociability of streets and neighbourhoods and may in time attract 'anti-social uses and behaviours' – for example, unsafe streets and higher crime rates, particularly in the maze-like pathway systems of many post–Second World War public housing projects.[24] From a place ballet perspective, one can say that the possibility of individual habitual bodies easily coming together in co-presence has been greatly compromised because the particular pathway configuration does not direct movement from less integrated pathways onto more integrated pathways that would then become spaces of animated pedestrian activity.

Relationships, Interconnections, Wholes, and Place Ballet

What does this discussion of lively urban place as interpreted through place ballet and space syntax say about relationships, interconnections, and environmental wholes interpreted phenomenologically? First, in terms of relationships, one can say that place ballet automatically gathers time, space, and people's needs through the taken-for-granted unfolding of bodily regularity. Both the result and the source of this tacit unfolding is a series of automatic interconnections: between an individual's routine and others' routines; between those routines and the settings, origins, and destinations in which and for which the routines unfold; between body-subject's actions and a supportive spatial configuration incorporating some pathways that are well used and lively, and other pathways, traditionally residential, that are less used and quiet. The result is an environmental whole that is integrated, ordered, alive, and a new entity of place considerably greater than its human and environmental parts.

This phenomenology of lively urban places indicates how a particular fit between people (specifically, habitual bodies) and world (specifically, particular pathway structure) supports physical co-presence and potential encounter that may facilitate sociability and a sense of community and neighbourhood. Hillier's demonstration of how a particular pattern of spatial configuration – the deformed grid – has the potential to found a nexus of lively pedestrian movement illustrates in a remarkably new way the basic phenomenological principle that people are immersed in world as world is immersed in people.

In relation to habitual bodies gathering in space that is transformed into place, Hillier's work concludes that a major need is *permeability* – the relative accessibility of a place, which in turn relates to the number of alternative routes running through that place and the potential amount of human movement, exchange, and interaction thus facilitated. Such an interconnected pathway network, on the one hand, encourages ease of access and greater spread of movement; on the other hand, a permeable network discourages inefficient movement and the frustration of impenetrability. Design-wise, the setting most likely to facilitate place ballet involves well-connected streets, small blocks, mixed uses, and humanly scaled buildings whose footprints, entries, and windows have a direct relationship to the sidewalk and street.[25]

In today's North American context, where the minimally permeable, low-density, functionally separated suburb is the norm, the need is fine-grained, mixed-use, gridded neighbourhoods that potentially have the power to rekindle informal interpersonal interactions, lively streets, and neighbourhood place ballet. One controversial example is the 'New Urbanism' – a design effort to create walkable, mixed-use neighbourhoods with coherent public spaces sustaining informal sociability.[26]

Having considered lively urban places as one way to focus the phenomenological meaning of relationships, interconnections, and environmental wholes, I next turn to Goethe's way of science as a means to explore a phenomenon of the natural world – the appearance of colour. With that discussion in place, I can conclude by seeking broader implications of these two phenomenologies, thus identifying more general qualities and patterns of relationships, interconnections, and wholes indicated by phenomenological explication.

Goethe's Way of Science

Though Johann Wolfgang von Goethe is much better known as a poet and playwright, he also produced a considerable body of scientific work that focused on such aspects of the natural world as light, colour,

Table 15.1. Questions to keep in mind for Goethean looking and seeing.

• What do I see?
• What is happening?
• What is this saying?
• How is this coming to be?
• What belongs together?
• What remains apart?
• How does this belong together with itself?
• Is it itself?
• Can I read this in itself?

plants, clouds, weather, and geology.[27] In its time, Goethe's way of science was highly unusual because it moved away from a quantitative, analytic approach to the natural world and emphasized, instead, an intimate first-hand encounter between the student and thing studied.

To illustrate Goethe's approach to seeing and understanding things in nature, I focus on his work dealing with light and colour because it offers perhaps the clearest explication of Goethe's style of phenomenological method. Sceptical of Newton's colour theory (which claimed that colours are contained in colourless light and arise, for example, through refraction in a prism), Goethe began his studies of colour in the late 1780s and published the results of his work, *Theory of Colours* (*Zur Farbenlehre*), in 1810.[28] The crux of his colour theory is its experiential source: rather than impose theoretical statements (as he felt Newton had done), Goethe sought a means to allow light and colour to reveal themselves directly through our own human experience.

To understand Goethe's style of looking and seeing, I focus on the prism experiments in part two of *Theory of Colours*. These simple but demanding exercises are a helpful way to introduce students to phenomenological looking, because a phenomenon is present – the appearance of colour in a prism. Although most people are unfamiliar with this phenomenon, it can be readily examined, described, and verified through sustained work with the prisms. Table 15.1 indicates the kinds of questions to keep in mind in doing these experiments and, for that matter, for all Goethean science.

Participants are asked to begin simply by looking through the prism, seeking to become more and more familiar with what they see. They record their observations in words and coloured drawings. Ideally, the experiments are done by a group of four or five, so that participants can share their observations and bring forth descriptive claims that other

Table 15.2. Some examples of accurate descriptive statements arising from looking through a prism.

> - Black, white, and uniformly pure surfaces show no colour through the prism; rather, colours appear only at edges, which can be defined as places of contrast made by darkness and lightness.
> - Colours, however, do not appear along all edges; rather, they appear only along edges that are more or less parallel to the axis of the prism.
> - The more marked and strong the edge of darkness and light, the brighter and more lively the colours.
> - Usually, the colours at the edges arrange themselves in two different groups: a yellow-orange-red group and a blue-indigo-violet group.
> - Less frequently, the colours green and magenta appear.

participants can then confirm or reject, drawing on their own looking and seeing. Gradually, the group moves towards a consensus of exactly how, where, and in what manner colours appear.

This process of seeing accurately is not easy or fast. At the start, many participants expect to see colour everywhere or, with vague memories of high school physics in mind, expect a full-colour rainbow to appear, which in fact does not readily happen. Once participants bracket their expectations and begin to really look at the colours as they actually appear, participants often present observations that are vague or inaccurate: for example, 'I see a halo of colour around all objects' or 'colours appear only where there is light.' Neither of these observations is correct; they indicate the misreading and imprecision into which beginners can fall.

In short, this process of looking requires continual presentation, corroboration, recognition of error, and correction. Eventually, however, group members can establish a thorough picture of their experience of colour through the prism, and end with a set of generalizations like the accurate descriptive statements presented in table 15.2.

Seeing and Understanding Broader Patterns

The exercise of looking through the prism just described is excellent for introducing students to the effort, care, and persistence required in Goethe's approach to looking and seeing, but his aim is considerably larger: to discover a theory of colour that arises from the colours themselves through our growing awareness and familiarity. Here, we move into a stage of looking and seeing that explores the wholeness of

Figure 15.4. The three cards to be viewed through a prism.

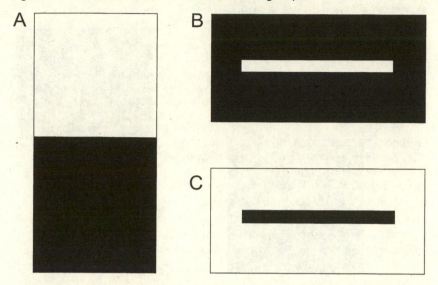

colour by describing in what ways colours arrange themselves in relationship to each other and to the darkness-lightness edge. This edge, as
discovered in the prism exercise described in table 15.2, seems to be a
prerequisite for any colours to arise at all.

To pinpoint such patterns and relationships, Goethe presents a series
of experiments using a set of cards with black-and-white patterns that
are to be viewed carefully through the prism and then to be recorded
accurately. The cards discussed here are illustrated in figure 15.4, and
instructions for their use are provided in table 15.3. figures 15.4–9 and
table 15.3.

The value of the cards in these experiments is that they provide a simple way to direct the appearance of colour, thereby providing a more
manageable and dependable context for looking and describing. Rather
than seeing colour along any edge, participants are now all looking at
the same edge displaced in the same way so they can be certain that
they will see the same appearance of colours.

In regard to card A, for example, we begin with the white area above
the black and, through the prism, look at the white-black horizontal
edge in the middle of the card. If the image that we see is displaced
by the prism below the actual card, then at the edge we see the darker
colours of blue above violet (see figure 15.5). If we turn the card upside

Figure 15.5 and 15.6, illustrating card experiments 1 and 2 (results of experiments 3a and 3b, not shown).

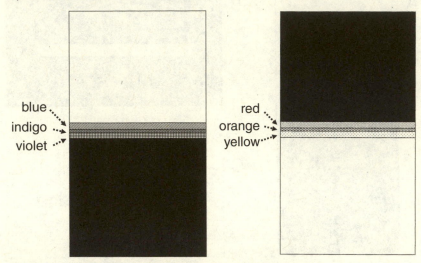

Figure 15.7 Illustrating card experiment 4.

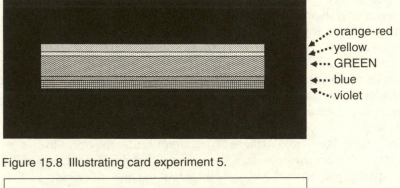

Figure 15.8 Illustrating card experiment 5.

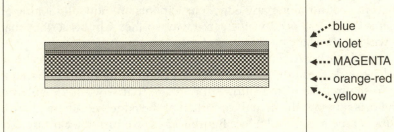

Figure 15.9. Goethe's ur-phenomenon of colour as evoked by a semi-transparent medium.

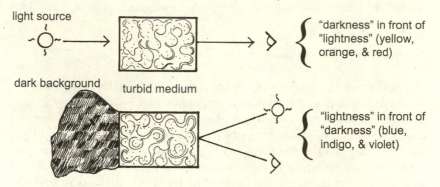

Table 15.3. Five prism experiments from *Theory of Colours.*

- **Experiment 1.** Hold card **A** with the white area above and black below. Making sure that all participants' images are displaced by the prism in the same direction (i.e., either above or below), locate the card's black-white edge in the prism. What colours appear along the edge? Draw and identify.
- **Experiment 2.** Invert card **A** so that the black area is now at the top and white is at the bottom. What colours now appear along the edge? Draw and identify.
- **Experiments 3a & 3b.** Repeat situations 1 and 2, but this time ensure that the image of the card's edge is displaced in the opposite way (if down before, now up and vice versa).
- **Experiment 4.** Look at card **B** so that the long axis of the white rectangle is parallel to the prism axis. Observe and describe the colours that appear on the upper and lower edges of the white rectangle. Slowly move card **B** until it is an arm's length away. As you move the card, observe and describe any colour changes. What *new* colour appears?
- **Experiment 5.** Using card **C**, carry through the same procedure as with card B. What *new* colour appears?

down so that black is above white, we now see something quite different – a set of lighter edge colours that, from top down, are red-orange and yellow (see figure 15.6).

As figures 15.7 and 15.8 indicate, the experiments with cards B and C are perhaps the most intriguing because they generate two colours not seen as regularly as in the dominant spectra of yellow-orange-red and blue-indigo-violet. As one moves card B farther away towards arm's length, there is a point at which the yellow and blue edges merge, and a vivid green appears horizontally so that the original white rectangle is now a band of rainbow (figure 15.7). For card C, a similar point is reached where the red and violet edges merge to create a brilliant magenta (figure 15.8).

Allowing the Parts to Belong

I have discussed a portion of the procedure that Goethe used to introduce participants to the prismatic appearance of colours. Now I want to highlight the style of looking and seeing more precisely and suggest how it might have value for exploring the natural city. In working in the way that Goethe required, it is important to emphasize that participants must be active in their seeing. They must not merely observe as passive spectators but plunge into the looking – they must, literally, 'pay attention' so that they see *with intention* rather than just having a visual impression.

For Goethe, however, these efforts of active looking and seeing are not enough. Once the participant gains familiarity with the particular patterns seen (for example, black above white generating red-orange-yellow), then the next step is what Goethe called 'exact sensorial imagination' – in other words, visualizing and thinking the phenomenon concretely in imagination. For example, I picture myself holding the black-above-white card, picture the displacement of the prism, picture the yellow-orange-red edge, then picture myself turning the card upside down and seeing the new edge of blue-indigo-violet.

Notice here that there is now an action that is simultaneously outer and inner as well as perceptual and cognitive – I re-experience my perceptual seeing but do it in my mind's eye. As Henri Bortoft explains, 'I am giving thinking more the quality of perception and sensory observation more the quality of thinking.'[29] What I have just encountered in perception is transcribed into an intellectual picture, but that intellectual picture is held to accurate transcription by the original reality of my perceptual looking and seeing.

An important result in Goethe's colour experiments is that we begin to realize various necessary connections among the colours – for example, we recognize that blue, indigo, and violet always appear together, as do yellow, orange, and red. In this sense, says Bortoft, we see colours 'belonging' in a non-contingent 'togetherness' that is not determinable from just looking alone. The perception here of necessary connection 'is the perception of a relationship as a *real* factor in the phenomenon, instead of being only a mental abstraction added on to what is experienced with the senses.'[30]

Moving Out into Nature

In regard to his prism experiments, Goethe realized that light and darkness were integral to the appearance of the colours. He saw the prism, however, as a complicating factor in that it was required for the colours to appear. If, instead, he could find some situation in nature where colours arose *all by themselves*, then he would be able to locate the source of colour in nature itself. He called such a foundational situation the 'ur-phenomenon' (*Urphänomen*) – the deep-down or primal phenomenon that marks out a necessary pattern of relationship.

In time, Goethe concluded that the ur-phenomenon of colour is the reciprocity of darkness and light or, more precisely, that colour is the resolution of the tension between darkness and light. Thus, darkness lightened by light leads to the darker colours of blue, indigo, and violet, while light dimmed by darkness creates the lighter colours of yellow, orange, and red. As Goethe poetically summarized the situation, colours are the 'deeds and sufferings of light.'

As figure 15.9 indicates, Goethe believed that he had discovered colour's ur-phenomenon in his observations of the sun, sky, and landscape. On clear days he noticed that the sun directly overhead at midday is a yellow-white, whereas the same sun setting is often orange or red. He also saw that the sky overhead is a brilliant, darker blue, whereas towards the horizon its blue shade grows lighter. In a similar way, he noticed that, when looking at a series of receding mountain ridges, the nearer mountains are shades of indigo and violet, while the ridges farther in the distance are blue.

In all these instances, Goethe interpreted the layer of atmosphere between him and the thing seen as a semi-transparent medium that, depending on the situation, works as a layer of light or darkness and thereby generates lighter or darker colours. In front of the white brilliance of the sun, this atmosphere is turbid and thus darker. Depending on its thickness, this translucent medium makes the sun's colour appear yellow at midday or red at dusk and dawn.

On the other hand, this same turbid atmosphere in front of the blackness of space or the dark green of distant mountain slopes works as a lightness. Thus the sky at the horizon, with more atmosphere between it and me than the sky directly above, is a lighter shade of blue than the sky above. Similarly, the mountain ridges farther from me have more atmosphere between them and me than the ridges nearer, so the distant ridges appear blue while those nearer are indigo and violet.

Unlike Newton, who theorized that colours are entities that have merely arisen out of light (as, for example, through refraction in a prism), Goethe came to believe that colours are *new* formations that develop through the dialectical action between darkness and light. Darkness is not the passive absence of light, as Newton suggested. Rather, darkness is an active presence opposing itself to light and interacting with it. Goethe's central aim in *Theory of Colours* was to provide a way to demonstrate first-hand this dialectical relationship and colour as its result.

Engendering Reverence for Nature

Conventional analytical science emphasizes a knowledge of primary qualities – i.e., features of quantity such as number, size, and position that can be measured and thereby transformed into a mathematical model. Goethe, however, sought a science of *qualities* – a method whereby colour becomes visible as intelligible *within itself*, i.e., without some external explanatory agency such as 'angle of refraction' or 'wave length' that lies outside colour as colour appears.

Rather, in Goethe's way of science, colours in everyday experience – for example, the colour edges made by the prism or the changing colours of sun and sky – are now understood to have an intrinsic necessity and therefore are understandable *in themselves*. He sought to locate, through direct experience, the relationships and interconnections among the colours. His resulting theory, as Bortoft emphasizes, is a phenomenology of colour rather than an explanatory model.[31]

There is nothing wrong with a quantitative science that gives attention to the progressive appearance of the natural world in its mathematical aspect, but this analytical interpretation is only partial. The natural world may be capable of appearing in other ways if approached accordingly. This is Goethe's great contribution: he pointed the way towards a complementary way of study that allows our thinking to enter into the coming into being of the phenomenon instead of analysing in second-hand fashion what has already become.[32]

For me, what is most inspiring about Goethe's *Theory of Colours* is its facilitating a kind of 'folding over' of natural phenomena so that things unjoined before now connect in relationship. Phenomenological geographer Edward Relph says that the best phenomenology is the 'gathering together of what already belongs together even while apart.'[33] *Theory of Colours* offers such a gathering admirably, fostering an awareness and understanding of colour that parties can see and agree on once they have worked through Goethe's experiments. The result might be called a phenomenology of intersubjective corroboration and a science of qualities.

It is also important to emphasize that today, Goethe's approach is being applied to many other topics in the natural world and is leading to innovative practical results. One example is ecologist Mark Riegner's pioneering efforts to use plants and animals as a means to 'read' the unique sense of place of particular ecological regions.[34] Another example is the work of animal researchers Wolfgang Schad[35] and Craig Holdrege,[36] who seek to render a Goethean phenomenology of animals through qualities of animal form, appearance, and behaviour. I particularly admire sculptor John Wilkes's efforts at a Goethean study of water and the crafting of fountain-like vessels he calls 'flowforms.' These vessels allow water to move in a lemnescate rhythm that not only is aesthetically attractive but also provides important ecological functions, including oxygenating water more quickly and thus having important value for waste water treatment.[37] For the natural city, Wilkes's work is an invaluable model because it demonstrates how handsomely crafted water features derived from the directed attention of Goethean seeing can integrate urban aesthetics and urban sustainability, urban art and urban practicality.

The Becoming of Parts Together

I now return to the original question of what interconnections, relationships, and wholes become phenomenologically and what this understanding might mean for the natural city. In the style of phenomenology I argue for here, the quest is 'right parts all of a piece' – in other words, a mutual coming to presence of parts and whole through a sustained effort to look, and resulting moments of insight in which one 'sees.'

This style of phenomenology is arduous in practice and uncertain in results. Bortoft identifies the central dilemma as the 'hazard of emergence.' On the one hand, a part is a part only if it contributes to the whole to which it belongs; on the other hand, the whole can emerge only if it allows the parts to appear.[38] As Bortoft explains, 'the whole depends on the parts to be able to come forth, and the parts depend on the coming forth of the whole to be significant instead of superficial. The recognition of a part is possible only through the "coming to presence" of the whole.'[39]

What is the foundational 'stuff' that grounds and allows for this coming to presence? For Bortoft, it is a situation in which all the parts have their proper place and can be together in a way that is real and non-arbitrary. In short, there is a genuine belonging that both sustains and reflects a whole, all part and parcel.[40] In my phenomenology of lively urban places and in Goethe's phenomenology of colour, there is an effort to locate and describe necessary relationships and interconnections that both contribute to and are shaped by a belonging together in which the parts are integral and have their place. The integral parts of place ballet are individual habitual bodies in synchrony with a supportive spatial configuration that generates animated streets and places. The integral parts of Goethe's colour theory are the tension between darkness and light, and the colours resulting from light overcoming darkness and vice versa.

In regard to the natural city, these two phenomena point towards contrasting dimensions of the urban lifeworld: on the one hand, bodily routines and city place ballet exist largely in the natural attitude outside of self-conscious awareness, while, on the other hand, discoveries evoked by Goethean science involve a patient, deliberate attention whereby taken-for-granted aspects of the world emerge reflexively. I would phrase this difference in terms of two contrasting modes of daily life – what I called in *Geography of the Lifeworld* the 'triad of habituality' and the 'triad of openness.' The former refers to the typical ordinariness and humdrum quality of everyday life, which much of the time involves unquestioned repetition and routine that most people, unless forced, are unwilling to change. In regard to the natural city, Jane Jacobs's vivid account of the hourly, daily, and weekly regularity of pedestrian life on New York City's Hudson Street is an archetypal example of the triad of habituality.[41] One fruitful means by which to introduce useful shifts in this triad is through thoughtful design of the physical environment. Such design is demonstrated, for example, by Hillier's space syntax work, which provides ways whereby careful manipulation of city streets' spatial configuration might generate invigorated urban places through place ballet.[42]

In contrast to the triad of habituality is the 'triad of openness' – those moments in everyday life when one is suddenly alert to the world in a more sensitive, intense way and experiences a sense of heightened encounter. As the above explication of Goethe's colour work indicates, his way of science can be an important tool for moving people into the triad of openness. By practising a way of encountering the world in an empathetic, participatory way, Goethe believes that what is taken for granted and thus unseen can reveal new, unexpected patterns. His method of looking and seeing can be practised at any time and in any place, including in the city. In this sense, the approach can direct one's attention to urban phenomena that, in the past, might have gone unnoticed. One ready urban example is coloured shadows, which are given considerable attention by Goethe[43] and appear when two light sources (one white) cast shadows thrown by an object – say a street tree. If, for instance, the illumination of a city streetlight is orange, the tree's shadow cast by the orange light and illuminated by some nearby white light is *blue*, even though there is no blue light anywhere near.[44] To see coloured shadows as one walks through the city at night is a small but memorable event, reminding one of the ineffable wholeness of the natural world, even in the most human-made of environments.

Goethe contended that, if one practises his way of looking and seeing, one might eventually discover how parts that before were seemingly unrelated – like the orange streetlight and the tree's blue shadow – might coalesce in underlying pattern and togetherness. I realize that, in our time of poststructural relativity, any emphasis on necessary relationships and interconnections founded on a non-contingent 'belonging' will strike some critics as an experiential essentialism associated with a conservative phenomenology that still believes in the 'things themselves.' On the one hand, I believe deeply that the relationships of necessity revealed by Goethe's colour theory and by place ballet are real lifeworld structures that can be discovered through careful study and description of typical environmental and place experiences. On the other hand, one must realize that place ballets and the significance of colour are always expressed through particular cultural, social, and personal filters. In short, there is always a lived dialectic between the more general and the more specific, between the foundational and the particular way the foundational is expressed in the real-world lives of particular people in particular places at particular historical moments. My personal study preference lingers with the foundational.

In this chapter, I have emphasized lively urban places and colour because I have a particular interest in phenomenological insights as they might reach into the world of praxis, including urban education, design, and policy. Phenomenological research on place ballet might not only sensitize individuals and groups to particular urban places that have important significance in their own lives, but might also offer practical means for strengthening those urban places through policies and designs sustaining permeable pathway configurations. Goethe's way of science might be particularly significant for appreciating the city, because the approach offers a comprehensive, intuitive means for encountering urban phenomena like light and colour. One discovers unsuspected interconnections among parts that suddenly merge together in wider patterns of relationship and meaning. One feels satisfaction intellectually but is also surprised and touched emotionally. One comes to appreciate the city in a deeper, more interconnected way.

In *The Four-Gated City*, novelist Doris Lessing writes that love is 'the delicate but total acknowledgement of what is.'[45] Her idea crystallizes the heart of Goethean seeing: that the mundane, little things of our world can house an unsuspected but miraculous wholeness that we can encounter, understand, and come to care for. I believe the greatest contribution that phenomenology can offer is to provide a systematic means for discerning this miraculous wholeness in all portions of the natural and human-made worlds. In terms of city matters, this means that a phenomenological style of looking and seeing might contribute to understanding the urban lifeworld more thoughtfully and thoroughly. Through that understanding, we might assure a more natural city wherein at-homeness and serendipity, ordinariness and extraordinariness all have their place.

NOTES

1 This chapter began as a presentation by the author at the 23rd annual symposium of the Simon Silverman Phenomenology Center, 'Renew the Face of the Earth: Phenomenology and Ecology,' held on 11–12 March 2005, at Duquesne University, Pittsburgh, PA. An earlier version of this chapter was published in *Phenomenology and Ecology*, ed. Melissa Geib (Pittsburgh: Simon Silverman Phenomenology Center, 2006), 53–86. The editors thank the Simon Silverman Phenomenology Center for allowing the author to draw on this earlier work.

2 Donald Worster, *Nature's Economy: A History of Ecological Ideas*, 2nd ed. (New York: Cambridge University Press, 1994), 22. In this book, Worster emphasizes that the central concern of ecology is 'the interdependence of living things,' though he also demonstrates that ecology as a science

often understands these interrelationships in a much different way from the 'ecological point of view,' which he defines as 'a search for holistic or integrated perception, an emphasis on interdependence and relatedness in nature, and an intense desire to restore [human beings] to a place of intimate intercourse with the vast organism that constitutes the earth' (82).

3 Reviews of the phenomenological contribution to environmental topics include Carl F. Graumann, 'The Phenomenological Approach to People-Environment Studies,' in *Handbook of Environmental Psychology*, ed. Robert Bechtel and Ara Churchman, 2nd ed. (New York: Wiley, 2002), 95–113; Peter Hay, *Main Currents in Western Environmental Thought* (Bloomington: University of Indiana Press, 2002), chapter 6; Robert Mugerauer, *Interpretations on Behalf of Place* (Albany: SUNY Press, 1994); and David Seamon, 'A Way of Seeing People and Place: Phenomenology in Environment-Behavior Research,' in *Theoretical Perspectives in Environment-Behavior Research*, ed. S. Wapner, J. Demick, and T. Yamamoto (New York: Plenum, 2000), 157–78.

4 Mark Riegner, 'Toward a Holistic Understanding of Place: Reading a Landscape through Its Flora and Fauna,' in *Dwelling, Seeing, and Designing: Toward a Phenomenological Ecology*, ed. David Seamon (Albany: SUNY Press, 1993), 211–12; David Seamon, *Dwelling, Seeing, and Designing*, 16. On a phenomenology of urban wholeness, see David Seamon, 'Grasping the Dynamism of Urban Place: Contributions from the Work of Christopher Alexander, Bill Hillier, and Daniel Kemmis,' in *Reanimating Places*, ed. Tom Mels (Burlington, VT: Ashgate, 2004), 123–45.

5 Bill Hillier, 'The Architecture of the Urban Object,' *Ekistics* 56 (1989): 5–21; Bill Hillier, *Space Is the Machine* (Cambridge: Cambridge University Press, 1996); Bill Hillier and Julienne Hanson, *The Social Logic of Space* (Cambridge: Cambridge University Press, 1984).

6 David Seamon, *A Geography of the Lifeworld* (New York: St Martin's Press, 1979).

7 Maurice Merleau-Ponty, *Phenomenology of Perception*, trans. Colin Smith (New York: Humanities Press, 1962 [originally 1945]).

8 Merleau-Ponty, *Phenomenology of Perception*, 138–9.

9 Jane Jacobs, *The Death and Life of Great American Cities* (New York: Vintage, 1961), 50.

10 William Whyte, *The Social Life of Small Urban Spaces* (New York: Conservation Foundation, 1980).

11 Jacobs, *The Death and Life of Great American Cities*.

12 David Seamon and Christine Nordin, 'Market Place as Place Ballet: A Swedish Example,' *Landscape* 24 (October 1980): 35–41.

13 Ray Oldenburg, *The Great Good Place* (New York: Paragon House, 1989).

14 Hillier, *Space Is the Machine*; Hillier and Hanson, *The Social Logic of Space*.

15 David Seamon, 'A Lived Hermetic of People and Place: Phenomenology and Space Syntax,' in *Proceedings, 6th International Space Syntax Symposium*, vol. 1, ed. A. Sema Kubat et al. (Istanbul: ITU, Faculty of Architecture, 2007), iii–1–16.

16 Hillier, 'The Architecture of the Urban Object,' 5.

17 Hillier, *Space Is the Machine*, 213.

18 Hillier's mathematical measures derive from configurational properties only; thus other important aspects of urban place – e.g., land uses, functional activities, building types, and user density – are not considered. Hillier claims to demonstrate that 'movement in the urban grid is, other things being equal, generated by the configuration of the grid itself' (*Space Is the Machine*, 5). He argues that 'the structuring of movement by the grid leads, through multiplier effects, to dense patterns of mixed-use encounter that characterize the spatially successful city' (6; see also 167–70).

19 Hillier, *Space Is the Machine*, 161.

20 Hillier and Hanson, *The Social Logic of Space*, 108–9.

21 Eventually, one must ask if, in the real place, the pathways of highest integration are actually the most used and the liveliest in terms of pedestrian activity. To answer this question, Hillier and his researchers have gone to the actual pathways and counted pedestrians. Overall, results indicate a high correlation between high integration values and animated streets. See Hillier, *Space Is the Machine*, 161; S. Read, 'Space Syntax and the Dutch City,' *Environment and Planning B: Planning and Design* 26 (1999): 251–64.

22 Hillier, *Space Is the Machine*, chapter 4.

23 Hillier, *Space Is the Machine*, 171.

24 Hillier, *Space Is the Machine*, 178.

25 One helpful effort to integrate spatial configuration with other aspects of urban place, including placement of functions and land uses, is Ian Bentley, Alan Alcock, Paul Murrain, Sue McGlynn, and Graham Smith, *Responsive Environments: A Manual for Designers* (London: Architectural Press, 1985).

26 Stephanie E. Bothwell, Andrés M. Duany, Peter J. Hetzel, Steven W. Hurtt, and Dhiru A. Thadani, *Windsor Forum on Design Education: Toward an Ideal Curriculum to Reform Architectural Education* (Miami, FL: New Urban Press, 2004); Peter Katz, *The New Urbanism: Toward an Architecture of Community* (New York: McGraw-Hill, 1994); Edward Robbins, 'New Urbanism,' in *Shaping the City: Studies in History, Theory and Urban Design*, ed. Edward Robbins and Rodolphe El-Khoury (London: Routledge, 2004).

27 The most complete set of Goethe's scientific writings in English is Johann

Wolfgang von Goethe, *Goethe: Scientific Studies*, ed. and trans. D. Miller (New York: Suhrkamp, 1988). For examples of recent Goethean phenomenology, see David Seamon and Arthur Zajonc, *Goethe's Way of Science* (Albany: SUNY Press, 1998). The best single overview of Goethean science, including its phenomenological significance, is Henri Bortoft, *The Wholeness of Nature: Goethe's Science of Conscious Participation in Nature* (Hudson, NY: Lindesfarne Press, 1996). For a helpful overview of academic evaluations of Goethean science, see F. Amrine, F.J. Zucker, and H. Wheeler, eds., *Goethe and the Sciences: A Reappraisal* (Dordrecht: Reidel, 1987); and 'Goethe's Delicate Empiricism,' a special issue of *Janus Head*, 8, 1 (2005).

28 Johann Wolfgang von Goethe, *Theory of Colours*, trans. C.L. Eastlake (Cambridge: MIT Press, 1970); Goethe, *Goethe: Scientific Studies*, 1988.

29 Bortoft, *The Wholeness of Nature*, 42.

30 Bortoft, *The Wholeness of Nature*, 99.

31 Bortoft, *The Wholeness of Nature*, 33.

32 Bortoft, *The Wholeness of Nature*, 214.

33 Edward Relph, 'Response,' *Journal of Environmental Psychology* 2 (1983): 201.

34 Mark Riegner, 'Toward a Holistic Understanding of Place'; Mark Riegner, 'Horns, Hooves, Spots, and Stripes: Form and Pattern in Mammals,' in *Goethe's Way of Science*, ed. Seamon and Zajonc 177–212.

35 Wolfgang Schad, *Man and Mammals: Toward a Biology of Form* (Garden City, NY: Waldorf Press, 1977).

36 Craig Holdrege, 'Seeing the Animal Whole: The Example of Horse and Lion,' in *Goethe's Way of Science*, ed. Seamon and Zajonc, 213–32; Craig Holdrege, *The Flexible Giant: Seeing the Elephant Whole* (Ghent, NY: Nature Institute, 2003).

37 Mark Riegner and John Wilkes, 'Flowforms and the Language of Water,' in *Goethe's Way of Science*, ed. Seamon and Zajonc, 233–52; John Wilkes, *Flowforms: The Rhythmic Power of Water* (Edinburgh: Floris, 2003).

38 Henri Bortoft, 'Counterfeit and Authentic Wholes: Finding a Means for Dwelling in Nature,' in *Dwelling, Place, and Environment: Towards a Phenomenology of Person and World*, ed. David Seamon and Robert Mugerauer (New York: Columbia University Press, 1989), 287.

39 Bortoft, 'Counterfeit and Authentic Wholes,' 287.

40 In part, Bortoft's understanding here derives from philosopher Martin Heidegger's distinction between 'belonging *together*' and '*belonging* together.' Martin Heidegger, *Identity and Difference* (New York: Harper and Row, 1969), 29. In the former situation, parts not necessarily of a piece are brought arbitrarily together. In other words, the parts are together but they

may not really *belong* together. The latter situation is more real, because the parts all necessarily belong together, and this belonging founds the possibility of really seeing how all the parts are together and the whole they make. One of the most effective aspects of Goethe's colour theory is its discovery of how particular colours '*belong* together' because of the light-darkness dialectic. Goethean science attempts to find this *belonging* together in regard to the particular phenomenon studied.

41 Jacobs, *The Death and Life of Great American Cities*, 50–4.

42 One intriguing aspect of place ballet is that, though it is grounded in the natural attitude and routine, it can also evoke novelty, excitement, and surprise. The serendipity of encounters, the possibility of newcomers and outsiders, the sense of place ambience – these qualities may give a taken-for-granted place a sense of exhilaration and allure, all housed in the triad of habituality.

43 Goethe, *Theory of Colours*, paragraphs 62–80 (29–37).

44 This appearance, Goethe claimed, involves the instantaneous tendency of the eye to supplement the dominant orange lightness with a blue – the complementary colour of orange – in the darker shadow; see *Theory of Colours*, paragraph 77.

45 Doris Lessing, *The Four-Gated City* (New York: Bantam, 1969), 10.

16 The City: A Legacy of Organism-Environment Interaction at Every Scale

ROBERT MUGERAUER

1. Nature's Place in the City: The Usual Viewpoint

That nature occurs in the city is an obvious thing to say. We all know that there are trees and birds and rain in the downtown areas, and grass and squirrels and a stream or two in the suburbs. Nature's place in urban areas seems unproblematic, and not especially worth further consideration. But, if we reflect on the 'usual' view, we note that, in fact, nature comes to our attention mainly through dynamic events. When a major snowstorm surprisingly hits the Carolinas, when a heat wave all but shuts down New York City and tempers rise along with the temperature, or, more tragically, when an earthquake shocks Kobe, Japan, or San Francisco, not only area residents but people all over take notice. At least for a while.

Other, smaller phenomena also result in notable experiences. The blossoming of cherry trees in Washington, DC, or dogwoods in Austin, Texas, provides a splendid ephemeral spring pleasure. The media have covered stories of falcons and hawks perching on skyscrapers in Manhattan in order to swoop down upon their prey. Apparently, hawks and falcons have adapted to the urban canyons. On a larger scale, nature envelops the city as climate. The typical regional climate helps define a sense of place: Miami and New Orleans are distinctive partly because their heat and humidity affect everything from architecture and clothing to food, street layout, and thus behaviour. Seattle's cool and humid environment is a dimension of a biocultural atmosphere that includes cafés and coffee everywhere, hooded sweatshirts, and large overhanging eaves on houses. The Nordic inflection of Minneapolis is bound up with its snow, its bright blue winter skies that come with the cold fronts, and the invitation to cross-country ski to avoid cabin fever in February.

Yet climate is not deterministic. Our buildings and habits respond to it, of course, but what we have made creates yet another environment. Hence we have become more sensitive recently to the darkening and wind patterns that happen when skyscrapers create their own local microclimates, or when the temperatures of urban areas generate experienceable heat islands, or when bounce light between buildings is so strong that it creates problems for neighbours, as happens even with such sophisticated designs as Gehry's Disney Concert Hall in Los Angeles. Those sensitive to educating us about urban environments, such as landscape architect Anne Winston Spirn[1] and others,[2] have been analysing these phenomena for quite some time.

On a planetary scale, researchers, professionals, politicians, the media, and many citizens are focusing attention on the implications of global warming, especially as it radically shifts climates, melting glaciers and raising ocean levels, leading to increasing flooding in some places and desertification in others.[3] Given the large percentage of the world's population living in urban areas and near sea level, concern with our excessive energy consumption and global warming is raising alarms in regard to urban changes and challenges. In addition to dealing with these huge natural and human problems, even more modest and manageable urban elements merit serious attention.

Complementing new and radical technologies and practices remind us how much we can learn from nature itself and from traditional vernacular responses. Classics such as William Whyte's *Social Life in Small Urban Spaces* (1980) demonstrate how parks and plazas work best when they provide alternative seating that can be used flexibly amid shifts from hot to cool to cold weather. A thriving tradition of ecological design exists.[4] The lessons of passive solar energy have been promulgated by architects and researchers; for example, Egyptian architect Hassan Fathy followed up his early work on the social-formal patterns of Gornea in Africa with an analysis of heat gain and loss through the passive effects of earthen buildings and wind flow in hot, arid climates.[5] Simultaneously, changing how we finance, plan, design, build, and maintain facilities to achieve lower life-cycle (long-term) costs, rather than merely short-term savings, increasingly integrates sophisticated siting, landscaping, engineering, materials, air-light control-circulation systems, and other dimensions to develop 'green buildings' that use the best of traditional and high-technology resources.

In all these ways, the presence and increasing importance of natural phenomena in the city are obvious and taken for granted. In addition to pragmatic planning, design, and construction problems, new issues are also raised at a theoretical level. For example, questions about the differences and relations between 'nature' and 'culture' (often posed in terms of 'nature versus culture') are being rethought. Current theories of social construction explore how both our infrastructure and our buildings shape our lives, and how 'nature itself' is a product of social and economic processes. That is, it increasingly appears that we may not only 'make' our physical environment: with our interpretive concepts and science-technological experiments, we actually construct what we take to be nature. Others argue, from a sharply alternative viewpoint, that nature and human culture are substantially determined by the physical characteristics of the world and the laws of physics and chemistry. The current belief that the genetic makeup of living beings, including humans, sets the course of life and its possibilities (even beyond the individual being to the social level) is an example of the view that nature determines culture – resulting in a significant debate as well as substantial misinformation.[6]

2. Nature Everywhere, at All Scales, at All Times: An Interactive View of Organism ← → Environment

(a) Organisms Shape or Construct Their Environments

As part of the usual view just discussed, we unreflectively go about as if what mattered were only the mid-range, phenomenal realm. This everyday attitude rests on faulty assumptions: first, that the organisms and environments with which we are routinely familiar (plants, insects, birds, fish, animals, people; meadows and forests, nests and hives, and cities) lie within the sphere of what we both understand and can control with our technology; and second, that the macro (for example, not only the cosmos, but climate) and micro (not only the subatomic, but the plethora of micro-organisms, and, until recently, the genetic) realms are at the limits of our comprehension and resist control. In contrast to the taken-for-granted experiences and perceptions outlined above, which certainly dominate our thinking and actions today, I want to argue on behalf of a richer viewpoint – in terms of the complexity and detail of the phenomena included and of the integration of the many dimensions and processes. I want to develop some of the ways in which a continuity or homology in organism-environment interactions exists across the micro, phenomenal, and macro (climatic) scales. This continuity is intelligible, and, if understood, could lead to more holistic theory and practices.

In fact, current research and reassessments in complexity theory, self-organization, phenomenology, and enactivist approaches to cognition correlate with Developmental Systems Theory (DST), constructivist interactionism, emergence, and co-evolution in their development of an epigenetic position, in contest with the performatist view (wherein development is understood to 'be performed by genes').[7] DST and its related approaches, as well as theories critical of neo-Darwinian natural selection theory, are coming to understand the interactive dynamic among organisms (of all sorts, including humans) and their environments.[8] Without belabouring the point, empirical studies and theoretically sophisticated interpretations demonstrate conclusively that such cases are widespread and have implications yet to be fully appreciated.[9] Not only humans, but organisms at all scales, modify and are modified by their environments in ways that are far more complex than are accounted for in dominant neo-Darwinian genetic-environment modelling. There are many common examples of small creatures changing their surroundings or external appearance for self-protection or for trapping prey.

As soon as they hatch, caddis fly larvae 'weave little tubes with silk-like material, then strengthen them by attaching plant material, particles of sand or gravel, or shells of tiny bivalves or snails, for example, to these tubes' – what is available locally also helps camouflage.[10] Tropical parrotfishes (*Scaridae*) sleep 'inside a mucous cocoon which they secrete for protection from nocturnal predators.'[11]

It is not unusual for such structures to be very sophisticated and complex, even in otherwise inhospitable ('impossible') environments. To give only two examples, 'the nest of the great reed warbler (*Acrocephalus arundinaceus*) is woven of dry, thin materials, moulded from inside with the bird's body, pushed out with the legs, and lined with soft material.'[12] Less well known, the amazing 'dwelling place of a water spider [is] an air-filled bell anchored under water by a net of spider's threads. *Argyroneta aquatica* lives its entire life underwater: she carries air with her, rising to surface only once a day [where she] traps an air bubble at the surface and pulls it down into a net she has woven.'[13]

Hornets' nests can be quite large and 'flexible,' as with *Vespa crabro*, which expands its nest, takes some parts down, and adds new ones.[14]

Even more complex, ants' nests often have 'chambers [that] reach far into soil below the nest, as is the case with the common brown garden ant (*Lasius niger*). As with bees, the nest controls temperature and humidity as workers tend the brood of eggs, larvae, and pupae in their cocoons.'[15]

Lest we overlook what is so close as to be hidden in plain sight, trees, too, interact with and shape their own environments. Through trunk, branches, and leaves above, and roots below, trees are intimately sites of elemental cycles. Water, carbon, oxygen, nitrogen – all components – interact, 'sustaining a balance of gases, water, and nutrients ... Tree roots penetrate deep to collect minerals and nutrients ... The soil also contains earthworms and insects, which maintain fertility by aerating and mixing the humus and soil' so that multiple systems and organisms are dynamically connected.[16] Indeed, as autopoietic analysis points out (pushing further than the previous sentence might indicate), the soil itself is already an organic-environment complex: 'Soil ... is not unalive. It is a mixture of broken rock, pollen, fungal filaments, ciliate cysts, bacterial spores, nematodes, and other microscopic animals and their parts.'[17]

(b) Development

Clearly, organisms engineer their environments. So what? Isn't this obvious? What new insights follow from the detailed documentation of the wonders of organisms' 'architecture' and environmental formation? A great deal: reinterpreting what we 'know' discloses new meanings. A first major area that is being affected by the empirical and theoretical shifts is development. When organisms shape their environments, they are also shaping their own development. Of course, the relationships between developmental and environmental factors are complex, and too little is understood about them. For all the importance of genetics – of which more shortly – it turns out that environmental factors can radically modify organisms 'in process,' as it were. This means that organic forms are neither as inherent-fixed nor as biologically generated-determined as might be thought. For example, both genetic makeup and environment shape the phenotype and development of *Drosophila* (the fruit fly, about which we know more than any other organism), as is well documented by studies of the effects of temperature on the number of eye cells that develop:

In general, the morphology, physiology, metabolism, and behavior – that is, the phenotype – of an organism at any moment in its life is a product both of the genes transmitted from the parents and of the environment in which development has occurred up until that moment. The number of light-receptor cells, or facets, in the compound eye of the fruit fly, Drosophila, is usually about 1,000, but certain gene mutations severely reduce the number of facets. For example, flies carrying the mutation Ultrabar have only 100. However, the number of eye cells also depends upon the temperature at which the flies develop; flies of the normal genotype produce about 1,100 cells at 15 degrees C, but only 750 cells at 30 degrees C.[18]

Generally, environmental factors such as light, diet, temperature, humidity, and local chemicals can be shown to modulate significantly the character and thus possibilities of activity of many organisms. At the same time, 'natural environments' are not merely fixed contexts within which organisms develop, because environments are partially constructed by the organisms themselves, as well as by their own forebears and other organisms. As we are seeing, closer attention to the two-way interactions between environments and organisms is resulting in better understanding of the ways organisms also actively shape their environments and thus their own development. Birds, for example, routinely construct their nests in a wide variety of ways, which has an impact on the kind of development that occurs in the young and on the very success of development. Less obviously, even trees modify their surroundings. This is the case with pine trees (such as the slash pine [*Pinus elliotti*], longleaf pine [*Pinus palustris*], and shortleaf pine [*Pinus echinata*]) and the acid soil that results from their dropped needles. The modulation of the accumulated acidity of the forest floor leads to changes in other organisms and the emergence of mutual systems, as when the trees become symbiotic with fungus:

> To compensate for [an acid forest floor and hard sterile sand] conifer tree roots have developed a symbiotic relationship with mycorrhizal fungus that provides the tree roots with nutrients in return for carbohydrates. Recent research has shown that these fungi can increase the growth rate of pine seedlings by 50 per cent.[19]

Similar phenomena occur with termites as well as with anthills. Among the 'most spectacular' and vastest of all such 'adaptive structures' are termites' nests.[20] The queen, king, workers, soldiers, eggs, and young occupy a complex of storage chambers in which they cultivate 'the mycelium of a mushroom (*Termitomyces*) on a compost of leaf or wood particles, allowing the young larvae to visit fungal beds.'[21] Or, in an anthill of the small red wood ant (*Formica polyctena*), hundreds of thousands of inhabitants, with a mortar of soil and body secretions, start below ground, cover openings, densify surface, line inside chambers and passages; they plug and unplug openings depending on temperature (which operate as do our windows) and move material from within to the top, so that interior humid material dries out and prevents mould formation. Thus, the mound helps to obtain sufficient solar heat in temperate latitudes.[22] Clearly, not just humans, nor larger creatures such as beaver and birds, but organisms generally build their environments, and do so in a way that also affects other organisms.

(c) Impact on Evolution: Niche Construction and Inheritance

The reinterpretation of organism-environment not only changes our understanding of development – the shaping of individuals – it also leads to rethinking the 'dominant' or received theory of evolution – the shaping of populations. The evidence uncontestably challenges many of the assumptions of conventional evolutionary thought. This can be seen clearly if we contrast the traditional, basic evolutionary schema with the new paradigm. In classical evolutionary theory it is taken that the environment provides the context that selects in or out mutating genetic characteristics, so that the organisms that best survive and reproduce are those that 'fit' their environment. In short, the genes are given internally (inherited), and are selected by the external environment. But, in light of what we are discovering about development, it is not the case that the environment is pre-given in any simple sense: it does not provide a 'niche' to be filled by organisms that best 'fit' to it.[23]

From our initial considerations on how the environment is not simply 'there,' we now can discern and elaborate two dimensions of – to use the proper name for this phenomenon – niche construction. We need to continue to develop and appreciate the first, basic aspect, which is that just seen in section 2(b): organisms actively shape their environments, changing them dramatically and pervasively. In addition, organisms are active participants in selecting what a niche is: that is, in what counts as or amounts to a niche for that organism. For birds that break clams to eat, rocks are a significant part of their environment; for those same birds, an asphalt roadway or sidewalk would serve the same function of providing a hard surface upon which to break the clam shells. In fact, as one can observe in the San Juan Islands of the Pacific Northwest, a roadway is better for this purpose. Shells dropped from 23 feet (7 m) break every time on the hard, flat surface, lying there until the birds swoop down to extract the clam. When dropped onto shoreline rocks, a large percentage of the shells are lost, from not breaking or from slipping down into unreachable places. Yet in this same environment, this roadway is not part of an ecological niche for birds that eat only flying insects (which in this case would neither be attracted to nor be otherwise plentiful at this site).

It is well worth noting that this recent theoretical and empirical reassessment confirms what already was argued some time ago by Maurice Merleau-Ponty (citing Weizäcker and Goldstein):

> Thus the form of the excitant is created by the organism itself, by its proper manner of offering itself to actions from the outside. Doubtless, in order to be able to subsist, it must encounter a certain number of physical and chemical agents in its surroundings. But it is the organism itself – according to the proper nature of its receptors, the thresholds of its nerve centers and the movements of its organs – which chooses the stimuli in the physical world to which it will be sensitive. 'The environment (*Umwelt*) emerges from the world through the actualization or the being of the organism – [granted that] an organism can exist only if it succeeds in finding in the world an adequate environment.'[24]

Susan Oyama, Paul E. Griffiths, and Russell D. Gray's masterful and stimulating overview of what the newly emerging interpretations mean is worth citing at length:

> The idea of construction through the interaction of many different factors is applicable to evolution as well as development, and it highlights striking similarities between the two processes. Just as there are no preexisting representations or instructions that shape organisms from within, there are no preexisting niches or environmental problems that shape populations from without. Evolutionary change is the result of interactions in which outcomes are codetermined, or co-constructed, by populations and environments with their own, often intricately interrelated, histories and characteristics; outcomes are not imposed by or prefigured in only certain interactants. Extended inheritance both increases the range of developmental outcomes that can be given evolutionary explanations and alters our view of evolutionary dynamics. If evolution is to change in developmental systems ... it is no longer possible to think of evolution as the

shaping of the organism to fit an ecological niche. Rather, the various elements of the developmental systems coevolve. Organisms construct their niches both straightforwardly by physically transforming their surroundings and, equally importantly, by changing which elements of the external environment are part of the developmental system and thus able to influence the evolutionary process in that lineage.[25]

Hence, it is argued that niche construction provides 'a bona fide inheritance system' that shapes future populations.[26]

The most cited example of this phenomenon concerns the many oviparous insects, where young are not born into a 'neutral' or random environment. Instead, the females lay their eggs on a food source. For instance, 'parasite wasps lay their eggs inside caterpillars, and the larvae slowly devour their living hosts before crawling out and weaving cocoons.'[27] Hence, though parasites are often thought of as beings that feed upon another in order to thrive themselves, in the case of the oviparous, it is the next generation that benefits from the modified legacy of a specific and appropriately nurturing 'living environment':

The wasp carries a caterpillar which she has paralyzed by stings to the nest, in the burrow, then deposits an egg on it and fills in the nest; she will return and check the nest, bringing more caterpillars if the larva has hatched and is eating.[28]

The realm of leaf-cutter ants is especially fascinating. There we see how, as they cultivate food for their own future generations, they are the desired 'prey' of others, which attempt to turn them into heritage incubators.

Leaf-cutter ants cut off a piece of leaf with their sharp mandibles and make their way home with their loads. Small workers ride home on pieces of leaf and repel the attacks of parasitic flies with wide-open jaws. The small parasitic flies would lay their eggs on the necks of the ants so that when the fly larvae hatch, they can burrow into the ants' heads and devour the contents … Those ants that manage to bring the cut leaves back cultivate their own food in special chambers by preparing compost beds for their fungus.[29]

Nor is this cultivation of white mould and future generations a minimalist operation, since a single colony of leaf-cutter ants can contain millions of workers and displace tons of soil.[30]

Since the environments that organisms themselves produce or modify (that is, those selected as relevant) shape the organisms' development and well-being, a self-organizing system unfolds that also needs to be understood over time. Since many of the major dimensions of environments that are genuinely interactive with a given organism are those into which next-generation organisms 'are born' and develop, these are precisely what amount to a 'heritage.'

> Niche construction starts to take on a new significance when it is acknowledged that, by changing their world, organisms modify many of the selection pressures to which they and their descendants are exposed, and that this may change the nature of the evolutionary process.[31]

In short, what organisms do in shaping their environments not only amounts to their shaping their own development (the ontogeny of individuals), but also to their modifying future generations – that is, the evolution of their own (and other) species.

The latter point about niche construction or engineering changing the conditions for other species is clearly not unusual, given the examples cited in this chapter. For example, in the case of the ants just noted,

> the collective leaf-cutting activities of such large colonies of [these major herbivores of the neotropics] can have enormous impacts on the surrounding environment ... in ways that may either harm or benefit other organisms ... [such as on the] growth and density of those species of plants that they exploit, as well as on those plants that grow in the improved soil of their nests and those species that rely on the ants to disperse their seeds. Moreover, leaf-cutter ants have glands that secrete substances that kill virtually all bacteria and fungi, except for the single fungus that they cultivate.[32]

Acknowledging, understanding, and absorbing these facts is new to evolutionary theory and research. In the old model, inherited genes are selected by environmental factors, period (figure 16.1). In contrast, the new model (figure 16.2) manifests a continuingly dynamic process, across generations: an organism comes to life in an environment, partly constructed by other organisms of the same and different types; the environment modifies the organism as an existing individual and genetically, so that offspring are affected; the genetic changes make a difference to the organisms in action; the organisms interact with the transformed environment as other organisms select those dimensions

Figure 16.1: Basic Evolutionary Theory: A given environment selects for genetic features which lead to the best fit to an ecological niche

Figure 16.2: Co-evolution and Development Systems Theory: Niche construction and an active role in selecting niche →inherited environments, so organisms modify their own and other groups' development and evolution

Environmental Selection

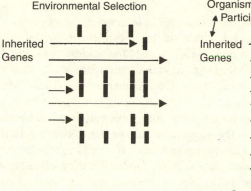

Organisms shape and inherit environments
Participate in environmental selection

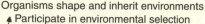

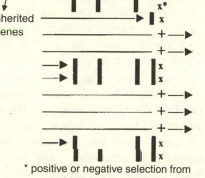

* positive or negative selection from now-added environmental inheritance is marked t or x

that might count as a niche and further modify that environment, and so on. In sum, empirical evidence and new interpretations move us towards an interactionist model of organisms ←→ environment.

A crucial aspect of the new view is seeing that we cannot accept the usual reductive view of genes as the basic and only 'atoms' of life that somehow replicate themselves and build up into organisms and their life courses. This position has been thoughtfully and energetically argued by Lewontin,[33] Levins and Lewontin,[34] Oyama,[35] Rose,[36] and many others.[37] At the very least,

It is clear that the bodies of animals and plants are transient agglomerations of materials derived from both of these flows [the flow of biomass through food webs as well as the flow of genes through generations], and not only for the obvious reason that living creatures must eat … to successfully reproduce. A more fundamental reason is that the very structural and functional properties of these bodies cannot be explained in terms of genetic materials alone. Between the information coded into genes and the adaptive traits of a plant or animal (i.e. between genotype and phenotype), there are several layers of self-organizing processes, each sustained by endogenously generated stable states, themselves a matter-energy flow. Genes are not a blueprint for the generation of organic structure and function, an idea implying that genetic materials predefine a form that is imposed on a passive flesh. Rather, genes and their products act as constraints on a variety of processes that spontaneously generate order, in a way teasing out a form from active (and morphogenetically pregnant) flesh.[38]

Further, and just as important, since niche selection and construction also commonly generate a heritage system, what organisms inherit cannot be reduced to the genetic. There also is the extra-genetic, which includes the immediate environs, the extended environment and life cycle, and the external phenotype.

That the phenomenon of niche construction, which includes a heritage effect, is more widespread than appreciated is seen in the fact that even trees function this way. For example, trees that benefit from being in local environs that are burned off (to change soil chemistry, eliminate competing vegetation, trigger shells or pods to release seeds, etc.) often thrive because their genetic structures and their environments have interactively resulted in shaping surroundings and conditions that promote success. A dramatic instance is found in the way the eucalyptus, with its gum and peeling bark, but resistance to fire, 'transforms its surroundings in ways that modify group lineage and development' by generating an environment in which fire is both more likely and to their benefit:

> Many eucalypt species have seeds that cannot germinate until they have been scorched by a bushfire. To increase the frequency of bushfires to the point where this system works reliably, local populations of eucalyptus trees must create forests scattered with resinous litter and hung with bark ribbons. They are carried aloft by the updraft as blazing torches and spread the fire to new areas.[39]

Beyond the immediate environment on which we have been focusing, the further question of what counts as 'life' needs to be re-examined in light of the new ideas about what is replicated and reconstructed over its course.[40] Whereas we normally consider the life cycle to be that of an individual organism, the phenomena of niche construction and inheritance make clear that what may matter is the life cycle of the entire colony or nest or mott (in part referred to as the 'superorganism'). We find evidence for this in the 'pheromone-mediated transmission of fire ant queen morphology.'[41] Similarly, in the case of quaking aspens (*Populus tremuloides*; Phylum: *Anthophyta* [*Angiospermophyta*]; Kingdom: *Plantae*), a 106-acre (43-ha) stand in Utah weighing 13 million lbs (6 million kg) and sharing a single root system has been nominated as the largest 'organism' on earth, with each genetically identical tree considered the stem of a many-treed body.[42]

As we are seeing, the external phenotype – one outside the bodies that actually carry them – though most obvious for humans, also is operative for many other organisms.[43] While this point is recognized even by those who argue for a determinism that I believe untenable (for example, Dawkins), considerable work remains to be done to understand the full extent to which, beyond specific sets of genes, not only other genes in the organism, but also future generations, and even other species are constituted by organisms and inherited constructions. Clearly, as we have noted several times in passing, it is not only that organisms of one kind shape themselves: regularly, organisms shape the 'earth' itself (the shared environment), each other, and, beyond the life cycles of individuals, future generations of others. The phenomenon, found across the range of life forms – from lichens (the combinations of fungus and either green alga or blue-green bacterium, which, as they grow, 'slowly turn solid rock inside out, into crumbling soil and living earth'), to mammals, to fish – is often breathtaking in scope.[44] As a parallel phenomenon, the snails *Euchondrus spp*, which 'eat endolithic lichens that grow under the surface of limestone rocks in the Negev desert ... are the major agents of rock weathering and also of soil formation in this desert.' This is due not to their consumption of lichens, but to the 'unexpected fact that these snails have to physically disrupt and ingest the rock substrate in order to consume the lichens. They later excrete the rock material,' depositing it 'on the soil under the rocks' at an estimated annual rate of '0.7 to 1.1 metric tons per hectare per year, which is sufficient to affect the whole desert ecosystem.'[45]

Though urban dwellers are usually oblivious to the pervasive production and transformation of soil by earthworms and tree roots that continually goes on beneath their feet, in the most dramatic and obvious cases, such as with beaver and their dams, we can directly see the 'cascade effect.' The beavers' dam

sets up a host of selection pressures that feed back to act not only on the genes that underlie dam building, but also on other genes that may influence the expression of other traits in beavers such as their teeth, tail, feeding behavior, their susceptibility to predation or disease, their social system, and many other aspects of their phenotypes, including, probably, the expression of another extended phenotype, the building of lodges by beavers in the lakes they create by their dams.

Dam construction may also affect many future generations of beavers that may 'inherit' the dam, its lodge, the altered rivers, as well as many other species of organism that now have to live in a world with a lake in it. For example, beavers can create wetlands that can persist for centuries. They can modify the structure and dynamics of riparian zones, and they can influence the composition and diversity of both plant and animal communities. Some of these consequences of niche construction may be just ecological, but some are likely to have evolutionary consequences as well.[46]

In the case of humans, much is passed along through language and culture, through our social institutions. This is precisely why libraries, schools, and entire cities are so important to us. That animals do probe and manipulate their environments and both provide and benefit from learning opportunities appears to be well documented.[47] The extent to which other organisms generate and pass on such genuine epistemic environments – dispositions, information, possibilities, etc. – via forms of communication or observable behaviour (which would not simply be preprogrammed genetically) remains a fascinating and pressing area for investigation with passionately invested arguments from several viewpoints.[48] In any case, there is no disagreement that cities can be fruitfully understood by way of the concept of external phenotype. As Manuel Delanda puts it, we can move from considering the individual human's endoskeleton to the urban exoskeleton, in which bricks are turned into homes, monuments, and walls. However, we also need to be cautious about comparing organisms and cities, especially insofar as 'organic' is often taken to mean 'in balance or stasis,' whereas both need to be considered 'as different dynamical systems operating far from equilibrium.' This is especially crucial in the case of cities, because the latter seldom are in equilibrium, given the flows of matter, energy, and money that pass into them.[49]

The combined new understandings of development and evolution that come about with new interpretations (which matter more in this case than radically new empirical studies, though the latter are generated by the rethinking) of niche construction, with its inheritance dimension, apply, as we have seen, to organisms in general. What we now see is that a dynamic, interactive relation exists among organisms and their environments. This relation has lasting consequences through the legacy that affects the lives, genetic features, and surroundings of generations on complex ecosystems.

3. Rethinking Nature and Built Environments: Continuity from Bacteria to Entire Cities

The above learning clearly marks a major gain in our knowledge about the relation of systems of organisms and their environments. One of the attendant insights is that there is a continuity of phenomena from micro-organisms to plants, animals, people, and cities, then to macro phenomena, such as climate. To return focally to where we began, to the issue of nature and/in the city, at least three points follow from what has been said.

First, cities need to be seen as complex, whole ecosystems, made up not only of the humanly built infrastructure, but of the networks of organisms at all scales. We need only think of recent work documenting the organisms-environments complexity that lies behind epidemics.[50] Recently reanalysed masterfully by Manuel Delanda in *A Thousand Years of Nonlinear History*, the basic phenomenon has been appreciated for almost 200 years. We can see this in Paul Pry's 1829 cartoon showing the organisms that a microscope could reveal in water – in this case, ordinary drinking water that was terrifyingly populated by little beasties. His caption read 'Monster Soup commonly called Thames water. Being a correct representation of that precious stuff doled out to us. Microcosm dedicated to the London Water Company.'[51] The major point was that after the 'cholera epidemics hit London in successive outbreaks: in 1832, 1848, 1849, 1853, and 1854,' it became understood that 'pathogenic organisms – bacteria, protozoa, worms, viruses, and fungi – are responsible for outbreaks of waterborne diseases.'[52]

Second, we may at times want to say, 'I know that,' or believe that we are back where we began. 'Of course, there is nature in the city, squirrels and rats and water.' Have we merely recycled what is common knowledge to no real gain? No, because we tend to 'forget' what we have learned, especially in that we do not really attend to the assumptions that are dramatically changed or to the implications that affect how we must do research differently and act pragmatically. In fact, we now explicitly face clear alternatives. With the new developmental systems theory, co-evolution theory, constructionism, and ideas concerning niche construction and selection, including legacy – all empirically grounded – we can, and must, rethink how nature is everywhere in cities, at all scales, and how organisms and environments are mutually dynamic, interactive. Further, these new modes of thinking can be joined with non-linear self-organization theory: for example, Maturana and Varela's[53] approach to autopoietic, auto-catalytic phenomena (and the variations increasingly described as self-organizational). This view was sophisticatedly developed by Delanda,[54] who helps explore what it means for cities to be understood as ecosystems where that means that they are open, dynamic, and discontinuous.[55]

Finally, these theories and empirical analyses are congruent with enactivist cognitive theories, which may both further insight into embodied cognition and also, reflexively, provide fresh thinking about our character as organisms interacting with our environments, in terms of ontogeny and evolution.[56] The development of this phenomenological-autopoietic approach is providing increasingly sophisticated analysis of how cognition and learning operate in our history-making practices, from the co-ordination of actions in pragmatic tasks, management, and computation to the cultivation of social solidarity.[57]

These insights not only better allow us to appreciate the complex historical development of ecosystems, and the biocultural-regional contexts of cities, but also bring us back to one of the initial concerns of this essay: climate and its full ecological impact on cities.[58] For two outstanding, but still typical, examples, we can attend to what the *GAIA Atlas of Cities: New Directions for Sustainable Urban Living*[59] and the exceptional *Adapting Cities and Buildings for Climate Change: A 21st Century Survival Guide*[60] compellingly present as our current problems and responsibilities. Cities are heat sinks or domes, generating, collecting, and holding heat in ways that are having dangerous effects. The chains of phenomena are familiar: solar radiation and energy dissipation from factories, air conditioners, and automobiles and other vehicles (whose running engines give off heat as well as other emissions in exhaust) heat up air and make it circulate. CO_2 and NO_x in the air act as greenhouse gases; concrete and tarmac store heat; concrete canyons are created between buildings. Cooling spaces adds even more air conditioning, which further increases ambient temperatures, as does mirrored glass, which reflects solar radiation, in an upward spiral of warming.[61]

Unpacking all these dimensions leads us to a genuine puzzle, if not

paradox: How do we plan for a city using knowledge about spontaneous, open, or self-organized phenomena, which are, by definition and
empirical reality, precisely those aspects that are not planned? This is an
especially important issue given that well-intentioned plans have gone
awry for thousands of years, often as the result of unintended consequences. In Taft, California, in the 1920s, for example, efforts by federal
government forces to exterminate mice had perverse consequences in
the form of mice by the thousands flooding over terrain that formerly
had been free of them.[62]

4. Questions of Healthy versus Maladaptive Cities

Is it possible to comprehend and develop cities in ways that do not
make them destructive to their surroundings and organism inhabitants? Though these are ancient questions with no sure answers, they
were pressed a century and a half ago by the Health of Towns Association, and again at the beginning of the twentieth century by the Garden
Cities Movement. Out of the latter developed the Regional Planning
Association of America (RPAA) and the idea of the 'city in the region,'
as distinct from the 'city and the region' (from whence came Ian McHarg
and Ecological Design). Currently, we have the fresh application of the
ideas of self-organization and the science behind Deleuze and Guattari
by Manuel Delanda.[63]

Delanda makes the point that whereas large animals once were the
most dangerous predators, for a long time they have been 'replaced'
by people, especially as concentrated in cities. Cities, which 'were ecologically deprived places, incapable of feeding themselves,' colonized
the surrounding regions and even other 'countries' in order to supply
themselves, to the point where, as Braudel put it, 'Europe was beginning
to devour, to digest the world.'[64] Is there no way to change cities from
being parasites on the countryside and resident and visiting organisms,
as is a wasp to the orchid? Is there no more sustainable model than
the one Americans have (fondly) inherited from Daniel Boone: explore
and settle territory that is new (to you, though others lived there before
you), use it up, and then move on?

There is no shortage of negative examples of the effect of development on the environment. When we ignore the natural circumstances
of urban development, when we mistakenly think that we can control
natural forces with our technology in cases where we cannot, and when
we generate and manage monocultures (whether in hybrid corn or

learning environments), we endure erosion, mudslides, floods, desertification, famine, epidemics, and serial collapses. Increasingly, it seems that our biggest settlements are the greatest disasters. The countrysides, which are treated as little more than supply bases for the cities, are themselves sites of famine. The huge urban areas with concentrated populations of all sorts of organisms are sites of epidemics, as bacteria travel in the guts of animals or within us as we move around the globe more rapidly than ever by means of cars and airplanes.

Yet, there also are successes. The heterogeneity of cities can be the scene of exceptional social and political tolerance, the opposite of the provincial and exclusionary. Cities can be gateways across cultures, geographies, and ways of life. As the meeting place par excellence of organism-environment interactions, cities can be the places in which immune systems develop resistance (tolerance) to otherwise harmful or even lethal 'germs' – bacteria and viruses. This is the city as a region of resilience. We have much to do: to begin, further study must be done of the complex systems of cities as open, self-organized 'markets' – for example, of cultural exchange or material trade; of economic flow; of networks of energy, food, and technology diffusion; and, as we have seen, of the interchange of organisms of all sorts with their surroundings. We need to critically examine whether it is helpful or dangerously misleading to develop the suggestive homologies between (1) exchange at a bacteriological level that can lead to greater immunization rather than epidemics; (2) linguistic hybridity, which unavoidably includes cultural-identity hybridity; and (3) urban heterogeneity as essential to social-political tolerance.[65] Then, too, we need to figure out how to integrate what the auto-catalytic teaches with what we do by planning and design.

It is useful to consider such positive examples. As a case of cultural-natural systems – in fact, multiple such systems – we can see how the self-organization of organisms and behaviours at all scales produces thriving lifeworlds, and how such emergencies also pose problems and offer possibilities when these spheres 'intersect' with one another. One such famous example should remind us of the influence of light on the development of differing numbers of eye cells in fruit flies, where the light also is a result of organisms' construction of local environments: Durham's case of adult lactose (in)tolerance, in which there is a

gene that allows some Indo-European races to digest raw milk as adults. First of all, variation for this gene does exist and is highly correlated with certain cultural patterns. High prevalences of this gene exist only in populations that today consume comparatively large amounts of fresh milk and possess ancient mythologies that both record and encourage adult fresh-milk consumption. In turn, these genetic and cultural materials are associated with environments of low ultraviolet radiation, where vitamin D and metabolic calcium are chronically deficient, that is, with environments where fresh-milk consumption can have positive effects.[66]

Among several possible explanatory scenarios, Durham lays out what he takes to be the most plausible:

As genes for LA [lactose absorption] were favored at high latitudes, more people could drink milk after weaning, thereby spreading the benefits of milk production and improving the local cultural evaluation of the memes behind the practice. The increased availability of milk, in turn, would have continued the genetic selection of LA genotypes, thereby augmenting the frequency of adult lactose absorption, the benefits of milking, the cultural preference for milk, and so on in perpetuity ... The cycle may have started as a continuation of routine infant feeding practices. Early on, the milk of dairy animals may have been tried as a supplement to mother's milk, increasing the volume of lactation, its duration, or both. By virtue of the (initially rare) LA genotypes, some recipients would have maintained lactose sufficiency beyond its normal lapse, continuing to drink milk and thereby avoiding rickets in their early years ... In particularly rachitogenic areas, the advantage to fresh milk consumption would have extended into adolescence and adulthood.[67]

So, there is Switzerland, with its wonderful alpine biocultural landscapes and cheese,[68] and German-Swiss Wisconsin, the self-identified dairy state, which produces large quantities of high-quality milk, cheese, and butter. When such coherent, complex lifeworlds come into contact with distinctly different ones, it is not surprising that a specific difference, though symptomatic of a fully systemic differentiation, is missed until serious problems arise. Adult milk-tolerant cultures which, with the best of intentions, sent milk products to help the starving in other countries were surprised that the results were disastrous, until it was understood that in most cultures, milk is not tolerated beyond the infantile nursing stage. Understanding that adults in Mediterranean cultures, for example, do not digest milk led to buffalo and Italian mozzarella. These non-lactose products are now safely enjoyed by the lactose-intolerant as well as by many who are tolerant and simply like the taste, having no idea of the cultural-biological background.[69]

Another dimension is found in the planning, design, and construction of green buildings and landscapes that are appropriate to the climate and to the dense cities that are emerging and that will dominate as the sites of human population in the future. There are more promising approaches than one might suspect, ranging from the modest but influential works of Pritzker Prize winner Glenn Murcutt, which 'touch the earth lightly,'[70] to the environmentally oriented design education of Victor Papanek[71] and the creative pedagogy of ecological landscape design and planning.[72] Considering the fundamental elements of water, heat, air, and light in urban sites opens a first promising answer to our question of how social policy and planning might learn enough from self-organizing systems to develop appropriate environmental strategies. The transfer would come as a result of understanding the city as we understand the natural global environment: as an open system, far from equilibrium.

As a result of information about global warming, the great tsunami in the Pacific, and the flooding of New Orleans, we have become much more aware of how important water is for a healthy city. In terms of scale, watersheds also emerge as non-arbitrary spatial spheres, since flooding usually occurs as a regional-urban phenomenon in which rivers significantly increase disease, erosion, and pollution – much of which is due to our sewerage, motor oil, and overused pesticides, which run off into the water systems and move downstream. (See figure 16.3.) As for fertilizer, so much nitrogen from its excessive use in the American Midwest drains off into the Mississippi River that a 'dead zone' has been created in the Caribbean. There, algae super-blooms cover hundreds of square miles in which there is not enough oxygen for fish, which die by the millions. Even the upstream portions are in danger, as we see in England, when storms from the North Sea hit the southeast coast, pushing seawater inland. As sea levels rise because of melting glaciers, the already unmanageable surges, up the Thames valleys, for instance, will increase, flooding both the countryside and London more seriously than ever before.[73] In addition to dealing with the fundamental causes of global warming, a wide range of smaller-scale interventions are needed to mitigate this hazard, to help manage and restore ecological systems to fuller resilience, and to enable us to learn more about their complexity and non-linear dynamics.

Simple yet effective remediation of urban watersheds shows the links

Figure 16.3. Urban-regional watershed, Seattle runoff into Puget Sound.

among water, soil, vegetation, fish, birds, and people. The movement towards green infrastructure has many variations to manage stormwater and drainage – to direct, slow, and filter runoff, allowing the conveyance of rainwater to places where it is less harmful or even needed. At one end of the spectrum we find elaborate underground collection facilities in which stormwater can be purified and reused, while providing wonderful miniature wetlands for enjoyment by humans and birds, as in the dense urban fabric of Potsdamer Platz, Berlin. (See figure 16.4.) Less elaborate forms include rural-suburban Prince George's County, Maryland, which took an early Low Impact Development approach, as did Seattle's Street Edge Alternative pilot project, in which the landscaping was dramatically changed by introducing grassed swales, 2 feet (60 cm) of grass shoulder, and over 1,200 shrubs and trees, as well as reducing road width by 6 feet (2 m) and having a sidewalk on only one side.[74] (See figure 16.5.) The new environment improves the network of water diffusion and filtration, substantially reducing polluting runoff from roads into Piper's Creek and from there into Puget Sound, thus helping water quality and wildlife. In addition, less impervious street cover reduces heat buildup and, through good design, calms

Figure 16.4. Stormwater collection system, Potsdamer Platz, Berlin.

Figure 16.5. Street reduction and landscaping mitigate runoff, SEA Street, Seattle.

traffic, making the area safer, quieter, and more conducive to positive neighbourly interactions.

If we carefully attend to the water systems, it is still possible to regenerate the urban riparian ecology and enhance the quality of life. For example, daylighting (uncovering so as to open to sunlight and wind) streams reverses the previous practice in which urban spring water and rainwater has been buried – channelled directly into culverts and underground drainage or sewer systems. This is achieved by bringing the flowing water back to the surface of the earth and replanting native vegetation along the banks. Daylighting allows for the rehabilitation of plant life, complex aquatic organisms and fish (including Coho salmon, whose impeded migration is one of the motivating factors for change in the Pacific Northwest), bird populations, and even larger creatures, such as beaver.[75] (See figure 16.6.) Greenbelts can be extended in corridors – often in the same locations as the stream and river systems – to provide the connected sequences of spaces that birds and other species need, rather than isolated patches, which prove to be non-sustainable islands in terms of thriving biodiversity.[76] The quality of our experience in such restored environments also is significantly improved, aesthetically and in terms of connection with the natural world. The pleasure people take in connecting to natural elements is immediately obvious, as is seen in the drawing power of Freiburg's *bächle*, an ancient system of stream management by small, paved, open channels that the city recently extended throughout the Altstadt as the residents affirmed their identity in terms of the green city.

Heat, air, and light are also critical to the phenomenon of energy use and the larger 'metabolic' relation of cities to their regions and the planet. As one thread to follow, urban energy exchange is amazingly complex. It is a classic example of multiple dissipative systems, with so many variable factors that traditional methods of study, though important, have not been able to interpret most of the unstable dynamics. Cities, of course, take in energy in many forms: natural and fuel-produced heat, food, and water, and processed materials, ranging from wood, steel, glass, cement, plastic, and paper to all the goods we consume. At the same time, cities produce and export large quantities of sewage, exhaust gases, and industrial and domestic wastes.

On the positive side of our continuing effort to address the problems, the new mode of interpretation and practice promises different materials, forms, and processes to better construct and restore healthy organism-environment dynamics, even enabling us to reread stories of

Figure 16.6. Stream daylighting, Ravenna Creek, Seattle.

Figure 16.7. Wind towers, Dubai, Arab Emirates Republic.

success and failure from our past, finding meanings in what may have been set aside or ignored. For instance, in regard to heat and air control, traditional technologies have much to teach. Beyond the lessons to be learned from passive solar control, already somewhat well studied and adapted in regard to earthen and stone buildings,[77] there is increased interest in thermal movement via heat chimneys or wind-catchers, towers long used in the Middle East to let heat escape during hot days and let cool air enter at night. (See figure 16.7.) Similarly, the shading and ventilation systems modifying heat and humidity in the tropics that have developed historically work well, and can be adapted to other locations. The re-examination of these fundamental principles and their adaptation with new materials and designs is proving beneficial in renovations of existing buildings as well as new projects.[78]

The same principles can be put into effect using the entire building envelope, a practice that has virtually become standard. Such design and construction uses double-wall and raised-floor systems with air in between: the heat rises and dissipates when it is hot; on cool days, the air remains stable and insulates the interior from the colder exterior. Research carried out by Battle McCarthy and others indicates that 'double-skin buildings can reduce energy consumption and running costs by 65 per cent, and can cut carbon dioxide emissions by 50 per cent in the cold temperature climatic prevalent in the United Kingdom' – information he directly puts to use with the wind towers and wall systems in his Ionica Headquarters building and Bluewater shopping mall in the UK.[79]

Hand in hand with the impact and control of heat is that of light. In a striking instance of change in a feedback system, better management of heat and energy use can result from better ways of providing proper lighting. Undesirable positive feedback from a non-linear system occurs when we continue our usual methods of providing interior lighting: when conventional buildings in hot climates are lighted in the customary manner, there is enormous and problematic heat gain. Often the largest source of heat in the building comes from light fixtures. To counter the excessive heat, air conditioning is added or increased, consuming even more energy and reinforcing practices such as sealing all windows so that users cannot disrupt the efficiency of the heating and cooling systems. To reverse the feedback from what amounts to an explosion of heat and energy consumption, light can be brought into the interior by several means. The floor plan can be changed by adding an atrium in the middle; or light shelves – simple horizontal elements placed above head level – can be installed, deflecting light from the windows at the outside edge of a building up to the interior ceiling (which then is re-reflected downward further inside).[80] This approach also encourages revisiting the air exchange systems.

The better circulation of air between wall and floor elements also eliminates the unintended incubators for mould spores, some of the major culprits in sick building syndrome. Recently, we have been surprised to find that many buildings initially designed and constructed to save energy by keeping in heat have been overly sealed; by not letting moisture escape, they have created warm, damp places between walls (or between ceilings and the floors above). This situation creates excellent environments in which bacteria, such as Legionella, and toxigenetic fungi, such as the notorious mould *Stachybotrys chargarum*, thrive, causing allergic and respiratory responses dangerous enough to occupants that the structures often must be destroyed.[81] In contrast, successful 'post–air conditioning' projects dealing with light, air, heat, and energy use in a sophisticated way are found in many parts of the world: for example, the Himurja office building, in Shimla (India), consumes almost zero energy during the day as a result of the integrated systems.[82] Economic as well as environmental features are turning in favour of such approaches: since over a 30-year period, half of a building's total costs are for energy and maintenance (as distinct from construction), initial investment in ecologically sound buildings can provide considerable savings in overall life-cycle costs, as is well demonstrated by many lesser-known but very competent high-performance buildings cited by Johnson Controls, such as Johnson Wax Headquarters and West Bend Insurance outside Milwaukee. In some cases, as in flood zones, escalating insurance rates are a powerful driver to new practices.[83]

The features considered here are not limited to homes and small or mid-rise buildings, but can be implemented in the mega-structures increasingly necessary to accommodate urban populations. (Eighteen hundred highrises were constructed in Asia alone during the 1990s.)[84] Some of the most exciting new environments – often called 'green skyscrapers' – demonstrate the viability of ecologically positive buildings as well as showing a beautiful new aesthetic. As with the aforementioned Potsdamer Platz in Berlin, air exchange can be managed throughout the great vertical rises. Among the structures making up the complex, the three buildings comprising the Daimler Benz Offices by Richard Rogers Partnership use natural ventilation and daylighting that operate according to the stack principles described here: by orienting the building to use prevailing breezes as well as by employing operative windows, large atriums, air inlets and outlets, an air plenum, external vertical shading devices, and solar shading provided by variable glazing. These features, along with passive solar energy, cut the facilities' energy usage and carbon dioxide emissions by more than 30 per cent.[85] Indeed, today's most sophisticated designs combine a great number of such ecologically improved elements.

Among the most amazing successes and works in progress are highrises in tropical southeastern Asia. Ken Yeang is a seminal designer and thinker on behalf of the natural city. He and his partner, T.R. Hamzah, have a wonderful record of ecologically and socially successful buildings. Their 21-floor tower in Penang, Malaysia, provides natural daylight by locating all office desks within 20 feet (6m) of an operable window, and by using sunscreens and walls that draw air inside and circulate it without the use of mechanical systems. This design reduces energy use by half and makes a stronger connection to the outside environment. Similarly, their Menara Mesiniaga in Selangor, Malaysia (1992), is designed so that

all of the windows facing east and west (the hot sides of the building) have external louvers to reduce solar heat gain. The north and south sides have unshielded windows, improving natural light. The elevator lobbies are naturally ventilated and illuminated, and a roof structure was designed to accommodate photovoltaic panels in the future. But of all the bioclimatic features, the vertical landscaping is the most representative of T.R. Hamzah and Yeang's approach ... it is used here on different floors in a staggered or spiral pattern, allowing the plants to receive maximum sunlight and rainwater. The vegetation cools the building and provides workers with a sense of connection to the outdoors and nature.[86]

Another example is Hamzah and Yeang's EDITT Tower in Singapore (1998) (see figure 16.8):

For a building of its size and height, the EDITT Tower has an unprecedented ratio of outdoor planted areas to indoor office spaces. The green spaces ascend from the ground to the top floors, and incorporate vegetation from surrounding landscapes to create ecological continuity. In addition to the greenery, which aids in cooling, air quality, and water maintenance (by filtering rainwater and serving as a site for sewage composting), the building contains a water-recycling, water-purification, and sewage-recycling system. As a result, it uses half as much water as most buildings its size.[87]

In light of the complexity of self-organizing systems, we have clearly been encouraged to stop thinking of buildings as autonomous. This is more than a rejection of the modern aesthetic of the autonomy of the artwork, where buildings are seen as sculptural objects; in fact, it explores the relation of buildings to each other as well as to natural systems and built infrastructure. Traditionally, cultures have learned how to maximize the benefits of community form so that buildings shade each other and pedestrian walkways from the sun, or provide openings for breezes, as is needed. This approach has led to the very interesting development of CHPs – combined heat and power stations. Small local power stations can be located in the 'centre of town,' generating electricity; the hot water produced in the process, which would be excessive waste to be dissipated in our usual energy-use patterns, can be piped into neighbouring homes and businesses where it is needed. By using the problems from one system to solve those of another, the process becomes a doubly positive asset in the neighbourhood context: reuse eliminates both wasting byproduct heat in one site and consuming separately generated heat in another. Since the system works best where buildings are close together and connected by short pipes, CHPs also promote a

Figure 16.8. EDITT Tower, Yeang & Hamzah, Singapore.

level of density that has other desirable social and ecological benefits, as argued for by the compact city, new urbanism, and related movements, and as demonstrated as successful in Helsinki, Stockholm, Stuttgart, and Rottweil, Germany.[88] Other examples are found in building complexes, where typical mixed use (offices, shops, residences, social and cultural facilities) is provided in environments that are energy sensitive and open to connection with nature. For example, Renzo Piano Building Workshop proceeded from the plan to redevelop exhibition buildings in Lyon, France, to generate Cité Internationale, a 'micro-city' open to the river, a tree-lined promenade, and the older parts of the city.

On an even larger scale, entire sectors of cities are being planned differently. Though it remains to be seen how much is a matter of public relations and advertising and how much turns out to be a reality, the interest in 'eco-cities' is running high. The conceptual planning certainly is ambitious: for example, Hamzah and Yeang have developed a master plan for an Eco-Tech City in Rostock, Germany, as have Ralph Johnson with Perkins & Will for an ecological campus complex at Luanda, Angola. China currently is of special interest because of its dramatically increasing industrial pollution and its simultaneous intense urban development (at present, half of the buildings now underway *in the entire world* are going up in China). While there are notable projects in Beijing and Huangbaiyu, most expectation is focused on Dongtan, an eco-city for 500,000 future residents being developed on an island near Shanghai.[89]

Conclusion: That Is, Further Questions

Do we need to learn to promote grassroots, bottom-up planning in light of what we have learned from self-organization – for example, as Durham concludes, 'that a major cause of opposition between genetic and cultural replicators is the imposition from above of habits and customs (or living conditions leading to certain habits and customs) that are maladaptive'?[90] Given that the contrast between the imposed (planned) and spontaneously-vernacularly developed is parallel to Delanda's own explication of centralized hierarchies of homogeneous features versus decentralized meshworks of diverse elements, we could press the need to examine the extent to which gateway cities (as distinct from central-place cities) promote complexly hybrid, resilient natural-cultural (rather than monocultural) environments, including politically-culturally tolerant societies.[91] We need to examine the alternative possible relations between discourses and practices of genetics, engineering, and bio-medicine on the one hand and capitalism's rapidly growing research-production facilities on the other in light of prospects for organism-environment well-being rather than exploitation.[92]

We return, then, to our fundamental concern of environmental-cultural well-being in urban-nature dynamics. A final positive direction would be seen in taking seriously the basic questions that are emerging, such as those above. Key questions still demand an integrated, holistic approach to be even partially answered: What is the natural city? How does it come about? How might it be maintained? As one approach to thinking the issue through, we can again look to the early and still critical *Ottawa Charter of Health Promotion* and lessons to be learned from the more than 500 cities pursuing 'healthy city' ideals.[93] We also can freshly investigate how new interpretations, theories, and empirical studies of organism-environment interactions such as are being developed by those unfolding DST, niche construction, heritage landscapes, co-development/evolution, autopoiesis, enactivism, and related approaches might provide new tools with which to conduct research, planning, and design. In the Preface to the new edition of his *How the Leopard Changed Its Spots: The Evolution of Complexity*, biologist Brian Goodwin articulates what may be the core lesson from our new understanding of how 'ecosystems, economies, communities, plants, animals, and health' all are characterized by 'complexity and unforeseen unpredictability':

> Instead of a primary focus on controlling quantities, the challenge for science is to cooperate with the natural creative dynamic that operates at the edge of chaos, to experience the qualities that emerge there, and to move toward a participatory worldview which recognizes the intrinsic values that make life worthwhile.[94]

NOTES

1 Anne Whiston Spirn, *The Granite Garden: Urban Nature and Human Design* (New York: Basic Books, 1984).

2 Victor Papanek, *The Green Imperative: Natural Design for the Real World* (New York: Thames and Hudson, 1995); Ken Yeang, *The Green Skyscraper: The Basis for Designing Sustainable Intensive Buildings* (New York: Prestel, 1999).

3 Sue Roaf, David Crichton, and Fergus Nicol, *Adapting Buildings and Cities for Climate Change: A 21st Century Survival Guide* (Boston: Elsevier, 2005);

Robert Mugerauer, 'Adapting Urban Settlements for Global Warming,' in *Symbiosis and Safety* (Kobe University Press, forthcoming).

4 Bart R. Johnson and Kristina Hill, *Ecology and Design: Frameworks for Learning* (Washington, DC: Island Press, 2002).

5 Hassan Fathy, *Natural Energy and Vernacular Architecture: Principles and Examples with Reference to Hot Arid Climates* (Chicago: University of Chicago Press, 1986).

6 R. Dawkins, *The Selfish Gene* (Oxford: Oxford University Press, 1976); E.O. Wilson, *Sociobiology: The New Synthesis* (Cambridge, MA: Harvard University Press, 1975); Richard Lewontin, *Biology as Ideology: The Doctrine of DNA* (New York: Harper Perennial, 1991); Richard Lewontin, *The Triple Helix: Gene, Organism, and Environment* (Cambridge, MA: Harvard University Press, 2000); E.F. Keller, *The Century of the Gene* (Cambridge, MA: Harvard University Press, 2000); E.F. Keller, 'Beyond the Gene but beneath the Skin,' in *Cycles of Contingency: Developmental Systems and Evolution*, ed. Susan Oyama, Paul E. Griffiths, and Russell D. Gray (Cambridge, MA: MIT Press, 2001); Steven Rose, *Lifelines: Life beyond the Gene* (New York: Oxford University Press, 1997).

7 Oyama, Griffiths, and Gray, eds., *Cycles of Contingency*.

8 Oyama, Griffiths, and Gray, eds., *Cycles of Contingency*; Robert Mugerauer, 'Enacting Color Vision,' IAPL Intensive on Steven Holl, Helsinki, forthcoming.

9 Juhani Pallasmaa, *Animal Architecture* (London: Academy Editions, 1994); Robert Mugerauer, 'Deleuze and Guattari's Return to Science as a Basis for Environmental Philosophy,' in *Rethinking Nature: Essays in Environmental Philosophy*, ed. Bruce V. Foltz and Robert Frodeman (Bloomington: University of Indiana Press, 2004).

10 Karl von Frisch, *Animal Architecture* (New York: Harcourt, Brace, Jovanovich, 1974), 43, 39 (plate 20). Throughout the chapter, I have modified von Frisch's captions to read as standard sentences; though I have rearranged the content, I place it within quotation marks to make clear that I am merely rewording what are his ideas and findings.

11 Astrid Witte and Casey Mahaney, *Hawaiian Reef Fish* (Honolulu: Island Heritage, 2005), 54–5.

12 von Frisch, *Animal Architecture*, 197, 176 (plate 80).

13 von Frisch, *Animal Architecture*, 34, 38 (plate 18); J. Scott Turner, *The Extended Organism: The Physiology of Animal-Built Structures* (Cambridge, MA: Harvard University Press, 2000), 120–1.

14 von Frisch, *Animal Architecture*, 61, 59 (plate 33).

15 von Frisch, *Animal Architecture*, 105 (plate 440), 109 (figure 47).

16 Mitchell Beazley, ed., *The International Book of the Forest* (London: Mitchell Beazley Publishers, 1981), 19, 121; Turner, *The Extended Organism*, 99–119.

17 Lynn Margulis and Dorion Sagan, *What Is Life?* (Berkeley: University of California Press, 1995), 19–20.

18 Richard Levins and Richard Lewontin, *The Dialectical Biologist* (Cambridge, MA: Harvard University Press, 1985), 90–3, 91 (figure 3.1; cf. 3.2, 4.1).

19 Beazley, *The International Book of the Forest*, 55; cf. 132–3.

20 Turner, *The Extended Organism*, 195–200.

21 von Frisch, *Animal Architecture*, 137, 132 (figure 57).

22 von Frisch, *Animal Architecture*, 107–8, 98 (plate 53).

23 The eucalyptus, which has come to dominate host ranges to the extent that it is seen as a noxious invasive species, provides a compelling instance in which we can appreciate that it makes little sense to talk of a 'vacant niche' – or else, as Sterelny and Griffiths point out, the damage done to ecosystems by invasive species becomes unintelligible. Kim Sterelny and Paul E. Griffiths, *Sex and Death: An Introduction to Philosophy and Biology* (Chicago: University of Chicago Press, 1999), 99.

24 Maurice Merleau-Ponty, 'The Reflex,' in *The Structure of Behavior* (Boston: Beacon Press, 1963), 13.

25 Oyama, Griffiths, and Gray, eds., *Cycles of Contingency*, 6.

26 Kevin N. Laland, F. John Odling-Smee, and Marcus W. Feldman, 'Niche Construction, Ecological Inheritance, and Cycles of Contingency in Evolution,' in *Cycles of Contingency*, ed. Oyama, Griffiths, and Gray, 118–20; Kim Sterelny, 'Niche Construction, Developmental Systems, and the Extended Replicator,' in *Cycles of Contingency*, ed. Oyama, Griffiths, and Gray, 336; L. Keller and K.G. Ross, 'Phenotypic Plasticity and "Cultural Transmission" of Alternative Social Organisms in the Fire Ant Solenopsis invicta,' *Behavioural Ecology and Sociobiology* 33a (1993): 121–9.

27 Carl Zimmer, *Parasite Rex: Inside the Bizarre World of Nature's Most Dangerous Creatures* (New York: Free Press, 2000), 48–50; Turner, *The Extended Organism*, 135–7.

28 von Frisch, *Animal Architecture*, 52 (figure 24a).

29 von Frisch, *Animal Architecture*, 117 (figure 51).

30 F. John Odling-Smee, Kevin N. Laland, and Marcus W. Feldman, *Niche Construction: The Neglected Process in Evolution* (Princeton: Princeton University Press, 2003), 3–5, citing B. Hölldobler and E.O. Wilson, *Journey to the Ants: A Story of Scientific Exploration – Processes of Inference Learning and Discovery* (Cambridge, MA: MIT Press, 1994).

31 Laland, Odling-Smee, and Feldman, 'Niche Construction, Ecological Inheritance, and Cycles of Contingency in Evolution,' 119.

32 Odling-Smee, Laland, and Feldman, *Niche Construction*, 5–6.
33 Richard Lewontin, *The Genetic Basis of Evolutionary Change* (New York: Columbia University Press, 1974); Lewontin, *Biology as Ideology*; Lewontin, *The Triple Helix*.
34 Levins and Lewontin, *The Dialectical Biologist*.
35 Susan Oyama, *Evolution's Eye: A Systems View of the Biology-Culture Divide* (Durham, NC: Duke University Press, 2000); Susan Oyama, *The Ontogeny of Information: Developmental Systems and Evolution* (Durham, NC: Duke University Press, 2000); Susan Oyama, 'Terms in Tension: What Do You Do When All the Good Words Are Taken?' in *Cycles of Contingency*, ed. Oyama, Griffiths, and Gray.
36 Steven Rose, *Lifelines: Life beyond the Gene* (New York: Oxford University Press, 1997).
37 We cannot take up here the critical and intensifying arguments about the extent and dangers of the reductive oversimplifications about the 'genetic': what genes are, how they 'operate,' that they in fact do not 'replicate themselves,' that actually 'the genotype simply does not exist' (Tim Ingold, *The Perception of the Environment: Essays in Livelihood, Dwelling, and Skill* [New York, Routledge, 2000], 255 ff). For a good overview of the major figures and positions, see, on the one side, Dawkins, *The Selfish Gene*; P.S. Kitcher, *Vaulting Ambition: Sociobiology and the Quest for Human Nature* (Cambridge, MA: MIT Press, 1985); on the other, Lewontin, *Biology as Ideology*; Lewontin, *The Triple Helix*; Oyama, *Evolution's Eye*; Oyama, *The Ontogeny of Information*; Keller, *The Century of the Gene*; and B.C. Goodwin, 'Constructional Biology,' in *Evolution and Developmental Psychology*, ed. G. Butterworth, J. Rutowska, and M. Scaife (Sussex: Harvester Press, 1985).
38 Manuel Delanda, *A Thousand Years of Nonlinear History* (New York: Zone Books, 1997), 112; cf. James D. Watson, *The Molecular Biology of the Gene* (Menlo Park, WA: Benjamin, 1976), 145; Stanley Kaufmann, *The Origins of Order: Self-Organization and Selection in Evolution* (New York: Oxford University Press, 1993), 525; Goodwin, 'Constructional Biology,' 176.
39 Paul E. Griffiths and Russell D. Gray, 'Darwinism and Developmental Cycles,' in *Cycles of Contingency*, ed. Oyama, Griffiths, and Gray, 195–6; cf. 204–05. On Snow gum (*Eucalyptus pauciflora*), Red River gum (*Eucalyptus camaldulensis*), and the scribbly gum (*Eucalyptus haemastoma*), see Beazley, *The International Book of the Forest*, 151–3.
40 A.F. Robertson, 'The Development of Meaning: Ontogeny and Culture,' *Journal of Royal Anthropological Institute* 2 (1996): 591–610.
41 Sterelny, 'Niche Construction, Developmental Systems, and the Extended Replicator,' 334; Keller and Ross, 'Phenotypic Plasticity and "Cultural

Transmission" of Alternative Social Organisms in the Fire Ant Solenopsis invicta,' 335–6; Paul E. Griffiths and Russell D. Gray, 'Replicator II: Judgment Day,' *Biology and Philosophy* 12, 4 (1997): 471–92.

42 Margulis and Sagan, *What Is Life?* (plate 21).

43 Laland, Odling-Smee, and Feldman, 'Niche Construction, Ecological Inheritance, and Cycles of Contingency in Evolution,' 119.

44 Beazley, *The International Book of the Forest,* 124–5; Margulis and Sagan, *What Is Life?* 181, 189.

45 Odling-Smee, Laland, and Feldman, *Niche Construction,* 7–8, citing M. Shachak, C.G. Jones, and Y. Granot, 'Herbivory in Rocks and Weathering of a Desert,' *Science* 236 (1987): 1098–9; M. Shachak and C.G. Jones, 'Ecological Flow Chains and Ecological Systems: Concepts for Linking Species and Ecosystem Perspectives,' in *Linking Species and Ecosystems,* ed. C.G. Jones and J.H. Lawton (New York: Chapman and Hall, 1995).

46 R.J. Naiman, C.A. Johnson, and J.C. Kelley, 'Alteration of North American Streams by Beaver,' *Bioscience* 38 (1988): 753–62; C.G. Jones, J.H. Lawton, and M. Shachak, 'Organisms as Ecosystem Engineers,' *Oikos* 69 (1994): 373–86; C.G. Jones, J.H. Lawton, and M. Shachak, 'Positive and Negative Effects of Organisms as Physical Ecosystems Engineers,' *Ecology* 78 (1997): 1946–57; Laland, Odling-Smee, and Feldman, 'Niche Construction, Ecological Inheritance, and Cycles of Contingency in Evolution,' 119; documentation by von Frisch, *Animal Architecture,* 266 ff. may seem tame compared with the competing interpretations of these researchers on the one hand and the critique by Sterelny, 'Niche Construction, Developmental Systems, and the Extended Replicator,' 335, on the other.

47 Sterelny, 'Niche Construction, Developmental Systems, and the Extended Replicator,' 334–5; Sterelny and Griffiths, *Sex and Death,* chapter 3.

48 Sterelny and Griffiths, *Sex and Death,* 335.

49 Delanda, *A Thousand Years of Nonlinear History,* 27–8, 104; Odling-Smee, Laland, and Feldman, *Niche Construction.*

50 William H. McNeill, *Plagues and Peoples* (New York: Anchor Press, 1976); William H. Durham, *Coevolution: Genes, Culture, and Human Diversity* (Stanford: Stanford University Press, 1991).

51 Anne Whiston Spirn, *The Granite Garden,* 135 (figure 6.2).

52 Steinberg, *Down to Earth,* 136.

53 Humberto R. Maturana and Francisco J. Varela, *Autopoiesis and Cognition: The Realization of the Living* (Boston: D. Reidel, 1980); Humberto R. Maturana and Francisco J. Varela, *The Tree of Knowledge: The Biological Roots of Human Understanding* (Boston: Shambhala, 1992).

54 Delanda, *A Thousand Years of Nonlinear History.*

55 Cf. Mugerauer, 'Deleuze and Guattari's Return to Science as a Basis for Environmental Philosophy.'
56 Maturana and Varela, *The Tree of Knowledge*; Francisco J. Varela, E. Thompson, and E. Rosch, *The Embodied Mind: Cognitive Science and Human Experience* (Cambridge, MA: MIT Press, 1991); Mugerauer, 'Enacting Color Vision'; Humberto Maturana, 'Biology of Cognition,' 1970, reprinted in Maturana and Varela, *Autopoiesis and Cognition*; Maturana and Varela, *Autopoiesis and Cognition*. Maturana's original work on autopoiesis, further developed by Maturana and Varela, is broadened from analysis of the nervous system and structural coupling, for example, to the effects of learning and interaction with the environment.
57 Charles Spinosa, Fernando Flores, and Hubert l. Dreyfus, *Disclosing New Worlds: Entrepreneurship, Democratic Action, and the Cultivation of Solidarity* (Cambridge, MA: MIT Press, 1997); Terry Winograd and Fernando Flores, *Understanding Computers and Cognition: New Foundation for Design* (Norwood, NJ: Ablex Press, 1986).
58 Robert Mugerauer, *Interpretations on Behalf of Place* (Albany: SUNY Press, 1995).
59 Herbert Girardet, *The GAIA Atlas of Cities: New Directions for Sustainable Urban Living* (New York: Anchor Books, 1992).
60 Roaf, Crichton, and Nicol, *Adapting Buildings and Cities for Climate Change*.
61 Girardet, *The GAIA Atlas of Cities*, 29; cf. Spirn, *The Granite Garden*, 50; Roaf, Crichton, and Nicol, *Adapting Buildings and Cities for Climate Change*; Proceedings, 2nd International Symposium on Design Strategy towards Safety and Symbiosis of Urban Space (Kobe: University of Kobe-COE, 2005).
62 Steinberg, *Down to Earth*, 147.
63 Delanda, *A Thousand Years of Nonlinear History*; Manuel Delanda, *Intensive Science and Virtual Philosophy* (New York: Continuum, 2002); cf. Mugerauer, 'Deleuze and Guattari's Return to Science.'
64 Delanda, *A Thousand Years of Nonlinear History*, 133.
65 See Delanda, *A Thousand Years of Nonlinear History*, 27–8, 107; Keller, 'Beyond the Gene but beneath the Skin'; E.F. Keller, *Making Sense of Life: Explaining Biological Development with Models, Metaphors, and Machines* (Cambridge, MA: Harvard University Press, 2002); Oyama, 'Terms in Tension: What Do You Do When All the Good Words Are Taken?'; Spinosa, Dryfus, and Flores, *Disclosing New Worlds*.
66 Durham, *Coevolution*, 282.
67 Durham, *Coevolution*, 283; cf. Delanda, *A Thousand Years of Nonlinear History*, 143.
68 Mugerauer, *Interpretations on Behalf of Place*.

69 Durham, *Coevolution.*

70 Mugerauer, *Interpretations on Behalf of Place.*

71 Papanek, *The Green Imperative.*

72 Johnson and Hill, *Ecology and Design.*

73 Roaf, Crichton, and Nicol, *Adapting Buildings and Cities for Climate Change.*

74 Steve Nicholas. '"Green Infrastructure" Puts Seattle on the Map,' *Seattle, Daily Journal of Commerce*, 25 July 2002.

75 Ken Yokom, 'Building Nature in Perceptions of the Past: Two Case Studies on Urban Stream Restoration in Seattle,' PhD dissertation, University of Washington, Seattle, 2006.

76 Patrick M. Condon, ed., *Sustainable Urban Landscapes: The Surrey Design Charrette* (Vancouver: University of British Columbia Press, 1996).

77 See Fathy, *Natural Energy and Vernacular Architecture.*

78 Arvind Krishan, Simon Yannas, S.V. Szokolay, and Nick Barker, eds., *Climate Responsive Architecture: A Design Handbook for Energy Efficient Buildings* (New Delhi: Tata McGraw-Hill, 2001); Roaf, Crichton, and Nicol, *Adapting Buildings and Cities for Climate Change.* I want to thank my PhD student colleagues – Sarah Dooling, David Hsu, Jayde Lin Roberts, J. Watson, Ken Yokom – for help in tracking down significant examples. Overall, as more and more research is done and more projects are designed, built, and documented, an increasingly rich archive from which to learn is becoming available. For more information on many of the examples cited here, and others, see especially David Gissen, ed., *Big and Green: Toward Sustainable Architecture in the 21st Century* (New York: Princeton Architectural Press, 2002); Simon Guy and Steven A. Moore, eds., *Sustainable Architectures: Cultures and Natures in Europe and North America* (New York: Spon Press, 2006); Catherine Slessor, *Eco-Tech: Sustainable Architecture and High Technology* (New York: Thames and Hudson, 1997); Maggie Toy, ed., *The Architecture of Ecology* (London: Architectural Design Profile No. 125, 1997); and Yeang, *The Green Skyscraper.*

79 Gissen, ed., *Big and Green*, 42.

80 Krishan, Yannas, Szokolay, and Barker, eds., *Climate Responsive Architecture.*

81 http://www.epa.gov/mold (accessed 23 May 2008).

82 Krishan, Yannas, Szokolay, and Barker, eds., *Climate Responsive Architecture*; Slessor, *Eco-Tech.*

83 Roaf, Crichton, and Nicol, *Adapting Buildings and Cities for Climate Change.*

84 Yeang, *The Green Skyscraper*, 114.

85 Toy, ed.,*The Architecture of Ecology.*

86 Gissen, ed., *Big and Green*, 106; cf. Yeang, *The Green Skyscraper.*

87 Gissen, ed., *Big and Green*, 108.

88 Girardet, *The GAIA Atlas of Cities*.
89 http://www.worldchanging.com/archives/004378.html (accessed 23 May 2008).
90 Cited in Delanda, *A Thousand Years of Nonlinear History*, 145.
91 Delanda, *A Thousand Years of Nonlinear History*, 30–1; Keller, 'Beyond the Gene but beneath the Skin.'
92 Robert Mugerauer, 'Reterritorializing Power, Life, and Money: Bio-Medical-Technological Built Environments,' 2006, IASTE Conference on Post-Global Environments, Bangkok, forthcoming.
93 Gissen, *Big and Green*.
94 Brian Goodwin, *How the Leopard Changed Its Spots: The Evolution of Complexity* (Princeton: Princeton University Press, 2001), ix–x.

17 Natural Cities, Unnatural Energy?

GAURAV KUMAR AND BRYAN W. KARNEY

Introduction

The nature of cities is to concentrate not just humans and human activities, but the consequences of those activities. No matter what the benefits of urban concentration are to the human population, there are nearly inevitable (and often detrimental) consequences to the natural systems. More specifically, this chapter considers the effects on energy use of concentrating human activities in cities. However, this is not so much a chapter about specific technologies, devices, or processes, though it does eventually advocate some specific strategies or policies. Rather, this chapter primarily contends that one of the most significant consequences of the concentration of energy-related activities is to create an emotional distance that tends to separate decision makers from the larger-scale consequences of their actions. Both implicitly and explicitly, the chapter argues that if we cannot find ways of reducing this separation – of bringing the scale of the human use of energy back into terms that are deeply meaningful – the quest for sustainability is likely to be ineffective, frustrating, or perhaps even futile. Thus our premise is simple: cities may be a natural extension of both human civilization and our collective intellect, but they risk reducing our awareness that it is nature itself that makes their sustenance possible. It is their very success that has, at least in the short run, emotionally, physically, and conceptually detached us from explicitly experiencing this reality.

The solution, if one is to be found, will be to make better decisions about how cities function, how they are evaluated, and how they transform. This decision process is a decidedly human activity. Indeed, whether implicitly or explicitly, humans continually size up almost everything, asking whether some action is worth the trouble. Depending on the context, answers range from obviously yes, to definitely no, to 'maybe, it depends.' Although as an academic exercise one well might debate the categorical extremes, it is the middle ground that is almost always the most interesting. The middle ground forces us to assess whether the likely benefits of an endeavour outweigh its expected costs. Of course, some sort of evaluation is inherent in the asking: decision processes and assessments require us to decide what we value. Our goal in this chapter is to examine the energy relations of the natural city through the lens of the question 'In what sense is it worth it?' More constructively, we consider how we can improve the benefits and reduce the external and internal costs of supplying and using energy in the urban context.

Certainly history indicates, and modern trends to urbanization support, that cities are 'worth it' overall. For the greater part of the history of civilization, survival has been a crucial force behind such decisions: the chances of survival were considered better for the group than for the isolated individual. But cities soon became not only a survival mechanism, but a way to enrich human life and experience. Indeed, people almost invariably operate on the premise that cities – complete with their sometimes controversial or problematic residences and shops – are a natural and expected human outcome.

Yet if we intentionally alter our environment, we ought to consider the way this touches on questions of ultimate survival, both ours and that of our planet's many other inhabitants. This thinking is surely at the heart of sustainability considerations. In what sense can cities be considered sustainable? Certainly they do allow us to pursue many activities and permit a degree of human specialization and cooperation that would otherwise be extraordinarily difficult to achieve. They facilitate scientific, creative, and artistic knowledge, and inculcate much that is worthwhile. Modern cities permit the freedom to conduct meetings, to go to the movies, to browse the Internet, to travel the globe, to share books and ideas, to exchange perceptions, to specialize in technical or social fields, and to promote our cultural evolution in a global context. Given so many positives, why is the future of cities in any doubt at all? And what bearing do cities, even natural cities, have on ultimate questions of human sustainability?

To answer these questions, we must recognize one key reality: cities not only do many beneficial things, but they inevitably do something more – they inherently isolate their residents from their larger environment and ecological contexts, the very contexts that make their life possible. For cities have seldom managed their own resources, or produced their own food or energy, or coped with their own waste. Yet every resident is sustained by these external flows. It is perhaps even questionable whether it is possible for the city to meet internally all its survival requirements. This chapter looks at how much this isolation, and thus the city's very measure of achievement, has disconnected inhabitants from the support systems that keep it vital. This disconnect is simultaneously a physical and an emotional one. It is circular, so that its consequences reinforce and isolate the city from its environment, its decision makers from the consequences of their decisions, and its populace from appreciating the true role of their environment in their daily lives. Could the sheer quantity of resources consumed and the energy needed to sustain a city preclude the possibility of a longer-term achievement of sustainability? Though building cities may be natural, their very success causes our contextual or environmental awareness to diminish. This means that the measure of a city's success is also a measure of its inherent risk: the successes that make a city worth sustaining are exactly those that risk its failure. Given this tension, we argue that special actions and measures are required to bring about a more balanced and holistic view. We present this argument primarily in the context of energy systems.

Measuring Success: Energy, Values, and Achievement

Since no environment is infinite, questions relating to the allocation of resources between various activities inevitably arise. How are such decisions made? Certainly, there is an explicit component, of those goals we can both articulate and discuss. But there are also highly influential implicit or unconscious dimensions. How we evaluate what is better, or even possible, inevitably involves a deep component of value systems. At the individual level, value systems are often hardwired in, being implicit in our snap judgments and early dismissals, but the reasons for these evaluations and assessments are often extremely hard to articulate.[1] To be convincing, sustainability must be embodied in the way we actually live, and thus must be incorporated into a gut-level understanding and expectation of the nature of the world. But this is exactly what we tend to lose when we are removed from the context of the ecological system, and thus represents a central conundrum in the quest to make the natural city more sustainable.

Energy is perhaps one of the most practical and universal (and yet still elusive) abstractions of the modern age. Energy is not only an economic commodity that we buy and trade, it is a conceptual framework that can (and should) be used to gauge the usefulness, viability, or character of many other things. Much like monetary currency, energy is conserved in the sense that it can be accounted for, in the way it flows between different systems, and in the way it transforms any system it resides in or moves through. Together, these attributes give energy an almost universal but implicit appeal, allowing energy to be used as a key measure of the value of a traded commodity.

Physically, energy is a general but complex concept, particularly since it often acts as the ultimate changeling. To a thermodynamics specialist, energy is not simply the oft-stated 'ability to do work,' but rather a general measure of the net way a physical system interacts (through heat and work) with its surroundings. Energy participates in a remarkable number of systems, whether embedded in the chemical bonds in food or in a tank of gasoline; it is transmitted in a single photon and in the warmth of a patch of sunlight. It is found in noise and vibrations, in the arrangement of atomic nuclei, and in the economically significant barrels of oil, litres of gasoline, or cubic metres of natural gas. Energy is found in an explosion, in the elevated position of a mass in a gravitational field, and in all forms of movement, from a gust of wind to the rush of water. Energy is found in the flow of heat, or in the ubiquitous but invisible pulse of an electrical current. All these forms of energy play a vital and varied role in both human and natural systems.

Yet one of the initial challenges that arises is that almost every one of these forms of energy is commonly expressed in different units. Like the currencies in the global economy, energy comes in a huge number of denominations and forms, some more universal and tradable than others, many of which have deep historical roots but may now be largely anachronistic.

Take one preliminary example. There was certainly a time when a term such as 'horsepower' was to people an intuitive and natural concept. One had a sense of the power, stamina, and effort associated with the work a horse could do, often dwarfing mere human effort, whether applied to till the ground, uproot a buried stump, or lift a heavy weight. But if one rarely sees a horse in action, let alone harnesses one, what does it mean for a car engine to be measured as 240 horsepower? To add numerical absurdity to this already difficult abstraction, what does it mean for a modern power plant to have the net output of 20 million horsepower? This distancing between current form and historical process creates challenges, and the problem is not unique to horses.

In fact, we largely ignore, or at least have no real feeling for, the human or embodied dimension of energy use. Electricity, in particular, has become almost the universal articulation of energy; we use it in countless devices and in innumerable ways. Many already plug in their cars. We pay for electricity in kilowatt-hours (kWh), but we seldom consider what such a term means. A kilowatt-hour is simply a thousand watts being used for one hour, making it worth 3.6 million joules. In fact, though inexpensive, a kWh is a great deal of human physical energy. To visualize this, imagine carrying two 25-litre water jugs (the water-cooler variety, or about 50 kg) up a long set of stairs. How high would you have to go to embed in them a kWh of gravitational energy? The answer is remarkable: you'd have to climb the stairs to the very top of the CN Tower in Toronto (not just to the observation deck), a height of 553 metres – not once, but 13 times! Even this basic unit is already almost too large to be encompassed in terms of mere human effort. Perhaps it would be more instructive to consider what this amount of energy would be worth in an economic context.

Yet economics provides little additional clarification. At today's prices, a kWh is bought for about a nickel; hardly equivalent to the back-breaking, water-carrying work we just entertained. In Ontario, the typical price of electrical usage is about 5.6 cents/kWh[2] for most residential and commercial uses. In Europe, the equivalent local price is between about 10 and 17 cents/kWh,[3] and at times of peak usage may be significantly higher, perhaps 10 times as much as the Ontario rate. Does that mean Europeans value electrical energy more than Ontarians do? Yet, even at triple the price, no modern city dweller would accept our hypothetical water-carrying employment. Through most of human history, only a slave could be imagined to perform such drudgery. The conclusion is perhaps a little premature, yet on the surface at least, our energy system behaves rather like an invisible workforce that has been enslaved to do most of our day-to-day activities. The trouble is that the resources that fuel our vast industrial appetite are less readily available than they once were. Also, large and sustainable energy sources are rarely found within urban areas. Rather, staggering amounts of urban energy are collected and imported from elsewhere, carried to cities through a vast network of electrical conduits, energy and gas pipelines, and transport tanker cars, before the energy is quickly and presumptuously consumed.

Fundamentally, the city's embodiment of energy is somehow disconnected from our intuition, our cognitive psyche. We seldom use a humanly meaningful reference point to estimate how much energy a kWh really is. In 2003, the electricity usage per capita for Canadians was some 17,200 kWh,[4] the third-highest in the world at that time. This is extraordinarily high, especially when we consider that the main space-heating and transportation sources are seldom electric, and thus not included. But how does one wrap the mind around such a huge number, itself conditioned on a base unit that is almost humanly inconceivable? How do we create a gut-level sense that to be sustainable, cities will need to learn to curb extravagant expectations, and that even the natural city must be gentler in its ecological tread?

Scales of Energy

What we urgently need to do is to go on an energy diet and reduce our energy intensity. This action could partially be accomplished by raising electricity prices not as a tactic to penalize users, but as an incentive for conservation. If cheap calorie-rich food is an indication, cheap energy leads us as a society to become energy obese. Consumption habits become deeply embedded in our expectations of what the 'good life' is, and curbing them is not likely to come easily. In this section, we reinforce the previous images with several others, all aimed at better bridging the gulf between the energy we actually use and those quantities for which we have some deeper feeling.

Overall, energy is not only a means for balancing equations and economies, it is a key index needed to balance the environment and our cities. But why has this role not been fully realized? Expanding on the previous food analogy, why are we oblivious to the scales of energy we consume? Perhaps a simple food illustration – a Mars bar – might provide some help. Remarkably, assuming a full conversion of chemical energy to work, and if one tolerates a slightly exotic image, there is enough energy in a one-dollar Mars bar to lift a moderately sized blue whale (weighing about 100 tonnes) by one metre. Imaging this – a Mars bar beside a blue whale – is an excellent image of such a disparity.

More generally, a useful metric in gauging the energy value of consumption can be created by considering approximately how much energy, in megajoules, a dollar would buy (recognizing that these values continually shift with time and location):

- candy bar (Mars) 0.9 MJ/$
- gasoline 35 MJ/$
- electricity 60 MJ/$
- natural gas 98 MJ/$

Since these everyday goods span two orders of magnitude, it is no wonder we have so little feeling for how much energy we consume. Added into this mix is the embodied energy in all the goods we use. These goods usually contain an inherent energy value, usually at best only partially represented by how much an object costs in economic terms. Clothes, books, silicon chips and electronic hardware, medicines, packaging, and electricity all have embedded energy values and pricing determined by how much slave-like work nature has been made to do. The energy we use is directly related to the limits of our human and technological growth. But have we exceeded these limits? Understanding how energy flows in our society would give us a starting point for exploring ways that a natural city might efficiently use energy. Energy conservation has become a catchphrase for the modern environmentalist, and rightly so. But reducing our energy imprint might be more meaningful if one could be physically aware of how much energy is worth. 'Worth,' it seems, comes in two forms: the first being that which we can internalize and embody within our cognitive patterns, and the second being monetary cost. Embodying our energy requirements is nearly impossible for modern humans, because we consume it on such a vast scale: from what we eat, amounting to a few thousand calories, to what we wear and use, to the amount of water, minerals, and bio-commodities we buy, to the cars we drive and the buildings we occupy.

To put the stated values in perspective, perhaps we need to further enlarge the range of images we use. Consider explosive force: a tonne of TNT has the energy equivalent of about 4,184 MJ – about $40 worth of natural gas. If you want to 'observe' this energy, you need watch Niagara Falls for only a few seconds (just over two seconds, in fact). Not only is there a fracture between our perception and the reality of our hunger, but the value of a given amount of energy is also influenced by its end use, in this case hydro power versus explosive power.

To more graphically underline the idea of energy as evaluation, consider the Colosseum in Rome. Gladiatorial combat comprising lethal weapons, charging chariots, whips, swords, slaves, exiles or convicts, and executions is hardly common these days – these combats were historically used as a political tool and as entertainment. How might one gauge the Colosseum's value? A historian might say that the Colosseum tells us of the mistakes and successes of the past, and is an imprint and proof of our development. An engineer might say that the materials used in construction are a testament to the technical skill of the prevalent civilization, informing us of the evolution of engineering technique. The economist might say the Colosseum is worth 10 per cent of all revenues collected from the tourism industry, and is a good investment both historically and presently. In *The Upside of Down*, Thomas Homer-Dixon[5] estimates the required energy: including only the farming and transport of food energy for the workers and oxen used over the construction period, and excluding other significant upstream and downstream energy requirements, still results in a staggering tally of more than 44 billion kilocalories of energy. Over 34 billion of these kilocalories went to feed the roughly 1,800 oxen engaged mainly in transporting materials. More than 10 billion kilocalories powered the skilled and unskilled human labourers, which translates into 2,135 labourers working 220 days a year for five years.

But what do such numbers really mean? Is 44 billion kilocalories equivalent to the energy in 2,000 pizzas, or 2 billion? It is actually about 184,000 GJ, equivalent to about 30,000 barrels of oil. With today's prices (or was it yesterday's?) this is worth about $3 million. In terms of gasoline energy, this translates to about 5.2 million litres of gasoline (enough to fill a couple of Olympic-sized swimming pools). Yet, in 2004, Ontario consumed 15.7 billion litres of gasoline,[6] or about 43 million litres a day. So the province of Ontario consumes about eight times the energy equivalent for building the Colosseum – in a single day!

Homer-Dixon goes on to say that our societies are based on these sorts of colossal flows of high-quality energy, without which the complexity of our life would unravel. Yet, recognizing our vulnerability is not equivalent to solving it. Is not building and development natural to humans? Yet that natural tendency implies a much higher usage and consumption of precious few resources. It almost seems that in order to conceive of a natural city, we are in conflict with ourselves: our natural tendencies versus our natural environment. But how are we to reconcile this conflict? Can the equilibrium point be reached without catastrophic imbalance, or equally dangerous overshoot?

The key thought is that humans used to have a much more acute sense of the natural embedded energy they consumed. Specialization within cities has broken the connection of manufacturing and usage. Ultimately, we must recognize that all human needs are served through nature and the environment. It is essential to acknowledge this isolation so that we may remedy it. A natural city must conform in some way to a constrained usage of energy, not simply because it is environmentally beneficial, but because it must reinforce the true costs of using that energy. It must ensure that the embodiment of energy is recognized as a natural part of human interaction. The focus for most metropolitan cities should not be only inwards, towards human activity, but also outwards, towards the environment. Measuring our success through internal metrics must ultimately relate to our collective impact on this sustaining environment. This is an absolute critical connection that must be enforced and then reinforced if we are to design and build natural, sustainable cities.

Societal Perspectives

Western society is apparently stressed on many fronts. Its populace may be well educated, well informed, and technologically advanced, but it has caused havoc in the global, environmental, and cultural realms. Our society seems inwardly driven; we are conditioned to think that the betterment of our lives and our individual being can be satisfied through consumerism. Most decisions made by the general populace via individuals ask the question 'How does it affect me?' Advertising and marketing gurus have spent obscene amounts of money to blossom the economy into such a perfect buying machine, a fantasy that has recently collapsed along with falling markets. The prevalence of personal transport, personal computers, personal accessories, and personal information is but a symptom of a much larger problem. On the financial and economic front, we are locked into a cycle of consumerism that seems insatiable, but we must recognize that everything we consume has environmental, social, and cultural dimensions as well.

Our conditioned nature seldom provides us with the foresight to ask, 'How does this affect others?' Whether they are buying a new car, purchasing a new home, maximizing their financial portfolios, or buying groceries, most people are concerned first about themselves. If instead they asked, 'Is this better for our society?' the decisions would become complex and even infeasible. While seemingly disconnected, such a consideration has a tremendous impact on our societal energy use, our energy footprints, and our communal sustainability.

Let us explore the sphere of influence of the relatively simple idea of buying local. Imagine, for example, if an entire community in the suburbs decided to buy only local produce for the spring and summer months. The initial buyers would pay a high premium, because the costs are borne by fewer people. But with time, the costs could be more evenly spread and the community's energy footprint reduced. To become more sustainable requires a large enough pool of initiates willing to 'do the right thing,' along with the mental change that prompts the rest of society to seek the betterment of the community, not just themselves. This 'unselfishness' does not coincide with Western societal values, so how are we to achieve this seemingly impossible goal? Artificial market drivers, for example, and policy are fairly effective influences. In the case of foodstuffs, after considering that it takes energy to manufacture the packaging, manufacture preservation agents, construct distribution centres, and provide local transport and storage requirements, the total energy consumption is sizeable. But what if many (or all) communities adopted the same policy? Can the true energy reduction of such action be measured?

Similar questions arise about water consumption as well, especially for water-intensive crops such as rice, to which one can associate an inherent water price. And since it takes energy to pump, channel, and construct irrigation, the real energy impacts are much more complex than those already stated. The above example does not consider the environmental or social costs. For example, fresh water being a scant resource for the paddy fields of India and China (a primary exporter) is in no way reflected in the price paid or the consideration given by consumers in the Western world. More recently, however, other factors, such as fuel and fertilizer costs, have been reflected in the global increase of rice prices. Buying a kilogram of imported rice affects the environment, the economy, and the very lives of the farmers producing it. Asking the same question again – 'How does this affect others?' – seems to have a larger sphere of influence than local buying habits. If such a small decision can lead to such a large web of complex interactions, how large might the sphere of influence of the natural city be, and can it be designed to minimize the negative impacts?

We need to recognize that we are dependent on our environment, that we exist within it, not outside it, that it provides us with everything we consume, and that if we are not mindful, we will destroy our only resource and seal our fate. A natural city is not a luxury, or an interesting concept confined to journals, but rather a critical necessity if we are to recover our collective connection with nature. Energy is able to capture the essence of our civilizations, the dependencies of our being, and becomes the true starting point for any endeavour to envision a natural city.

EnerGuise

We have explored the truly astonishing scales of energy in our lives, as well as society's altruistic, yet limited, perception on energy consumption. Part of the reason for the ignorance of externalities is that energy use is often well disguised: not simply by form and function, but temporally as well. Energy is a part of every activity, not just the ones we plug into a wall socket or fill with gasoline or diesel. Are we fully aware of the embedded energies that go into the manufacturing of the appliances themselves, or of the social consequences of purchasing the product? This seems to be a major roadblock universal to Western ideals: the fact that 'improvement' or 'efficiency' is not context specific and is typically valid only in an isolated system. As a relatively simple example, what does the 'efficiency' or 'power consumption' of a 60-inch plasma LCD television mean to most users? In most cases, the total power consumption is higher than for a conventional television. And even if it were not (as may be the case in the near future), the rating does not represent the higher manufacturing costs associated with the product, which is substantially more energy intensive. Some may argue that this true cost is captured in the higher price of the product, insofar as it is imported, and the labour may have been fairly cheap. In this example, energy has disguised its intensive manufacturing past with a frugal-use future.

This embedded energy value seems to be disguised not just from the social perspective but even economically, both factors being interconnected and codependent. This energy that is disguised – EnerGuise – is not free, as is discussed later in more detail. Yet, even ignoring the embedded energy, most people are oblivious to energy's role. If asked about the number of ways in which energy is measured, many people may be able to name several common units. But we can measure energy in calories and kilojoules, megatons of TNT and kilowatt hours, barrels of oil, miles per gallon, degrees Celsius, Kelvin, Watts/m^2, and the ever-popular \$/litre or \$/kWh. We measure energy in chemical bonds and fission reactions, spectra and wavelengths of radiated waves, and quanta packets of light, candle lumens, and sound intensities. We measure energy in human dimensions, such as 'cars' or 'household' or even the vivacity of paintings and exhaustion of the human body; in planetary systems, cosmological constants, and the mysterious dark matter of the universe; in ordinary foods, extraordinary senses, urban and rural greenspaces, nature reserves, and the atmosphere of a metropolitan city. Subjective though some of the measurements may be, when mingled with objectively quantifiable ones, these collectively trace a common link: beneath both layers of perception lies a very real flow of differing forms and quantities of energy. A painting may be vibrant because of the wavelengths of colours it reflects, but a similar observation may be made of distant galaxies. A complex web of interacting energies is constantly shifting, evolving, and unfolding. These EnerGuises may provide a way for a natural city to recognize, enhance, and map its energy flows both internally and externally to its natural environment. In designing a natural city, such considerations should play a big role, because they will influence how goods and services are perceived and thus influence the question of whether a natural city is being founded on unnatural externalities.

Sustainability

Recognizing the scales, perspectives, and disguises of transforming energy for the natural city inevitably leads to the idea of mapping its inputs and outputs, or its sustainability. The energy a natural city consumes could be mapped using collective arrays of inputs and outputs, yet envisioning a sustainable future may not be so simple. Any concept of sustainability works on the premise that by mapping such inputs and outputs of various components and converging where the loop is closed, where the goal is efficiency (environmental, social, or economical), maximization might be achievable. But is it really? For example, consider the power infrastructure of the natural city. Perhaps it might all come from renewable energy, such as geothermal or solar or wind. Which might be termed more environmentally efficient: to decentralize power production, so that each household generates its own electricity, or to have a centralized wind farm or solar station? Wind turbines have come to be seen as cumbersome and problematic to track power usage, but solar power is subject to cascading failures and blackouts. Are true economies of scale possible, or are they largely a side effect of more concentrated risk? Suppose our modelled natural city opts for the first choice of decentralized power production. What happens if household production breaks down? In winter, this means many people may be without power and therefore be at great risk. Moreover, one must consider where all of that infrastructure will be built, how it will be shipped, and how it will be assembled.

Tools such as life-cycle analyses may give us an idea of what the trade-offs between centralized and decentralized power production may be, but may say little about the reliability of the design, the accuracy of the results, or the externality aspects that extend beyond the boundaries of the study. And even if some of these questions could be addressed, the next hierarchy of connections must be accounted for. How could everyone afford their own electrical production costs? The problem now engages the political, legislative, and economic realms of the natural city; the same is true for centralized production. Socially, environmentally, and economically, it would be like having a million small problems to solve instead of a few large ones. Sustainability, then, is a guide to evaluating the trade-offs a natural city would encounter, but is not the only tool that needs to be considered. Sustainability's strongest ideal is that it advocates preventive approaches, not simply for engineering or design, but along social avenues, such as preventive medicine, sustainable architecture, and self-sustaining economies.

The Modern City

Before exploring how a natural city might work, we must understand how cities presently function. Although cities are as unique and varied as wine or cheese, they all have rather high population densities and rely on the transportation of materials and people. Cities also tend to be function specific, where certain parts are dedicated to certain tasks, such as industrial areas, manufacturing plants, artistic districts, shopping complexes, nightlife areas, and nature parks. It becomes easy to see that from an energy point of view, these areas have varying requirements (not accounting for residential living). Why not design utility infrastructure that recognizes these differences and maximizes usage?

There have also been significant changes in the way materials and energy flow through the city. As the city expands, the area encompassed by its borders generally increases in a much higher proportion, as opposed to its interface with other jurisdictions. This means that the ratio of flow of materials and energy to the serviced area is constantly increasing. At some point, this ratio becomes too high and a smaller subsection or jurisdiction may be formed. But what exactly is this ratio? Can it influence the design of a natural city?

Large cities generate vast amounts of waste, and this, too, must be accounted for. A lofty goal for a truly natural city might be to reduce its waste to zero. It is conceivable in theory, but perhaps impractical. There is no alternative for treating bio-hazard waste, for example, save incineration, perhaps to produce power. A natural city may also consider its streets and infrastructure as breeding grounds for various flora and fauna. In the same way that bicycle and trekking trails, pedestrian walkways, and high-occupancy vehicle lanes are designed to meet the needs of the populace, natural cities can be designed with urban wild-life in mind. Many species of birds, animals, and plants are surprisingly adaptive in such environments, and with a little help may flourish.

The Energy Picture

In terms of energy, the modern city gobbles up a fair bit, but it also radiates a lot of energy back into its environs. This counter flow is generally toxic to at least some degree, being in the form of waste heat, waste sludge or sewage, toxic chemicals, runoff, and many other unusable or at least unviable forms. Modern cities also tend to form urban heat islands because of their many manufactured surfaces, which are also partly responsible for vast amounts of chemicals being washed into the urban watershed. Cities in colder climates tend to use a lot of energy for space heating in the winter and space cooling in the summer. Hotter cities tend to have a more generalized cooling pattern of very high peak day usage and less intensive night-time usage. Nonetheless, the energy intensity of the natural city needs to be mapped to attribute energy usage to particular types of industry so that it can be decreased.

These high-quality energy flows are used at exorbitant rates because of the low economic cost of the resources; cities will almost certainly require more energy in the future. What makes these basic facts all the more troublesome is that the quality of both the resources and the energy we harvest is decreasing. While newer technologies usually end up creating novel problems, there is neither a roadmap nor an agreed-upon destination for human development. The need to develop newer technology does not imply an ultimate purpose for the impressive array of our inventions. While acknowledging that a natural city has many more dimensions than energy itself, all of these dimensions – be they social, economic, techno-centric, bio-diversity, or cultural evolution – are based on the assumption that a natural city has significant high-quality flows of energy. Without such a flow, the basic conditions and standard of living would degrade, overshadowing the very need for a natural city.

To develop towards a truly natural city, energy flows must be understood and then reduced so that the city's dependence on natural resources is reduced. As demonstrated through the Colosseum example, the energy needs of the past were minuscule compared with the energy needs of the future. Any examination of the world's primary energy consumption[7] shows a steady increase over the better part of the last century. What is unclear is whether this growth is natural for the human race. Presupposing that it is, what can be done to reduce our flagrant use of nature's resources? The energy picture really raises this question: How can we simultaneously use less while providing more?

Creativity and Technology

Creative ideas abound and are perhaps one of the few avenues that may provide significant advances in opposition to so-called conventional thinking:

(a) Modern building materials, for example, tend to be far removed from nature; in most cases, natural processes are unable to break them down. Nowadays, building materials are more often recycled, or the aggregate used from old demolished buildings.

(b) Mining a city's electronic and technological wastes to recycle them into new components is another solution to increasing resource consumption. All electronic equipment, such as circuit boards and microchips, has accumulated to the point that it constitutes a vast (but complex) source for silicon, copper, tin, and zinc.

(c) End-of-life manufacturer accountability is yet another option that provides cyclical material processes, but is becoming progressively more economically viable, particularly since virgin resources are increasingly more expensive and more difficult to find.

We have come far in our quest for progress and development, but are dangerously close to letting progress slip into disaster. Besides moving through the Industrial Revolution and continuing on towards global change today, such avenues as biotechnology, nanotechnology, and nuclear experimentation all represent real risk.

The limits of our technologies are complex to define. But borrowing from the analogy used for signal reception, once the noise of a technology becomes increasingly louder than the signal and the externalities of that technology's intended function, we have reached a limit.[8] In most cases, however, the danger is that this limit is ill defined or invisible. Sometimes, one limit may even be traded for another. The green revolution, for instance, has induced genetic modification of food produce, but has traded genetic diversity for replicable high yield and productivity, often at the cost of compromising many of the natural defences an organism had for variability in conditions and stresses. Antibiotics have led to the eradication of many diseases and have helped produce the well-being of several generations, but have been traded off against the body's decreased natural immune response and the creation of superbugs that threaten to initiate major epidemics. Granted, many of these consequences could not have been conceived of in the past, but as we try to learn from such lessons, we can anticipate such developments of our present arsenal of technologies. We are quickly learning, for example, that the information age has led to proliferation of technologies that may allow us to boost productivity, but increase stress levels as well. In this case, the limit is ill defined. One might ask at what limit of stress does the average person's productivity start to decrease, and how much does technology contribute to that reduction? A natural city must acknowledge and engage such questions.

Designing the Natural City: Conceptual Ideas

Part A – The Energy Hive

Before we discuss design alternatives for the natural city, let us consider if any other natural cities already exist. Understanding how they function and what drives the equilibrium state, we can start to build a framework for the anthropogenic natural city. To better illustrate how cities need to be augmented, changed, or designed, let us look at an ecological analogy using a colony such as a beehive, an ant hill, a termite mound, or a coral reef. A common biological theme is that the harvested energy is on a scale that does not overload or undervalue the nature of the organisms. Their environs exist in their collective linkages. When a 'natural' colony realizes that resources are scarce, essential activities are prioritized and a shift takes place among its members either to conserve resources or to spend them to locate more food. In other words, there exists a balance in natural colonies to regulate internal mechanisms based on external stimuli, and not the other way around.

Natural cities need to function in much the same way. An ant colony or beehive will establish an equilibrium point where growth is no longer possible. While these insects have reached their peak efficiency, human beings can make much better use of the resources they currently harvest. Basically put, human beings have found ways to exploit nature so that it promises unlimited growth, breaking the feedback connection with the environment. To re-establish this feedback, an energy mapping is proposed that could illustrate the high-intensity energy flows through a city. Inputs and outputs of energy should be mapped (analogous to industrial ecology) such that they would outline the critical and non-critical imports and exports to surrounding jurisdictions and wastes expelled into the environment. This would facilitate more comprehensive holistic metrics to be used as performance criteria. This energy-hive mapping could also be interfaced with economic and social models to become a predictive tool in assessing overall impacts. The iterative nature of such an endeavour would have significant bearing on the policy development and review process.

The mapping itself might become complex, with each inflow connecting to several outflows and vice versa, much the same way a comb in a beehive is connected to several others. Since energy flow is interconnected and codependent, this implies that a change in one aspect or component of the flow would also affect others. Larger, quicker networks mean that effects are felt far and wide and may travel quickly – but may also mean that small, positive changes may have larger positive repercussions. Performance indexes such as resiliency and robustness can now be quantified and benchmarked. The energy hive would prove useful in establishing a model of the internal energy flows of the natural city, but we need the model to extend beyond the walls of the natural city into the external environment.

Part B – Energy Banking

Connecting the internal energy flows with the external requires us to ask ourselves: How much energy are we hoarding and what is the cost to our environment? How much have we withdrawn from nature and when must we replenish it?

The idea here is that since the natural city will have inflows and outflows of energy, perhaps we might treat them as deposits and withdrawals, with the bank being nature itself. Most people understand the concept of banking: deposits, withdrawals, interest, and assets making up the net worth value. While we obtain much useful work out of our natural surroundings, like any bank, we have a bit of slack to play with. Our ecosystem contains buffers that are able to deal with a certain amount of polluted deposits and material withdrawals. Even better, it may seem for a time that we are not incurring any significant service charges or loss of credit. Yet, in nature, all of our unpaid interest charges in some form of cashable IOUs seem to be accruing, and as the stock market events of October 2008 so dramatically reminded us, any system that is falsely sustained, or that runs long-term deficits, tends to become unstable and prone to sudden collapse.

But as we allow nature to slave for our needs, we begin to get collection calls from the bank. Communicating with us through messages about holes in the ozone layer, global climate changes, drought and the scarcity of water, the loss of irrigable land and crops, and decreased diversity, nature is surely telling us that it is high time we started making payments. We are likely rapidly exhausting the buffer that has helped us survive. The danger is that we have collectively leveraged so much, we may not be able to pay it back at all; who can guarantee or underwrite our loan? The momentum of the interest rate and a large loan means we may be liable for foreclosure or worse. Bankruptcy, in this case, means that the bank goes down as well – a virtually unimaginable crash and decoupling of our entire ecosystem, on both local and global levels.

But perhaps we can use this banking analogy to create a constructive tool. Building biodiversity, creating natural parks, bettering air quality, and doing such general natural enhancements can be related to a common sustainability index or performance metric. Consider that these improvements are all part of the same portfolio, but represent various types of assets. In the financial world, profitability and positive net worth are two main performance criteria. Applied to the realm of environmental sustainability, this approach seems disconnected, because there is no common denominator between the different assets and thus no framework to evaluate the value or trade-offs between them. Unlike the financial world, where assets and money are largely interchangeable, it is inherently impossible to have such a perfectly valued system for the environment. Biodiversity and human health are not readily interchangeable 'assets,' but surely it is possible to have a much closer approach than the one we have now.

Holistic Approaches

The phrase 'holistic approaches' has in recent times been applied loosely in many cases. Instead of an explicit definition of what is meant by the term, illustrative examples would perhaps better serve our current purposes. From the energy perspective, simple concepts such as space heating and lighting seem at the outset to be disparate from each other, but in reality they are not. For example, the recent ban of incandescent light bulbs in Ontario, with the aim of switching to compact fluorescent ones as a means of being more sustainable, has come under some scrutiny.[9] In colder climates, incandescent bulbs provide the secondary benefit of electrical heating in winter, thus offsetting to some extent space heating that may be derived from natural gas, which has higher greenhouse gas emissions. Of course, the point is not to stop analysis, but to offer analysis that is comprehensive in order to be prescriptive.

Since conventional methods lack the ability to account for externalities and links between various performance criteria, the natural city needs to be designed using tools and benchmarks that address such relations via holistic mapping criteria. In the environmental context, our disconnection with nature means that the indications of our society going over the tipping point are in some cases blatant yet ignored, and in other cases masked and subtle.

Another example of a non-holistic and analytical sleight-of-hand is the recent obsession with automobile efficiency. Consider, first, that even if an automobile's efficiency were significantly higher, would the result automatically be a lower environmental impact as opposed to public transit? Does efficiency in any way reflect the embedded energy due to the manufacturing process, or consider whether trips taken are worthwhile? In order to achieve higher efficiencies, one idea is to build cars that are much lighter. A lighter car is more efficient, since a greater ratio of the available power moves the occupants. But the more pressing part of efficiency reporting has to do with CO_2 emissions. Most manufacturers (and consumers) report only fuel efficiency (L/100km) as the ultimate performance criterion – a good performance indicator for non-electric and non-hybrid vehicles. So lulled are we by such figures that we use them even for electric or hybrid vehicles, not stopping to consider that fuel efficiency may be the wrong metric for them. While fuel efficiency is informative, it cannot be applied simplistically to electric cars, since they also draw some power from the grid. It is as if recharging the electric battery comes for free, both economically and environmentally. Even when the appropriate measure is used (such as grams CO_2 equivalents) in places such as Western Europe, these are still reported as direct conversions from the fuel efficiency components only. In reality, the efficiency of electric cars would depend on the supply mix of the region as well as the internal fuel efficiency. Notice that this says nothing about battery life, long-term waste disposal issues, battery and electronic reprocessing, or embedded manufacturing energy.

Holistic approaches can be effectively used to influence both policy making, on the large scale, and public understanding, on the local level. But even holistic approaches have their limits. Consider, for example, the hypothetical situation where a large portion of personal transportation is made up of 'environmentally friendly' electric cars. In fact, the government of Canada had been offering an eco-rebate program (up to $2,000) for fuel-efficient vehicles that included electric cars.[10] The reason supplied for discontinuing the program was that Canadian retailers had started offering many more fuel-efficient vehicles, which was the prime goal of the program. Holistically, however, the program had an unintended trade-off; fuel-efficient vehicles tended to be imported cars, resulting in a substantial drop in the sales of North American products and over-supply due to manufacturing. Going back to our example, a large portion of electric cars may have other impacts as well. A significant shift to electric cars would require a major increase in total electrical power production requirements, not accounting for transmission and line losses. Where might all the extra electrical energy come from? Renewable sources only? Does a vehicle's fuel efficiency metric have any real bearing for this example? Obviously, this discussion exposes only the tip of the gas emission iceberg, but effectively demonstrates the need for holistic criteria in all sectors when designing a natural city.

Another challenge with respect to setting holistic performance criteria for the natural city is decreasing its energy imprint. The city's power-generation infrastructure represents a substantial portion of all energy consumption. But how should each type of generation technology be evaluated? It is obvious that the answer cannot be 100 per cent solar energy or 100 per cent wind energy, since both are intermittent sources and are inherently unreliable; it is highly unlikely to be 100 per cent nuclear or 100 per cent hydro, because of massive capital costs involved for such development, not to mention public acceptance and land-use footprints; it cannot be 100 per cent geothermal or coal or natural gas, either. Each technology brings its own set of possibilities and costs, all of which need to be integrated into the social, cultural, and ecological environs of the city. Solar power in a predominantly cold or rainy city may not be technically effective, but development of nuclear power for a relatively small population would be equally unviable, even from a technical perspective alone.

The trade-offs between these differing technologies need to be evaluated, not because there is a precedent to build a natural city, but because it is a responsibility we owe to future generations as well as to nature itself. Human development in the natural city will also involve other trade-offs, to which end animal hunting and breeding grounds need to be conserved, ecological webs need to be monitored, manufacturing energy intensities need to be addressed, and long-term health hazards need to be analysed. But the real question is whether it might be possible to achieve progress through far fewer repercussions; if not, where is the balance point?

To illustrate the problem of the balancing act, consider that for every kWh of energy generated, there is an environmental cost. Say this cost is in terms of trees felled, oil drilled, gas burned, or some other transaction. As power generation increases, so do the marginal rates of these environmental costs. At some point, these costs must balance each other out: that is, the costs of harvesting the resources must reach the point where they outweigh the utility of the end good or service. But how are we to equate environmental costs with economic ones? How many trees felled must equal the revenue of producing a sheet of paper? Is it one, 10, or 100? What if there were only 1,000 trees left? Or only 100, or only 10? And how do we compare the differing measure associated with differing sources? It is these hidden consequences that dynamically alter the decision maker's understanding, with the consequences nearly always being hidden as well.

The goal of these approaches is ultimately to be able to construct a map of how implemented decisions ripple through the ecology of the natural city, through both social and environmental domains. Since such connections inherently imply trade-offs, by evaluating them we can start to recognize how the interfaces between technologies interact with each other and with society. The real driving force for the following section is that without the proper framework in place, without the ability to ascertain the potential trade-offs between different courses of action, particularly with respect to energy, the natural city may fall victim to the drawbacks of conventional wisdom and methods. Accounting for the limits of our technologies as much as possible, and integrating the social dimension into the planning process, we may develop a framework that is sustainably progressive yet recognizes its own limitations as well.

Energy Metrics and Strategies

While keeping in mind that the natural city exists in a larger context, that our object is to preserve this environment as best we can, the following energy metrics are proposed as a preliminary guideline to better understand the impacts of generational infrastructure.

(a) The $/kWh production metric has been used in the past to categorize such infrastructure over the lifetime of a project. Notice, however, that it may not include upfront construction costs or non-traditional environmental costs. To compensate, some financiers establish a break-even cost within a time constraint. In parallel, an equivalent energy break-even cost can also be included, at least in terms of the facility's embedded energy. Note that for non-renewable sources (and nuclear ones), this break-even time will never truly be positive, since the fuel will always contain more energy than the output. This Energy Return on Investment (EROI) can then be mapped into the associated environmental costs and carbon footprint of the facility itself.

(b) One measure of the environmental cost is the greenhouse gases in CO_2 equivalent per kWh of energy production (CO_2 emitted /kWh). Associating a cost (say $10–$100/tonne of CO_2 equivalent) with every kWh of energy produced helps to gauge which strategy might prove better. If we were to calculate the market price for carbon, we could simply look at the price for petrol or crude oil. This is the price we are willing to pay to use the carbon; such a price will be substantially higher than where current policy sets carbon pricing. Using this marginal cost (it changes with time) in the planning process as an environmental burden then puts renewable and non-renewable energy on a more level playing field. Though we may not have to actually pay this cost, it allows us to gauge the sensitivity of our own dependence on fossil fuels.

(c) Yet another metric is measuring the tonnes CO_2 emitted/kWh of energy over the life cycle of a project. This should be done for all effluents released due to the entire process of energy production. CO_2, NO_x, and SO_x are airborne climate change–inducing factors; others, including toxic chemicals, oils, and biogenic agents, may be released into the environment through water waste, mine tailing, or other solid wastes.

(d) Other criteria to use with respect to energy include reliability and resiliency of the network itself. Quantifying this value is possible, and many approaches exist that can map this value as a function of cost. Reliability must also factor in: the idea of energy storage or a buffer system that is able to contribute to the reliability of the network that stabilizes it as and when required.

(e) Another important consideration is the end use of the produced

energy. For example, heating in cold climates may come from natural gas furnaces, district energy, or direct electrical heating. Each of
these strategies has a certain amount of environmental impact. District energy requires significant underground piping infrastructure.
Natural gas results in greenhouse gas emissions, as does electrical
heating (depending on the electrical supply mix). The absolute differences between these emissions would be a function of the natural gas
efficiency and the supply mix of the whole system. In cases where the
supply mix is mainly hydro or renewable energy, it may make better
environmental sense to heat spaces using electrical loads as opposed
to natural gas, but such strategies are rarely evaluated, if at all. Heat
pumps, for example, are considerably more efficient than resistance
heaters. Such considerations should drive the total overall policy decision. The total system costs need to be evaluated, not simply the com-
ponential ones.

(f) Other factors, such as conservation and demand side management, must be used as alternative strategies. Policy may also consider
market drivers that artificially inflate resource costs to their truer values. In other words, higher gasoline prices may actually prove beneficial in the long run – thus, perhaps policy makers should be artificially
inflating the price of gasoline rather than trying to subsidize it. The
challenge is to find the right pricing.

(g) Other resource usage costs must also be integrated into the
planning scenario. Upstream and downstream consequences, such as
increased water usage and land and mining resource depletion, also
need to be integrated.

The system as a whole must be studied, with links between components drawn out so that sensitivities to the assumed inputs can be
analysed and predicted. These energy metrics and strategies would
serve as tools in a toolbox to tweak and bolt together integrated solutions that are not limited to their immediate scopes and implementation vicinities.

Framework

It is necessary to form a conceptual framework through which a natural
city might be envisioned and designed. The main goal for this framework is not to envision a 'solution' that strictly prescribes predefined
parameters, but rather to use it as a tool to guide the many possible
combinations of actions and their unfolding over time. Adaptivity

(accounting for the small as well as the very large) is crucial, as are practicality and effectiveness. In terms of energy, the most useful metric is efficiency. Trading one form for another, more usable form is the primary aim of most energy transformative systems – the foundation upon which most cities and societies are constructed. The following points list the criteria such a framework might incorporate.

(a) The interconnection of our society elicits trade-offs – to recognize this point is the first 'natural' step.
(b) The interconnectedness is part of the problem, but can also be part of the solution.
(c) Actions that go with the grain of human nature should be advocated wherever possible.
(d) An independent, holistic, and common-denominator sustainability index is crucially needed.
(e) Iterative benchmarks that constantly spur and encourage betterment of the techno-social architecture are needed. Such benchmarks try to:

   (i)   Consider general improvement criteria for specific target projects – common to many/all developments;
   (ii) Explore how the different components and cogs of a natural city might interact, and their consequences;
   (iii) Map the selected criteria to a common network in order to explore the ecological evolution of the city;
   (iv) Encourage diversity within the realm of every criterion to better the chances of the city's evolution; and
   (v)   Actively measure and record the improvement criteria at the local/specific level.

Some traditional benchmarks a natural city should strive to maintain include the following:

(a) Higher intensities [jobs, people, greenspace, and recreation]/km^2
(b) Utility planning and transportation that include minimizing ecological impacts and life-cycle energy consumption as part of every objective and policy decision.
(c) Local and municipal governing of pollution [air and water] within the city.
(d) Conservation and demand management of energy, even if that means increasing the price of energy goods and services.

(e) A creative environment where the incentives and open debate on innovative actions can be discussed as a prerequisite to implementation. This discussion must be as unconstrained as possible, must include public input, and is vital to the growth and development of a natural city.

Future Solutions

Creating an Energy Map

Based on the framework outlined, it is easy to recognize that the complexity and interlaced nature of our society, technology, and environment are truly astonishing. The effort required to trace externalities through an entire technological system, its society, and its environmental context until the loop is closed is staggering, even for small systems. In most cases, these interactions do not result in an equilibrium state. At best, we can evaluate the largest trade-offs between them, and ask the right questions that allow us to recognize such externalities. One of the more novel ways to do so is to track time flows of energy, balancing the inflows and outflows wherever possible. In this way, an *eco-social energy map* can be created for many of the processes that take place in a natural city.

Energy Tags

Yet another way (with some strategic research) is to brand all products and services with an energy intensity label, the units being embedded energy/Base unit or service provided. This energy intensity would, at the very least, enable consumers to choose environmentally sustainable alternatives; it would be the energy equivalent of rating entertainment media, or the branding of health food, or even be analogous to fuel economy or efficiency ratings. Unlike ratings such as Energy Star or similar standards that simply measure what the future consumption would be, this would include the energies embedded during the manufacturing process. Such interactions are incredibly complex and diverse; quantitizing them is the first step towards understanding their true roles.

Conclusion

Even when all the above-mentioned analyses have been carried out, the true complexity of the network is not easily revealed. Included in these criteria are the mundane yet critical factors of financing, lead times, and economical viability. Superimposed onto these factors is the proposed strategy itself. An innovative technical solution might suddenly become more viable if a few components were changed or the efficiency of the process was increased. The environmental damage might be negligible if, for example, construction were to take place in an arid desert. Other factors, such as quantifying the reliability or robustness of the proposed solution, guarantee a long-term return on investment, including environmental externalities. Perhaps the resiliency of the system cannot be traded off under any circumstances because doing so would represent a breach of national security. Such interactions are not easy to describe, predict, or map.

Other strategies, such as conservation and demand management, increasing energy efficiency, creating legislative or policy constraint, updating codes and standards, encouraging zero-carbon, zero-net energy, and energy standards such as Passive Haus or LEED (Leadership in Energy and Environmental Design), are essential tools in building a natural city. But we must be wary; just as in the electric car example, we must ensure that the sustainability of such developments on a small scale does not lead to large-scale problems.

We can predict such problems, and combat and improve our strategies by mapping the high-intensity energy flows through their transformations. This approach would yield a preliminary roadmap to navigate the world of dynamic changes. The decision process used when building a natural city must come from without, not within, the outward context being the essential component in mapping the city's externalities. It is simple to understand that the energy that powers the city springs from the natural resources surrounding it, and that the ability to tame and harness this energy requires the recognition of that ultimate imbalance. The artificial world that we create within a natural city is dependent on this external world to sustain itself. The second law of thermodynamics cannot be violated: for all the naturalness within a city, there must be an equal amount of irreversible destruction elsewhere.

NOTES

1 Willem H. Vanderburg, *The Growth of Minds and Cultures: A Unified Theory*

of the Structure of Human Experience (Toronto: University of Toronto Press, 1985).

2 http://www.theimo.com/imoweb/marketdata/marketToday.asp. (Prices are updated daily.)

3 http://www.worldenergyoutlook.org/2006.asp (accessed 8 December 2008).

4 http://earthtrends.wri.org/index.php (accessed 8 December 2008).

5 Thomas Homer-Dixon, *The Upside of Down* (New York: Random House, 2006), 48–50.

6 http://www.ctv.ca/servlet/ArticleNews/story/CTVNews/20050928/gas_consumption_050928?s_name=&no_ads= (accessed 8 December 2008).

7 BP Statistical review of world energy June 2006 (XLS). British Petroleum (June 2006): http://www.bp.com/liveassets/bp_internet/globalbp/glopalbp_uk_english/reports_and_publications/statistical_energy_review_2006/STAGING/local_assets/downloads/spreadsheets/statistical_review_full_report_workbook_2006.xls (accessed 3 April 2007).

8 Willem H. Vanderburg, 'The Most Economic, Socially Viable, and Environmentally Sustainable Alternative Energy,' *University of Toronto Bulletin of Science, Technology and Society* 28, 2 (April 2008): 98–104.

9 Tyler Hamilton, 'Switching Off Incandescents a No-brainer?' *Toronto Star*, 17 March 2008: http://www.thestar.com/article/346692 (accessed 8 December 2008).

10 Steve Rennie, 'Ottawa Scraps Clean-Car Program,' *Globe and Mail*, 29 February 2008: http://www.theglobeandmail.com/servlet/story/RTGAM.20080229.wh-feebate-0229/BNStory/specialGlobeAuto (accessed 8 December 2008).

18 Children and Nature in the City

SARAH J. KING AND INGRID LEMAN STEFANOVIC

'Even though it's a big city, nature pops up everywhere.'
          – Mohammed, grade 6 Toronto public school student

Introduction

In planning our urban environments, it is becoming increasingly important to explore how values and perceptions affect decision making. Unless those attitudes are better understood, it will be difficult to modify behaviour realistically to encourage more sustainable living patterns or to successfully design natural cities in a way that generates a true sense of place.

It is that motivation to better understand taken-for-granted values and perceptions of place that inspired a recent research study to investigate perceptions and values of visitors to the Lake Ontario Waterfront Trail. The trail consists of an over 600-km stretch of small roads and trails from Niagara to Kingston that allows for a unique uninterrupted biking or hiking experience through rural and urban areas along the northern shoreline.[1] The aim of the project was twofold: to better understand the extent to which people value such an opportunity to engage with environments that reflect the interplay between cities and natural areas, and to generate recommendations for future planning and policy development.

While the initial phase of the project was concerned with the perceptions of adults, specifically those who had travelled the trail from end to end, it became evident that children's voices were far too rarely included in public policy discussions of this kind. As a result, we decided to turn to a group of children ages nine to 14: they were old enough to express their views in a coherent manner, but young enough to engage in unstructured play within their lived environments. A portion of the trail to the west of Toronto was identified as one that provided a focused area for study, since it is often perceived as aiming to integrate the urban with the natural.[2]

In working with children, we were not interested in undertaking a large-scale quantitative survey of their views. Instead, the aim was to identify workable class sizes and to walk portions of the trail with these students, to non-intrusively observe their spontaneous patterns of interacting with natural and urban environments, and to gradually elicit their explicit reflections on what nature in the city 'is' – and what it 'ought to be,' as expressed through essays, drawings, and photographs. Overall, the project provided another small contribution to the increasingly significant discussion that has emerged in recent years about how children interact with their environments, and what this finding might mean for public policy and planning.[3]

A Project to Explore Nature in the City with Children

The project involved approximately one hundred schoolchildren ages nine to 14, from two public schools and one private school, all located to the west of the downtown Toronto core. Students were drawn from grades 6, 7, and 8. Two schools were located in close proximity to a marsh or other ecologically significant landscapes; one class focused on students' special needs. Overall, the group as a whole reflected diverse cultural traditions from lower- to upper middle-class neighbourhoods, with both new Canadians and those whose families had been in Canada for many generations. In the face of this diversity, our strategy remained consistent: to allow opportunities for the students to engage with the Waterfront Trail both through spontaneous play and through reflective classroom assignments, using their experiences together with us on the Lake Ontario Waterfront Trail as a focus of study.

Our hope was to elicit the children's taken-for-granted beliefs about urban nature and to impose our hopes and expectations as researchers as little as possible. To this end, we endeavoured to design a research protocol that was open-ended and that allowed the children to shape their own responses. In every case, our researchers worked in teams of two: one person took the lead in facilitating the research process, while the other observed the children's play and documented it photographically.[4]

After meeting with each group of children in their classroom, we began by visiting the trail together and spending unstructured time: walking, playing, chatting, and exploring the local green spaces along the trail. During this time, the children engaged with their local settings in a variety of ways. Our documented photographic and written observations of this unstructured play constitute the first set of data for the project.

Once we had spent at least 30 minutes in unstructured play, we moved into the first structured reflection. One exercise required that each child be given a picture frame cut from brightly coloured construction paper. The children were invited to think about what nature is like in cities, and to choose something they noticed that represented for them what 'Nature in Cities is … ' They then 'framed' that image with their cut-out, enabling the rest of the group to see the picture they had selected. A tour of the impromptu art gallery followed, with recorded discussion of the chosen images, and reports from each 'artist' about his or her image and what it represented. Finally, a camera documented the framed image itself. These pictures of what 'nature in the city *is*,' and their accompanying descriptions, formed the second subset of our data.

In the case of a private school where we worked, students were provided with a Global Positioning System and digital cameras, rather than construction paper picture frames. Despite the sophisticated technology, the aim was the same: to capture a significant image of what 'nature in the city *is*' for them, and to describe their impressions.

With each group, we returned to the children's classrooms for further discussion. In some cases, children shared with us the treasures they had brought back from their walks along the trail. The contents of back pockets revealed rocks, sticks, bits of bark, and a collection of cherry blossoms. Classroom discussion invited reflection about what nature in cities *could* be like, and what the students would have liked to do and experience on the Waterfront Trail that was not possible.

The children were then invited to write or draw their impressions about what 'nature in cities *should be*.' Descriptions of their work and what it meant to each student were also recorded. These paragraphs, poems, drawings, and descriptions of what nature in cities *ought to be* formed the third subset of data.

As will become evident in the following pages, our general findings suggested that the more unstructured time children spent in unstructured (wilder) spaces, the more sophisticated their observations were of the natural world and their relationship to it.

Observations of Children at Play along the Trail

One of the schools we visited runs along a residential street and into a manicured park at the mouth of a major river. The park itself consists of lawns with flower beds, concrete paths, and trees, but no playground. Along the edge of Lake Ontario is a retaining wall built of large boulders that extend to form a jetty out and over the water. The children were drawn immediately to climbing and clambering over the rocks along the water's edge. Girls and boys often played separately. The girls were drawn to one another, walking along the paths and talking in small groups, though some of them were eventually drawn to the rocks. The boys climbed out along the rock jetty as soon as we arrived, pitching rocks into the water. As they wandered away from the water's edge, one of the boys threw down his soccer ball and they used the park's turf as an impromptu soccer pitch. (See figure 18.1.)

A nearby creek is channelled into a three-foot-wide concrete bed as it flows through the park and into the lake. Some of the boys demonstrated their agility by leaping from one side to the other. In many ways, we found that among this pre-teen group, preparing themselves for the

Figure 18.1. The allure of rock jetties.

social challenges of high school, play was not particularly uninhibited. The clear exception was evident once the students found themselves near water, at which point it seemed that their guard went down and spontaneous play defined the moment.

A second school with which we received permission to work was located beside a significant ecological marshland and conservation area. The Waterfront Trail runs past the school, along a boardwalk through the naturalized area of the marsh to the edge of the lake, and then into the more manicured grounds of a nearby park. The school has a hiking club, so many of the students know the trail well. Some have even worked on its upkeep.

The grade 6 children with whom we visited this portion of the trail were once again drawn to the water – though on this occasion it was the marsh, visible from the boardwalk, that caught the students' attention first. They were fascinated by the huge carp that live in the marsh, and watched them thrashing about in the reeds for food. When one child spotted a nesting mother duck with her young, the children gathered quietly around to peer at them. Once the children reached the pebbled beach at the lake, the favourite activity was skipping rocks along the water's surface.

As we moved onto the treed lawns and beaches of the nearby park, most children swarmed the play structure, while some took quiet moments alone on the sandy beach, or on a small rock jetty. The splash pad had been turned on for the summer, and the children gravitated towards it. It was only the teachers' authoritative demands that prevented the children from leaping into the spraying water.

One small class of students had spent many hours at this marsh over the course of the school year, learning about and experiencing its complex living systems. They had used the trail for recreation, and also as the focus for a major school project for the year. These children moved along the trail much more slowly than others with whom we travelled, stopping to examine plants, insects, flowers, and snails; to listen to bullfrogs; and to watch the fish, the birds, and the water. They spent a long time hanging over the edge of the boardwalk, talking, laughing, and pointing out marsh life. They climbed the lookout tower that had been built as a part of the boardwalk, and spent time investigating the marshland environment from their new vantage point. Where the boardwalk rose into a bridge, some of the children scaled down underneath and enjoyed the cave-like space.

When we reached the beach, these children not only skipped stones, but also were far more actively engaged with their environment, climbing trees and jumping over fallen ones. One boy, finding a small stream running into the water, dammed it up with a piece of board he found on the beach, experimenting with the changes he could make to the watercourse. The children played for a time on the playground equipment, but were most excited to take us off the main trail to their favourite spot: a dirt trail leading through the forest to a footbridge over a creek. There, they explored at the creek's edge, dropped things from the bridge into the water, and manoeuvred across the creek along fallen logs, which they used as bridges.

As we watched the children from these various groups spend time on the trail, it was clear that the students from this particular class engaged in the most creative and wide-ranging free play, and were the most likely to notice the minutiae of the natural world. Other children certainly exhibited some of this engagement with the world of the trail, but were much less likely to notice the small creatures or details of the landscape surrounding them. All of the children exhibited the same playful pull towards the water, but others took less notice of the minutiae of urban nature and explored the areas to a much lesser degree than the students who were well informed from their daily interactions with the trail and marsh.

Some of the reasons for this variation in response might lie in age discrepancies. The grade 8 students were, no doubt, beginning to feel the social pressures of adolescence and may have been less likely to engage in active play. Nevertheless, age is not the only explanation, since the nature of the green space itself is very different in the various communities that we studied. The park near one of the schools, where students were less actively engaged in their explorations of the trail, is highly manicured. There is no marsh, no bullfrogs, no nesting baby ducks to engage the children. There are no pebbles to skip across the lake. The children climb the rocks and leap the creek, but their drives to experience more are stymied by the nature of the place in which they find themselves. These differences that were observed in the nature of the children's being at play were further confirmed once we considered their explicit, formal reflections about nature in cities.

Nature in Cities Is ...

Beautiful

In the 'Nature in Cities *is* ...' photo exercise, the children used brightly coloured picture frames (or, as mentioned, in one case used digital cameras) to capture 'snapshots' of their experiences of nature in cities, to frame images that they felt were significant. We have analysed these pictures and their accompanying descriptions thematically, looking for common ideas that were explicitly expressed or implicitly conveyed. We were also intrigued by a small number of pictures that were interesting not because they represented ideas commonly expressed by many children, but precisely because they conveyed unique or distinctive insights and impressions.

A major theme that emerged in our analysis of children's photos and descriptions of what 'nature in cities is' related to the *beauty* of the natural world. Some students shared verbal descriptions of their own personal aesthetic experience of nature. Others were intent on capturing images of what they viewed to be the beauty of pristine nature. In all cases, the students characterized nature in cities as something positive, and attempted to convey the importance and beauty of 'the natural' through their images.

In one case, a child took a picture of dandelions in the lawn of the park, because they 'look beautiful.' In another, a child lay at the base of a tree and took a picture looking up the trunk into the branches, which were just beginning to leaf. When asked why this picture was selected, the child explained, 'I looked at the tree. And it's nice. I don't know … ' The depth of emotion made up, in this instance, for the lack of verbal sophistication.

Sometimes, this aesthetic view of nature was expressed with a different emphasis. For example, Cory, a grade 8 student, carefully composed a picture that he believed captured the important elements of the park in their beauty when he wrote, 'its got the water fountain and then you can see the whole park in this view, behind the water fountain, and it looks really nice.'

A grade 6 student, Amanda, composed a photo that included 'trees, rocks, water and the beach … and it's got most of the things that are in nature.' The attempt to capture multiple elements of a park setting in their natural beauty was common throughout the pictures.

Those students who had spent much time in the adjacent marshland setting throughout the school year led us away from the constructed spaces of the park to take photos in their favourite, 'wilder' places, including areas with fallen trees, wildflowers, and the creek – significantly different from the earlier photo of dandelions in the lawn. Their descriptions of the pictures that they chose were often sophisticated, reflecting a deep engagement with place: 'My name's Nicholas and I chose this picture because it shows nature as growing and beautiful and colourful … The water, half of the tree's falling down, the rocks, the leaves falling off the trees, and the beautiful flowers over there.' Another student took a similar photo at the same spot and reflected, 'I chose that because it's exactly like Mother Nature. Fallen down tree, you know, water, lots of flowers. That's why I chose this.'

As researchers, we were unaware that this highly naturalized part of the park existed, and we enjoyed being led through it by these knowledgeable children. The students engaged with our conversation about nature in cities largely because it was an opportunity for them to share a favourite place.

Nature as Pristine

Among the students' pictures that attempted to convey natural beauty, some stood out because the students who created them naively described their pictures as capturing pristine, untouched nature in some way. For example, a student took a photo of an expanse of lawn with planted trees (some mulched at their bases), a paved path, and a building off to the far right. She then said, 'I've got a picture of perfect natural wildlife and nature with no man-made by-products or anything like the rest of the city, and I think that's really what nature is.'

Despite her statements to the contrary, every element in her picture was clearly constructed, planted, or shaped by human effort, though it is possible that some of the oldest trees in the background pre-date the park's construction. To this child, a manicured park represented 'perfect natural wildlife.'

An experienced local teacher of this age group suggested to us that these examples can be explained by the lack of real experiences of wild nature among urban and suburban children.[5] Peter Kahn has explored and drawn out the deeper consequences of this problem in his discussions of Environmental Generational Amnesia.

> I think we all take the natural environment we encounter during childhood as the norm against which we measure environmental degradation later in our lives. With each ensuing generation, the amount of environmental degradation increases, but each generation in its youth takes that degraded condition as the nondegraded condition – as the normal experience.[6]

Kahn characterizes Environmental Generational Amnesia as a source of environmental complacency and of distorted meanings of environmental concepts. In our study, children attempted to express the meaning of the natural, but their experience was sometimes so limited that they mistook managed nature for wildness. They knew to value wilderness settings, but did not understand them in a meaningful way because of their lack of exposure to such environments.

In order to overcome the problems of Environmental Generational Amnesia, Kahn contends that we must help children to experience more 'pristine' instances of the natural world, although he holds that we must also recognize 'that children construct knowledge and values not only through interaction with a physical world (with nature) but through interaction with a social world and with social discourse.'[7] In his view, we need not necessarily escape built environments; instead, our amnesia (and that of our children) can be overcome by prolonged and thoughtful engagement with aspects of the natural world within our local settings – with bugs and weeds and dandelions, as well as through protecting wilderness areas.

We need to find ways to thoughtfully engage with nature within our cities, recognizing that 'children's earlier forms of knowledge are not wrong but incomplete and are capable of being transformed into more adequate forms of knowledge.'[8] The somewhat distorted images and interpretations of 'pristine' nature we were offered demonstrate the need not for *correction*, but for further engagement with these children in uncovering a 'natural' world that, inevitably, infuses the local urban environments that they experience on a daily basis.

Nature Described through Relational Experiences and Metaphoric Expressions

For the children who had had earlier opportunities for deeper engagement with natural landscapes surrounding their school, the photo exercise constituted a similar opportunity to share their own special visions of nature in the city. Two boys took pictures of the creek and its banks. Bryan reported, 'I chose this picture because it reminds me of at my cottage because we have this creek at my cottage that I always go to in the summer … We usually go either frog-hunting, minnow-hunting, having some fun.'

Simon also evoked memories of past experiences when he remarked, 'I just took this picture because it's really nice and we've played in this. It was fun … We hunt and fish, and stuff … sometimes people will take off their shoes and socks and walk in it. 'In describing this particular creek, the aim was to provide much more than a simple inventory of beautiful elements. In the cases of Bryan and Simon, the boys spontaneously wove meaningful past memories into their present experiences of place. When they were invited to expand upon their remembrances, the creek that lay before their eyes became linked, through their animated discussion, with happy times from elsewhere. That our visions of nature are both historically and socially embedded in lived experience is evident through these kinds of stories.

Some children were intent upon describing nature in the city in terms of a more complex *interplay* of distinct characteristics. Sarah, for instance, framed a picture that balanced a shady spot under a tree with the bright sunny beach, 'because half of it's really calm and then the water's more [active].' Eric created a photo of a tree fallen across the creek, with tiny new shoots growing out of the old trunk: 'And the reason that I chose this picture is because I thought that it's interesting how the tree has been sort of wrecked and now you see it's trying to recreate its little branches and stuff and things are growing on it.' That nature in cities is, to use Eric's words, 'sort of wrecked' and is trying to recreate itself in many small ways is no small insight!

Whether through aesthetic appreciation of natural environments, or through a recognition of environmental complexity, one cannot help but notice that all the children with whom we worked seemed, at some point, to want to describe nature in cities in a positive light, as something balanced or thriving. In some instances, those descriptions held nature in high favour, precisely because it was being distinguished from built settings. In other cases, however, students were able to envision an intersection between the natural and the urban, as we see below.

The Intersection of the Natural with Built Elements

A small but significant number of students composed photos that highlighted the *integration* of natural and built elements. These students focused less on retrieving or highlighting specific natural elements that were defined as existing independently of human intervention, choosing instead to explore the dynamics between grown and built forms.

Along the Waterfront Trail, where we spent time with these three groups of children, one can see the skyline of the City of Toronto when one looks out over Lake Ontario. Anchored by the iconic shape of the CN Tower, and with the tall stacks of a coal-fired electricity generating station in the foreground, the skyline of the urban core became a counterpoint to the elements of the park within which we stood. While for some students the city remained simply a backdrop ('the park, and the city, Toronto, in the background'), or an aesthetic trope ('with the fog around the CN Tower, it sort of reminded me of a cloak'), others used the skyline to make more complex points. Carly's photo includes the park and the Trail in the foreground, and in the background the lake-shore and skyline, with apartment towers and the generating station rising above the trees on the shoreline. She says, 'All along the shore part, you can see trees and then you see buildings so it looks like the city in the park.'

Mohammed took a photo similar to Carly's, but focused only on the water and the view of the shoreline and skyline. He explains, 'Even though it's a big city, nature pops up everywhere ... You have these urban buildings and factories and stuff, but nature's all around.' It seemed to us that these children were attempting to demonstrate another way in which the beauty of nature in cities can be appreciated: through the balance of natural and built elements in the city.

Adam took a picture that focused the viewer's attention on the human elements in the immediate surroundings of the park. Adam's picture included the lawn, trees, and walkways of the park, bounded by a row of cars and minivans in the parking lot. When asked why he composed the picture as he did, Adam replied, 'I think that here [in the park], it's mostly trees and cars.' This observation is astute; in most of the waterfront parks in this area, there are great green expanses of lawn, and great grey expanses of parking lot, so people can park their cars while they enjoy the park. The parks are, in a very real sense, 'mostly trees and cars.'

The Place of Pollution

Though most students focused on a positive view of nature in cities, some held a more dystopic view, attending to issues of pollution and dirt. In the words of one student,

> This is Sarah's picture and she says she picked the dirty part because it shows how dirty the lake is and to tell the community that they should stop the pollution of the water.

> I'm taking a picture of a coffee cup stuck in between a couple of rocks. And I picked this because it shows how people we don't know in the city are polluting our parks.

In this second case, the student captured an iconic item of Canadian culture (and of Canadian litter): the Tim Horton's disposable coffee cup. While there was some garbage, for the most part, the parks that the children visited were tidy and manicured. In the water where Sarah took her picture, there were certainly rocks and some mud from the jetty, but the 'dirty' water with which she was concerned was not clearly polluted in the direct sense that she seemed to intend. Pollution is certainly an issue in such a heavily urbanized environment, especially one in which a coal-fired generating station has been producing emissions for many years. On the other hand, at this stage of their education, these children did not have a solid grasp of the invisible challenge of particulate and effluent pollution. Litter and mud could be seen, and so perhaps were more easily understood.

Nature in Cities Should Be ...

The concern with cleanliness and pollution was a central theme of the children's pictures and paragraphs describing what 'Nature in cities should be ...' The primary characteristics of ideal urban nature, as the children described them, included clean water, air, and play spaces, such as those described by Vikram in this poem:

> Nature and cities should be
> In complete and total harmony
> With clear skies and clean air
> And trees that are never bare ...

For most of the children, their concerns about pollution of natural spaces were expressed through discussion of litter and garbage. Nasreen wrote, 'Nature in cities should be like nice and beautiful. It should be clean and tidy. I think that our city is half clean and half dirty because of all the garbage that's everywhere and people throw garbage everywhere and don't clean it properly.' Among many of the students, cleanliness and pollution stood out, above all else, as a concern as the students looked to the future.

In the exercise 'Nature in cities should be ...', children were encouraged to imagine that anything was possible, and to depict in their drawings and writings the best union between the built and the natural that they could imagine. For the majority of students, their answers did not depart in any significant way from their past experiences. Drawings often depicted parks similar to the ones they had visited, with the addition of animals, trees, and litter bins. Carly's picture exemplifies this. Her drawing includes a beach, trees, animals, a pathway, and homes;

placed at the centre of the drawing, as if to emphasize its central importance to her ideas, is a large garbage can with a recycling symbol on it. (A second garbage can is found at the right side of the drawing.) Carly describes her picture as being about 'how everything's together, and everything's cleaner.'

Along with their concern for litter and pollution, in this exercise children emphasized the importance of structured spaces for play, and of ensuring the safety of the natural and human worlds. Interestingly, some children expressed concern not with the fact that natural elements might harm people, but that people might harm nature. They suggested that the natural world needs to be kept safe from the destructive impact of human beings:

> Nature in our cities is unsafe I think. Anything can just walk across the street and get trampled or chased up a tree. Nature should be protected better. Even our trees are being torn down. Either by a man being paid to chop it down or an innocent kid snapping some branches or stepping on a bush. Nature should be more free. Not so confined. (Stephanie)

Stephanie's concern for the safety and freedom of nature implies that protecting nature requires placing limits on human behaviour. Among children who expressed concern around safety issues, only one was concerned for the safety of people (i.e. safe play structures for children). The rest were, like Stephanie, concerned for the safety of the non-human world.

Providing opportunities for play and fun-filled activities was the final most common issue raised by children as they thought about what nature in cities should be. This was especially true among the children who chose to use a drawing, rather than a reflective essay, to express themselves. Most of the pictures of what 'Nature in cities should be ...' included pathways, swing sets, climbers, and sandy beaches (some even with beach volleyball courts!), along with trees, fish, birds, and sometimes even the Canadian iconic image of a beaver. These pictures often appeared to be idealized (and litter-free) images of the parks that the children had, in fact, visited. Milva's picture clearly demonstrates this view: she drew a broad expanse of green lawn, bisected by a paved pathway and by a creek, with a gazebo, a typical children's playground, a water fountain, and the requisite garbage can.

Milva's is one of many pictures that emphasized the importance of recreational space in urban environments. We noticed that in most of these pictures, the recreational space the children drew was highly structured, designed to control the behaviour of park users, very much like the spaces the children play in every day. Frequently, the drawings included depictions of a path for bikes and skateboard use, as well as for strolls. There is often a bridge crossing bodies of water. There is a playground and a garbage can for litter.

In the students' eyes, the ways people are to enjoy this sort of space are clearly predetermined. For instance, Jamie drew a picture of two people on a beach, looking out over the water, with a playground to their left and a pile of rocks to their right. A bird is perched upon the rocks. As Jamie described his picture, we recalled how the children had enjoyed climbing on the rocks at the shoreline, and so we asked him whether the children could play on the rocks he had drawn. He reluctantly indicated that this might be possible, but he made it clear that the rocks were 'mostly for the birds.' The play structures had been designated, in his eyes, as being most appropriate for the children.

Taken together, these central themes revealed a somewhat controlled view of the relationship between humans and nature in cities, one in which the behaviour of people must be restrained in myriad ways in order to ensure that nature can thrive. This view of the ideal relationship between humans and the non-human was exemplified in the writings of another student, Amreen. In her paragraph, she captures all of the concerns discussed above: play, safety of animals, safety of people, litter, and cleanliness.

> Nature in cities should be a clean place to enjoy ... Kid[s] can play and adult[s] can relieve stress or just relax. It can be a place to ride your bike or to hang out with friends ... There should be benches and safe playgrounds. People should not litter or else the water will get polluted and many animals can die ... There should [be] more garbage cans around the main areas so people can litter less. Nature in cities should be fun!

In a context where children largely spend their time in urban parks with structured spaces, perhaps it is not surprising that their ideal does not stray far from their experience.

Kahn's conception of Environmental Generational Amnesia suggests that 'as we lose daily intimate positive affiliations with nature and accept negative experiences ... as the norm, we suffer physically and psychologically, and hardly know it.'[9] Among these children, the issue is not simply that some of them see constructed park spaces as untouched nature. Many of these children are losing the opportunity for creative, unstructured play, learning instead that the most appropri-

Figure 18.2. Manicured nature: One child's vision.

ate way for them to be in relationship with the natural world is through experiences that prioritize safety, cleanliness, and order. In these children's experience, not only is nature highly controlled, but they themselves must also learn to be highly controlled, for the sake of everyone's well-being. (See figure 18.2.)

This controlled view of the relationship between people and nature in cities was challenged by a small number of children who drew pictures of their vision of nature in cities. Their pictures seem to represent an alternative view in which humans and animals enjoy nature together, there is lots of unstructured free play, and litter is not a central concern. These children share an emphasis on play with their peers, but their pictures suggest that children should be playing along creeks, on fallen trees, in forests, and on play structures. They depict children playing with dogs, with birds, as well as with one another.

An unstructured view of how nature should be in cities is clearly represented by Simon's drawing. Simon drew a creek in a forest, with a pathway and a bridge across the creek. Ropes and swings hang from the trees, and a fallen tree provides an alternate route across the creek. He has drawn people and dogs playing; the only person using the pathway has just dived from the bridge into the creek. This forest playground is clearly a sanctioned play area, as the city has erected some signs. As well as a notice against littering, the signs read 'No leashes for dogs at all times' and 'Swimming very aloud [sic]'. Simon elaborates,

> This is my picture. It's not done, but it's just a forest and you can play in it. You don't have to stay on the path. And you don't have to have leashes for your dogs. There's basically no littering, it's a $10,000 fine. And you swim in there and stuff. And just climb on all the trees and cross the rivers – with that tree – just so you can play around and stuff.

Because of his rather liberal and accommodating teacher, Simon and his classmates have had the opportunity to experience the joys of leaving the paths in the park and playing according to their own inspiration. In this regard, Simon's vision is a reflection of earlier time spent within the wilder marshland surroundings, with plenty of time for unstructured play.

Our experience was that, while other children from the same school played in the same parks, they were not offered the same time and freedom to explore. Without such time for unstructured play, the children's views of nature appeared to be noticeably more controlled and manicured. That being said, we also found that few children attempted to express intimate relationships with nature, or to describe in detail the kinds of special moments in the outdoors that so many adults reflect upon as important parts of their childhoods.

Such a finding is, perhaps, to be expected. In her article 'Spots of Time: Manifold Ways of Being in Nature in Childhood,' Louise Chawla argues that peak childhood experiences of nature, those 'magic' or 'ecstatic' moments, are experienced as a 'preverbal state of being' that are hard for an outsider to observe, and impossible for children to express.

At their best, these ineffable forms of experience fall among what Little has categorized as children's 'sweet nothings' (one of the reasons for the common dialogue between parent and child: 'Where have you been?' 'Out.' 'What did you do?' 'Nothing.').[10]

As adults, Chawla notes, many look back and describe the special experience of these spots of time as something that provides them with strength or calm throughout their lives. In our research, we found that the children's reflections about their experiences of nature were not as rich as the play we observed; this was especially true in the second reflective exercise, which took place in the classrooms. Children's spontaneous engagement with the natural world betrayed a strong connection with the environment that was not often captured in their reflective exercises.

Children and Environmental Research

Our observations drawn from the time we spent with approximately a hundred middle school–aged children along the Lake Ontario Waterfront Trail seem to suggest that the more free play children have experienced, and the more their play takes place in wild or unstructured spaces, the deeper their environmental consciousness. In our qualitative project, we asked children for their reflections about nature in cities, and observed them at play in the 'natural' park spaces closest to their schools. The children's thoughts about how nature in cities is and should be often mirrored their experiences of play on the trail: where children spent their time in manicured spaces, their expectations of nature were focused on order and cleanliness; where children spent free time in wild or unstructured spaces, like the class that explored the creek at the rather extensive marsh nearby, their observations and understandings of non-human nature were more complex and nuanced. While we cannot draw firm conclusions from these correlations, it does seem significant that none of the students from the latter class, who had spent time in 'wilder' environments, had a misplaced vision of manicured park spaces as 'untouched nature.'

This correlation between lived experience of the natural world and environmental moral reasoning may appear obvious, but is perhaps also often forgotten by those planning parks and play areas for children. Free play cannot be replaced with virtual experiences; discovering exotic animals in zoos or watching documentaries on the Discovery channel does not have the same positive effect on children's development as clambering on trees and across creeks: 'Just as real life does not consist primarily of car chases and exploding buildings, quotidian nature is much more about grasshoppers in the pigweed than it is about rhinos mating on a pixellated screen.'[11]

Stephen R. Kellert argues for the importance of direct experience with nature, suggesting that 'A natural world of imagination and vicarious experience can be emotionally dysfunctional if not balanced by contact with the actual and real of ordinary and everyday life.'[12] From a consideration of the available evidence, Kellert concludes that virtual and indirect experiences of nature simply do not have the same developmental effect on children and adolescents as do the local and actual.[13]

Our study suggests that unstructured free play in unengineered environments has a strong positive effect on children's ability to appreciate the complexities of the natural world. This observation is supported by the work of other authors, such as Robert Michael Pyle,[14] Kellert,[15] and

Richard Louv,[16] and also by Kahn, whose discussion of Environmental Generational Amnesia suggests that the development of children's environmental moral reasoning can be enriched by sustained interaction with the natural world and 'daily intimate positive affiliations with nature.'[17] Based on these thoughts alone, we might begin to suggest ways of building and reclaiming cities that promote such experiences for children, in order to support the development of their environmental moral reasoning.

Louise Chawla, an environmental phenomenologist who has done much work focused on the nature of children's environmental experiences, argues (as do we) for the importance of allowing time for free play in wild spaces because of the magical or mythic experiences these times can engender. Chawla documents how important it is when 'children can have this sense of absorption and power without trespassing on carefully managed adult domains,' because this freedom can positively affect children's sense of agency, identity, and the richness of their emotional lives.[18] This experience of magical play, the absorption of children in the moment, with the release from the worries of their larger lives, can be healing. One study suggests that, among children with attention deficit disorder, 'children with greener play environments showed less severe symptoms in general, and children functioned better after activities in green settings.'[19]

This finding is especially interesting to note as we reflect on our time with a small group of children who had been identified as having moderate learning disabilities. In their own independent classroom, their teacher had made time in the wild an explicit part of these children's educational routine. Intriguingly, we found these children to be the most relaxed and the most insightful when it came to complex expressions of the value of the natural world in urban spaces. This finding may be a further tentative illustration of the positive benefits of direct lived experiences with nature.

Chawla also highlights the importance of allowing some risk taking among children, in the regular context of their daily play activities. Risk taking, which so many children can be attracted to as a part of play, 'invites a heightened awareness of the environment and a sense of power in overcoming danger.'[20] In the absence of some sense of risk, children may become bored and alienated, and they may not develop mastery of their own skills in the natural world. To be sure, no wise adult wishes to expose children to dangerous environments, but that is not really the point. Rather, controlled environments such as playgrounds and playing fields frequently do not allow children to develop a sense of agency and responsibility, as they limit the opportunities for appropriate risk taking.[21] It is important to find a balance between safety and exposure to the complexities and wonder of the natural world, which generally cannot be compartmentalized into neat, orderly spaces.

In Kellert's words, 'direct experience' provides the opportunity for children to be in contact with the natural environment, outside of human structures or planning.[22] Upon review of the current research findings in this area, Kellert concludes that such experiential learning is important for 'cognitive development, especially during middle childhood and early adolescence';[23] that it 'occupies a surprisingly important place in a child's emotional responsiveness and receptivity' during middle childhood;[24] and that direct experience of the outdoors, especially in unfamiliar and wild spaces, has a major positive influence on the character and personality development of teenagers.[25] Drawing upon the work of Rachel Sebba, Kellert suggests that the opportunity for a relationship with the natural world places the child in a relationship with a phenomenon that is changing in continuous and unpredictable ways, prompting the child's 'adaptive and problem-solving responses.'[26]

Given this understanding of the importance of children's unstructured free play, as exemplified in our research along the Lake Ontario Waterfront Trail, it seems easy to agree that 'we need to design our cities with nature in mind, in view and within grasp.'[27] As we undertake the project of the natural city, we must resist the impulse to overdesign, to manage every space so carefully that we leave nothing for the free expression of our children. The kinds of spaces and places we need to create are not only park spaces and green roofs; in the natural city, we can also benefit from ditches, marshes, and perhaps even vacant lots: 'nothing is less empty to a curious, exploring child than a vacant lot, nothing less wasted than waste ground, nothing more richly simmered in promise than raw ground. Yet too many adults seem to have forgotten the vacant lots of their growing up years.'[28]

When we 'save' wild places, we often preserve the wild right out of them by correcting drainage, landscaping, or adding playgrounds and playing fields.[29] Pyle argues that we need to resist this impulse for improvement, and begin to see 'waste' ground as a treasure. Our research suggests that children require spaces in cities where they can play freely, experience risks, and encounter wildness on the smallest scales: the wildness of water and fish and weeds. Time in these spaces has positive effects for children's environmental moral development, and also for their broader wellness as human beings in the world.

The inspiring part about being with children is that one's focus is so clearly directed towards the future and towards positive possibilities.

Our children's well-being depends upon a healthy planet. Sustainable cities that inspire awe of both the built and the natural environments are a significant part of that equation. If we heed the call, we will recognize that each one of us has a role to play in ensuring our own, as well as our children's, environmental future.

NOTES

1 The study was funded by the Social Sciences and Humanities Research Council (SSHRC), Canada, as well as the University of Toronto's Faculty of Arts and Science, which helped to support continuing work with children beyond the three-year SSHRC project.

2 For instance, Hazel McCallion, mayor of Mississauga, located to the west of Toronto, has taken a strong stance in favour of preserving natural areas within urban corridors. In her words, 'our official plan designates natural areas for protection and when development applications are proposed, the City acquires natural areas so that they can be preserved.' See http://www.world-mayor.com/results05/interview_mccallion.html (accessed 2 November 2008).

3 For a sense of the kind of interest this theme is generating, see the journal *Children, Youth and Environments*. Visit http://www.colorado.edu/journals/cye/ for more information (accessed 2 November 2008).

4 Ingrid Stefanovic and Sarah King were alternately facilitators of these groups. Lois Lindsay and Bruce Sexsmith did excellent work documenting the children's participation. We thank them for their invaluable assistance.

5 Jean Gilmore, personal communication, 10 August 2008. In Ms Gilmore's work, this lack of outdoor experience prompted her suburban school community (near to our research site) to begin taking its grade 7 students out of the city to a children's camp for three or four days every spring.

6 Peter Kahn, 'Children's Affiliations with Nature: Structure, Development, and the Problem of Environmental Generational Amnesia,' in *Children and Nature: Psychological, Sociocultural and Evolutionary Investigation*, ed. Peter H. Kahn, Jr, and Stephen R. Kellert (Cambridge, MA: MIT Press, 2002), 106.

7 Kahn, 'Children's Affiliations with Nature,' 113–14.

8 Kahn, 'Children's Affiliations with Nature,' 114.

9 Kahn, 'Children's Affiliations with Nature,' 113.

10 Louise Chawla, 'Spots of Time: Manifold Ways of Being in Nature in Childhood,' in *Children and Nature*, ed. Kahn and Kellert, 215.

11 Robert Michael Pyle, 'Eden in a Vacant Lot: Special Places, Species, and Kids in the Neighbourhood of Life,' in *Children and Nature*, ed. Kahn and Kellert, 319.

12 Pyle, 'Eden in a Vacant Lot,' 128.
13 Stephen R. Kellert, 'Experiencing Nature: Affective, Cognitive and Evaluative Development in Children,' in *Children and Nature*, ed. Kahn and Kellert, 145.
14 Pyle, 'Eden in a Vacant Lot.'
15 Kellert, 'Experiencing Nature.'
16 Richard Louv, *Last Child in the Woods: Saving Our Children from Nature-Deficit Disorder* (New York: Workman Publishing, 2005).
17 Kahn, 'Children's Affiliations with Nature, 113.
18 Chawla, 'Spots of Time,' 216; see also R. Hart, *Wildlands for Children* 14, 1 (Stuttgart: Landschaft + Stadt, 1982): 34–9; and K.R. Olwig, 'The Childhood "Deconstruction" of Nature and the Construction of "Natural" Housing Environments for Children,' *Scandinavian Housing and Planning Research* 3 (1986): 129-43. Cited in Chawla, 'Spots of Time.'
19 A.F. Taylor, F.E. Kuo, and W.C. Sullivan, 'Coping with ADD: The Surprising Connection to Green Play Settings,' *Environment and Behaviour* 33, 1 (2001): 54–77, cited in Chawla, 'Spots of Time.'
20 R. Hart, *Children's Experience of Place* (New York: Irvington, 1979); J.F. Porteous, *Landscapes of the Mind* (Toronto: University of Toronto Press, 1990); and Louise Chawla, *In the First Country of Places: Nature, Poetry and Childhood Memory* (Albany: State University of New York Press, 1994), cited in Chawla, 'Spots of Time,' 217.
21 This point brings to mind the case of the City of Toronto, where, some years ago, almost all play structures were removed over the course of one summer, as it had been determined that their design and manufacturing did not sufficiently reduce the risk of playing on them. Then began the long, slow process of raising funds for new play structures, which seem 'boring' to some, as all opportunities for risky or exciting play have been thoroughly minimized. On the other hand, at one school we know of, the first serious injury of a child (a broken arm) took place in the first week after the installation of the new play structure and new playground surface: no one helped the children to develop a sense of appropriate play on the new structure because it was supposed to be so 'safe.'
22 Kellert, 'Experiencing Nature,' 118.
23 Kellert, 'Experiencing Nature,' 122.
24 Kellert, 'Experiencing Nature,' 126.
25 Kellert, 'Experiencing Nature,' 138.
26 Kellert, 'Experiencing Nature,' 140.
27 Kahn, 'Children's Affiliations with Nature, 114.
28 Pyle, 'Eden in a Vacant Lot,' 306.
29 Pyle, 'Eden in a Vacant Lot,' 321.

Conclusion

We come to the end of a journey that has inspired reflection on how we might move forward in conceiving of a more 'natural city.' Glimpsing through the lenses of philosophy, religion, social and political ecology, architecture, history, and anthropology, we have ultimately looked to our contributors to shed light on nothing less than how best to uncover a *new ontology of the city*.

Certainly, the term 'natural city' is not simply meant to replace other concepts that emphasize the need to build in a more 'green,' 'healthy,' 'livable,' or 'sustainable' manner. Instead, we acknowledge the need of multiple narratives as a condition of wise action. These deliberations about a natural city are meant to provide an additional essential set of interpretive frameworks for continuing meaningful dialogue.

Perhaps more importantly, the concept of a 'natural city' is meant to remind us that fundamental, taken-for-granted paradigms and world views – often bypassed in discussions of urban planning and design precisely because they are hidden and implicit – ultimately drive policy making and decision making within our human settlements. In the absence of a rethinking of essential *ways of being* within our cities, we risk engaging merely in busywork and denying the vital significance of the very interpretive horizons that frame the questions we ask and the answers we derive in the building of our cities.

This volume addresses some of these deeply rooted paradigms that prevent us from moving ahead in planning our natural cities and points to new directions. For instance, a number of authors reflect upon the nature and scale of dualistic world views and the schisms between 'natural' and 'urban' environments that constitute fundamental barriers to genuine sustainability. Others look to history, literature, and non-

Western religions to unearth clues for a more thoughtful cosmology within which to situate the planning of a natural city. Some deconstruct popular concepts, such as 'global cities' or the civic role of women, in an effort to rethink the human and environmental interface within urban settings.

Uncovering embodied knowledge of place – from soundscapes, to implicitly understood pathways, to the phenomenology of colour or the expressions of sacred, ancestral landscapes – reminds us that a natural city is never simply a theoretical construct but an ontological expression of our very ways of being-in-the-world. Learning from the ecology of organism-environment interaction means building upon lessons derived from the earth itself.

In inquiring about actual city designs, from India to China, we are presented with case studies that allow us to learn from our mistakes as well as our success stories. If older, organic settlements managed to better preserve an urban way of life that was also respectful of the environment, how might we grasp these pre-thematic visions in order to better plan our future cities?

Exploring ways in which to take large-scale consequences of energy use and interpreting them within a clear, human horizon of significance means, once again, benefiting from knowledge strategies that are no longer abstract but deeply embodied and, in that sense, deeply meaningful. Moreover, the fact that paradigms of urban living are already in place within our youths' imaginations reminds us of the urgency of addressing ways of thinking that operate not simply within governments, industry, or the corporate sector, but also from the time children begin to explore their environments and frame them in a certain way. There is a need to recognize that education is not simply a matter of transmitting ecological knowledge, but of supporting embodied ways of being within our natural world.

In addition, the fact that cities are 'grue-like,' and thereby inherently temporal rather than static, reified entities, reminds us that an ontology of the natural city is itself never a fully accomplished affair. The job of defining and building human settlements that more meaningfully integrate the 'urban' and the 'environmental' within a genuine natural city remains a task in progress, although it is one that must begin within a rethinking of world views, as this book has begun to do.

In closing, let us recognize that, in many ways, the givenness of the earth draws us towards the ultimate and impenetrable mystery of existence. No matter how much we try to control and dominate the world around us, the earth exceeds our grasp. As previous chapters have shown, even when we try to set up barriers between our cities and the natural world, that world makes its way back in because, in the end, the earth is the very condition of the possibility of our existence.

Writer Peter Ackroyd reminds us that 'the city is built upon lost things. It is constructed in a literal sense on the ruins and debris of the past; it towers above forgotten underground rivers and discarded tunnels. It is built upon old graveyards and burial pits.'[1] As this volume suggests, reintegrating 'nature' into our cities means more than increasing parklands or tinkering with minor conservation strategies; instead, it means shifting horizons: placing the city within the context of the surrounding landscapes and, indeed, the universe itself, rather than bulldozing the soil to accommodate artificial constructions. It also may mean allowing a sense of history, tradition, the common good, and the sacred earth, rather than merely developers' dreams and the quest for 'world class' status, to permeate the progression and direction of our urban lives.

Certainly, more remains to be said. How might an ontology of waste and trash affect the notion of a natural city?[2] How might transportation decisions be made on the basis of a more insightful interpretation of human understanding and sense of place? What sort of ontology of water can emerge through the prism of a natural city? This volume has begun the process of deliberation on these and similar points. We invite our readers to continue the dialogue as we collectively appropriate lessons learned and strive to imagine, create, and inhabit urban spaces where social justice, ecological integrity, and civic empowerment flourish, and an openness to wider mysteries of both the earth and the cosmos can be found within city limits.

NOTES

1 Quoted from *The Times*, 7 October 2006, in *Underground: London's Hidden Infrastructure* (London: The Building Centre, Store Street, 2008).
2 For a fascinating introduction to this topic, see Greg Kennedy's wonderful book, *An Ontology of Trash: The Disposable and Its Problematic Nature* (Albany: State University of New York Press, 2007).

Contributors

W. Scott K. Cameron grew up amid the rocks and trees of northern Ontario before taking up philosophy at Queen's University and finishing his PhD at Fordham University. He took a visiting post at Loyola Marymount University in Los Angeles, where he is now a professor – though after seventeen years he still feels like a visitor in the dry Southwest.

John Cobb taught at the Claremont School of Theology from 1958 to 1990, and then retired to Pilgrim Place. He has devoted much of his career to promoting the thought of Alfred North Whitehead and its implications for theology, economics, and biology.

Frank Cunningham is Emeritus Professor of Philosophy and Political Science at the University of Toronto and a researcher and senior adviser at the university's Cities Centre.

Hilary Cunningham is Associate Professor of Anthropology at the University of Toronto. Her current research is based in northern Ontario and focuses on what she terms 'gated ecologies.' She is particularly interested in how the creation and implementation of borders and boundaries around conservation areas are linked to particular conceptualizations of nature.

Bruce Foltz, Professor of Philosophy at Eckerd College, draws on the history of philosophy (especially ancient Greek, Byzantine, and Russian philosophy) and contemporary European methodologies to address issues in environmental philosophy and the philosophy of religion. He has authored a number of books and articles in these areas. He serves as executive editor of the journal *Another City*, and is co-editor of a major forthcoming collection of articles by Orthodox philosophers and theologians entitled *Toward an Ecology of Transfiguration*.

Trish Glazebrook is Professor and Chair of the Department of Philosophy and Religion at the University of North Texas. She received her PhD from the University of Toronto and publishes in Heidegger studies, ecofeminism, development studies, ancient philosophy, and philosophy of science and technology.

Shubhra Gururani is Associate Professor of Anthropology at York University. Her research focuses on the cultural politics of nature, place, and gender in agrarian and urbanizing India. She is currently conducting ethnographic research on the politics of land and infrastructure in Gurgaon.

Bryan Karney is currently Associate Dean of Cross-Disciplinary Programs in Engineering and Professor of Civil Engineering at the University of Toronto. He is a director in the consulting firm HydraTek and Associates Inc. He has for almost thirty years researched the design, analysis, operation, and optimization of various water resource and energy systems. He is interested in the assessment and measurement of overall system performance, measurement, monitoring, policy issues, and decision making.

Sarah King holds a PhD from the University of Toronto and is currently a SSHRC Postdoctoral Fellow at Queen's University's School of Environmental Studies. Her research focuses on the role of cultures and religions in relationships between humans and the rest of nature, with particular attention to the experience of place, and to relationships between settlers and indigenous people in Canada.

Gaurav Kumar is a Business Portfolio Analyst in Engineering and Project Delivery at Hydro One Networks Inc. He has an MEng from the University of Toronto, has worked as a project manager for distributed generation investors, high-voltage breaker replacement programs, business planning, and work execution, and is actively involved with studies in compressed air energy storage.

Kenneth Maly is Professor Emeritus of Philosophy and Environmental Studies at the University of Wisconsin-La Crosse. He also teaches part-time in philosophy at the University of Guelph, is general editor of the University of Toronto Press's New Studies in Phenomenology and Hermeneutics series, and has an active Tibetan Buddhist practice.

Robert Mugerauer is Professor and former Dean at the University of Washington's Department of Urban Design and Planning. His most recent books are *Heidegger and Homecoming* (2008) and *Environmental Dilemmas* (2008). His current research projects focus on urban ecology and on the relation of environmental design to health and well-being.

Richard Oddie is a musician, writer, and teacher living in Hamilton, Ontario. He holds a PhD in Environmental Studies from York University.

Stephen Bede Scharper is Associate Professor with the Centre for Environment at the University of Toronto and the Department of Anthropology, University of Toronto, Mississauga. His research and teaching are in the areas of environmental ethics, environmental world views, and religious ethics and ecology. He is the author of *Redeeming the Time: A Political Theology of the Environment* and co-author of *The Green Bible*. He currently serves as a faith and ethics columnist for the *Toronto Star*, and has contributed over 400 reviews and articles to various popular and academic journals.

David Seamon is Professor in the Department of Architecture at Kansas State University. He is an environment-behaviour researcher and editor of *Environmental and Architectural Phenomenology*.

Vincent Shen is Professor and Lee Chair in Chinese Thought and Culture in the Department of East Asian Studies and Department of Philosophy, University of Toronto. His research interests lie in the areas of Chinese philosophy, comparative philosophy, phenomenology, and philosophical problems of technology, culture, and religion. He has published a number of books including *Confucianism, Taoism and Constructive Realism*; *Philosophy of Paul Ricoeur*; *Technology and Culture*; *Generosity to the Other: Chinese Culture, Christianity and Strangification*.

Ingrid Leman Stefanovic is Professor of Philosophy and former Director of the Centre for Environment at the University of Toronto. Her

research is in the area of environmental and architectural phenomenology, and projects typically investigate how values and perceptions drive decision making. A book on this theme is entitled *Safeguarding Our Common Future: Rethinking Sustainable Development.*

Peter Timmerman is Associate Professor in the Faculty of Environmental Studies, York University. He works extensively on environmental issues ranging from climate change to nuclear waste disposal. Much of his current research is on environmental ethics and various religious traditions – recent publications include articles on the Buddhism of John Cage and Zen responses to biogenetic manipulation – and participation in projects on the ethical foundations of ecological economics.

William Woodworth *Raweno:kwas* is Mohawk, Six Nations of the Grand River, and resides in Toronto with his partner Paul and dog Bo. He is an architect and executive director of the Beacon to the Ancestors Foundation. He teaches aboriginal culture and architecture at the University of Waterloo's School of Architecture.